American Folk Music and Folk Musicians Series

Edited by Ralph Lee Smith and Ronald D. Cohen

Photo by Jim Robinson.

Ballad of an American

The Autobiography
of Earl Robinson

Earl Robinson

with

Eric A. Gordon

American Folk Music and Musicians, No. 3

The Scarecrow Press, Inc.
Lanham, Md., & London
1998

SCARECROW PRESS, INC.

Published in the United States of America
by Scarecrow Press, Inc.
4720 Boston Way
Lanham, Maryland 20706

British Library Cataloguing in Publication Information Available

Library of Congress Cataloging-in-Publication Data

Robinson, Earl, 1910–1991
    Ballad of an American: the autobiography of Earl Robinson / Earl
Robinson with Eric A. Gordon.
        p.   cm. — (American folk music and musicians: no. 3)
    "List of works and discography by Earl Robinson": p.
    ISBN 0-8108-3433-2 (alk. paper)
    1. Robinson, Earl, 1910– . 2. Composers—United States—Biography.
I. Gordon, Eric A., 1945– . II. Title. III. Series.
    ML410.R6247A3 1998
    780'.092—dc21   97-33023
    [B]   CIP
                                                                       MN

♾™ The paper used in this publication meets the minimum requirements of
American National Standard for Information Sciences—Permanence of
Paper for Printed Library Materials, ANSI Z39.48–1984.
Manufactured in the United States of America.

For my parents
Victor and Naomi Gordon

—E.A.G.

CONTENTS

Section Six: 1972-1981

Section Seven: 1982 to Now

ACKNOWLEDGMENTS

Generous grants from Jessie Lloyd O'Connor, and from the Puffin Foundation Ltd. ("dedicated to the continuing dialogue between art and the lives of ordinary people"), made this book possible. They are deeply appreciated. We also thank Victor M. and Naomi B. Gordon for their thoughtful, timely, and patient support.

Gwen Gunderson did research for this book at an early stage, organizing papers and conducting interviews. Her efforts helped substantially. Kathryn Butzerin also offered numerous suggestions.

Many people helped in different ways, telling anecdotes, reminiscing about old times, supplying tape recordings, offering housing, granting permissions to reprint letters and lyrics, providing moral and material support. Their assistance is gratefully acknowledged. Jill Ansell, Beatrice Arkin, ASCAP, J. Marx Ayres, Judy Bell, Louisa Bowen, Charlotte and Perry Bruskin, Bette Jean Bullert, Larry Buzecky, Marie Carter, Pietro Castelnuovo-Tedesco, Robert Carl Cohen, Ronald D. Cohen, Sarah Cooper, Norman Corwin, Sarah Cunningham, Josephine Hayes Dean, Mary Ann Dempski, Charlotte Diamond, Wayne Friedlander, Steve Gilbert, Carolyn Goodman, Archie Green, Manuel Greenhill, Ernest Harburg, Alfred Hayes, Waldemar Hille, Daniel Hovey, Esther Hovey, Sean Killeen, Wolfgang König, Miles Kreuger, Millard Lampell, Millie Lent, Harold Leventhal, Rose Wortis Lewis, Sam Locke, Paul Loeb, Michael Loring, Albert Maltz, Stewart Manville, H. Stanley Marcus, Michael Martin, Harold Matson Co., Zoraya Mendez, Eda Reiss Merin, Betty Millard, Robert N. Miller, Arcie Nishkian, Bob Norman, Brent Oldham, Richard Partlow, Vern Partlow, Maurice Peress, John Randolph, Paul Robeson, Jr., Duane Robinson, Hazel Hawley Robinson, Jim Robinson, Perry Robinson, Ruth Martin Robinson, Shelly Romalis, David Rosen, Waldo Salt, Evelyn Sasko, Oscar Saul, Proletta Schatz, Robert Schneideman, Joan Schulman, Pete

xii   Acknowledgments

Seeger, Miriam Sherman, Charles D. Stackhouse, Harvey Stackhouse, Robert Steck, Viola Kates Stimpson, Mary Suggett, Lori Elaine Taylor, Raymond Teichman, Edith Tiger, Eric W. Trumbull, Mary Tyler, Abigail Van Buren, Joanne Ver Straten, Arthur Vogel, Jeffrey Vogel, Frank Wilkinson, Joseph Wortis.

The authors thank those who read all or parts of the manuscript: our hard-working and forgiving literary agent Frances Goldin, and Ralph Lee Smith and Ronald D. Cohen, our editors at Scarecrow Press. Also Rick Barnett, Jim Cramer, Frederic A. Gordon, Ilse Gordon, Victor M. Gordon, Miriam Painter, and Earl's two sons, Perry Robinson and Jim Robinson; and the members of the L. A. Writers Group, who provided innumerable helpful suggestions: Peter Cashorali, Steve Johnson, Rondo Mieczkowski, Kieran Prather, Stuart Timmons, and Mark White.

Along the road to publication, it became necessary to convert the computer files for this book from one system to another, and to prepare the manuscript in camera-ready form. Assisting in this complex, painstaking, and time-consuming process, and gratefully appreciated here, were Shon Encinas, Michael Jessen, Craig Morgan, and Edward M. Salm. My dear and faithful friend Stephen F. Roff devoted days upon days of expertise and commiseration to the success of this project, for which I am eternally grateful.

Permission to quote from letters and lyrics has been secured whenever possible. The following credits have been specifically requested:

"Black and White," by Earl Robinson and David Arkin; "Same Boat, Brother," by Earl Robinson and E. Y. Harburg; "Pioneer City," by Earl Robinson and Millard Lampell; "If I Am Free," by Earl Robinson and Lewis Allan; "I Kissed a Communist," by Earl Robinson and Lewis Allan; "Ride the Wind," by Earl Robinson; "Song of Atlantis," by Earl Robinson; "I Been Thinkin' About J.C.," by Earl Robinson; "The Flying Squadron," by Earl Robinson and Oscar Saul. Re-

SERIES EDITORS' FOREWORD

by Ralph Lee Smith and Ronald D. Cohen

Earl Robinson, composer of "Joe Hill," "The House I Live In," "Black and White," *The Lonesome Train*, and *Ballad for Americans*, is a major figure in twentieth-century music. He was also one of the most affable and charming, full of honesty and a warm sense of humor. In this book, largely written by Robinson and completed by Eric Gordon after Robinson's death, one takes a musical tour of America that extends from union halls and left-wing political groups of the 1930s to Broadway, Hollywood, the urban folk revival, and the New Age ethos of the 1980s. Along the way, one meets scores of the famous and near-famous, but none is more engaging than Robinson himself. Gordon accurately describes him as "a naïve believer in common decency whom cynicism had never touched."

Robinson was a folk-style composer and performer throughout his long career. His account of the politically inspired music scene of radical New York in the 1930s is a fascinating tale that only he could tell. Arriving in New York in 1934, Robinson immersed himself in the musical and theatrical worlds of left-wing groups, providing songs for unions, activist organizations, and the radical stage. His influence was immense and permanent. When he entered the scene, trained musicians with an orientation in European beaux arts traditions were struggling with the problem of how to compose "proletarian music" for the masses. The masses showed a distressing tendency to view these earnest efforts with virtual indifference. Robinson fitted the right key to the lock. Drawing from American folk music traditions of which many "proletarian" composers had little knowledge, Robinson created music and melodies that proved to be the right vehicles for popularizing the messages of justice and equality.

His personal knowledge of the radical music scene was

immense. His description of left-wing musical activity of the period is like a trove of sunken treasures brought to the surface. Among the things that one will find in this book are the reaction of black Communists to Leadbelly, and how Leadbelly reacted to their opinions; how "Joe Hill," the most famous of all labor songs, was written; and how a radical song about Abraham Lincoln got into the book for the Broadway musical *Hellzapoppin*.

The love that Robinson had for America finds extensive and beautiful expression in his music. His obvious patriotism makes even more incredible the tale he tells of the postwar days of congressional witch-hunting and the blacklist. It is scarcely believable, but true, that the FBI's file on this person who so deeply loved his country ran to over a thousand pages.

In his later years, to the distress of some of his old political comrades-in-arms, Robinson moved from left-wing politics to occultism and New Age beliefs. Eric Gordon correctly comments that, rather than representing a discontinuity in his intellectual and artistic life, Robinson's happy exploration of the New Age world reflected his lifelong, open-minded search for unifying themes in human life and experience.

INTRODUCTION BY A LONELY COLLABORATOR

by Eric A. Gordon

"For a long time I have put out the notion of living to the age of 140," Earl Robinson says toward the end of this book. "At that time I will look around and see how things are. If they're okay, I'll stick around. If not, I'll go someplace else."

Numerous times, in both private and public settings, I had heard Earl rehearse this plan for the rest of his life, and I knew it had to be included in his autobiography. Sometime in 1990—just after he had returned to live in his native West Seattle for the first time since 1934—Earl began sounding a new note. So in the manuscript he extended his thought, adding, "But I have lately decided there is nothing magic about the number 140. I might choose to go some sooner. Who knows?"

Sure enough, within a year, Earl was dead—or in his expression, had "moved to his new address." On July 20, 1991, at 7 p.m., Earl was driving his embattled but sturdy two-door '78 Datsun on Admiral Way, just blocks from his home. At the intersection of Manning, where the City had erected a confusing passing lane amid a stretch of new road construction, he met head-on with a four-wheel drive vehicle operated by a middle-aged man who the police said had been drinking. The impact killed Earl if not immediately, then likely within minutes. The shock doubtlessly protected Earl from feeling any pain. The officers on duty guessed that had he been wearing his seatbelt, he might have survived.

Earl had not intended to be gone long: He carried no wallet and no money on him. It's almost as though he had left the house just to keep this appointment. Friends found his television at home brightly blaring to no one. A few weeks after this incident, the other driver—a man deeply grieving for his late wife and for his own failures, and now subject to criminal prosecution—took his own life.

Earl Robinson's death lengthened a chain of recent losses in American music: Within two years, Leonard Bernstein left us, then Aaron Copland and Elie Siegmeister, and a few weeks after Earl, Alex North, the distinguished film composer, then William Schuman, all of them friends and colleagues. As the Nineties unfold, very few survive from the ranks of composers and musicians of the Thirties and Forties, many of them identified with the left-wing and other "people's" movements that attracted millions to their side. That generation taught us as a nation what American music could sound like, freed from European domination.

I met Earl while researching *Mark the Music: The Life and Work of Marc Blitzstein* (St. Martin's Press, 1989). I had interviewed him at length about his friendship with Blitzstein, and about the times and causes that had captured both of their imaginations. In 1988, when I completed my manuscript, I asked him to review it for possible errors or misinterpretations. I had originally intended to sum up Blitzstein's life with a reference to his opera *No for an Answer*, ending on a note of protest against injustice. I owe to Earl my concluding citation of Blitzstein's setting of an e. e. cummings poem, "yes is a pleasant country," for Earl believed that Marc ought to be remembered on an upbeat—as surely Earl would want to be as well. I regret that I didn't respond more favorably when Earl asked me how receptive I felt to psychic experience, for if I wanted, he said, he could put me in touch with Marc now.

When Earl proposed that I collaborate on his autobiography, I had no reservations. After working for so long in cold isolation from my subject, Earl presented me with the opportunity to join forces with a living legend, the composer of *Ballad for Americans*, "Joe Hill," "The House I Live In," "Black and White," and so much more. Even if he had "gone native" with the metaphysical stuff—Earl lived in California from 1966 to 1989—I knew that after the stricter materialism of Blitzstein's mind, I would appreciate the active engagement with a markedly different set of assumptions about the nature of experience. Nonetheless, Earl's story bore strong continuities with the Old Left I had studied. Interestingly, not long after Earl moved from California back to Seattle, I moved from frenetic New York to California myself.

Earl in fact wrote most of this book. Some chapters, like the Roosevelt White House visit, appear here very much as he wrote them—well rehearsed anecdotes and memories finally committed to the typewritten page. In a very few cases, like the painful farewell to his wife Helen in 1963—a loss he suffered for the rest of his life—I had to reconstruct a narrative from letters and diaries. I edited, trimmed, and shaped the material. Always, I asked questions, my prodding and probing uncovering many long-forgotten details.

Earl had an unsettling penchant for resolving uncertainties by holding up both hands, closing his eyes tight and pondering the question. Then one hand would fall and he'd say "1934" (as opposed to "1935"), as though Clio, the muse of history, had intervened on his behalf. I did not entirely share his confidence in this methodology for arriving at the truth, so I also spent many months living with Earl's vast collections of papers, finding sheet music, contracts, concert programs and reviews, background material Earl consulted for his compositions, scrapbooks bursting with crumbling newspaper clippings, awards, photographs, transcripts of interviews with Earl and others associated with his career, and thousands of letters to and from performers, friends, family, and colleagues. My notes from this research, and from various interviews I conducted, complemented Earl's memory.

The end result is not the definitive musicological or biographical treatment Earl deserves and may receive one day, but it is a first-person document of a most lively time in American history, this troubled and exhilarating Twentieth Century. At the same time, with its frank discussion of difficult subject matter, such as his Communist Party membership, his marital infidelities, or his acceptance of New Age psychology and philosophy, this book exposes Earl in ways perhaps few autobiographies do, to negative judgment and opprobrium. He felt that whatever good he had achieved in his life could not be extricated from his faults. Rather than censor his life, he left it to history to sort out his worth as a creative talent and as a human being.

At points in Earl's autobiography I tried to tuck in some passages emphasizing what a pioneering role he had played in the course of our musical life—how *Ballad for Americans*, for instance, unleashed a virtual flood of vernacular choral writing for both radio and the concert hall by such composers as William Schuman, Blitzstein, Copland, Bernstein, and others. In another place, I suggested that *The Lonesome Train* is a first-rate piece of American music that merits a new lease on life through a fresh recording. Earl deleted these observations with his characteristic mix of modesty and immodesty: "It's true," he said, "it's true. But it's for others to say, not me."

Earl and I together reviewed almost everything in this book except for the additions to the manuscript concerning the FBI. From the moment we began our collaboration, I urged Earl to retrieve his FBI file to see what we'd find. At long last, in April and May 1991, after some pushing on the part of Earl's congressional representatives, almost a thousand pages of Earl's dossier arrived in the mail. Earl pored through it all and made comments on each noteworthy page. Aside from the FBI file itself, Earl's comments make for fascinating and sometimes amusing reading, as he discovered how frequently FBI agents flubbed their work: For years, to cite a small detail, they kept repeating the fiction that he had blue eyes, not brown— evidence that bored G-men would sooner copy from previous reports than use their own powers of observation. Earl also came to realize, with more bemusement than anger, how huge and pervasive was that bureaucracy that for all the middle years of his life spied on him, reported his movements and activities, played an unending series of dirty tricks on him, and prepared for his eventual detention in one of a network of federally maintained concentration camps.

Our working relationship could not have been more satisfying. Earl had enjoyed many happy experiences of artistic collaboration with such lyricists as Yip Harburg, Lewis Allan, and

John Latouche, while I had never shared my craft so intensely with another person. We aimed to create a readable, human account of a life, that goal superseding all agendas of personal ego. Along the way we shared trips, meals, sleeping quarters, movies, concerts, birthday parties and holidays, political rallies, friends, and good times.

Not once did either of us feel threatened or insecure, though to be sure we had some thorough discussions on many points. Earl had never publicly admitted writing "Quiet Man from Kansas," a tribute to Communist Party chief Earl Browder with words by Mark Hess. It took some vigorous debate to persuade him to let go of his old secret. In another place, talking about his colleague, singer and songwriter Lee Hays, who lived with the Robinsons for nine years in the 1950s, it seemed to me time finally to acknowledge Lee as a gay man. But Earl had never actually seen Lee having sex with a man—and had never discussed it with him; so he was reluctant to speak untruly of him, possibly harmfully. I countered that in this day and age it was no harm to affirm someone's homosexuality. We compromised, and the book has Earl believing that Lee "was probably homosexual."

Earl could be at once sophisticated and naïve. Reading his letters from the 1940s, when he organized the People's Songs movement on the West Coast, I discovered a man of almost combative strength, who convincingly argued his views against a broad background of current events and esthetic and political philosophy. Though his commitments lay firmly in his belief in people, his faith in the Communist Party sometimes stifled his natural empathy. At a later point he dropped his attachment to ideology and tried reaching out through the personal growth movements, and through his explorations into the psychic. In this latter phase he entered realms that disturbed some of his friends on the left—who somehow never grasped how gullible they themselves had been. Their distress at Earl's new course kept them from appreciating his more recent compositions based on ancient Armenian mythology, Atlantis, dolphins, St. Francis, Jesus, and other New Age subjects.

Earl's rare qualities and often startling contradictions made him an eagerly sought-after companion with a flexible, dynamic, inquiring mind. He could be goofy and irreverent and earnest, simultaneously and on the same subject, this charming, white-maned octogenarian who just wouldn't go out to pasture with all the tired old liberals.

To the end, he inspired a deep love, especially when he performed. His naturally sweet voice had weathered, to be sure, but possessed great stamina and could hit all the high notes his songs demanded. His delivery seemed free of all artifice, and though some of his repertoire went back more than fifty years, he gave it a freshness that made it seem as though it had leapt off his keyboard only yesterday. He basked in applause, and sometimes when he stood up from the piano, grinning ear to ear, his old shy stooping stance reappeared, and one could see there still the gangly kid from Seattle, the trusting believer in common decency whom cynicism had never touched.

Not long before he died, Earl gave a lecture-recital about Joe Hill, in the course of which he gave the definition of a pro: "Someone who knows what he wants and knows how to get it." In the main Earl did know what he wanted: to compose music and create works of art that would inspire and create dialogue with the public. He welcomed commercial success when it came, but it did not sway him from his course of honesty (as he saw it). Earl never wrote a piece of music that exploited the sorrier instincts of humanity, and but rarely a song that sought success only in the marketplace. These traits, combined with his political outspokenness, guaranteed him a more modest livelihood than his talents might otherwise have earned him. But he slept well at night with a clean conscience. What Earl wanted was at all times, and at whatever sacrifice, to guard his personal and artistic integrity.

One time, in the summer of 1990, I asked him to join me on a visit to an art gallery exhibition of industrial design and poster art from the first exciting years of the Soviet régime, a period he had heroized for long years. Afterward, I asked him if in these days of Gorbachev and perestroika he didn't see some rejuvenated future to those old ideals. He stopped in the middle of the street, oblivious to the passing traffic. "My friend," he pronounced, pausing for effect and leaning his wide-eyed face into mine, "Socialism is a dead duck."

Yet Earl never denied or disparaged his past. Uniting Old Left and New Age, Earl passionately wanted humanity to come together—mystically, perhaps—in some manner of global cooperation. That feeling found expression in Communism in the first half of the century, and the Age of Aquarius in the second. Yet no firm line divided these periods: Just as he had written music for FDR in 1944, and for Henry Wallace in '48, he wrote a presidential campaign song forty years later for Jesse Jackson, that he sang all over the country with undiminished glee.

So here it is. Earl's life story is a tapestry of art, politics, and spirit, that illuminates many of the major debates and struggles of our nation's history. His songs endure. They can inspire us all. That for sixty years he conducted his prophetic searching with a ceaseless, irrational optimism surely lends us a little more courage to look forward with hope.

A MOMENT OUT OF TIME

For ten years, since the late 1940s, when the House Committee on Un-American Activities (HUAC) started harassing Hollywood screenwriters and artists, you could never tell who the Committee would go after next. Year after year, I waited for the other shoe to drop . . . on me. Well, along about Spring of 1957 HUAC decided to rake up some muck in the New York music world. For four days, beginning April 9th, Honorable Representatives from several of these United States held forth at the federal courthouse at New York's Foley Square. Their subpoenas had fallen upon some forty-odd individuals. A few friendly witnesses talked about their days as Communists in the ranks of musicians' Local 802, confirming what HUAC wanted to hear: that these repentant former left-wingers now stood "unequivocally opposed to every aspect of Communist ideology."

HUAC reveled in these cathartic recantations that suggested nothing so much as a medieval auto-da-fé. But thirty-seven of us provided a different kind of public theatre. We refused to answer HUAC's questions as to membership, former or present, in the Communist Party—claiming the right not to incriminate ourselves, guaranteed by the Fifth Amendment to the Constitution. For most of those who "took the Fifth," HUAC sniping resulted in an immediate loss of work and income. Except for the boiling oil and the stretching rack, HUAC was truly the American Inquisition.

My hearing on April 11th, conducted mostly by HUAC staff attorney Richard Arens, and brightened by occasional intrusions from Tennessee Rep. James B. Frazier, Jr., California's Clyde Doyle, and Missouri's Morgan M. Moulder, lasted about an hour. The children's chorus I directed at New York's Metropolitan Music School attracted their attention, for HUAC perceived in music a particularly insidious and diabolical mechanism by which Communists indoctrinate the young.

MR. ARENS: Mr. Robinson, how old are these children you teach?

MR. ROBINSON: Between six and eleven, and then a sort of teen-age group that goes up to about fourteen.

MR. ARENS: Do you teach them any revolutionary songs?

MR. ROBINSON: This is what I teach . . . the *Ballad for Americans*, and *The Lonesome Train*. Some are my compositions, some American folk songs. Sometimes we go across the border and take a foreign folk song, too. I explain to them that this is for the purpose of getting to understand other countries better. As Mr. Doyle said the other day, music is an international language.

MR. DOYLE: A universal language.

MR. ROBINSON: Pardon me. A universal language.

MR. DOYLE: I am not an authority on music, but I know that much about it.

MR. ROBINSON: O.K.

(Mr. Doyle made sure I understood his well considered thoughts on music.)

For a brief moment in the national spotlight, my entire and intermittently illustrious career in American music came down to one simple question. For the culture-hounds, nothing else mattered: Was I a Communist?

Let us hear from our intermittently comprehensible Representative again, and from my chief inquisitor:

MR. DOYLE: Show me one poem or one song where you have deliberately set to music or otherwise that the American schoolchildren, for instance, or the Americans, shall support the Constitution, and so forth. Do you see what I'm getting at?

MR. ROBINSON: I have a song called "The House I Live In." That is America to me. It has sold millions and millions of copies. It has been sung by most of the

big singers in the country at one time or another. This
says:

> *What is America to me?*
> *A name, a map, the flag I see,*
> *A certain word, democracy.*
> *What is America to me?*
> *The house I live in,*
> *The plot of earth, the street,*
> *The grocer and the butcher,*
> *The people that I meet.*

The middle section goes on, "The words of old Abe
Lincoln, of Jefferson and Paine, of Washington and
Roosevelt."

MR. DOYLE: Mail me a copy and I will pay you
for it, gladly.

MR. ROBINSON: The biggest line in it is, "A
dream that has been growing for a hundred and fifty
years." This has been sung. School kids know it. You
should know it.

MR. DOYLE: Why, then, do you tear down this
theory by this sort of thing? Why do you tear down
that magnificent conception of our country?

MR. ROBINSON: I am not tearing down. I have
never torn down.

MR. DOYLE: I beg to differ with you. You are. I
say mail me a copy of that, and I will pay you for it,
gladly.

Richard Arens had certainly tired of this exchange and
now began to wind up the hearing.

MR. ARENS: I want to clear the record on one
thing, Mr. Chairman. Are you now a Communist?

MR. ROBINSON: Do you expect me to answer
that?

MR. ARENS: Yes, I would like to have you deny it
while you are under oath.

MR. ROBINSON: . . . I don't feel this Committee
has a right to pry into these kind of things, and also to
try to make me seem subversive, when every bit of
work I have done in my life has been in defense of
America and helping America, I feel that you have no
right to try to put me in that kind of light, and I decline
to answer.

The hearing shortly concluded. I left that dark courthouse,
moldy with the foul vapors of intimidation, and strode into
the bright American sunlight of a sweet spring noontime.

Yes, I had been a Communist for more than twenty years.
And yes, I had done all within my powers as a composer and
singer to insure that my great country fulfill its inspiring promises to her people and serve as a beacon to the world.

For this they tried to make me an outcast in my home.

SECTION ONE
1910-1934

MY BEGINNINGS IN SEATTLE

So the time has come to move back into Robinson history, a story of music and politics, notes and words, unions, democracy and war; presidents and minstrels, Old Left, New Age, men and women whose turn in the sun I was privileged to share. The Ballad of an American.

Even beginnings demand beginnings, as our biblical sages knew when they recorded chapters of begats. On the Robinson side the traceable history goes back to my great-grandparents and no further. One came from Wales, the others from various states along the Eastern Seaboard. The generations tracked a gradual movement westward, most of the Robinsons settling in Michigan around the towns of Mears, Hart, Fennville, Ganges, and Plummerville. No one of particular distinction, and no identifiable family occupation stands out among them.

My mother's family, the Hawleys, are of far greater interest. On her father's side, records preserved in various British archives go back to the mid-1600s. For several generations, Hawleys identified with the early Quaker movement. In the 1830s a Henry Hawley emigrated to America, settling for a time in Brooklyn. Letters that have come down to us indicate that he and his wife Jane were interested in spiritualism and clairvoyant phenomena—perhaps I inherited something from them. Later Hawleys went to Michigan, where they specialized in fruit farming.

Going back from my mother's mother, a number of other family names come into the picture. Certain branches can be traced more than a thousand years to the time of King Alfred in England and Charlemagne. Apparently there were some knights among them. The Putnams counted themselves among the earliest settlers in America. Quite a tribe of them lived in Salem, Massachusetts, in 1692-93 at the time of the witchcraft trials. The proceedings split the family apart. Some became accusers, even against their own cousins. One woman who objected was herself jailed for being a witch, but managed to escape to England. John Putnam supported the trials but, trying to be fair, defended those he judged wrongly accused. Joseph Putnam staunchly opposed the trials, denouncing them as so much ignorance and superstition. A later Putnam, Israel, was a famous hero of the American Revolutionary War. We know of at least two forebears killed in the Civil War.

Mommer made musicians of us

Morris John Robinson, my father, was a man of many parts. He gave his height as 5'8"—he wasn't quite—and he never had an ounce of fat on him. Immensely competitive as an athlete, he loved to win at whatever he undertook. He was graduated from the University of Michigan law school in 1904, but after a year practicing law and not liking it, he turned to Sears Roebuck. He worked himself into the Sears correspondence department in Chicago, and married my mother-to-be, Hazel Beth Hawley in 1908. After they'd passed a year in a four-room flat in Chicago, Mom's Uncle Tim Plummer gave the young couple a pair of lots with a two-room house in the Ravenna district, then outside Seattle—he had paid $10 for the lots at a tax title sale. So they moved there, anticipating a new Sears store starting up. For $500 they created a four-room house with an attic, and had a well dug for another $100, all of which they paid off in installments. I was born into the new house on July 2, 1910, and named for Little Earl, my father's brother who died at the age of four.

I can uncover few things of real importance to write about in my earliest years. The advent of World War I in 1914, when I was just four years old, made scarcely a ripple in my consciousness. I can remember being admonished by my mother, "Eat your oatmeal, the starving Armenians—," just the merest foreshadow of my later absorption with that noble people in my folk opera *David of Sassoun*. But the war supplied some songs we used to parody lustily. "Over There" was such a one, with its "drums tum tumming everywhere." It took me a long time to get the meaning of "Tooby-ware, Tooby-ware." My folks supported the war. My mother, however, was less taken in than my father by the Wilson slogan, "Make the world safe for democracy."

And the Seattle General Strike, coming when I was nine years old, might just as well not have happened for all the impression it made on me. I never heard of the powerful Industrial Workers of the World movement in the Northwest—the Wobblies—until long after I reached New York and joined "the movement" in my twenty-fourth year.

So I look to music for my early memories. Mommer was naturally artistic. She had a fine sense of color in her painting, played piano well enough to teach a large number of students, including my sister, my brother, and me. I caused her great frustration by my five-year-old inability to hear or sing differences in pitch. It appears I was an enthusiastic monotone. When she tried to get me to sing lower, I stooped down to my hands and knees and sang the same pitch. When she said higher, higher, I would rise on tiptoes, stretch my voice and neck, all the while singing the same Johnny one-note. I learned to hear and sing different sounds only when I got into first grade at the Lafayette School in West Seattle.

It was on piano, at age six, that I started to show some talent. I began improvising my first composition, "Ghost Dance." It began with slow, separated spooky thumps on a low G. Faster action still on G. Then a rising theme in G minor appeared. With dramatic stops and starts, the dance theme grew and developed excitingly. "Ghost Dance" never became anything beyond a childish exercise, but it was important to me once.

My mother's high musical nature led her into studying harp, violin, organ, and cello—on which she became expert enough to play in a local symphony. She filled our house with the sound of her music. We three kids grew and proliferated in our musical tastes. Mommer used to insist on our practicing every night right after dinner, while she cleaned up. Her subterfuge successfully made musicians of us, because all the while we thought we were getting out of doing the dishes! My brother Duane, two and a half years younger, graduated from piano to flute, which he played excellently, till he discovered the saxophone and clarinet, and began going professional. He also dabbled in guitar and learned bass so he could do dance jobs for pay. These days, Duane is a horn man. He never left music, though he got a doctorate in sociology and a masters in social work, and became an inspirational teacher and counselor.

Like me, my sister Claire, three and a half years younger, stuck closer to music. Both of us became excellent pianists and both took up violin and later viola, for essentially the same reasons: The high school orchestra had a plethora of pianists but needed fiddlers. I took violin for four years, enough to be able to play second violin in high school and a weak viola in the University of Washington symphony. Claire became professional on both instruments, taught piano, and for a time was a music copyist in Los Angeles. To this day Claire remains involved in music in Seattle, gracing quartets and orchestras with her presence. We three often played classical trios for flute, violin, and piano, and quartets with Mommer on cello. And the whole family sang.

On his two-week vacation from Sears every year, Dad took the family "out to camp." We drove around the state, pitching tent sometimes in a different spot every night. In time, my folks tired of constantly moving, and we began staying longer in places like Fish Lake, where we . . . fished. Eventually, they bought land between Allyn and Grapeview on Puget Sound. My grandfather John Robinson built our cottage there in 1926, where we still went "out to camp." There in Puget Sound we kids all learned to swim.

Around an outdoor fire, my father came into his own. The black sheep in this musical family—all he could play was the mandolin and he didn't read music—he picked and trilled, and sang a beautiful tenor harmony to "Smile a While," "Girl of My Dreams," "Sweetheart of Sigma Chi," "Tenting Tonight," and countless other old numbers, including the almost-folk songs of Stephen Foster. We kids learned to harmonize at these folksong fests where Mommer played a cool ukulele accompanying Dad's mandolin. Those enchanting times formed a solid base for the join-in type of singing which I was to encourage later in my entertaining career.

Inspired putterer

I tended to take assurance from my father and a lack of affirmation from my mother. One time he came home from work and my mother instructed him to take me down to the basement and give me a beating for something. My resourceful old man took a stick and beat hard on the newel post of the stair, hissing at me, "Yell, yell!" so my mother would be satisfied that I was being punished properly. In psychic communication with my Dad eighteen years after he died, we reminded one another of this incident. "I couldn't hit you," he said. "I love you, boy." In accordance with the standards of the day, however, we never hugged each other, just shook hands.

As a musical person, Mommer was my first inspiration. But I had a book of spirituals that I used to play and sing, and only years later did Mommer ever mention how much she liked listening to me.

As a role model, my father was more important to me. He taught me how to garden organically, and I felt proud to be helping him. We chopped and sawed a lot of wood for the fireplace, standing on opposite ends of a long crosscut saw, him teaching me to pull, not push, and let your partner pull in turn. I got to love the sound of the saw so much I later built a fugue on it for an orchestral piece.

Dad never wasted a scrap of garbage. It all went into the humus pile. A dead branch, fallen off a tree, Dad would cut into small bits with his knife that he kept so sharp, and he'd plow it back into the ground. "When you take from the earth you gotta give back to it." We kids had the job of cleaning the starfish from off the beach at our camp—starfish ate the oysters that grew there—and he'd spade them into the soil under the fruit trees. Good fertilizer.

An inspired putterer, Dad even wrote a little philosophical essay about it:

> The primary object of puttering is the passage of time with calmness and tranquillity. . . . One of the cardinal principles of correct and inefficient puttering is saving everything; all junk is valuable puttering material. . . . A true putterer never accepts pay for his stuff, advice or time; the satisfaction is in producing the needed things and fixing the fixable things, doing something for his fellow man.

I tried to follow my Dad faithfully in athletics. He had caught for his Olivet College baseball team. I became catcher for our neighborhood West Seattle club. He was an excellent wrestler, pinning men much bigger than himself. With me he'd let me win at least enough so I wouldn't get discouraged. Though small, I was able to win many contests where my speed and wiriness overcame bigger boys. And as my old man was a great open field runner, so I became one on the football field, playing both tackle and touch. Duane and I formed a tight team—Duane was fast and an excellent pass catcher—and our passing attack plus my open field ability mowed down many a neighborhood combination of larger boys.

Still, this never translated into my making the varsity or even the second team in high school. My size—just ninety pounds as a freshman—ruled me out, perhaps ordaining my becoming popular more through music than athletics, though I did make the sophomore basketball team, and pursued that sport intramurally through high school and college.

I remember my father politically as a righteous liberal. He used to assert with passion, "It's wrong for ten percent of the country to have all the money and ninety percent to have nothing." As a lifelong Democrat, he was once persuaded by the party to run in the Republican primary—to "keep the Republicans honest." Their candidate being secure and otherwise unopposed, Republicans according to Washington law could and would cross over and vote for the reactionary on the Democratic ticket, thus ensuring an election contested on more conservative terms. So Dad's candidacy forced the Republicans to stay in their own primary.

At Sears he eventually became head of the inspection and correspondence departments (answering dissatisfied customers), and thought of himself as close to general manager. But the Depression came along and in his twenty-fourth year of employment, just short of twenty-five and a lifetime pension, a man came out from Chicago headquarters with a broom. At a very healthy fifty-five, Dad had his choice of a demotion, to become a snooper on his fellow employees, or to resign. He promptly resigned.

Dad fondly wished that Duane and I would go to Michigan—he served as Michigan Alumni Association secretary-treasurer in Seattle almost to his passing in January of 1969, at age eighty-eight. I never seriously considered it, but clear up into college time did see myself as following in his footsteps at Sears Roebuck. One summer, during high school, I tried finding a job for some weeks, unsuccessfully. Then Dad said, "Why don't I get you a job at Sears?" I picked orders on roller skates—fun for a while, at ten dollars a week—until one day, rounding a corner, I skated straight into one of the managers. From then on it was no more roller skates, and no more fun either.

At age fifteen I got my license. My driving career included accidents, many tickets over the years for speeding and other traffic misdemeanors, falling asleep at the wheel, attendance at traffic schools, and culminated (1975) in two nights in a hospital. I found myself forever trying to institute a change in my driving habits, but the old habits persistently kept creeping back. In my eightieth year, when I moved and had to give up my California license for a Washington one, it took me three exams to pass the test.

Concerning sex, I was the veriest neophyte. Committed to athletics and music, I had little inclination for girls. Early on I would satisfy my romantic feelings by arranging to walk by a dark-haired beauty named Marjorie, and tip my cap as gracefully as I could. Almost any response from her satisfied me deeply. Later I embarrassed a lovely girl named Katherine by saying hello with exaggerated emphasis every time we passed in the hallway. If she, or any other girl, had answered with anything like my enthusiasm, I think I would have been scared to death. I was just not ready—a slow learner.

A BACHELOR OF MUSIC
WITH A NORMAL TEACHING DIPLOMA

I entered college a little too soon. Accustomed to getting A's and B's in high school without having to work at it, I was lost in my freshman year at the University of Washington. Also I had a misplaced conception of what to expect from college. I thought I wanted to build toward a job at Sears Roebuck, and prepare to be a businessman. I ignored my whole musical direction, believing that music is okay—fine, even—but not to make a living.

Music harmony, duck soup

All set to enroll in business administration, on the way to the university I had a partial change of heart, and I signed up for liberal arts instead. The subjects I chose reflected this dichotomy. An economics course represented the business side of me; hard and uninteresting, I barely passed it. An English course, including some creative writing, was the liberal arts part of me; I got a B. Two courses in geology represented I don't know what, I guess an attempt to expand my horizons. I failed one and got a D in the other, though after college I became fascinated with the subject again. In short, I flunked out.

During the semester I stayed out, I had to earn a good grade in a correspondence course in order to be accepted back. So I took music harmony. It was duck soup for me to get a B+. I re-enrolled into the Music Department. At the time, I put myself down some for this: I had failed to cut the mustard as a business major, failed my father. I'd taken the easy way, which wasn't "right." In retrospect I realized that I had finally found the exactly correct spot for me.

I latched on to all the music courses available, studied music history, delved into Mozart and Bach. I deeply appreciated recordings by a singer named Paul Robeson. That voice truly grabbed me. His singing the Negro spirituals, in particular "Motherless Child," made a profound impression. It is still difficult to express the effect of his voice in words at all adequate.

11

One must hear it. He was only a voice to me, but I was to meet and become friends with him nine years later.

I sang plenty too, in choral classes, and later with the Men's Glee Club. Few thrills in the world compare to singing in a massed choir, but one that does is writing for massed voices. I practically got drunk on Wagner in Mrs. Louise Van Ogle's enthusiastic class, which illuminated the marvelous leitmotifs of the *Ring of the Nibelungen*. The excitement of understanding this music has thinned out with the years—Wagner is not what he used to be; perhaps he never was.

Most importantly, I studied advanced harmony with Carl Paige Wood, and began breaking the rules against parallel fifths and octaves. I carefully pointed out in my composition exercises that I did this because I liked the sound, and became annoyed when Mr. Wood's grader insisted on red-penciling the parallel octaves that I had explained I wanted. Still, to this day I find myself watching for parallels in my composing. It's good to first learn the rules. You know better what you are doing when you find it necessary to break them. I took counterpoint and composition with George F. McKay, taking great pleasure in producing continuous contrary motion in the counterpoint exercises.

Meantime I refined my piano playing, studying privately with Mrs. Van Ogle, the Wagnerite. A grand lady, she took me through Bach and Chopin, Rachmaninoff, Schumann, Mac-Dowell and Mozart. I learned enough viola to play with the university symphony—poorly, I fear, but they needed me.

Along with developing my classical piano, I became involved with dance music. From my senior year in high school, I performed with the Blue Knights, a band which played around Seattle and the Puget Sound area. I was quite proud of being able to pay more than a quarter of my university tuition from dance bookings. The Blue Knights also included my brother Duane on clarinet and tenor sax. Believe it or not, the Blue Knights are still around in 1991, playing for West Seattle High School reunions and other celebrations. Sixty years after our beginnings we continue to set people's feet tapping, throw mean licks, and play the golden oldies and many modern tunes.

Late one night in an after-hours club following one of our gigs, I heard a black blues band for the first time. This music, in the flesh, was not commonly heard in Seattle, and it impressed me profoundly. So playing with and arranging for the Blue Knights led me in a jazz-blues direction. From Duke Ellington's recordings I became a disciple of his. Later I came to know him and many of the other great black and white jazz artists. And I could wholeheartedly encourage my son Perry, who has become a genius (proud father speaking) on the jazz clarinet.

Four-eyes

A private struggle of mine leads back to the musical. I tried to handle a congenital nearsightedness without resort to glasses. Back in the third grade it was clear that something was wrong with my eyes. I would squint to see, later discovering I could pull one or both eyes out to the side, and would be able to read the blackboard or see at the movies. With the help of my mother, who didn't like the look of glasses on me any better than I did, I rejected them in favor of the Dr. Bates system. Bates believed in exercising the eyes, left and right, up and down, practicing looking cross-eyed, to strengthen them. I learned something I can do to this day, look cross-eyed with one eye and straight with the other. I also worked on an eye chart to try to see the words at a greater distance every day. My eyes improved to where on a bright day I could see 20/20. Actually, I memorized the chart and hypnotized myself to think I was seeing perfectly, because the improvement did not last. I would stretch my eyes, squint all through high school up into college, in a heroic effort to look "normal."

This fear of looking bad ("four-eyes") obsessed me. A dance orchestra job forced me to straighten out. This sax man, head of the band, noticed that I was not reading the piano charts but improvising a lot, some okay, some not. And I would lean way forward to see the score. One night he simply said, "Robinson, you need glasses," implying that if I didn't get them I could lose my job with him.

With glasses my playing miraculously improved, though I still took them off on dates with girlfriends, driving at night one-handed as usual. I had to leave Seattle finally to accept myself as a four-eyes.

Practical advice

As an anonymous liberal arts student majoring in music and minoring in history, I made efforts to fit in with the university mores. A couple of fraternities rushed me, but when I saw that Greek life involved a solid amount of money, I backed out: I couldn't legitimately ask my father to support my joining. This was for the rich, and we were more working class. Thinking it compulsory, in the fall of 1929 I joined ROTC, the Reserve Officers' Training Corps, which we dubbed the "rot corps."

My father advanced the tongue-in-cheek theorem, "Never let your studies interfere with your college education." So I followed his advice by hanging around the YMCA, where all kinds of discussion flowed freely. My new friend Neal Miller was a true source of practical information for this budding searcher for clarity in the Depression Thirties. He instructed me thoroughly on evolution and Darwinism. He backed me strongly when I confronted my old Presbyterian minister from West Seattle on the nature of God as both a jealous and a loving being. All the good reverend could tell me was, "You must have faith." Eventually I resolved my religious crisis by turning toward atheism—right in the middle of the YMCA! In retrospect, however, I'm glad my folks sent me to Sunday school, though they didn't themselves go to church. It gave me a sense of connection to world history, plus a superficial knowledge of the Bible, beginning with Matthew Mark Luke John, Saddle a horse and all get on.

Most practical of all, Neal told me how I could get out of ROTC by espousing pacifism, being sincerely against all fighting. This I found not hard to do, and after eight months, in June 1930, changed from ROTC to P. E.

A girl I knew from a psychology class invited me on a double date. Hortense and I sat in the back seat of the other couple's car, free to neck as we wished. She nestled in my arms, ready and a-waitin' . . . for what? I wondered. I couldn't bring myself to kiss her until I had said some loving words. And I had no words. We sat in that awkward posture for an hour until it came time to leave. I took a lesson from that experience. I would make a point in the future of saying some love words whether I felt them or not, in hopes that the act of speaking would unloosen the Earl yearning to be free of repression.

I blamed my mother for this inability to love. The very word didn't exist in our family's vocabulary, although my father managed to convey love to me from time to time better than my mother. My mother's message, delivered to me around my college time, came out like this: "Men are beasts, and women do not enjoy sex." She said it over and over, sometimes with a laugh, so it wasn't quite serious, but effective nonetheless.

Only later did I learn what a libertine my old man had been. How much my mother knew, and how much she covered up for him as "respectable" wives so often would, I'll never know. Her take on the behavior of the sexes obviously came from close personal experience. I wound up blaming my mother for my inability to get laid, and for implanting in me a negative view of my sexual drive. Now that I am taking more responsibility for creating what happens to me, I realize that I am the one who made it not happen. It would be five more years and New York before I lost my virginity. And in some ways, conditioned both by adulterous father and reproaching mother, I turned into the "beast" she warned I might become.

I took the music education/normal diploma program fairly seriously, for nearly everybody in the music department understood that the only sure way to use your college education well was to become a music teacher. Becoming a concert pianist or a composer, which I most wanted to do, seemed highly unrealistic. Teaching didn't intrigue me much, but I took all the music education courses and fulfilled the classroom requirement. For half a year I taught third, fourth, and fifth grade music at Whittier Elementary School in Seattle, and another half year I taught orchestra and glee club at Ballard High School.

For two summers I worked selling magazines for a company out of Portland. A team of five or six of us college students traveled all over Washington, Oregon, and Idaho under the stewardship of an experienced salesman. The first summer we sold *Good Housekeeping*, which didn't move so well. The second summer I sold *Delineator*, a women's style magazine. It may not have been a better rag, but I had developed a slicker spiel, offering to play something on the piano if the lady bought a subscription. I made $300 that second summer, pretty good money in those days, plus got to see the whole Northwest.

Once when I hitchhiked down to Portland, I got picked up by this guy who immediately started wooing me. Before long, he pulled off the highway. First he kissed me. It was delicious, my first real experience at it. Then he went down on me, but after fifteen minutes, he couldn't stimulate an erection. "If I could only get you on a bed," he told me. That thought didn't do much for me either. I just wasn't interested.

The summer between junior and senior years, a job turned up at Mammoth Lodge in Yellowstone Park, working as a "pack rat," meeting guests as they drove in, and installing them in cabins, serving them, building fires in the morning, emptying their slop jars (we called this "shooting their wild ducks"). The most important part of the summer was the valuable experience I gained as an entertainer. The workers ("savages") put on shows for the "dudes" every night. I sang, acted, even did some adagio dancing with a beautiful girl, Lorinne. The job was supposed to last all summer, but after a month, the lodge cut back its personnel: Depression, you know. So Earl was out of a job.

Johnny, Jack, and Mary Lou

Three especially talented friends of mine were constant companions. Johnny Rarig had perfect pitch and in the men's glee club would magically hum the correct note for our a cappella numbers. He later became a fine commercial arranger and composer in Los Angeles. He still plays piano gigs in Mariposa and Yosemite. Jack DeMerchant, a man of enormous musical talent with many gifts, discovered a quite good tenor voice in me, and had me singing high C's and C sharps almost before I knew it. After World War II he had an operatic quartet called the Troubadours that toured widely and garnered excellent notices. Sometime in the 1980s I lost track of him.

Mary Lou Schroeder (now Wright) was the organist of our group. Today she is organist, choir conductor, and music director of a big church in Pittsburgh. I was less than a perfect model of academic accomplishment, and I owe Mary Lou an enormous debt, for she spent hours and hours copying out my parts and manuscripts. We truly loved each other, so much so that when Jay Wright came into her life, a year or two after graduation, Mary Lou told him she couldn't commit to him because of me. So he came to see me, and went back saying I didn't want to marry her, but he did. Johnny, Jack, Mary Lou, and I would gather at the dinner table, tune our water goblets to different notes on the scale, and play tunes with our spoons. Summertime, we'd sit around a beach fire after a nighttime swim, stare into the flames and philosophize on Music, Life, and the Future. Mary Lou wrote to me recently: "We all came to the conclusion that we wanted our music to be real and vital, not just ivory tower and technical masterpieces—and that we couldn't do that unless we delved into EXPERIENCE and knew personally what all the feelings of humanity were truly like."[1] Typical college musings. But I took it all very seriously.

I stayed in college for five years, the last two highlighted by interesting contradictions. For one thing I was engaged in an ever more determined effort to find a girl with whom I could lose my virginity. Joan, a high school senior, liked me a lot. We were both pitifully uneducated. We often sat in my

Model-T Ford coupe, with no back seat to which we could retire. I remember romantically telling her one time that I was playing Beethoven's Fifth Symphony on her breast. Her friend, whom she told everything, exclaimed, "I wish my boyfriend Jim knew music!" But nothing more happened with Joan.

The biggest of contradictions had to do with my future on graduation. I was spreading my wings a bit as a composer in my junior and senior years. My first real composition, for two trumpets and two trombones, I called *Rhapsody in Brass*, and submitted it—unsuccessfully—for a scholarship at the Malkin Conservatory of Music in Boston. Each of four movements I designated by a color: Gray, in a sad, dirgelike mood; Green, which made use of Irish folk songs; Blue, singing the blues on a theme stated in the first movement; and Red, fiery and exciting. The only performance of this *Rhapsody* took place on a concert of new American music March 2, 1934, sponsored by our college music club.

This piece set in motion a style of composing that I have not really forsaken to the present day. I continuously ended up writing music with a program. Give me words of significance, poetry that sings, theatre, film, dance, any kind of action that asks for a musical underpinning, and I can compose just fine. It took a long time before I stopped apologizing for my inability to write pure music.

For the composers' concert that George McKay assembled in my senior year, I invented a more elaborate program piece. In line with my growing jazz orientation I composed *Symphonic Fragment* for an orchestra with one oboe, three clarinets, bassoon, three trumpets, three trombones, tuba, percussion, and piano. A standup bass was the only string instrument I allowed. As a result of my antireligious "studies" at the YMCA, I conceived the idea of the Church, represented by a reed organ (three clarinets and the oboe) playing an old hymn tune, struggling to maintain itself amid the conflicting forces of modern society, symbolized by the rest of my orchestra. The Church never had a chance: The organ is overcome and drowned out by the piano and the brass. In retrospect I doubt that I effectively demonstrated my antireligious position. I never wrote out my intentions for the printed program, and some confusion existed over what the hymn tune was supposed to mean. *Symphonic Fragment* is important because it points toward the road I would travel in my music. Not necessarily against religion—because I reversed this in later years—but toward songs of protest.

Note

1. Mary Lou Schroeder Wright to Earl Robinson, September 23, 1988.

SLOW BOAT TO CHINA

Equipped with my Bachelor of Music and my Normal Teaching Diploma upon graduation from the University of Washington in June of 1933, I found only one job opening in a small Oregon high school. I might have been hired because I offered to start an orchestra in after-school hours. I didn't pursue it, though. This being the depth of the Depression, it seemed the one thing the country did not need was a music teacher. So I figured I had the choice of becoming a concert pianist, which promised a life of practicing five to eight hours a day, or a composer, and I decided for the latter. It was a brave gesture toward freedom, for I still took some time discovering myself as a composer.

Lo and behold, an invitation came from Canyon Lodge to work the same pack rat job at Yellowstone that summer. Among the guests I met a big wheel at the Eastman School of Music, where I imagined going to study composition. I put a lot of energy into this plan, but it never worked out. I was a heavy hitter and pitcher for the Canyon Lodge baseball team, but the main interest for me was the entertainment we offered the guests in the evening. I sang, acted in skits, played piano, arranged songs for the house orchestra, and danced adagio.

Back in Seattle, my father got me another job at Sears, lifting 90-pound rolls of wrapping paper and wire. I took satisfaction in my own strength, but I wanted to compose, and I would arrive home at night too tired to even sit down at the piano. I quit the job after a few months, took a room across town, rented a piano, and studied with Berthe Poncy Jacobson. The best teacher in Seattle, she had been a student of Ernest Bloch in Geneva. Working with me on the César Franck *Prelude, Chorale and Fugue*, she taught me a method of striking the bell tones that I have never forgotten.

A demonstration of Life Itself

In March 1934 I grabbed the offer of a job in an orchestra aboard the *President Jackson* bound for the Orient. It involved playing salon and classical music for the dinner hour, and dance tunes after dinner. I sang popular songs through a megaphone at the piano, carrying on my Blue Knights experience. Most important on this five-week trip, I lifted my head above the staid lower middle-class life I had always led, and saw my situation from 5,000 miles away across the Pacific Ocean.

The first night out to sea, coming out of the Strait of Juan de Fuca—you can imagine we capitalized on that name for more than one dirty joke—we hit a tremendous storm. Waves twenty feet high. The power, complexity, and contrapuntal quality of the water fascinated me. I saw the storm as an incredible demonstration of Life Itself—the life I had not been living up to then. I pictured myself standing on the sidewalk watching life go by, in all its stunning richness, and I wanted to be a part of it, composing, helping to create and mold. The waves would build and build to fantastic climaxes, smashing against each other, then break into millions of tiny atoms, only to build again and again. I saw it as a great symphonic composition. (In the movie *The Young Toscanini*, the maestro himself had this same fantasy of conducting a sea symphony while crossing the Atlantic as a young man of just about my age.)

On this trip I bought a guitar from a passenger for two dollars. How could I lose? It influenced and informed my serious composition from then on. The guitar, banjo, recorder, or accordion, all folk instruments, found their way into nearly every piece I wrote. Besides which, that guitar—a lot more portable than a piano—helped me become a folksinger. And that is how I first became known and made my living for many years, much more than on the piano, which I always considered my primary instrument. That guitar helped me to gather folksongs wherever I went, and truly understand and assimilate the music of my country.

The ship took us to five ports on the way out, and the same in reverse on the way back: Tokyo, Kobe, Shanghai,

Hong Kong, and Manila. We remained at most two or three days in each city. In Tokyo, I got fitted for silk shirts made to order with my monogram, and by the time we returned there the shirts were finished. In Japan I remember being struck by the way the colors were so different from ours, more primary, yet subtler and bolder. In Hong Kong I made another attempt to lose my virginity. Still wasn't ready.

I forget how it came about, but somehow I had lunch in Shanghai with the second best tennis player in China. I bought cloisonné vases there, a teak chest, and an embroidered shawl that lay over my mother's Steinway for many years after. Visiting Shanghai was an eye-opener in my political education. The city was divided up into several foreign concessions— German, British, French. I took a rickshaw to the American concession, located behind a wall twenty feet high. There, in this city of eight million Chinese, I actually saw a sign posted: "No Chinamen or dogs allowed." Fifteen years later I quoted this to people who wondered about China going Communist.

SECTION TWO
1934-1939

UNION SQUARE: I JOIN UP

Scarcely a week back in Seattle from the Orient, on April 29, 1934, I set out cross-country in a Model-A Ford jalopy owned by Franz Brodine, the ship's orchestra leader. We meandered our way to New York to see Franz's wife Cecilia, a painter who had remained there on a previous trip. With us came old college friend Johnny Rarig, excellent piano player and composer, who played a mellifluous clarinet. With Franz's violin and my guitar we made a trio, collecting and playing folksongs across the country.

Discovering a lifelong truth
This trip, like seeing the Orient, opened my eyes still wider. First we traveled south, camping where we could, to San Francisco, Berkeley, and Yosemite. "Johnny and I walked downtown and wandered down Main Street," I wrote in my diary about Los Angeles, May 8th. "Many Negroes—homosexuals by the dozen—quite a cosmopolitan town." On to Arizona and the Grand Canyon, New Mexico, Texas, and Oklahoma. In Little Rock we stayed with Johnny's friends, the Beans. From the diary, May 20th:

> Fine people. They gave us a lot of interesting sidelights on the "nigger," his life, habits, activities, why he is held down, etc. Stories galore—Southerner's attitude is the same as it was in the Civil War. They consider the nigger shiftless good-for-nothing but they like him and evidently have an understanding of the general lower class of Negro. The thing they do not do as I see it is to stimulate any feeling of pride in himself or in his race. He is made to feel inferior and always treated as such.

Thus my consciousness began to be prodded by these new environments. The Beans even managed to set up a gig for the three of us one night with the Little Rock Symphony—Franz joined the second violin section, Johnny sang one number, and

27

I played a piano piece. Memphis, Nashville, Knoxville, Lynchburg, Richmond. May 23rd: "It is becoming increasingly apparent to me that people are the important thing in this world." There it is: At age 23 I had discovered a lifelong truth. We took a month to reach New York, and it cost me just thirty dollars.

Once we arrived in New York, we managed to scrape together a little money by playing club jobs and small concerts. I still had the idea of further studies at either Juilliard or the Eastman School of Music, but it turns out I never went near either place. Instead, I gravitated down to Union Square. Back in Seattle I had read Albert Halper's book about it. Here was the life! The seething conflict drew me into its orbit, the clashing ideologies, the naked police violence against the workers and unemployed, the tension ready to snap at any moment. Here was the answer, emotional and intellectual, to all my questioning.

Out of that grab bag of causes on Union Square soapboxes, I found the Communists the most effective. They were more disciplined fighters; they had a practical program of united action to force unemployment insurance from the government; and they led the first union of the unemployed. They had a vision of a socialist America, promoted through good papers, the *Daily Worker* and the monthly *New Masses*, with excellent, recognized writers. I watched the cops move their car in on a demonstration in Union Square, admiring with indignant horror how well they did their job. I saw a cop go berserk, clubbing a man into insensibility, then arresting him.

Getting into action

The Communists organized a crowd at the Waldorf-Astoria Hotel for a protest demonstration to free Ernst Thaelmann, the German Communist leader imprisoned by Hitler. I exercised my curiosity and attended. Along came an equestrian troop of police, sweeping their nightsticks indiscriminately. I got hit pretty decisively with a "love tap" on the tailbone. I felt so angry and insulted that I decided to "convert"

then and there. That June of 1934 I joined the YCL, the
Young Communist League. The fact that my backside hurt for
two days reinforced my conversion.

I went home to a single room I shared with a young black
man, Harry, and started on a mass song. I set the people's
chant to music:

> *Down with fascist terror!* (repeat)
> *Down with fascist murder, etc.*

Though this song didn't go any place, wiser heads having
determined that fascism in the U.S. wasn't all that imminent in
this second year of Franklin Roosevelt's presidency, it proved
salutary and educational for me. I was finally getting into action with my music.

I bought and read Communist publications, accepting
these texts as Bible. From my father's contempt for politicians,
from my college friends' doubts about authority and religion,
from my travels to the Orient, from seeing how the poor black
Southern farmers were forced to live, a host of questions had
taken root in my mind. Only now could I see that my mind
had been developing along as most young minds do, gradually
expanding with greater knowledge of the world. Except now I
saw that solutions to the crisis existed. I had a system to hang
onto, a vision to fight for.

My political education moved fast once I got into the
movement. I spent valuable time around the office of the ILD
(International Labor Defense), who campaigned tirelessly to
free the Scottsboro Boys. These nine young black men—boys,
really: the youngest was thirteen—were being framed on
charges of raping two white women in Alabama. The case,
taken up in 1931 by the Communist Party, became a cause célèbre and lasted for many years. ILD members took time to
educate me on what it meant to be born with a black skin in
white America. You were a second-class citizen with no rights
a white man was bound to respect. In the South horrible conditions of poverty and disease for the rural tenant farmers

added to the Jim Crow race discrimination, but even in the
North widespread segregation was more the rule than not.
Every time I fell back, in word or deed, on the image I'd been
brought up with—the black person as a happy-go-lucky type to
be tolerated and somewhat patronized—I had my attitude
roughly but compassionately brought into line.

Pauline Shriftman, the woman who recruited me to the
YCL, told me about the Workers Laboratory Theatre. I went
down to their loft on East 12th Street, to be welcomed by
Steve Karnot, who had studied with the immensely gifted director Vsevolod Meyerhold in the Soviet Union and played at
the International Theatre in Moscow. His column "From a
Director's Notebook" used to appear in *Workers Theatre* and
New Theatre magazines under the name Etienne (French for
Steven) Karnot. He became my Marxist "guru." I became fascinated by the logical, satisfying beauty of dialectical materialism, the Marxian method of analysis whereby an old thesis
butts up against a new one, and fresh syntheses eternally
evolve out of contradictions in society. This still has much
force for me though I have drawn away from the Communist
movement.

I have copies of letters I sent to two old Seattle friends
when I could no longer contain the enthusiasm over my conversion. I pointed out how, in the midst of starvation and
drought and people going naked, the government plows under
every third row of cotton, and slaughters cattle by the thousands. How they cut back on relief budgets at a time when
1,500 new families a day in New York were applying for sub-
sidies. How, years after World War I had ended, Washington
was spending 85 percent of all the money coming in from taxes
building armaments of steel and chemicals "in preparation for
another holocaust which will cause the last one to appear in
the light of a kissing game and post office party."

> Now possibly you are pricking or have pricked up your
> ears long ere this with the insidious thought, Ah,
> Communist propaganda, I smell a red, the underhand

Moscow gold campaign. Probably you have heard that I
have turned Communist. And that is right. Besides admitting it I am proud of it. But I am not especially trying to communize you. It doesn't matter so terribly
much whether you get interested in the party or not.
The important thing is that you understand and realize
or make a definite effort to understand the situation of
today. Especially in its relationship to yourself. Where
are you going to be when this country declares war?
With approaching fascism which is becoming the inevitable last resort of capitalism are you going to submit
quietly or are you going to be part of some group or
other which is fighting it? Are you going to ignore all
the things I have mentioned about the present situation
or are you going to understand the reasons and causes
behind all the graft, corruption, starvation and want
and try to better it? [1]

No, subtlety was not my strong suit.

Later that summer and into the fall of 1934 the Workers
Laboratory Theatre (WLT) and its "shock troupe," a smaller
unit prepared to jump into action at a moment's notice, accepted me into the collective. We had our studio on the
ground and first floors of a building on East 13th Street between Broadway and University Place. A couple of blocks
away the collective shared living quarters, where I took turns
cooking. We used to feed eight people on a dollar a day, and
we ate well. Sometimes we'd get testy over the chores. One
day a notice appeared on the kitchen bulletin board, reading,
"Dishwashers of the week, the pots are filthy." The next morning someone had replied, "From the dishwashers to the House
Manager, Greeting. Tell the cooks to stop cooking beans without water."

Incidentally, though it was totally unimportant to us at the
time, it's interesting that Curt Conway, Rhoda Rammelkamp,
and I were the only non-Jews in the collective. Sophie
Kniznick, a magnificent woman later known as Sophie Saroff,
cleaned and otherwise kept our quarters. Her eight-year-old

daughter, bearing the eminently revolutionary name Proletta, was always scrambling around the building.

Just two weeks after I joined the theatre, the whole shock troupe decided they needed a vacation. Ready as I felt for invigorating activity on the streets, I suddenly had two weeks to kill. I hitchhiked to Michigan to spend the time with my grandparents, Ed and Jane Hawley, on their fruit farm. Mother joined us there. In my eleventh year I had passed a beautiful summer there: I owned a lamb, I trapped rats, and got kicked by a horse. Well, this time I came loaded with Communist ideology and a burning desire to communicate it. Mommer referred to me as a "Bolsheviki" and Grandma threw up her hands in astonishment and disbelief. Grampa Hawley always paid for work done, and I earned some money picking cherries. I kidded around with some pre-teenage girls picking in an adjoining tree. When they started the childish chant, "Eeny meeny mynie mo," I chimed in without thinking, "Catch a nigger by the toe." I recoiled, shocked and contrite for using that forbidden word. Overwhelmingly penitent, I had nobody to commiserate with or apologize to. The girls didn't even notice.

Another memory of that vacation is harder to explain. By then deeply into the dialectical method of thinking, I looked for evidence everywhere. I found it one day watching a slow leak from a garden hose in my grandparents' sloping driveway. The water dripped down, taking time to build up behind small dirt obstructions, but eventually finding a way around or over the top. The relentless movement of the water symbolized the power of the working class, continually dammed up, its force constrained by the greater power of the capitalists. Yet the proletariat ceaselessly, unstoppably marched toward socialism. How did I get all this out of a hose? I don't know, but I got it, and the process satisfied me immensely.

Theatre is a weapon

In this richly creative period, totally at one with the struggle for socialism, our lives obeyed the slogan "Theatre is a weapon in the class struggle." Event after event confirmed this and gave it life. A strike was a sacred obligation. Hearing of one, we would drop everything any time of day or night, pick up a few or no props, gather our subway tokens and head for the action on waterfront docks, street corners, at factory gates, and in tiny meeting halls, to sing and play for the workers, to give them courage in their fight for a better world. Among our main tasks, we supported the unemployed councils in various trades. It was fun. And we felt useful. Since the WLT had been founded, in 1929, the collective had created some eighty short plays for agitational purposes, and we estimated our total audience, since the beginning, at a quarter of a million.

I mentioned subway tokens, which ·f I recall right cost a nickel. Well, this being the Depression, times came when I didn't even have a nickel. I had long suppressed these incidents, but in 1991 when I retrieved my FBI file, there they stood in black and white on the page: my two arrests, March 19, 1936, and again May 20th, for using slugs instead of tokens. The first got me a fine of $2 or two days in jail. I guess that second time I figured lightning never strikes twice . . . but it did. The second arrest got me $10 or three days. I scraped up the fine somehow.

I directed choral drama for WLT. As one of my first projects I taught the actors simple arrangements of black songs with the idea of putting on an epic, carrying the black people from Africa up through the Scottsboro case. This epic involved immense musical possibilities—tomtom rhythms, slave dances and songs, spirituals, blues, and militant protest songs. I made bare subsistence wages, got room and board and no spending money, but felt so much happier than I would be in a classroom. Here I could teach and study the truth, not what the school superintendent told me to.

I had direct experience with black workers in an unusual way. I got a job as an orchestra pianist on a ship out of New York that stopped at Miami and Galveston. The best part of the trip was at night, going up to the bow, where the all-black crew gathered. I talked with them passionately about Communism, how it would take shape, with none of the race discrimination that characterized the shipping industry at that time. Now earlier that year, in May, Harry Bridges and his longshoremen in the San Francisco Bay area had inspired a general strike, which led to one of the best unions ever, the National Maritime Union. Profoundly moved by this awesome solidarity, I tried to persuade the East Coast seamen to take similar action; I later learned that one of these fellows shortly became an organizer with the NMU.

Inspired by the mass action in San Francisco, with my "guru" Steve Karnot I wrote "Song of the Pickets" in a vein popularized in Germany by the composer Hanns Eisler, of whom more anon.

> Oh you victims of the blackjack,
> Of the teargas and gun fire,
> Tho' you died in pain
> You will live again
> In the actions of your comrades.
> We will carry on the battle,
> We will answer blow for blow
> Against the fascist hand
> Of the bosses' band,
> Bloody butchers of our leaders.
> To the boss we fling our answer:
> Workers of the world, UNITE!

In the fall that year we gathered around the piano one night at the theatre to make a song. We took as our theme a strike tactic invented by the Textile Workers, the flying squadron. A shop would go out on strike, and a few workers would pile into their trucks and cars and even bicycles, and throw up a picket line at another factory in a neighboring town. So that whole shop would go out too, because they were ready but just needed something to spark the fuse. This tactic transformed a small strike in one plant into a major, industry-wide demonstration of power that involved nearly half a million workers.

To a surging rhythm I improvised at the piano, a collective group led by Peter Martin, Oscar Saul, and Lou Lantz threw in verses.

The projected East Coast seamen's and longshoremen's strike did not come off, but for a year or more we sang the song wherever we performed. The New Singers, a leftist vocal ensemble conducted by Lan Adomian, picked it up and gave it a more polished choral treatment on concerts at the New School for Social Research and Steinway Hall. In 1935 the *Workers Song Book No. 2*, published by the Workers' Music League, included it in a four-part chorus version, along with my blatantly proletarian "Song of the Pickets."

"Flying Squadron" came into use most excitingly when the young warehouse workers of Local 65 went on strike in the garment district of New York. It was electrifying to turn on these young strikers with verses like

> *We'll tie the city fore and aft,*
> *They'll have to ship their freight by raft,*
> *Make way for the flying squad.*
> *We're going to make those bosses sign*
> *With an iron picket line,*
> *Make way for the flying squadron.*

And before we'd get to the last line we had hundreds of excited workers shouting back, "Make way!" Needless to say, for a performer—an actor and a composer—this passionately alive experience was worth ten Juilliards or Eastmans.

As the theatre's acknowledged but untitled music director, I worked to develop the shock troupe as a chorus, while helping them as solo singers to realize their musical potential. I accompanied them on guitar for the street and strike bookings and remained at the piano for the in-theatre revues which had already reached an advanced satiric and political level by the time I joined the theatre. One such was *Sweet Charity*, by Jack Shapiro, with music by Ruth Burke, which focused on the way the Red Cross, Salvation Army, and other charitable organizations helped to maintain capitalism.

Unquestionably left-Communist in character, our election revues roasted every capitalist candidate, not excluding New York City mayoral contender Fiorello La Guardia. Before the election we called the revue *Who's Got the Baloney?* Again by the Shapiro and Burke team, it made its points almost entirely in musical spoofs, attacking even the Socialist Party candidates who were not red enough for us. After the election, with its inevitable defeat of the workers' candidate, it was *La Guardia's Got the Baloney.*[2]

I wrote music to an election song for Communist City Council candidate Israel Amter, and for another more generic song, "Vote Red":

> *Election Day the big boys come*
> *And slip you fat cigars.*
> *They'll promise you a lot,*
> *A chicken in every pot.*
> *They'll kiss your kids and buy you beer,*
> *And tell you you'll be rich next year.*
> *Two months later, whaddya got?*
> *No more chicken,*
> *Not even the pot.*

One particularly effective thing the theatre did was help to run the pageants at Madison Square Garden. The Party would absolutely fill the place for the annual Lenin Memorials and would rely on us cultural workers for the majority of the program. The connection between art and politics became very clear in the Thirties. My song "Horace Greeley," hot off the guitar to words by Jack Shapiro, occupied a prominent place in one of these rousing pageants. Jack made the logical transformation from the 19th-century editor's famous expression "Go West, young man" to "Go left, young man." Another time I wrote "Quiet Man from Kansas," about the Party's General Secretary Earl Browder, that we sang at the Garden. Songs and chants from the YCLers would punctuate the proceedings. Here is a fine example:

> Give a yell, give a yell,
> Give a good substantial yell.
> And when we yell we yell like hell,
> And this is what we yell:
> Organization,
> Education,
> Solidarity,
> C-O-M-R-A-D-E
> Are we in it? Well I guess.
> YCL! YCL! YCL! Yay-ay-ay!!!

In this intensely exciting political scene, with our left-wing audience there ready and waiting, the revolution right around the corner, I resisted, somewhat unsuccessfully, becoming an actor. My job was music, I told myself. So I would be wholly present to bang a gong for a dramatic dance chant called "Free Thaelmann," which we'd present not just in the theatre but on the streets of the Lower East Side. We'd mark off a section of the sidewalk, and our audience old and young crowded up close or hung out of their windows—box seats!—intensely interested in the way we linked the fight against fascism to the American struggle to organize the unorganized. I also took over from Herbert Haufrecht at the piano, playing his score for the V. J. Jerome play *Newsboy*.

In case anyone's interested, at the ripe old age of twenty-four I finally lost my virginity that spring of 1935. It was Sally's first time, too. I met her in a left-wing theatre class, and we slept together off and on for about four months.

Notes

1. Earl Robinson to Carl Tjerendson, August 5, 1934.
2. In his autobiography, *A Life* (New York: Alfred Knopf, 1988), Elia Kazan says (p. 108) that the earlier version had been pro-La

Guardia; Party orders came down to change the line, then the play became anti-La Guardia. All of which forced him to question the independent spirit behind Theatre of Action and edged him further away from the Communists. Kazan did move away from us, but he is quite mistaken about the play, which was always anti-La Guardia.

THEATRE OF ACTION

If the Workers Laboratory Theatre had acted more or less frankly as a Communist unit, we prepared to widen our scope somewhat when the United Front policy came into being. In this new period, the Communists did not give up their organizational identity, but instead of polemicizing so much against other factions on the left, we decided that in order to resist fascism, we had better make productive alliances with other groups. The German experience chastened the whole worldwide Communist movement: There, the Communists fought so much against the Social Democrats all through the rise of fascism that they tragically underestimated the main danger. So we changed our name to the Theatre of Action and organized an impressive Advisory Council that included bona fide leftwingers like Clifford Odets, Albert Maltz, and Mike Gold, as well as others not so left-identified, such as Moss Hart, Erskine Caldwell, Alfred Kreymborg, and Lee Strasberg.

I become a Broadway actor

As of May 28, 1935, the WLT became the professional Theatre of Action when we produced our first full-length play, *The Young Go First*, at a Broadway house, the Park Theatre at Columbus Circle. Elia (Gadg) Kazan, a Communist then, but out of the Party later that year, came down from the Group Theatre to co-direct with Alfred Saxe. The play took the position that the Civilian Conservation Corps camps—part of the Roosevelt New Deal "make-work" plan—were militaristic and semi-fascist in character: The food was bad, the working hours long, the officers in charge were drunks, adequate transportation for recreation in nearby towns was unavailable, and the boys got their $25-a-month pay docked for very minor infractions.

The origins of this play are interesting. A young teenager named Arthur Vogel came to us one day, looking for Alice, whom he had met the night before at a party he had seen listed in the *Daily Worker*'s "What's On" column. In those days four or more young people would "shack up" in an apartment they could afford together, and they'd throw a rent party whose admission was either 25 cents or something for the apartment, like a couple of rolls of toilet paper. Alice auditioned for us, but by the time Arthur arrived, she had already left, never to be seen or heard from again. We asked if Arthur acted, directed, wrote, or what. He didn't do anything. But as we drew him into conversation, he began telling scenes of life in a CCC camp. He'd just come out of a seven-month stay in the hospital, due to an injury on his ankle suffered in one of the camps. We asked if there had been any strikes there, and he said yes, one time all the boys saved up their hard boiled eggs from breakfast, and later that day fired them in a massive volley against the camp director.

His delivery was less than compelling, but we asked him to put his ideas into play form for us, with the help of Peter Martin, our chief playwright. Because he had so much material to work with, a one-act play turned into a three-acter with nine scenes. Charles Friedman, on our executive board, also got involved with the writing. The leading Communist playwright John Howard Lawson invited the three of them up to his old colonial house in Moriches, near Montauk, Long Island, whence they emerged only three weeks before our scheduled opening with a play. The incidents were based not only on Vogel's experiences, but also on others from camps in five different states. The eight characters came from different ethnic backgrounds, all of them picked up for work at the Blue Hill Mountain Camp from various relief agencies in New York. By the end of the play, the boys organize and win their demands. The script, incidentally, is credited to George Scudder, a name literally picked from the phone book. Arthur Vogel/George Scudder later went on to a varied career in the theatre as writer, producer, and director.

I allowed myself to be pushed into becoming an actor. I performed creditably, mostly just by playing myself. At least none of the critics singled me out or named me negatively. The other cast members included Stephen Karnot, Will Lee, Perry Bruskin, Ben Ross, Nick (he preferred Nik) Ray, Curtis Conwaye (later known as Curt Conway), Edward Mann, David Kerman, and Harry J. Lessin. We all joined Actors' Equity and became activists in it. Ours was reportedly the first play to give rehearsal pay—the same five dollars a week we received normally. During the run, under our Actors' Equity contract, we got $25 a week.

The play was not a hit. Neither was it a flop. Most of the first-line drama critics attended a Hollywood farce called *Knock on Wood* that opened the same night. But we did get a number of reviews. On the minus side, the *Herald Tribune*: "Even a sympathetic audience found it hard to accept the naïve suggestion that the government camps are such salt mines of human exploitation as the authors suggest, although its members were patently more than anxious to do so." Other critics cited the episodic structure.

Among the plusses, the *New York Sun* called *The Young Go First* an "exceedingly fine production," saying, "The sets designed by Mordecai Gorelik are among the most efficient and interesting I have seen this season, and the direction of Alfred Saxe and Elia Kazan leaves little to be desired." John Mason Brown in the *Evening Post* added that the play was "acted with great reality by a likable set of young players who do not appear to be acting at all inasmuch as they seem themselves to be such authentic, healthy and happy graduates of the kind of outdoor life that is lived in CCC camps." (It seems he missed the point of the play.) Mike Gold, *Daily Worker* columnist, was quoted in the *Post*: "I've seen several of the CCC camps, and I know this stuff is true to life."[1]

A mixed but prescient notice appeared in *Variety* (June 12, 1935): "There are several actors in the troupe who can develop easily and prominently. One youth, Nik Ray, looks like a film bet, and another, Will Lee, may eventuate a comic to be reckoned with. But the play is bad, very bad." Nik did indeed go into film, but as a director: Some of his credits include *They Live By Night*, *Johnny Guitar*, *Rebel Without a Cause*, *The Sav-*

age Innocents and *Lightning Over Water* (with Wim Wenders).
Will Lee is best remembered for his years on *Sesame Street*.

The theatre cost us $250 a week to rent. To save money,
we worked out a deal with the unions whereby we hired only
two stagehands at scale, while the actors did the rest. Various
organizations that bought benefit houses provided ushers, such
groups as the Mosholu Branch of the Friends of the Soviet Union, the Committee to Support Southern Textile Workers, the
Bath Beach Branch of the American League Against War and
Fascism, and the International Workers Order—to give an idea
of the breadth of left-wing life in New York at the time. The
play ran five or six weeks in that unbearably hot theatre. With
air conditioning we might have played longer, but in those
days only the really big hit shows played through the summer.
Before we closed we did a special Friday matinee so that the
casts of other socially-minded plays could attend, like *Awake
and Sing*, *Waiting for Lefty*, *Till the Day I Die*, and the recently
closed *Parade* and *Black Pit*.

Theatre of Action's going professional produced a lot of
changes socially and politically. For instance, we upped our
standard of living. Charles Friedman had talked a wealthy
handbag manufacturer into leasing a building for a year on
East 27th Street between Third and Lexington avenues, to
serve as our living and working space. There each of us had a
separate room. The changes reached a "dialectically" new pla-
teau when the whole group went into the Works Progress
Administration's Federal Theatre Project in late March of
1936.

We made one last effort to retain our independent Theatre
of Action status by producing *The Crime*, a play by Michael
Blankfort on a complex labor betrayal theme. This was significant personally because of the way I was directed, again by
Gadg Kazan and Al Saxe. I had the part of a Spanish-American
War veteran. Kazan instructed me to stand ramrod straight,
with military bearing. This counteracted my forward-leaning
stoop which probably had its genesis in my pre-glasses days as I
sat at the piano trying to see the notes.

In *The Crime*, a labor leader becomes a rat. We gave only two performances before it dawned on us that, however psychologically shrewd a portrait Blankfort had drawn, we simply did not want to expose any negative side to the labor movement that would discourage workers from joining. Michael Blankfort later went to Hollywood as a screenwriter. Interestingly enough, he ratted on his old friends in 1952 when he testified as a friendly witness before the House Un-American Activities Committee. A touch of foreshadowing?

Note

1. All reviews, May 29, 1935.

CAMP UNITY: JOE HILL, LEADBELLY AND LINCOLN

The summer of 1936 was an enormously creative and fulfilling time for me. Bob Steck, director of Camp Unity, about 50 miles north of the big city in Wingdale, New York on Lake Ellis, approached me to come up. I would be in charge of the music program, allowed not only to compose, but encouraged to start musically Americanizing the movement—something I had been feeling the need for since I first joined up two years before, but hadn't clearly thought out. The poet, later novelist and screenwriter Alfred Hayes served as the dramatic director of the camp that summer. And Sophie Kniznick, who had taken care of the Workers Laboratory Theatre gang, took charge as assistant manager, holding sway in the kitchen for many a season. Her daughter Proletta ran the bookstore and newspaper stand. I remember how some of the Jewish campers used to delight us with their cheerleading:

> Mit a U, mit an N, mit an I-T-Y,
> Unity, Unity, Ay Yi Yi!

Helping the movement become more American

By 1936, the Party had begun growing out of its earlier sectarianism. It had adopted the United Front strategy, trying to pull together all antifascists. It felt that a closer identification with the home-grown tradition of revolution and protest would help the movement become more American, less dominated by immigrants or their first-generation children. In Stalin's language these were "cosmopolitan" types—by this he mostly meant Jews—who deprived the national movement of a certain authenticity. For when all is said and done, Stalin basically threw out Lenin's proletarian internationalism and substituted a Great Russian chauvinism. His emphasis on the national dimension affected all Communists worldwide, though at the time I did not have this understanding. Indeed, I would

45

not take one iota away from the wonderful international quality that had characterized Party life: I remember deeply enjoying the "Party picnics" where the ethnic groups from Russia,
Greece, Italy, Poland, Yugoslavia, and other countries would
play and sing their own music, apart from each other yet
bound together by the struggle for a better world.

In my job, which I took on happily, I dug out American
folk songs with working-class content, like "Wanderin'" and
"Paddy Works on the Railway," promoted the book of *Negro
Songs of Protest* collected by Lawrence Gellert, and popularized
the blaring folk Americanism of the Industrial Workers of the
World (the IWW or the Wobblies)—"Hold the Fort,"
"Commonwealth of Toil," "The Preacher and the Slave," "Pie
in the Sky," and the contents of the little red songbook the
Wobblies put out "to fan the flames of discontent." These
songs became American C. P. (Communist Party) standards.

To aid in this noble project I directed the Camp Unity
Chorus, an ever-changing amateur group organized every week
from among the campers. Tuesday night at the end of the dinner hour I would proceed through the dining room banging on
a tray with a knife, chanting in my loudest voice, "Chorus,
Chorus, come join the Chorus, back porch of the dining hall,
if you can talk you can sing." From close to a thousand people
in camp, about two hundred would show up for rehearsal.
Though they weren't expected to read music, I had mimeo-
graphed the words, and we'd begin preparing a program. By
the end of a week of nightly rehearsals the numbers had
shrunk to around a hundred voices; but a moving, often rousing choral program would adorn the Saturday evening's presentation for campers, staff, and weekend guests.

A profound demonstration of dialectics emerged from this
choral work with amateurs. *Quantity changed into quality.*
Large numbers of voices seemed to guarantee success. The
stronger, purer, on-pitch voices naturally took the lead, meeting the reasonably high standards that I set, and encouraging
the weaker voices to give their best. People who in their childhood had been called monotones, admonished in music classes

by insensitive teachers, "You be a listener," found themselves singing powerfully, beautifully in concert with the others. Of the two to three thousand singers who joined the Camp Unity choruses during the two summers I was there ('36 and '38), I only had to ask one person to leave, a young man whose ear was so untrained that he couldn't hear himself singing.

Accepting the line

Let's face it, Camp Unity was a Communist camp. The party line predominated and most of the thousands who came there understood this. So what was this party line that I found no trouble at all in wholly accepting? First, a congenial acceptance of all races, creeds, religions, and political persuasions, a welcoming attitude not all that common in America during those years. Only if you were fascist-inclined would you have difficulty fitting in, but then that would be *your* problem. Working people, especially those in struggle, were considered comrades. Bigotry and anti-Semitism were not just frowned upon, but actively opposed. We looked down on capitalism as the root cause, not just of fascism and racism, but of the Depression wherein 17 million were unemployed out of a nation of 100 million.

The party line included a whole-souled devotion to the Soviet Union, the only country to have carried through a successful revolution against capitalism, the first workers' state run by and for the working people and the peasants. The Party did not have to twist my arm or coerce me in any way. I bought the whole scene, thrilled to the apparent Soviet success in collectivizing agriculture and creating a secure industrial base through five-year plans. I delighted in the picture of a nation transforming its 90 percent illiterate into reading, writing, thinking, loving human beings. Heroism is deeply moving to me, and I cried at the robust Soviet films which celebrated first the Revolution and then this giant reconstruction of a whole country, 200 million souls leading the world. And all without benefit of a single capitalist, in fact with the active opposition of the "uppah clawsses" around the world.

The Soviet achievement in building their first subway in
Moscow exhilarated us on the American left, especially when
they decorated the station walls not with commercial ads but
with murals and works of art. We sang about it at Camp
Unity, using what we called "buffoons" to tell the story. This
is the old dramatic trick of heads and hands poking through a
curtain and manipulating doll bodies. The song written by Lou
Lantz to the tune of "Tavern in the Town" runs like this:

> *There is a marvel in the town (in the town),*
> *The Moscow Metro underground (underground)*
> *Down in Moscow's sands*
> *It was built by workers' hands*
> *Engineers, volunteers, built it all.*
>
> *With our Shock Troop flags unfurled*
> *We have challenged all the world*
> *We have shown unto the scoffers*
> *How the workers build.*
>
> *We built with workers' might and main (might*
> *and main),*
> *We planned it with a worker's brain (worker's brain),*
> *And for workers' use and not for bosses' gain. . . .*

In the Camp Unity and Party atmosphere of the '30s we
waxed enthusiastic about everything Soviet, including Lenin
and Stalin. The only negative information about the Soviet
Union came from the capitalist press, which had demonstrated
their bias countless times since the Revolution. So kill me: I
cannot remember being aware of any excesses of Stalin that
could not be explained in those days as merely reactions necessary to sustain socialism.

An addendum here, in no way attributable to party line, is
connected with my sex life. At Camp Unity, a place of free
and fast relationships, I made up for my twenty-four and a half
years of virginity with a quiet vigor. Reflecting on it now, I

imagine that many of the women I met that summer felt unin-
hibited away from home and parents—and boyfriends. And as
idealistic young Communists, they probably considered the
old-fashioned ways of chaste courtship and traditional marriage
depressingly bourgeois compared to the open culture of free
love. I know I felt that way. For some of the Jewish women, of
whom there were many at this camp so close to New York, an
affair with a genuine WASP, one in a leadership position,
however humble, may well have broadened their social horizons: I might have played a part in "Americanizing" their
party experience. Again, I'm only guessing.

If we found no fault with the Soviet Union, we had at the
same time a tremendously open and positive approach to
America, its revolutionary past and its ongoing history. There
would be a socialist America one day, coming about through
struggle, possibly revolution. Of this we felt convinced. General Secretary of the Communist Party Earl Browder's pamphlet "Communism is 20th Century Americanism" effectively
symbolized what the movement meant to me. I might point
out that though I speak in this book about music and theatre
primarily, artists in every other field also felt the same way:
Parallel campaigns in literature, dance, film, visual arts (such as
the populist murals of the 1930s), also thrived. In these Depression conditions almost anyone with a heart wanted to contribute somehow to solving the country's problems.

I received a sketch that summer with satirical lyrics about
Franklin D. Roosevelt. Two pro writers, Lesan and Gabrielson, had done this piece where FDR was Noah, and he and his
New Deal were trying to put the capitalist Ark together. I remember scoring this piece in detail, including a dance tune
where I added lyrics of my own, and producing it on stage at
Unity. Later on I worked with Harold Rome for the International Ladies Garment Workers Union, the ILGWU, on an
early version of *Pins and Needles*, the union musical that
opened in November 1937 and wound up running for an incredible three years on Broadway. Besides sharing duties with
him in the two-piano orchestra for the tryouts, I contributed

the FDR-Old Man Noah skit. The ILG included this Roosevelt satire at first, but later removed it as they began to accept and to be accepted by FDR. And I think Hecky Rome was much happier as the principal writer-composer on the final version of *Pins and Needles*. Rome wrote a populist man-in-the-street song called "Franklin D. Roosevelt Jones," and Al Hayes and I came up with a posh, upper-crust takeoff on it, "Herbert C. Hoover Snaithe." When Hecky heard about it he asked where the hell we got the name Snaithe, and we told him: out of his own Yale College classbook!

Another writer of importance there at Camp Unity was Abel Meeropol, better known by his nom de plume, Lewis Allan (I'll refer to him both ways). We began an ongoing collaboration that summer of 1936 which lasted, with certain intermissions, for more than forty years. The first two lyrics of his that I set to music were "May I Dance Without My Pants?"—an appropriate Depression number—and "I Kissed a Communist (Was My Face Red!)":

> *I always read the paper "for people who think."*
> *I never dreamed that I was even pink*
> *Till one lovely evening in the public parks*
> *I met a stalwart fellow whose kisses left their—Marx.*
>
> *I kissed a communist, was my face red!*
> *I was accursed by Mr. Hearst*
> *And Arthur Brisbane almost burst*
> *'Cause I kissed a communist, was my face red!*
>
> *The Liberty League said they could tell*
> *That I was under Stalin's spell.*
> *The daring vigilantes and the D. A. R. so bold*
> *They even searched my panties to find some Mos—cow—*
>   *Gold.*
> [Here I interpolated strains of Rachmaninoff's well-known Prelude in C sharp minor.]

I kissed a communist, was my face red!
I'm under suspish by Hamilton Fish
'Cause I kissed a communist.

Abel possessed an inexhaustible ability to turn out topical lyrics. Some did not excite me, however, and I'd give them back. Undaunted, he made his own music. His own songs— tunes and lyrics—included "Is There a Red Under Your Bed?," "Beloved Comrade," and a song of the Abraham Lincoln Battalion, all in minor keys, which he seemed to prefer. From the beginning he insisted on his own music for his song of a lynching, "Strange Fruit." This proved smart of him, for his mournful tune was taken by Billie Holiday, who sang and recorded it with immense power and pathos. She sang it as an intense blues, but in such an understated way that some questioned whether she understood the lyrics. But she did, all right. Her own life, with the discrimination she suffered, had prepared her well. Billie's singing made it a tremendous tour de force.

A useful song

I mentioned reviving some of the old IWW songs as part of our effort to Americanize the movement. One Friday night in late June, that summer of 1936, we planned a program of Wobbly songs like "Hallelujah, I'm a Bum," "Solidarity Forever" and songs of the Swedish-born Joe Hill (born Joel Hagglund, also known as Joseph Hillstrom)—"Pie in the Sky," "There is Power (in a Band of Working Men)," "Mister Block," "The Rebel Girl." Joe Hill was a labor organizer, executed in 1915 by firing squad in Salt Lake City after his conviction on a trumped-up murder charge brought by the State of Utah to squelch the IWW. He also wrote excellent songs.

Joe Hill cannot legitimately be called a composer—here I speak as a composer. His power is in his lyrics; the tunes he mostly stole, like Woody Guthrie. (I intrude here my advice to budding composers. Steal all you want, but only from the best places.) I sometimes compare Joe Hill in this respect with Johann Sebastian Bach. Frequently, in order to supply the music needed each Sunday at church, Bach would make use of, i.e., steal, a tune from the folk, from the street. Outfitting it with proper biblical words, he would arrange it as a chorale. Being a genius, his work lasted for the ages.

This is not so far away from what Joe Hill did. In his job, not so structured as Bach's, but no less important to him, he created songs for the working people, music to help and inspire them in their struggles. The news got around. When the Southern Pacific railway workers faced a strike, for raising their wage from a dollar to a dollar and a half a day, a strike that they foresaw would keep them out on the bricks for eighteen weeks or more, they knew they would need help. There could be backsliders among their ranks, facing loss of income for that long. Needing to support wife and kids, they might be tempted to scab—than which there is nothing lower or more contemptible.

And when they heard about this traveling Wobbly poet named Joe Hill, they called on him and he responded magnificently. He took a railroad folk song about an engineer named Casey Jones who ran his train through to a glorious wreck. He transformed him into a scab, who after dying in the wreck, went to heaven and scabbed on the angels . . . and was appropriately "sent to Hell a-flyin'," ending up shoveling sulfur!

The afternoon of our Friday-night campfire tribute to the Wobblies, Alfred Hayes gave me this poem of four-line verses he had published two years before in *New Masses*. I went into a tent with my guitar, and in about forty-five minutes emerged with a song. Al's words could certainly stand on their own as a poem in strict iambic meter, but for my purposes it seemed right to repeat the last line—better for joining in on, and the key to shaping a more finished tune.

> *I dreamed I saw Joe Hill last night*
> *Alive as you and me.*
> *Says I, "But Joe, you're ten years dead."*
> *"I never died," says he.* (Repeat)

"The Copper Bosses killed you, Joe.
They shot you, Joe," says I.
"Takes more than guns to kill a man,"
Says Joe, "I didn't die." (Repeat)

From San Diego up to Maine
In every mine and mill,
Where workers strike and organize,
It's there you'll find Joe Hill. (Repeat)

I've skipped a few stanzas, but the first one comes back to end the song.

I sang it that evening, but only a true clairvoyant could have foreseen anything like its subsequent popularity. It didn't get much applause, though I had put all my heart into it. I had no thought at the time of its being anything beyond a useful song to fit in with the Joe Hill campfire. But the next morning, a few people came around, saying, "That's a pretty good tune you have there. Could I copy out the words?" Which of course I gladly obliged.

That night something rather stupendous was born. Before the end of summer, we began hearing about "Joe Hill" being sung at a New Orleans Labor Council. Then they used it on a San Francisco picket line. "Joe Hill" went to Spain that fall with the American volunteers of the Abraham Lincoln Brigade to help inspire the fight against Franco.

Bob Miller published the song in 1938. I credit Michael Loring as being the first person to sing "Joe Hill" publicly. That same year he recorded it, with me at the piano, for Musicraft. I recorded it myself with guitar for the Library of Congress. A WPA Federal Music Project concert devoted to my music at the Brooklyn Museum included it, and the left-wing baritone Mordecai Bauman sang it at Town Hall in 1939.

At first the publisher refused to have "Joe Hill" reprinted in any of the myriad of labor songbooks that appeared in those days. Pete Seeger complained to me about this situation: "It's a blight upon working class culture. Son of a bitch. Well, it's the system." Eventually Bob relented—or people began to ignore him. "Joe Hill" is by far my most reprinted song. One collection that included it, *Songs That Changed the World*, identifies the song as "the 'spiritual' of the union movement," which I like just fine.[1]

Ben Dobbs, a progressive American I knew, had fought in Spain and later with the U. S. Army during World War II. Assigned to the OSS, he had the job of contacting the Italian partisans prior to our invasion at Salerno. Provided with all the necessary papers and identity cards, he managed to make contact. But the Italians were unimpressed with him or his papers.

"How in hell do we know who you are?" they said (in rough translation). "We live under Mussolini. Your papers are shit."

So Ben cudgeled his brain. How to prove his honesty—that he was in truth reliable? In desperation, he began singing, "I dreamed I saw Joe Hill last night. . . ."

"You're okay," said the partisans.

If I'd been more of a businessman, I would probably have exercised greater control over the song—aside from singing it at just about every appearance I ever made for more than fifty years. After a while I lost track, though I am continuously reminded of it up to the present day. It became free as a bird, traveled on its own like a folk song, composer and poet mostly forgotten. One labor school put out a booklet of *Workers Songs* with "Joe Hill"—"Words: Earl Robinson, Music: Traditional." Yep, that's how it traveled, every which way. But times came, years later, when "Joe Hill" saved both Al Hayes and me from going dead broke.

Go to the memorial service for almost any left-wing old-timer and you'll hear "Joe Hill" as the anthem everybody knows. Mouthing Al Hayes's simple, precious words, tears come to people's eyes as they recall the bristling times and audacious movements of their youth, when the spirit of Joe Hill pushed them on to courageous acts of solidarity.

So many stories, lies, and legends built up, and torn down, around Joe Hill: Books written to show that maybe he did kill the storekeeper, that it wasn't a frameup after all. More books to prove it *was* a frameup, with Joe deserving to be enshrined as an authentic, Swedish-born American hero (which I believe). Meanwhile, our song keeps moving on, translated into a dozen languages. Not long ago, Pete Seeger sent me a tape he'd received from Cuba, where a whole chorus does it in Spanish.

I suppose that for fifty-five years my close identification with this song has served to almost pass Joe Hill's mantle to me, though this could be said of others too, like Woody Guthrie or Pete Seeger, or later Bob Dylan or Phil Ochs. (Woody once wrote a "Joseph Hillstrom" song which never went very far.) I am proud of popularizing the Joe Hill saga, and I don't doubt that some of his legendary aura lit up my own career. But in truth there is no mantle. Each of us is unique. The important thing is that our song lasted and lasted, encouraging each new generation to study Joe Hill's life, and find in it the strength to keep up the struggle. As he said when he was about to die, "Don't mourn, organize!"

A troubadour from Fannin Street

To supplement our entertainment, we often brought fresh talents up from New York or elsewhere. Many of them at the beginning of their careers gained valuable experience performing before Camp Unity audiences. Dancer Pearl Primus came. Also the black singer Napoleon Reed, whom I accompanied on the piano. The afternoon of his recital, I was rehearsing with him when Louis Pasternak, the camp manager, and Bob Steck, the director, walked into the hall. Now Pasternak ruled with an iron hand, and his politics were insistently "correct." As Reed launched into "I Got Plenty o' Nothin'" from *Porgy and Bess*, Pasternak interrupted to say that such a demeaning image of Negroes would be totally inappropriate at Camp Unity and would have to be scrapped. Bob and I motioned to the singer that he'd have to go along. When Reed started the next number on his program, a spiritual, again Pasternak objected: too otherworldly. After Pasternak voiced a third objection, the six-foot-two singer inhaled deeply and in a smoothly modulated

tone said, "Mr. Pasternak, I must insist that you leave the theatre and desist from your opinions, or I shall leave on the spot.
If I am to take orders from you, I'll have no repertoire left." It
was the first time I had ever seen Louis Pasternak bested.

When I heard we had a chance of getting Huddie Ledbetter
to visit and sing for us at the camp, I got some excited. This
fabled troubadour, known professionally as Leadbelly but at
that time not so well known in the North, had been a prisoner
on chain gangs—he had been convicted of assault with intent
to kill—and with the help of folklore collector John Lomax
had sung his way to freedom. He knew hundreds of songs
ranging from dancy numbers like "Green Corn Come Along
Cholly," to work and chain-gang songs like "Take This Hammer, Carry It to the Captain"; and from the Fannin Street red
light district of Shreveport, Louisiana, songs for and about
prostitutes—"Yellow Gal," and Frankie, who shot her man
Albert (not Johnny in Leadbelly's version) who was "doin' her
wrong." Fannin Street was one of the very few places a black
singer could make a living as an entertainer.

This latter category created some trouble in Camp Unity—
songs like "DeKalb Blues," "Ella Speed," songs of bad women
and gun-toting gamblers. Even with his occasional jail song,
the protest could barely be discerned through his dialect. As
for myself, I was absolutely uncritical about this man of such
obvious and tremendous talent. Anything he sang was all right
with me. The beauty and freshness of his imagery, the power
of his voice, the driving rhythm of his 12-string guitar, totally
mesmerized me. It mattered not a whit to me that he threw in
little buck and wing steps, used terms like "nigger," "yallow
gal" and "brown skin," and obsequiously passed his hat at the
end of numbers (only a few months before, he had been on
welfare in New York City).

But in the Communist Party we had a rather exalted, ideal-
ized picture of the Negro as a faultless person of dignity and
substance, a person steeled in the struggle against second-class
citizenship and the minstrel-show Step'nfetchit image. Paul
Robeson represented this kind of man. But Huddie Ledbetter

didn't exactly qualify. While possessing his own strength, Huddie had learned through a struggle for bare survival to be totally respectful to white people, to play the happy-go-lucky fool when necessary. His song to Texas governor Pat Neff was exactly the kind of pleading that would gain him a reprieve in 1925, after six years of a thirty-year murder rap at Shaw State Prison Farm. As was his song to Louisiana governor O. K. Allen, that John Lomax recorded at the State Farm in Angola in 1933. Early on at Camp Unity I asked Huddie not to call me Mr. Robinson. So he switched to Mister Earl, and embarrassed me with that for maybe a year or two before the comrades persuaded him to drop this habit. (He continued addressing the younger Lomax, twenty-seven years his junior, as Mister Alan.)

The morning after Huddie's first concert, the camp was in an uproar. Instigated by the camp's handful of black Party members, there was strong criticism of Leadbelly, of me, of the white leadership that would allow such a thing to happen. "Why does he put on that minstrel act?" "The man's an Uncle Tom." "An insult to Negro women!" "As bad as Step'nfetchit." "The very name Leadbelly perpetuates a chauvinist stereotype, all brawn and no brain." And so on.

"Leadbelly is my stage name," Huddie explained. Along with Ironhead, Clear Rock, Black Samson, Lightnin', Steam Shovel, all names given to or adopted by black workingmen of the Deep South, Leadbelly is an honorable name denoting indestructibility in the face of hardship—and this from a heftily built, muscular figure with great arms that lifted and swung that 12-string guitar like a ukulele. The point was lost, however, on the Northern urbanized black Communists who had come to the Party believing with good reason that it would be a bastion of strength in their life-long fight for equality, a sanctuary against discrimination. Leadbelly's appearance evoked too closely the spiritual-singing, goody-goody slave mentality. Why, even the blues were considered a relic of the slave past.

The majority of Camp Unity, while enjoying Leadbelly's music, tended to side with the black minority, and I came to see their point. Huddie himself came to the rescue. It turned out he had already written a rousing song for the Scottsboro Boys. Just a little delving below the surface uncovered a deep and abiding protest, integral to all his singing.

Well, the second night we put on Leadbelly, it was the same Huddie but a different program. Though a case could be made that his songs of prostitutes were a form of protest, he didn't sing any of those. Instead came more chain gang songs, "Midnight Special," and the evening culminated in his magnificent "Bourgeois Blues." After Alan Lomax had spent an unsuccessful night in Washington, D. C., trying to get lodging for Huddie and his wife Martha while he recorded his songs for the Library of Congress, Leadbelly roared out the lines

> *In the home of the brave, land of the free,*
> *I don't want to be mistreated by no bourgeois-ee.*
> *Lawd it's a bourgeois town,*
> *Oh-o-oh, it's a bourgeois town.*
> *I got the bourgeois blues,*
> *I'm gonna spread the news all around.*

Incidentally, his pronunciation of that word was closer to "bush-wah."

Huddie hadn't been long out of state prison. After a while he got used to a new kind of freedom. Acquaintance with progressive-minded people who accepted him as a man and an equal, and praise by discriminating critics, all combined to wear off the minstrel edges. In time a new Leadbelly came forth, a tower of dignity, who stood before audiences at nightclubs, at countless folk festivals, over the air, and in album after album of new and exciting music. One time I shared an evening with him out in California. During a discussion period following our presentation, someone asked him: What would you say is folk music? Leadbelly rose, pondered, and replied, "Well, sir, the only way I can define it, it's that folk music that the folks sing and keep on singing and just keep on singing no matter what." So much for the professors.

One sad thing about his later period was his failure to get into movies. In any decently-run society, Huddie would have been a natural film star. His looks and his remarkable personality came across best in a small hall—close up, where you could see him and understand his words better. Movies would have really brought him to the big audience he naturally wanted. He hung around Hollywood for a year and a half but, as he sang, "There's a lot of Jim Crow in the moving picture show."

As a folk-based composer, I became strongly influenced by Huddie Ledbetter. With that marvelous 12-string guitar, he added his innate power and originality to the barrelhouse style he had studied in Shreveport with a man named Pine Top. "That's what I wanted to play on guitar, that boogie woogie piano bass," he said. "And I got it out of the barrelhouse on Fannin Street."

I took symphonic ideas from him. With no imagination at all, I could hear in Leadbelly the entire bass, cello, tuba, and trombone sections of an orchestra. For many years after that first meeting at Camp Unity, I would go to the master, listen, and study his records again and again when I had a composing job that demanded something of the blues power so inherent in him. The Black Church section of my *Lonesome Train* cantata is one of my tributes to him.

I owed a debt to Huddie for the use of words as well as music. When John Lomax first brought him to New York, audiences had some trouble understanding him. Huddie solved this by talking explanation between the verses, with his 12-stringer still noodling away underneath. The talk became integral to the song, and a new work of art would emerge. Listen to his "Frankie and Albert" for a demonstration. In line with my theme, "Steal all you want, but only from the best places," I incorporated the Leadbelly style in my very next song.

Abe Lincoln, Revolutionary

In my efforts to compose on suitably American themes, I had been looking for lyrics of substance to set to music, and by and large not finding them. The writers for the little poetry magazines generally floated out on Cloud 7 somewhere, trying desperately to be original, while cogitating their navels. Lyrics such as "Joe Hill" by Alfred Hayes came few and far between. So when I came across Earl Browder's pamphlet "Communism is 20th Century Americanism," I found myself latching onto his quotations from Abraham Lincoln's First Inaugural Address. These words, with their deep American significance, grabbed me in the gut:

> *This country with its institutions*
> *belongs to the people who inhabit it.*

Then for balance, I added

> *This country with its Constitution*
> *belongs to us who live in it.*

Lincoln again:

> *Whenever they shall grow weary*
> *Of the existing government*
> *They can exercise their constitutional right*
> *Of amending it.*
> *Or their re-vo-lu-tion-ar-y right*
> *To dismember, or overthrow it.*

(When I perform the song today, I sing "we" instead of "they.")

I set Lincoln's words to a catchy tune, though it really seemed as if they set themselves. Then Al Hayes and I surrounded them with folksy verses that, Leadbelly-like, made use of talking as well as singing. We made a statement on Lincoln that lit him (speaking theatrically) in ways that may have gone a little beyond his original intention. We placed Old Abe as "an honest man," "a working man," "a thinking man," "a great tall tree"—though for a time he "wavered and shook" on the slavery question because "he wanted peace between the states."

The Republicans for years called themselves "the party of Lincoln," so we compared him to today:

> *But Abe never crawled when the showdown came*
> *Like some people now who take his name.* . . .

Lincoln emerges a revolutionary, his democratic message ringing loud and clear, as the audience joins in on his words.

"It may take a bit longer for poetry of this kind to get around," I am quoted four years later in reference to this song,

> but if it has an idea which is close to the thoughts the majority of people are thinking—and is written in a style which is not too much at variance with their experience, then it will find them and contribute to their lives. And if it has music with it (and the same qualifications go for the music) then it will reach the mass audience, conservatively speaking, about five times as fast and five times as effectively.[2]

"Old Abe Lincoln" found acceptance at Camp Unity as no big deal, just the simple, 20th-century truth of the matter. When we brought it into New York that fall, however, it made quite a splash. My actor friend John Lenthier took it to Spain, where he sang it with the Lincoln Brigade, and where he died fighting. Along with "Joe Hill," it became part of the first presentation of Cabaret TAC, a Theatre Arts Committee antifascist revue, begun in New York City in the fall of 1938. We appeared Sunday nights, when the theatres went dark, at the Chez Firehouse on East 55th Street off Broadway. George Abbott produced that first TAC show as a benefit for medical aid to Spain and China. Norman Lloyd, Charles Weidman, Jay Williams and Hiram Sherman participated, among others. To give an example of our concerns and fears at the time, I quote a number "It Can't Happen Here," sung and danced:

> *It can happen in Gallipoli,*
> *In Afghanistan or Tripoli,*

But in dear old Mississipoli,
No, it can't happen here.

"Old Abe Lincoln" was sung by Lief Ericson, and recorded by myself (with guitar) for the Library of Congress and by Michael Loring (who also did "Joe Hill"), with me at the piano. Both songs shortly went into print with the Hillbilly publisher Bob Miller. One workers' songbook that reprinted it says, "The verse words are by Alfred Hayes and Robert Earl and the music by Robert Earl." That's me: At the time I was delicately hiding, being in the employ of the Federal Theatre. I tried not to be *too* clever, because I did want people on the left to know it was me.

Michael Loring and I used to trade verses and get the audience to sing along on Lincoln's words. Herein lies an unexpected tale. Cabaret TAC was quite exciting to Broadway, and the biggest wheels came to see it. In the audience one night was none less than Lee Shubert, who owned half the theatres on Broadway. Al Hayes and I got a call one morning from William Morris, a leading agent, referring us to the Shubert office. "He's interested in you boys," we heard; but Morris gave us no advice on how to negotiate with fancy producers.

So we two lefty neophytes presented ourselves, in June of 1938, to be greeted warmly by Shubert's chief assistant, a Mr. Kaufman. I sang not "Abe Lincoln," but political lyrics written to "Yankee Doodle" that Al and I had done in one of our Camp Unity revues. This intrigued Kaufman. While waiting for Lee Shubert to show, all the while reassuring us that "Mr. Shubert is interested in you boys," he would buttonhole whoever came into the office with this great idea of Hayes and Robinson setting political lyrics to old P. D. tunes—material in the Public Domain (you don't have to pay for them). As an example, to the tune of "John's Brown's Body" he chanted, "We'll hang Franklin Roosevelt to a sour apple tree"! I became educated that afternoon to some of the hate and distrust with which the Establishment regarded Roosevelt. In 1938 we on the left had no particular love for the President, but the

Shubert organization apparently wanted to use us in an *anti*-Roosevelt manner. Which did not sit very well with Al and me. As we agonizingly reappraised the situation, Lee Shubert finally appeared. Reminding me of satiric cartoons of Rockefeller, he came in rubbing his hands excitedly. Yes, he wanted "us boys" to write a new kind of musical for him. "We want you to do a show about the modern-day conflicts," he said, "the conflict between the Communists . . . and the Reds!"

To this day, I don't know for sure what he meant by that proposal. Could he have got wind of the very real but esoteric war between the C. P. and Trotskyist positions on permanent revolution in the Soviet Union? Anyway, he picked the wrong "boys" to do his job. Al and I felt too thunderstruck to laugh at the time, but we showed little enthusiasm, leaving Shubert's office with our integrity—and without a sale. At least not then.

Still, Shubert had been impressed by "Abe Lincoln," especially by the audience joining in on the chorus. This was clearly a commercial property, and he wanted it—we could hardly believe our ears—for a zany, low-comedy vaudeville evening called *Hellzapoppin*, the Ole Olsen and Chic Johnson "Screamlined Revue" at the 46th Street Theatre. In no position to turn down royalties, we gave him our fine revolutionary song. They arranged it gospel-style, for a black quartet, the Charioteers, making the song as patriotic as possible. Three of the quartet sang "My country 'tis of thee" in march rhythm, while the fourth scatted the radical Lincoln words more or less incomprehensibly, six nights and two matinees a week, and also on radio a couple of times. We heard later that even with this obfuscation, people in the audience almost fainted at the "re-vo-lu-tion-ar-y right to dismember, or overthrow it" line. As for royalties, the show paid $25 a week on "Abe Lincoln," delivered to Bob Miller, the publisher, who kept half. Every week Al Hayes and I subwayed up to his office in the Brill Building to collect our $6.25 apiece.

To give you another idea of how the left point of view was not nearly so isolated then in America as later on: In May 1938 the Communist Party USA opened its 10th national convention at Madison Square Garden. A chorus of 500 sang "Abe Lincoln," and CBS Radio broadcast the whole opening ceremony! Can you imagine that happening today?

In subsequent years, I sang "Abe Lincoln" hundreds of times in concert. But come the McCarthy period, I stopped. The word "revolutionary" could be used only with the utmost opprobrium. Shamefully I admit I was scared to utter it. Accused of being un-American, I tried so hard to maintain a patriotic stance. So Abe stayed on the shelf for a time.

Suddenly, in the early 1960s, the blacklist over, I saw a chance to program "Abe Lincoln" while singing for black students at a college in Florida. Thinking that these young people would be more sophisticated on Lincoln, would know that he at first did not want to free the slaves, that he indeed "wavered and shook" before committing himself to the Emancipation Proclamation, I gave a little speech on the subject before presenting the song. I included the figures from Carl Sandburg's *Lincoln: The War Years*:

> The Bible, including the Apocrypha: 926,877 words.
> Shakespeare's complete works: 1,025,000 words.
> Lincoln's speeches and writings: 1,078,000 words.

I added the comment, "Anyone who talks this much is going to speak out of both sides of his mouth some of the time."

I almost completely mistook this audience: They didn't know the truth about Lincoln. But when I invited them to get on board the revolutionary chorus, they started clapping, offbeat gospel style, to the rhythm of the words. And I learned that I was writing rock way back in 1936, and didn't know it!

Notes

1. Pete Seeger to Earl Robinson, September 3, 1941; Wanda Willson Whitman, ed., *Songs That Changed the World*, New York: Crown, 1969.

2. Donald Ogden Stewart, ed., *Fighting Words*, New York: Harcourt Brace, 1940, pp. 30-31.

FEDERAL THEATRE DAYS

Comes now the story of the Works Progress Administration, its Federal Theatre Project, and my part in it. To understand this scene properly it would be good to have some facts on the situation in America in the 1930s. Consider first what it meant having 17 million unemployed out of a nation of 100 million. More than twice that number were affected—wives, husbands, children, older people. Half the hundred million had to be intimately affected by what was called "the Depression." As Will Rogers joked, "You couldn't miss it, it was in all the newspapers at the time."

Desperation spread across the land. Unemployed Councils sprang up and demonstrated forcefully, often confronting police violence, for home relief. A new organizing giant, the Congress of Industrial Organizations (CIO), came into being, breaking with the old American Federation of Labor (AFL) system, where the narrow, individualistic crafts often found themselves fighting each other instead of the employers. The CIO, under the no-nonsense leadership of John L. Lewis, organized the workers of entire industries. The mine workers, the steel workers, the rubber, auto, electrical, machine, and communications workers all initiated immense and successful union drives. Working people became a force to be reckoned with. Communists selflessly threw themselves into the labor movement, often led it, and sometimes infused it with passionate vigor. At times we believed a revolution was around the corner. If and when the workers should be ready, we would help point the way.

Under Depression conditions, the Democratic Party became the acknowledged defenders of the working people and lower middle class. Never anything but capitalist—the Communists let no one forget this—the Democrats put up as their 1932 standard-bearer the demo-aristocrat Franklin D. Roosevelt. FDR saved the country from a radical revolution, engineering changes that seemed far-out radical to the Establishment and led to many accusations of his being a Red himself.

To prevent national collapse, he urgently created jobs, put money back into circulation, and moved the country toward full employment. Roosevelt and his New Deal, with hardbitten opposition from the class he was saving, began a massive public works program, an alphabet soup plan with PWA, WPA, CCC, NRA, and the rest. He put people to work, building roads, museums, schools, public buildings, parks, Boulder Dam, TVA. And he began a truly remarkable thing. The government decided to pay artists to sculpt and paint. They paid writers to write. They paid dancers to dance, composers to compose, and musicians to make music. From the simple idea of paying people to do what they did best there came a flowering of the arts the like of which America has not seen before, or since.

As a body the Theatre of Action determined to go onto the Federal Theatre Project in March 1936. We had to individually prove that we were jobless and poverty-stricken—not hard to do for any of us. We joined as the One-Act Experimental Theatre and scheduled three plays, *The Great Catherine* by Shaw, *Snickering Horses* by Em Jo Basshe, and *The Miser* (starring Will Lee) by Molière. We presented this triple bill at the Daly Theatre on May 13, 1936. Though well acted and directed, it proved the demise of our theatre. In essence, we couldn't retain the revolutionary spirit of our pre-Project days. Our steady Project salary of $23.86 a week comforted but did not challenge us. As for me, I had little to do as music director, so I would be out of a job. After a short run of the plays, the One-Act Theatre disbanded and our members scattered to other more viable companies within the Project.

Our little Theatre of Action production of *Newsboy*, directed by Al Saxe, was an unsung forerunner of the style and content of the popular theatre of the late Thirties. Our energy flowed into concepts like the Living Newspaper, the exciting documentary theatre which made a sensation with plays such as *Injunction Granted* and *Triple A Plowed Under*—plays about real people and real social issues. Perhaps the best remembered play of that kind was *One Third of a Nation*, after Roosevelt's famous

1937 Second Inaugural speech on the "ill-housed, ill-clad, ill-nourished."

Once the One-Act Experimental Theatre closed that May, I accepted the position at Camp Unity. I got back on the Project in the fall, assigned to the Music Department copying other people's scores, having to start from the bottom up as a would-be theatre composer. Even when paid for doing it, music copying and extracting parts are drudgery for the musician. Every composer gets stuck with it; some even come to like it. But for me it was a tedious setback.

Aaron Copland, my teacher

Musicians sympathetic to the left, and to the Communist Party, had organized the Downtown Music School, where they taught instrumental performance, choral singing, music history and criticism, and composition. Some distinguished people got involved with the school in those heady days: composers Marc Blitzstein, Henry Cowell, Wallingford Riegger, Charles Seeger, and Elie Siegmeister; and pianists Joseph Machlis and Aube Tzerko, to mention a few.

Aaron Copland, who had written a prize-winning song called "Into the Streets May First," offered to give a year's private composition instruction to the student submitting the best instrumental work and mass song. Blitzstein and Israel Citkowitz, a good composer with a small output, judged. With a piece of "factory music" that I composed and orchestrated, and some of my Theatre of Action songs, I won the competition. For a year, beginning in September 1935, I brought Copland everything I wrote and he would review it. He never told me how to compose, but he would introduce me to music that successfully achieved similar purposes. Once I brought in a jazz-style fugue, and he played for me Darius Milhaud's *La création du monde*, a concert piece that uses jazz.

Our relationship continued beyond that year. Three years later, when he heard my *Ballad for Americans*, he found fault with only one chord: He thought the refrain "You know who I am" sounded too schmaltzy-commercial. Aaron was also honestly interested in my opinion of his work. I once described a piece of his as "nervous," and though he never said a word, I noticed a greater lyricism in his subsequent work. A couple of years later, Copland wrote what may be his most popular work, *A Lincoln Portrait*. As in my own song "Abe Lincoln," it combines speech and music, a technique that he freely borrowed from me, and even quotes some of the same Lincoln quotes I had used. "Earl," he said, "I'm stealing some of your thunder." So it is proper to say that we studied with one another.

I learned much from the best mass songs of those days; in minor keys, they came from the German antifascists Hanns Eisler and Bertolt Brecht. I met Eisler in New York occasionally, and got to study with him later on in California. I remember one thing he used to say to our Composers' Collective: The workers don't carry a piano around with them. In other words, if you write a mass song with a harmonized piano accompaniment, be sure to make the vocal line enough of a tune so that the common worker can sing it. This from a student of Arnold Schoenberg, the twelve-tone master.

Many of the Composers' Collective members tried earnestly to create mass songs for the workers, and their efforts had elements of the heroic. These composers, all strong individualists, had been trained to guard their own style and originality. Many felt more sympathetic to the twelve-tone system than to the folk approach; in fact, drawn more to dissonance than to consonance, they actively disliked and disparaged folk song. For these people to put aside the "bourgeois prejudice" of individuality, agree to work as a collective in order to reach a new audience of untrained workers, and endure the sharp criticism of their peers, required an advance to a new human level, a restructuring of esthetic values, a submergence of self in favor of the larger goal. For artists brought up in Western ego-culture, this was indeed not far from heroic.

The *Workers Song Book* of 1934 put out high hopes for transforming the proletarian musical ear. Citing the revolutionary songs of Eisler, Shostakovich, Jacob Schaefer, Stefan Wolpe and others, "sung everywhere by huge masses of class-conscious workers," the Composers' Collective truly believed that a new anti-bourgeois musical movement was a-borning. About the recently formed workers' choruses they could write: "Their gargantuan appetite for new music, their delight in attacking technical difficulties that cause their bourgeois contemporaries no end of trouble, makes composing for them the highest kind of calling." In context this statement sounded less delusional than it reads today, for in 1934 we saw a worldwide militant workers' movement on history's horizon.[1]

Yet in truth, few songs written during this period ever captured popular attention—"Death House Blues," my contribution to the cause of the Scottsboro Boys, being no exception. I used verses from Lawrence Gellert's collection of *Negro Songs of Protest*, and Peter Martin added militant words to the chorus:

> *Paper come out done strew duh news*
> *Nine po chillun moanin Death House Blues*
> *Nine nappy heads wid big shiny eye*
> *All boun in jail and frame to die*
>
> *White workin man gonna set them free,*
> *Black workin man gonna set them free,*
> *All workin men gonna set them free,*
> *Workin men and the ILD.*

If little music written in the Composers' Collective ever genuinely reached the masses, still we honed our talents for the greater work to come. Charles Seeger, Wallingford Riegger, Elie Siegmeister, Aaron Copland, Marc Blitzstein, Alex North, Henry Leland Clarke, Norman Cazden, all went on to distinguished careers. The first great works that followed on the heels of the Collective's demise were Blitzstein's brilliant labor opera, *The Cradle Will Rock*, and Copland's school opera, *The Second Hurricane*. I soon produced some notable successes myself.

These pieces worked because by the late 1930s the composers had learned how to set words in a natural, American idiom without forcing them into weird, ungrateful harmonies with wide, leaping intervals. Part of the reason was political. The world situation had become so urgent that we just couldn't wait for the masses to catch up to us and our cherished modernity: We had to communicate our global anti-fascist viewpoint *now*. That meant simplifying—or better, clarifying.

As an example of this kind of immediacy, a distinguished committee of sponsors got together to produce Kenneth White's script *Who Fights This Battle?* With a musical score by Paul Bowles, it treated the current political situation in Spain, with a strong leaning toward the Communists opposing Generalissimo Franco. It received five September 1936 performances in a hotel ballroom to benefit the Ministry of Education of the Spanish Republic, raising just under $2,000, a sizable sum in those days. That was literally just weeks after the Spanish Civil War had broken out. I served as music director, playing piano and organ and conducting the chorus. Norman Lloyd and Nik Ray starred in the show.[2]

In the theatre field, the left coordinated its nationwide activity through the New Theatre League. At the Adelphi Theatre on a Sunday night, January 31, 1937, we presented a topical satirical revue called *Pink Slips on Parade*, an evening of 24 separate numbers, with music by Kenneth Hunter and myself (performed by Percy Dodd & His Royal Syncopators). Muni Diamond wrote the book and directed. My old Workers Laboratory Theatre friends Will Lee and Perry Bruskin played in the cast. The number "Doin' the Demonstration," to Lewis Allan's words about people organizing to save their jobs, constituted my most memorable moment in that show. Today it's hard to imagine so much talent going into a show for just one night and no residuals to broadcast the message widely and pick up the expense.

Composing for Federal Theatre

I would have felt more frustrated with the music copying, but I met Helen on the pay line one day in November 1936. After that, everything started changing. I talk about Helen more in the next chapter, but she must have been good luck, because in late winter, shortly after our marriage, still at my copy desk, I got a call from Lem Ward, a talented director fresh onto the Project with the express purpose of directing John Howard Lawson's *Processional*, a play about a West Virginia mining town during a strike with no fewer than 81 performers. The Theatre Guild had originally produced it on Broadway back in 1925, and included a tune by Gershwin for a miners' band. Mordecai Gorelik, who designed the revival, described

> [t]he garish backdrops of the cheap burlesque stage . . . , the scenic inspiration for this cartoon fantasy, which re-lated the events of a mine strike in terms of jazz. Miners, soldiers, the Ku Klux Klan, an agitator, a Man in a Silk Hat, a reporter, took part in a furious merry-go-round, proving Lawson's thesis that "the Twentieth Century is exciting to the point of chaos."[3]

The musical job here proved a challenge on several fronts. First, we couldn't get the rights to the Gershwin tune, so I had to write a Twenties-style melody to substitute. From the begin-ning of my career, I needed words or ideas, expressed through theatre, dance, or film, to get me going. For all my best songs, I got the words securely in mind before sitting at the piano. I also thought I needed a piano, a crutch not only then but well into my composing career. I broke through both phobias by taking long walks through Williamsburg, where Helen and I were liv-ing with her folks. I roamed through the empty streets down under the Williamsburg Bridge, and I'd hum, sing, and scream my *Processional* tune until I had it clear in my mind. John Houseman, visiting the show in rehearsal one day, pronounced my tune "charming." The *New York Times* said that my score "sets the tempo of *Processional* as well as that of 1925," placing me on a level with Gershwin![4]

About "pure" music vs. "program" music: I used to believe that only the Russians—Shostakovich, Prokofiev and the rest—could write "pure" music because they had solved the economic problems with socialism. Living sort of like angels in paradise, they could let music tell its own story, while we, under conditions of capitalist decadence and exploitation, had to direct all our artistic efforts at changing the system. How wrong I was in retrospect: The Russians had not solved all their worldly problems by any means, and artists need to feel creatively free under any system.

Because of my work on *Processional*, I had to skip the summer of 1937 at Camp Unity. I took only two weeks off from the Project to go to Camp Kinderland and write a musical. Similar to Camp Unity, Kinderland also had Communist sponsorship, but as the name indicates, it served younger children. Perry Bruskin remembers a getting-up chant that the Young Pioneers used to recite at Camp Kinderland, with a New York Jewish accent then pretty common:

> *Gerrup! Gerrup! Gerrup for exercise!*
> *You need a healthy baree* [body]
> *To fight the parasites! HEH!*
> *Gerrup!, etc.*

The musical was my first chance to work with Jules (Julie) Dassin, the dramatics director that summer at Camp Lakeland, the adult part of Kinderland. With good lyrics by Julie and Nathaniel Buchwald, it satirized Tammany Hall and New York politics. We had a "Tin Boxes" song (considerably before "The Little Tin Box" of *Fiorello*) that made fun of the graft system. We danced and shouted the smashing finale, "Stop That Tiger!" to the (stolen) tune of "Hold That Tiger," a popular song we used to play the hell out of in the Blue Knights band.

When I got back to the city, I faced another challenge with *Processional*. Lem Ward emphatically did not want a pit orchestra in plain sight of the audience. To the disapproval of the musicians, who never got to see the show, he placed the orchestra in a room more than fifty feet below the Maxine Elliott stage. Speech cues came in via radio transmission, and the conductor signaled when to play. A speaker broadcast the music into the theatre, timed precisely so the unseen orchestra could accompany the miners and their tune. Though viewed with dire fore-boding by everyone in the music department, I'll be damned if it didn't work.

Howard Barnes wrote of *Processional* in the *Herald Tribune*: "an emotional thrust . . . that makes the current Broadway exhibits seem extremely anemic by comparison." John Dos Passos called the musical score "excellent—in tone with the general charcoal drawing effect."[5] It enjoyed a respectable run of 81 performances from October 1937 to March 1938. Lem Ward went on to direct the classic of the Living Newspaper shows, *One Third of a Nation*, and was in demand on Broadway before his untimely death in 1942.

Militant music

The year 1937 saw the founding of the American People's Chorus, expressly "for the development of the People's Front." The International Workers Order gave me a room with a piano and five dollars a week to start an IWO chorus. One person came the first week, two the next, then a few more. By the end of the second month we had sixteen people rehearsing "Abe Lincoln," which opened an important concert on February 6, 1938, arranged by Marc Blitzstein as a benefit for *New Masses* magazine. Emcee Orson Welles introduced us in impressive tones, calling my song an example of "militant music," a subject on which he claimed some authority, having just directed Blitzstein's *The Cradle Will Rock* on Broadway.

Of course, I also claimed some authority in that field, for thousands of people sang my "May Day Song" at the annual march, which in the late Thirties used to draw half a million workers down Broadway. To an upbeat marching step we sang

> *Once a year we hear the sound of marching feet,*
> *Marching all together down the May Day street.*
> *Come and join the crowd that is so proud to say*
> *This is our own day, yeah.*
> *Come on and march. Come on and march.*
> *Come on and march on May Day.*

Goodbye to blues, goodbye to sorrow,
We're marching today, we're marching tomorrow,
For a roof overhead,
For our bed and our bread,
Come on and march on May Day.

With all due respect, my May Day tune became far more popular and lasted for many more years than Copland's "Into the Streets May First," a more crafted type of art song.

The chorus grew to 150 members at its height, some recruited from the best of the Camp Unity singers, and grew in power and influence as well. The five dollars from the IWO lasted just a month, after which the chorus became self-supporting, with dues and booking fees. I felt motivated to create something to take the place of the Theatre of Action shock troupe, a musical weapon to support the class struggle. We built up to legitimate concerts, which included an audience singalong on some new number usually composed by me. One of our most memorable concerts took place at the World's Fair on IWO Day (October 22, 1939) in the Hall of Peace—a wryly named venue, as World War II (without U. S. participation yet) had broken out the month before.

I felt happiest and most fulfilled when the National Seamen's Union invited us to sing in their soup kitchen as part of their strike activity. We sang "Flying Squadron" as well as "Joe Hill," usually making up new lyrics to fit the particular strike. I learned well in the Theatre of Action. To this day I am at the ready, with piano, guitar, or unaccompanied, to sing for a legitimate strike. It still is a sacred call which must be answered if at all possible. In 1987, I sang in New York for the Musicians Union opposite Radio City Music Hall, with which it had a conflict.

My first experiences with film scoring came during this period of the late 1930s, a rich time for documentaries. A radical production group called Frontier Films made *People of the Cumberland* about the Highlander Folk School in Tennessee, a place where local people learned union organizing and other ways to take some control over their lives. Alex North and I collaborated on the score, which used the American People's Chorus. Completed in the spring of 1938 by directors Jay Leyda and Sidney Meyers, with commentary by Erskine Caldwell and Ben Maddow, and photography by Ralph Steiner, it ran at the Cameo Theatre in New York for two weeks, and had further showings around the country.

In collaboration with the United Auto Workers and the CIO, Frontier Films also made a 33-minute documentary, *United Action*, an account of the summer of 1939 strike at General Motors, the background, the events during the action, and the final settlement. John L. Lewis, leading CIO organizer, appeared in the film—originally a silent, but the UAW officers wanted sound. So the director took a print to Frontier Films. They put a spoken commentary to it and added my chorus singing "The Flying Squadron" and other labor and folk songs. Over one scene of particularly heinous police brutality, I had a soprano solo singing a sweet, ironic "My Country 'Tis of Thee."

George Sklar's play *Life and Death of an American* was the biography of a typical worker—born 1900, died in the 1937 Memorial Day Massacre in South Chicago—who uncovers the myth of upward mobility and finds poverty in the midst of plenty. J. Arthur Kennedy played the lead. Alex North and I worked together on the score. We each chose parts we found congenial and collaborated in the overall production. I had more of the songs of social content, and Alex had more of the incidental music.

In the summer of 1938 I managed two jobs at once. While working on the songs for *Life and Death*, retaining my position and the standard $23.86 a week on the Project, I resumed my old job at Camp Unity, directing the choruses every week and discharging my musical duties faithfully. The Project mailed my checks to Wingdale, New York, the town nearest the camp. I confess that I went against the rules, circumventing Project regulations by taking another salary (Camp Unity paid $15 a week). At the time it seemed okay: I met all the deadlines on both jobs and never shortchanged anybody. I still feel a little twinge of guilt, but that came long after the fact.

Life and Death of an American opened at the Maxine Elliott on May 19, 1939, with sets by Howard Bay. According to Erwin Piscator, the genius refugee director from Nazi Germany, it was "the most superb stage production he had seen in America."[6] The show ran only very briefly, however, until the closing of the Federal Theatre Project in June.

"Ballad of Uncle Sam"

I met the writer and poet John Latouche in 1938, when we both submitted songs and sketches to the Project's musical *Sing for Your Supper*, produced by Robert Sour and Harold Hecht. Anna Sokolow choreographed; her then-husband Alex North also wrote music for the show. Coby Ruskin and Norman Lloyd acted in it, also Peggy Coudray, the zany Mrs. Mister from *The Cradle Will Rock*. Lighting by Feder, also of *Cradle* fame. Very loosely, over the course of eighteen separate skits, the theme of the show is Uncle Sam producing a musical to put unemployed performers to work.

In a real sense Latouche and I had been looking for each other. Ever since my success with setting Abe Lincoln's speech to music, I had been wanting to try on Franklin Roosevelt for size. From where I stood I could see that FDR was doing for America just what the country needed. And I wanted to acknowledge that musically. I looked at his "one third of a nation" and other pregnant sayings. But John had already been thinking of writing a history of this land.

So we were made for each other. And because *Sing for Your Supper* had Uncle Sam as its central character, we called our piece "Ballad of Uncle Sam." After he is seen enough by the audience, doing his experiment in show biz production, Uncle Sam is buttonholed by the ushers, the costumers and others who are never seen on stage, whereupon they start asking him questions. "Who are you?" "Where are you from?" And out of these questions comes a musical history of the United States.

Only twenty-four at the time, John had won several poetry prizes at Columbia, and had written sketches for *Pins and Needles*. For one season, since he knew four languages well, he served as interpreter for the Ballet Russe. He took a couple of weeks with the words and I needed a month for the music. While composing, giving musical shape to John's words, I saw certain possibilities. After his section where Uncle Sam says, "I'm English, French, German, etc.," I added, "And that ain't all. I was baptized Baptist, Methodist, etc." I never needed to take any public credit for words, but between John and me I'd occasionally remind him of my part. And he'd say, "But I could have written that!"

Harold Hecht put the "Ballad" into rehearsal immediately, scheduling it as the finale of the revue. And there lies a long, agonizing tale. *Sing* rehearsed and rehearsed, then went back to more rehearsal, for *thirteen months* before opening at the Adelphi on April 24, 1939. Gordon Clarke sang Uncle Sam—after we'd gone through eight actors for the role.

It is tempting to blame this delay on the Republicans and Dixiecrats in Congress who had sniped at the Project from its inception. The infamous Dies Committee on Un-American Activities, forerunner of McCarthy, leveled its most violent attacks on the Project, in particular *Sing for Your Supper*. They made sweeping public accusations that the press dutifully played up with little or no refutation, though at the core I believe that they principally objected to black and white actors dancing together in the show. Martin Dies, Texas Democrat and anti-Communist demagogue, wanted to subpoena the actual sets, but that proved impractical. They got hold of the script instead. Dies called the "Ballad" "an American version of the 'Internationale.'" And an angry Congressman Clifton A. Woodrum, Democrat from Virginia who chaired the House Sub-Committee on Appropriations, stood on the floor of the House and swore, "I have here the manuscript of *Sing for Your Supper*. If there is a line or passage in it that contributes to cultural or educational benefit or uplift of America, I will eat the whole manuscript."

Concerning the long rehearsal period, the FTP was not without fault.[7] I stayed with the show the entire time and can say that our "Ballad" survived with most of its spirit intact. But other numbers and songs would lose core personalities to Broadway or elsewhere and have to be dropped or replaced. The director consistently underutilized a brilliant young dancer in the show who eventually was fired for being uncooperative. His name: Gene Kelly.

As predicted, the House voted June 15, 1939, 373 to 21, to end the Federal Theatre. The entire theatrical, film, and arts world rallied to prevent the Senate from going along, but without success. As of midnight June 30th the Project was abolished. In *Sing for Your Supper* the song "Papa's Got a Job" (music by Ned Lehac) served as the first act finale.

> *Ain't it lucky, ain't it swell,*
> *I ran all the way home to tell,*
> *I'm so happy it's just like ringing a bell—*
> *Papa's Got a Job!*

In Brooks Atkinson's *New York Times* review, he had called this number "one of the most stirring sketches of the season" and "modern theatre at its best."[8] At the final performance, the show stopped at that point. The production manager came to the footlights and solemnly announced, "Yes, Papa had a job, but they're taking it away from him at twelve o'clock tonight." So the 150 people on this show, and the thousands more across the country in Federal Theatre, went back to the unemployment lines from which they'd been rescued.

The closing of the Project, in the middle of "my" two shows, *Life and Death of an American* and *Sing for Your Supper*, seemed tragic. John Latouche felt distraught at the death of our "Ballad" after sixty performances. The reactionaries in Congress had triumphed. But I am cursed with what some might call a Pollyanna attitude, and I didn't see defeat. I knew the "Ballad" was good and could stand apart from the theatre, because I had already led my chorus in it as a concert piece. I sensed in my bones that it would serve me as a model for future compositions: the topical or historical cantata. Somehow "Ballad of Uncle Sam" would be heard from again.

Notes

1. Aaron Copland reviewed the songbook in *New Masses*, June 5, 1934, the same issue that published his song "Into the Streets May First."

2. An excellent source for this period is Eric Winship Trumbull, "Musicals of the American Workers' Theatre Movement, 1928-1941: Propaganda and Ritual in Documents of a Social Movement," Ph.D. dissertation, University of Maryland, 1991.

3. Mordecai Gorelik, *New Theatres for Old*, London: Dennis Dobson Ltd, 1947, p. 308.

4. Review by Lewis Nichols, *The New York Times*, October 14, 1937. See also Brooks Atkinson, "Symphony in Jazz Time," *The New York Times*, October 24, 1937.

5. Tony Buttitta and Barry Witham, *Uncle Sam Presents: A Memoir of the Federal Theatre, 1935-1939*, Philadelphia: University of Pennsylvania Press, 1982, pp. 162-163.

6. Jay Williams, *Stage Left*, New York: Charles Scribner's Sons, 1974, p. 228.

7. See Hallie Flanagan, *Arena: The Story of the Federal Theatre*, New York: Limelight Editions, 1985; John O'Connor and Lorraine Brown, eds., *Free, Adult, Uncensored: The Living History of the Federal Theatre Project*, Washington, D.C.: New Republic Books, 1978. Also Buttitta and Witham, *Uncle Sam Presents*.

8. Review by Brooks Atkinson, *The New York Times*, April 25, 1939. The review does not mention our "Ballad."

ME AND HELEN

I met Helen Wortis on a Federal Theatre pay line in November 1936. This nice *heymish** girl behind me started a conversation. "You remind me of a friend of mine," she said. "She's an artist and comes from Seattle." My ears pricked up at the mention of my home town, and they stayed up when she told me her friend's name, Cecilia Brodine.

"Why, yes, the famous musical Brodines of Seattle," I replied. "Voltaire on accordion, Julia on cello, Russell on bass, and my good friend Franz the fiddler, who took me out of unexciting lower middle class West Seattle and opened up a new world to me with a job in his orchestra on the *President Jackson* going to the Orient. And in whose car I came to New York, the place I had to go, the Mecca!" Some of this may have tumbled out of me; at least my excitement must have shown when I met Helen.

About a year younger than me, and a delicious 5 foot 4, with soft brown hair and matching eyes, Helen began well the relatively simple process of taking charge: of me, of us, and this new relationship. I was ready, though I didn't realize it consciously. The previous summer at Camp Unity, with its plethora of women so totally available, had disposed me toward something deeper in my relationships. It wasn't a sexual thing at first. We talked, Helen especially, and I did a lot of listening.

We worked in separate departments of the Project, across from each other on the same floor. I languished in my unfulfilling music-copying, while she designed posters and programs. I loved watching her at work, how deftly she handled materials, how well she captured people in a quick sketch or cartoon. A true artist. I found myself looking forward to meeting her after work. With me her willing subject, Helen gently took me into her consciousness, and into the life of her family and friends.

---

* Yiddish: homelike, warm, accepting

81

Only part of me was truly present

Being taken in physically presented more of a problem. I
had taken a room out in Brooklyn with a male friend, where it
wasn't appropriate to invite Helen. She lived with her folks,
and couldn't enjoy intimacy with me at home, even late at
night, because her father, still protecting his 25-year-old daughter, might walk in on the proceedings. We would neck till all
hours of the night, but never consummate. So I would see her
home on the subway to Grand Street in Brooklyn, even after I
had gotten a small room of my own in Manhattan. I accepted
this situation, and would go home frustrated but happy somehow. One rainy daytime Helen and I walked around the
streets of the city looking for something to do, and she finally
had to suggest that we could go to *my* room. The idea had
never occurred to me! Perhaps it was a holdover from my
mother's counsel: A girl like Helen wouldn't enjoy sex, and it
would have been beastly for me to force it on her.

I began to think it would be nice to live together, maybe
get our own apartment. Had it been left to me, that is all that
would have happened. The concept of marriage just didn't figure in. Now Helen's sister Bea and her painter husband Dave
Arkin had eloped back in 1929. The first time I visited them,
Bea listened to my plan for living together, took me aside and
said, "Why don't you get married?" No pressure, just the easi-
est thing to do. I forget if Helen or I proposed.

Later I saw that I had not gone into this arrangement
clearheadedly. Still young and immature at twenty-six, having
only recently conquered my virginity, I needed more space
than marriage afforded me. I continued trying to score with
women, constantly testing and challenging my manhood, in
this way perpetuating the career of my old man. For me, issues
of love, sex, and fidelity had not yet sorted themselves out; I'm
sorry to say, truthfully, they never have. I guess that will have
to wait until my next incarnation. I felt naughty "stepping out"
on Helen, but never fathomed how my habitual Don Juan
complex kept me from realizing my full humanity in wholehearted commitment to my life partner.

A highly developed but narrow view of my mission in life presented another obstacle to marriage. In retrospect, Helen showed herculean restraint and clarity beyond the moment, because when we were about to be married, I sat her down in a little coffee shop in Manhattan and earnestly explained that music would always be first with me. Music and the movement, and she should understand this. It is embarrassing now to admit how stupidly unromantic I was, but that characterized our movement mood then: With "the revolution" just around the corner, we didn't feel we should tie ourselves down to lifetime bourgeois family commitments. As a Communist herself, she could accept my priorities, though she'd have preferred a more traditional marriage. A long time later it percolated through my noggin that music and the movement and a romantic marriage were not mutually exclusive; they could work together just fine.

After an unglamorous two-month courtship, we took Bea's advice. We went down to City Hall on our lunch hour, with two witnesses from the Project, and got hitched by a city clerk. It would have pleased Helen's family if we'd gotten married in style, but neither of us wanted a religious ceremony, she being Jewish and me being gentile and both of us nonpracticing. Also, in our political circles we had ambivalence about the marriage institution and all its hypocrisies. We did it the least conspicuous way we could, and didn't even tell our families till after the deed was done. I don't remember much about it, except the date February 17, 1937: Only part of me was truly present.

As our only splurge, we took an apartment on 72nd Street for $50 a month—a lot of money in those days. We figured we could handle that with our two $23.86's a week. But the rules of the Project disallowed pulling more than one salary per family. So we stayed there one month, then moved to Williamsburg to live (on my salary alone) with Helen's folks, and prove that two could live as cheaply as one.

A gentile among Jews

By now I had come to see that, alongside a few black activists and the strong groups of foreign-born, Jews were the body and the yeast of the leftwing movement, certainly in New York and the larger cities in the East. Jews without money, they permeated our cause with humor and compassion. I learned that there were other Jews, linked up with the enemy, labor baiters, Red-haters, social fakers, although the gentiles were also well represented among these. In the Wortis family, the Jewishness indelibly informed their lives, but they were anti-nationalistic, and certainly not Orthodox. We separated people out not by race or religion, but by their relation to the working class (Us) or the capitalist class (Them).

My friendship with Helen's father, Harry (Pop) Wortis, a jeweller by profession but a musician/singer/composer in reality, became deeper and more challenging and satisfying than what I had with my own father. Reading not a note of music, he would sit in the back of his Grand Street jewelry store between customers, playing the little organ he had there. He sang all the parts of the songs he composed, songs for a better world, or his Dreyfus cantata, celebrating the famous Jewish martyr, persecuted and finally vindicated. This Dreyfus piece finally came to be written out by Waldemar Hille (Pop called him Vladimir), the gentile composer and organist at First Unitarian Church in Los Angeles. I once encouraged Pop to enter a contest sponsored by a synagogue in L. A. to set the Jewish religious service to new music. Of course he had the traditional prayers in his veins and with my help he wrote a very Jewish-sounding service. I sat down with him for a week writing down what he sang, and arranged it for keyboard. It didn't win the contest, but earned second place.

Pop was the consummate incompleat musician. A natural, self-trained baritone with beautiful falsetto notes, he appreciated and knew all about voice production and opera singers good and bad. He gave me some singing lessons which wisely began where I was and carried me further. "Never force. Let the voice float, flow gracefully," he counseled. I say Pop was self-trained, but this isn't exactly so, for Pop's father, Wolf Wortis, was a cantor in old Russia, and a natural folk composer. Pop would often hum-da-dee a joyful folk tune that he remembered from his father's inexhaustible repertoire. Another song, simple and moving, expressive of the tragic strength not just of the Jews but of the whole human race, I later unconsciously incorporated into the "Wake, Sing Sorrow" number in my folk opera *Sandhog*.

At the age of 80, Wolf Wortis came to America to live with his son. Pop brought him to the Metropolitan Opera, where he sat with tears streaming down his face. When Pop asked what was wrong, his aged father said, "I never thought I'd hear such singing until I got to heaven." Wolf lived a saintly life. His friends would chastise him for living in a house that didn't keep kosher. He answered, "What's good enough for my son is good enough for me." All this took place before I came into the family, but legends grew around his memory.

One more thing about Pop. He also fitted me for glasses more than once, this being another string to his bow, which he studied and practiced as an adjunct to the jewelry store business. He would supply glasses for the less complicated cases in Williamsburg, turning over the more difficult problems to a specialist.

With Helen's mother Selena I can't say I developed a strong attachment. Alsatian-Jewish, she spoke both German and French impeccably. She regularly took out the great works of literature from the library: Balzac, Goethe, Schiller. Of her domestic talents Pop used to say, "She cooks like an Aryan." In her highly assimilated family, there ran quite a streak of Jewish anti-Semitism. Some of them became Christian Scientists. She acted a bit superior toward outsiders, and indeed toward her own peasant husband. Yet this good woman did her duty and could be relied on. And she was no reactionary either: She took her children to hear radical speeches on birth control, and lectures by labor leaders Elizabeth Gurley Flynn and Eugene V. Debs. In the '40s for a time she and Pop became members of the Communist Party. Once Pop took me aside and said reflectively, "Don't have too much sex. You don't really need it, you're better apart." Their separate beds may have been Selena's idea. We didn't take the advice.

With Bea and Dave Arkin I sang and made songs. A man of many talents, Dave realized himself most completely as a poet. He wanted to be a folk singer but his inability to tune a guitar sort of slowed down his progress. Their son Alan has made a big name for himself as an actor.

The oldest Wortis child, Irving, died suddenly at the age of 32 just a few months before I met Helen. Joe Wortis, Helen's other brother, is a Marxist psychiatrist. A protégé of Havelock Ellis, he had been analyzed by Freud himself, an experience he recounted in a book.[1] He wrote another book, *Soviet Psychiatry*, which explains how Marxian scientists apply dialectical materialism to the inner life.[2] (Many horrible revelations later, we now understand that Soviet practitioners often used psychiatry for political, punitive ends, but that is a distinct aberration from the theory.) Helen looked up to Joe not only as a big brother, but as a doctor, though in the latter role he acted very much the scientist and technician, and not much of a handholder. A baritone like his father, he sang everything from Schubert to Eisler to show tunes and union songs. Helen's other sister Rosella, a schoolteacher for long years, never seemed to enjoy life.

Beyond Helen's immediate relatives was a gang of extended family members, most of them politically committed, for whom I felt a real love. The family took special pride in Rose Wortis, daughter of Pop's sister Chaya. She joined the revolutionary movement quite young (assuming her mother's maiden name), organized for the ILGWU, got involved in a romance with Communist writer Mike Gold, though she left him after a time and then never married. She had visited Russia in 1922 as a delegate to the Fourth Congress of the Communist International, and had met Lenin personally. For years she served as a member of the Communist Party's Central Committee. A warm and down-to-earth person, she never allowed her high position to get in the way.

Thus began a partnership with LIGHTS and shades, UPS and downs. I emphasize the positives, which were many and rich. But I cannot ignore the problems, most of them of my own making. It took till after Helen's passing, twenty-six years later, for me to realize that I could have given much more to her than I did. We were so cool and Marxist-materialist-rationalistic that we never even said to one another, "I love you."

I have gone through times of beating my breast about my unfaithfulness, but I hung in with her, and loved her unspeakably well. I like to believe that Helen got much of what she wanted out of the marriage.

The birth of our son Perry, on September 17, 1938, was a touch-and-go situation. All through the pregnancy, Helen was very sick with toxemia. As long as the fetus was inside, her life lay in danger. The doctors waited almost too long before inducing delivery. Perry came in at three pounds, ten ounces, and lost an ounce a day for the first four days. They gave him one chance in ten of living. Helen couldn't nurse him, so there was controlled rejoicing as, fed with an eye dropper, he began gaining those ounces back. He stayed in the incubator for three weeks. He went on to gain perfect health, however. He is named, according to a venerable family tradition of keeping names going, after my great-grandfather Perry Robinson, who died in 1863. After the war we adopted our second son, Jimmy.

A powerful deposition

Some seventeen years after we married, Helen wrote down some observations about "my genyus, that dope" (that means me). Deep affection for me dwells in these words alongside her sardonic teasing, but the upshot remains that I made myself hard to live with.

> My husband is a musical genyus; he writes strong songs,
> love songs, patriotic songs that would melt a stone.
> Whole audiences swoon from him, people from 2 to 80

follow him, write him, adore him; people of other lands know his music. At home, however, he is a funny 'un. He possesses anything but genyus. He gets up like a bank clerk on permanent disability—he is an uninspired getter-upper. He does like any average schmoo, only worse.

Does he ever say, "What a beautiful day, I love the rain, how lovely you are, don't go to work today, let's you and me do something silly"?   No, he never says anything romantic at all. Yet his music swoons people, I'm telling you. He spends his day at the piano playing much too loud. Someone once said how wonderful it must be to hear music being made. Well, all it means is that I can never use the living room. It's full of him, and if not of him, then his letters; it means when he's here if I talk to him he never hears so he might just as well be out on a job. I think he's there, but he's really not.

Unless he's home at the piano, he's out leading choruses, giving lectures, singing, needing; he comes home in the wee hours with big circles under his eyes, white face, and runs for a sleeping pill; he has a weak bladder and keeps running to the bathroom all night, and me being a light sleeper. And sometimes he goes on a whirlwind tour for a month or so, comes home with sustenance for a couple of months, but needs a long time to recuperate. He sings concerts full of stuff to make people full of confidence, and the world is fine if we only knew it, and ours is a proud heritage. After the concert everybody goes out and does good except him; he collapses in a heap almost on the front doorstep. I pick up the pieces and put them to bed till the next such episode.

When we get out to the country he won't take nice leisurely walks through the pasture: he looks for an impossible mountain to climb and leaves me to tend to the kids while he climbs it. He comes down definitely suffering from lack of oxygen and he's proved something: that he hasn't learned to enjoy the simple pleasures.

He'll take his children's chorus and he'll take the loudest bunch of monotone loud squawking kids and inside a short while have them singing in harmony and

eating out of his hand. He doesn't like them a bit. The
parents say, ah, how he must love children, he does so
much with them. Confidentially, though, he does this
for the $15 involved.

Helen's deposition is a powerful thing. She is too tough on
me regarding the children. I could scarcely have worked with
them over the years only for the money (it was often less than
$15). But on reviewing the body of Helen's letter, I do take
responsibility for being thoughtless, and for acting the male
chauvinist a lot of the time. In accordance with the usual practice in that era, Helen made my work possible by handling the
domestic side of life, while I did little to promote her as a career woman. I have improved considerably since her passing,
but her insightful letter is a sharp reminder of how far I had to
go—and still have.

Notes

1. Joseph Wortis, *Fragments of an Analysis with Freud*, New
York: Simon & Schuster, 1954; reprinted by Charter Books, 1963.

2. Joseph Wortis, *Soviet Psychiatry*, Baltimore: Williams & Wilk-
ins, 1950.

SECTION THREE

1939-1947

BALLAD OF UNCLE SAM

In '76 the sky was red,
Thunder rumbling overhead,
Bad King George couldn't sleep in his bed,
And on that stormy morn,
Old Uncle Sam was born. Some birthday!
Old Sam put on a three-cornered hat,
And in a Richmond church he sat. . . .

Thus opens the number which overnight brought me quite
a lot of fame and some fortune.

A short eleven minutes

When Norman Corwin, the radio genius at Columbia
Broadcasting System, had me play and sing for the CBS brass
the "Ballad of Uncle Sam" (from the defunct Federal Theatre
Project's *Sing for Your Supper*), a prophetic thing happened.
Bill Lewis, vice president, exclaimed, "Wouldn't Robeson
knock the hell out of this!" Well, the fates smiled on us: Paul
Robeson had just returned to the U.S. after a series of triumphs
abroad. He'd done *Othello* at Stratford, England, and he'd sung
concerts to universal acclaim all over Europe, from France to
the Soviet Union, not forgetting performances in Spain in the
midst of the Civil War for the soldiers of the Abraham Lincoln
Brigade, there to fight Franco fascism. His reputation stood at
its highest point. The red-baiting attacks came later.

CBS had already tried to get Robeson to appear on their
new show "Pursuit of Happiness," which Corwin directed, but
his price came too high. After they heard the "Ballad" they
decided to pay it—a thousand dollars, I believe. Of course, not
everyone at CBS fell for the "Ballad." For the musical director,
numbers were supposed to last three minutes. That's what he
was used to, and he let me know in no uncertain terms that the
"Ballad" ran too long and had to be cut to a maximum of four
minutes before going on the air. Taking him seriously, I at-

tempted the impossible, managing to cut two or three lines of text, but no music. Finally I took the problem to Corwin. He proved most supportive. "Leave it the way it is," he said. And "Ballad" stayed a short eleven minutes. I say "short" because to this day people cannot believe that this musical synopsis of our country's entire history doesn't go any longer than that. Norman Corwin renamed the piece *Ballad for Americans*; Uncle Sam remained in the lyrics, however.

So Robeson and Robinson came together, producing a confusion of names and identities that has lasted up to the present. Numerous times I'd show up for a booking and they'd look at me puzzled, and say, "Oh, but Mr. Robinson, we thought you were colored!"

One time I had a performance out in Brighton Beach at an International Workers Order (IWO) center. I pushed my way through the jammed hall to the stage. There, over the proscenium, a huge sign greeted me: EARL ROBINSON, FAMOUS NEGRO BARITONE. When I got on stage, I apologized for failing to meet their expectations. "I'm only a tenor."

I went up to Paul and Eslanda's (Essie) apartment in a section of Harlem called Sugar Hill, where other prominent and well-to-do black people lived. The first words out of Robeson's mouth were "I know one of your songs." Turned out to be "Joe Hill." He had learned it in England, when he acted with a labor theatre in the play *Plant in the Sun*. I found this quite remarkable, because "Joe Hill" was only three years old at the time.

Robeson and I rehearsed every day for a week. I never worked with a more cooperative person. He continually checked with me how I wanted a phrase sung, a line read. If I ventured that a section might be stronger, or softer, Paul would say, "You got it!" and give what the part called for.

We had just one disagreement. Pitch. He insisted on moving everything he sang down a full third, a fourth, occasionally a diminished fifth. I put up some argument, not only because I felt so used to the key of E in which I wrote the *Ballad*, and in which my American People's Chorus had sung it dozens of times, but also because I knew that he had the notes in the higher range. He actually sang as much baritone as bass.

"Paul, you can sing it up there," I cried.

"Yeah, but I don't like it." And he explained plaintively that as a folksinger he had to have the song in a bass key comfortable for him. To clinch this he told me that the Russians had actually transposed the already low arias from *Boris Godunov* down to his key! "Seems like you might be able to do the same for me, huh?"

Ballad for Americans went out over CBS at 4:30 in the afternoon of Sunday, November 5, 1939. It came last on the program. Burgess Meredith read Norman Corwin's words of introduction to our piece:

> What we have to say seriously can be simply said. It's this: Democracy is a good thing. It works. It may creak a bit, but it works. And in its working, it still turns out good tunes, good news, good people. . . . Life, liberty and the pursuit of happiness—of these we sing.

Columbia pulled out all the stops. Norman Corwin produced and directed, Mark Warnow of "Your Hit Parade" fame conducted, Ralph Wilkinson did an excellent orchestration (in Robeson's key), and a young Lyn Murray, at the start of a more than fifty-year composing and arranging career, handled the chorus.

Fireworks went off. More than 650 people in the studio audience—including several members of Helen's family—stood and applauded for ten minutes. CBS switchboards were jammed in New York and Hollywood for two hours. "Where can we get that music?" they asked. Five hundred letters came in the next few days.

The piece became an instant hit. *Readers Digest* called it "the finest piece of American propaganda." Novelist and playwright William Saroyan said, "You have revealed what radio can and should be. Let it go on like that until everybody realizes what a great country this is." *Time* magazine called me "a two-fisted, not-too-widely recognized minstrel from the State of Washington."[1]

Robbins Music Corporation took the *Ballad* for publication. They sold 20,000 copies of the sheet music in the first year, and got MGM to pay $4,000—half to Robbins, a thousand each to Robinson and Latouche—for using it in *Born to Sing*, a silly kid actors' movie where a composer in jail could get out only if his work was performed. Thus *Ballad*, outlandishly choreographed by Busby Berkeley in geometric formations involving pyramids and revolving stages, and sung by Douglas McPhail, became the hero's "Midnight Special" finale. The movie was "precocious without being entertaining," said the *New York Times*; "With the exception of the 'Ballad for Americans,' tagged on the end without much rhyme or reason, it is dull and not infrequently embarrassing." I am inclined to agree, but at the time the film got some raves, too: "musically thrilling," "a winner in its class," "this musical hit is in the groove."[2]

Robeson began singing the *Ballad* everywhere he went, beginning with a repeat on CBS on New Year's Eve. Following that broadcast, *Variety* gave it this boffo writeup:

> The song is a masterpiece of authentic American love of country and puts to shame much of the radio writing that has recently been palmed off in praise of democracy. This one tingles with electrical energy, indomitable Yankee optimism and a fine faith in everyday people as against the snobbish and the entrenched minority. Half-song, half-recitation and a steady upbuilding dramatic wallop, the Ballad will no doubt be heard many times.[3]

Many times, indeed. Jules Bledsoe, Lawrence Tibbett, James Melton, and hundreds of others gave the piece countless performances over the next several years. (In his biography of Marc Blitzstein, my collaborator Eric describes the September 1943 British premiere in Royal Albert Hall, by a battalion of black army engineers—and a white soloist. Blitzstein prepared the chorus and Hugo Weisgall conducted the London Symphony Orchestra.) I believe that *Ballad for Americans* played a significant role in weaning our choruses away from the standard classical European repertory, which is fine, but not truly representative of what American composers can do. Seattle heard the piece that first year in June at the Washington State Music Teachers Association convention at the Masonic Temple, and Big Paul sang it in November at the University of Washington's Meany Hall, his long-time friend Lawrence Brown at the piano.

When Nathaniel Shilkret conducted it on Victor Records, he asked my advice on a chorus. Naturally, I recommended the American People's Chorus, the hundred-strong amateur group I had started two years before (soon to grow to over 200-strong), and I re-rehearsed them in Robeson's key. They performed magnificently on this definitive recording, and the chorus earned $200 for it. A full-page ad for the records came out in the *New York Daily News*.[4] By the end of the year 1940 the album had sold more than 40,000 copies, enough so that RCA dropped the price from $2 to $1.50. In *Redbook*, composer and critic Deems Taylor recommended our *Ballad* as his number one choice of the month. The left-wing Timely Records company cleverly released my set of *Songs for Americans* at the same time, so that they could be advertised, promoted and reviewed together. (This set included my "Abe Lincoln," "Joe Hill," "John Brown," and "Horace Greeley," plus traditional songs "Grey Goose," "John Henry," "Jesse James," "Kevin Barry," and "Drill Ye Tarriers Drill.") Forty years later, the National Academy of Recording Arts and Sciences put that first *Ballad* album in its Hall of Fame "honoring recordings of lasting qualitative or historical significance."

Unofficial national anthem

An interesting complex of circumstances occurred that summer of 1940. The Republican Party asked the publishers for the right to perform *Ballad* at their national convention in

Philadelphia on June 24th. Under the liberal standard-bearer
Wendell Willkie, the Republicans were trying to compete with
Roosevelt. Out of our hands by then, we had no say in the
matter. We learned later that the Republicans had asked Robeson to sing and he turned them down, so they got Ray Middle-
ton instead. The press reported that speakers quailed at being
scheduled after the *Ballad* because they feared anything they
said would be depressingly anti-climactic.

Perhaps Big Paul was making plain that he didn't care to
be coopted by the Republicans, but he had another good reason: He was singing our piece with the New York Philharmonic Symphony Orchestra at New York's Lewisohn Sta-
dium the same night, with Hugh Ross's Schola Cantorum and
the all-black Wen Talbert Choir. A *New Yorker* reporter called
on John Latouche and me to ask what we thought about the
Republicans singing our ballad.

"Flabbergasted," said Latouche.

"It's the weirdest thing I ever heard of," said Robinson.

"We wrote the *Ballad for Americans* for everybody, not
only Republicans," said Latouche.

"Especially not only Republicans," said Robinson.[5]

It had been only a year before that Congressman Clifton
A. Woodrum had promised that "if there is a line or passage in
[*Sing for Your Supper*] that contributes to cultural or educational benefit or uplift of America, I will eat the whole manuscript." I wonder if it tasted good.

Interestingly enough, *Ballad for Americans* also got used the
week before at the Communist Party Convention. It had become an unofficial national anthem.

Voice of America

The forces of reaction had tentacles reaching into all walks
of American life, not least into the entertainment industry.
That summer of 1940 the Hollywood Bowl booked Paul to
sing the *Ballad*. I returned to my home town of Seattle for the
first time since 1934, happily enduring my CBS fame. "Home-
Town Boy Makes Good," read the headline in the Seattle Sun-

day *Times*, whose reporters came to the airport to interview me as Helen, our son Perry, and I stepped off the plane. I drove down to L. A. mainly for the Robeson performance on July 23rd, with the Philharmonic Orchestra and the Hall Johnson Choir. As composer of the piece, I attended a breakfast given by the Hollywood Bowl Association on the morning of the concert. Paul didn't show up, but I didn't think much of it, figuring he was busy or sleeping late. That afternoon I asked him, "Where were you this morning?"

"Where was I what?" he answered. Turned out, he had not been invited—the star of the show, the only person aside from soprano Lily Pons who could guarantee to fill the Bowl.

Another upsetting thing happened. Paul's agent, whom he had assigned to find him a hotel, came back after two hours saying that there wasn't a hotel in town with a room for Robeson. Paul's attitude was magnificent. He said, "Go back and try again." This time, after two and a half hours of phoning and searching, the agent came back with a successful report. He had found a deluxe suite at the largest hotel, the Beverly Wilshire, for $100 a night (probably $1000 today), which Paul could have *if* he registered under a different name.

Now very few would criticize if Paul simply said, "The hell with you." He had all kinds of private homes he could stay in, both black and white friends who would have been delighted to put him up. But he chose to take the Beverly Wilshire under an assumed name, pay the deluxe rent, and arrange to spend a few hours every afternoon sitting in the lobby, where he could be easily recognized.

He explained why: To open the way for Marian Anderson, Roland Hayes and anyone else to have a place to rest their heads when they next came to Los Angeles. And this did the trick. The hotels were open to black guests from then on.

Racism is an evil virus in America. Its roots lead back to slavery times, its influence pervasive, its effects still devastating. Paul Robeson confronted and opposed it, worked with dignity and intelligence to defang and finally destroy it wherever he met it. In this noble but difficult campaign, *Ballad for Americans* proved a powerful ally. For a black man to keep saying, "You know who I am," ending up claiming to *be America*, contradicted the way most people thought and acted. Yet he, Big Paul, was accepted universally as *the* voice of America. If a few disagreed, they kept it to themselves.

So if my career received a vigorous jolt into public recognition by Paul Robeson's singing of *Ballad for Americans*, it can be said that his career and the cause of equality also got a lift. Within a few months I began hearing about performances by high school and university glee clubs, community choruses, children's choruses, church choirs, black and white, Jewish, all over the land, including my West Seattle High. And with each singing of the piece, with Big Paul there or a thousand miles away, *his* America hung in the concert hall like a great fraternal, democratic aura.

I received some very sweet reports from teachers who played the records for their classes. The four-sided album on 78s ended each side with "You know who I am," so that kept the kids guessing. Once, after the third side, while the teacher turned the record over, a kid was heard to mutter, "I bet it's the Lone Ranger!"

In the early 1940s, the *Ballad* developed a life of its own apart from Big Paul. MGM put it into *Born to Sing*. Lawrence Tibbett performed it on NBC. Spoiled by Paul's rendition, I considered Tibbett a little "operatic," and discouraged him from sustaining his note on "I - I - I - I am the et ceteras . . . ," but he went ahead and held it out anyway, remarking that he rather resented the term "opera" being spoken with disdain. Bing Crosby recorded the piece beautifully on Decca, and his version sold another 20,000 copies. I remember gently exaggerating the Crosby style when I described his crooning to friends:

> *In '76 the sky was re-eh-ed,*
> *Thunder rumbling overhea-eh-ed,*

sliding up into that "ed" sound. By the way, he sang it in the lower Robeson key. With all the radio play *Ballad* received, I figured it was about time I received some royalties, so I joined ASCAP in December 1940. Not too long after, my listing first appeared in *Who's Who*.

Once the war began, my old friend Arthur Vogel (author of *The Young Go First*) was a sergeant in charge of recreational activity at Fort Monmouth, New Jersey. His commanding officer came to him one Friday afternoon with an emergency: He had $8,000 to spend before Monday morning, otherwise the money would have to be returned to the general funds. Could Sgt. Vogel do it? The CO assigned Arthur a truck and driver and they drove to New York City. There he spent $4,000 on a magnificent set of sound equipment, another couple of thousand on forty smoking stands, and he bought paint for theatrical sets. Late Sunday night they passed a Sam Goody's record store just about to close. Arthur went in, looking for *Ballad for Americans*. Yes, they had it. But wasn't the manager shocked when Arthur said, "I'll take a hundred copies"! Of course, they weren't in stock, but by 8:30 Monday morning they were ready for pickup, and that used up the $8,000. Those hundred sets of records found their way into every corner of Fort Monmouth. Those soldiers heard my *Ballad* till their heads swam.

In my papers I have a letter that H. Stanley Marcus (of Neiman-Marcus in Dallas) sent to Simon Sakowitz (of Sakowitz Brothers in Houston). Marcus had just bought 75 albums of the *Ballad* and presented them to all the public schools in Dallas "in order to encourage tolerance among the school children." The gesture apparently succeeded hugely, and he recommended that Sakowitz do the same. "I am sure you can get the records at wholesale cost, and I personally recommend it to you as a good civic investment."[6]

After the war, Big Paul transferred from Victor to Columbia Records. Victor responded by withdrawing Robeson's *Ballad* from their catalogue—cutting off their nose to spite their face, because the *Ballad* was still selling well. Unofficially, the reason was that Robeson's left leanings had begun to fall under criticism. The recording remained unavailable for nearly fifteen years (except for pirate editions which paid no royalties), not because Robeson went Communist, but that he went Columbia!

Ballad for Americans un-American?

In 1940, after the war in Europe had begun, but before the U.S. entered it, I stood with the left's peace policy. During that period I appeared at Moose Hall in Seattle for the anti-war Washington Commonwealth Federation, mentioning how I'd rather have my songs sung before that group than before any other political party. A leaflet promoting the event stated that a manuscript of *Ballad for Americans* had been sold off to benefit the Communist Party's magazine *New Masses*. It seems also that a local high school had dramatized the *Ballad*.

These facts were set forth in a letter addressed to the Federal Bureau of Investigation on December 7, 1940, according to a page in my FBI files that I obtained in 1991. The correspondent asked the Bureau's opinion regarding the suitability of a leftwing composer's work for high school presentation.

On December 12th the FBI wrote back saying that the Bureau confined its work "to the investigation of violations of Federal laws and other matters of a kindred nature." Very correct and succinct, no?

Not exactly. For it appears that just around this time, the FBI caught wind of my political opinions (not that I kept them a secret), and decided that one day I might be a dangerous character. This is clearly what they had in mind by "other matters of a kindred nature," for my political thoughts and activities certainly represented no "violations of Federal laws." From that time on, for a period that lasted over 35 years, the FBI went to prodigious lengths to follow me, spy on me, study my movements, my friends, my marriages and family, attend my performances, clip newspapers, intercept telegrams and mail and phone calls, keep track of citations of my name, advise embassies abroad of my travels, log my magazine and newspaper subscriptions.

It took thousands and thousands of hours' worth of work to research and amass this information, which yielded no fewer than 1,150 pages that they sent me, plus many more pages they withheld for vital "national security" reasons. As we now know, the FBI kept such files on half a million people on the left, only for exercising their legitimate constitutional rights. The cost of such a taxpayer-subsidized program, especially when administered by a monstrous hypocrite the likes of John Edgar Hoover, is truly staggering. It comprised half the Bureau's budget in certain states.

Right at the beginning of my file appears a letter (April 26, 1941) from old J. Edgar himself to Assistant Director E. J. Connelley in New York, stating that I am being considered for "custodial detention," in other words, a round-up of supposed subversives without benefit of trial. Curious, right at the height of my popularity with *Ballad for Americans*. The timing can actually be traced to President Roosevelt, who extended these fact-gathering privileges to Mr. Hoover in light of the clear and present wartime danger. But from the beginning the FBI concerned itself far more with the left than the pro-Nazi right.

Every time my name appeared on an organizational letterhead as a sponsor for some benefit, it would be duly recorded in my file—ditto in the files of all the other names. License plate numbers of people visiting my home were written down, likewise when I visited someone else of interest to the FBI. Bureau agents placed hundreds of pretext phone calls to my home, or to places I worked, to ascertain current addresses, occupants of my home, occupations. Agents acting undercover stole mailing lists and recorded their names. Agents showed up at demonstrations to photograph, to take down names and license plates.

Bureau employees clipped dozens of leftwing and mainstream newspapers, including many in foreign languages, to see whose names could be culled and cited, what concerts and benefits had been announced, what open letters to the Governor or to the President were published. If 150 names appeared, you may be sure that 150 pages were prepared for entry into 150 different files. The labor involved! (I like the lingo the FBI used on a rubber stamp applied to these articles: "Clipped at the seat of Government." At least someone had a subtle sense of humor.)

The FBI also shared its data with other government agencies, and vice versa. Whenever I applied for a passport, the State Department passed the information I gave to the FBI. The Post Office and the Draft Board freely shared what they knew about me, the Justice Department handed over petitions to save someone's life or commute their sentence; nongovernment entities such as the telephone company gave full cooperation as well. The FBI served the House Un-American Activities Committee (HUAC), feeding its investigators every juicy tidbit that would help prove my disloyalty. And the FBI spawned the careers of many an anti-Communist journalist, supplying background information to besmirch names and reputations by the hundreds.

Much as the files reveal about the endless hunting for Reds under the bed, about our national phobia of the left, evidence shows the FBI as extremely careless and inattentive. Even though large swaths of blacked-out passages and agents' names decorate these thousand pages, it's obvious that many agents repetitively quoted previously gathered information, even when patently wrong. For example, in "eye-witness" reports of concert appearances, I am described as blond and blue-eyed—I have always had brown eyes and my hair was brown, too—an error made early on by some bureaucrat and endlessly recycled. More striking evidence that the agent supposedly at my concert was instead home with his wife or out with his girlfriend in some motel, is that I am frequently identified as colored, or Negro. Now I have no objection in principle, but for a fact-gathering body to be in such error so often makes me wonder what we taxpayers were getting for our money!

What do I *feel* about all this, fifty years later? Mostly a sadness over the awful waste of time, resources, and talent. I'm not bitter about it personally—there's too much water under the bridge for that now. It does make me wonder what kind of a country we would have today, not to mention what kind of career I might have had, without J. Edgar Hoover lording it over us all. And I feel very eerie, looking at those blacked-out names of agents, both FBI and undercover, who worked with me side by side in organizations and clubs, who shared platforms with me, who knew intimate details of my life. This kind of spy culture keeps people apart, breaks down a sense of community, forces us to question who we can ever fully trust. It's profoundly destructive to the spirit.

From time to time I shall refer to my FBI file as it sheds light—or darkness. One good thing, it reminded me of many a name, many an organization doing good work over the course of thirty-five years to keep this the "land of the free, and the home of the brave."

Notes

1. *Readers Digest* and Saroyan, quoted in "Paul Robeson Broadcast Brings Cheers from Vast Radio Public," *Daily Worker*, November 20, 1939; *Time*, November 20, 1939.

2. T. S., *The New York Times*, February 19, 1942; *Motion Picture Herald*, January 24, 1942; *Variety* and *Hollywood Reporter*, January 21, 1942.

3. *Variety*, January 10, 1940.

4. *New York Daily News*, May 14, 1940.

5. *The New Yorker*, June 29, 1940, has a slight variation on the dialogue.

6. H. Stanley Marcus to Simon Sakowitz, March 20, 1946.

CONCERNING CARL SANDBURG

Bu-u-r-rning

True hero worship is what I felt for old Carl after reading *The People, Yes* in 1939. The book truly blew me out. I absolutely had to make contact with him. It wasn't easy. He didn't answer my first two letters. Finally, after sending along my Abe Lincoln song (I knew he was a sucker for Lincoln), I got a precious postcard, typed, addressed "Dear Steve," a name I later learned that he bestowed on a man he felt okay about. He signed it Carl, giving tacit permission for a friendship to develop. I took a train out to his home in Harbert, Michigan.

I had already started working on songs with Paul Ashford for a projected musical on *The People, Yes*. And I brought along the book with voluminous questions for Carl. We got along well and my music impressed him. I had built a strong cantata around his refrain "In the folded and quiet yesterdays/How many times has it happened," which spoke of the martyred ones throughout history who, instead of receiving plaudits and thanks for their noble work, were tortured, beaten, and executed. Into his powerful poetry I inserted names of the martyrs chanted by the chorus, names like Joe Hill, Sacco, Vanzetti, Joan of Arc, and Galileo.

After I played this for old Carl he delivered himself of a most beautiful pair of sentences in his slow and measured tones. "I bu-u-r-rned when I wrote those words. You bu-u-r-rned when you did the myoo-sic."

Fall of 1939, permission from Sandburg in hand, with some of the material already written and even broadcast over WABC, I applied for a Guggenheim fellowship, *The People, Yes* as my project. I had in mind a new kind of people's opera, using the widest possible variety of homegrown American musical forms—minstrel, vaudeville, musical comedy and revue, folk songs and dances, county fair magician acts and patent medicine salesmen, chain gang and work songs, Arkansas

Traveler and cowboy ballads, hi-de-ho choruses, you name it, all fused into an epic with folk heroes such as John Henry, Paul Bunyan, Abe Lincoln, and Johnny Appleseed. Technically, the opera would integrate film, radio and living newspaper formats, mass chant, solos, ensembles, and choruses. The central theme was that throughout history, kings, dictators and empires have risen and fallen, but the people go on forever. I recruited some name references—Lillian Hellman, Hallie Flanagan, Aaron Copland, Herman Shumlin, H. V. Kaltenborn, my old Washington music professors, and some important critics. I knew that many applicants sent in proposals year after year without success; in my case it helped that just as I met the Guggenheim deadline, the Sunday *New York Times* gave a prominent three paragraphs to my opera. And that fall and winter, all hell broke loose with *Ballad for Americans*. Lo and behold, in March of 1940 the $2,000 fellowship came through.

With renewed determination I forged ahead. Eventually, Paul Ashford and I stopped working together. I had set many poems to music, had begun developing scenes and characters, and had communed closely with Sandburg. But we couldn't really find a cohesive stage work in the material. After the excitement of *Ballad for Americans*, I remained in New York, and Norman Corwin moved to Hollywood. I tried to finish the new piece with Norman and me working long distance. He had independently established good relations with Sandburg, having already dramatized *The People, Yes* on radio, developing satiric elements that the poet had only hinted at. Sandburg's "Tower of Babel" became a solid base for one of Norman's radio shows, and his fine invention of the "Three Stuffed Shirts," representing reaction throughout the ages, was brilliant. In the spring of '41 the Guggenheim Foundation granted me a $1,000, six-month extension to complete the work. Enough material existed for Norman and me to offer half an hour of it on CBS—May 18, 1941, with Burl Ives and Everett Sloane—and various other segments at one benefit or another.

I made a second trip out to Harbert, Michigan. Sandburg treated me to (in his words) a "luncheon of plain proletarian baked beans with a classy divertissement of goat's milk." It was—jumping ahead for a second—right after my cantata *The Lonesome Train* had been broadcast, with Pete Seeger on five-string banjo. I was raving about it as the only truly American instrument. Then a beautiful thing happened, which I'll permit old Carl to relate in his inimitable manner. This is from a letter about me (Erll) to Norman Corwin, March 24, 1941.

> Comes out then Erll has been on the lookout for such a banjo and no luck. So yrs truly reaches over, tipping back in his chair, into a corner behind two guitars and a Filipino 3-string fiddle and produces a banjo t[ha]t yrs truly has had going on 30 yrs, not playing it for 20 yrs because a guitar had priority. So he hands this identical banjo to Erll with a brief and pointed speech: "You are the one man in the USA to have this and I give it to you quoting the Cossack proverb: He owns the wild horse who can ride him." So we wrap it in a burlap bag, nickel plated with a tight drum, long narrow fretboard, a honey. Nobody else could have taken it away like that. It was like a good deacon giving away an adopted child, that had always been well behaved, to another good deacon who pledged to bring it up well behaved and godly.[1]

I treasured this gift for years, then finally misplaced it. I have trouble holding onto material things to this day.

With Norman, too, the collaboration proved only half successful. We never could develop a story line for that moving but plotless book. The image of the tower as a home for humanity, the "biggest housing project ever seen," with its accompanying "Six-Hour Day and Five-Day Week" hit song, was mighty indeed, especially when we got Burl Ives to broadcast it live one February evening of 1942. Instead of blaming God for shuffling all the languages and bringing disorder to the tower's builders, we showed the stuffed shirts as responsible. I found a third collaborator in William C. White, and we retreated to his Saranac Lake home for several weeks in July 1941 to pull the whole thing together.

Amazing unity

With all I'd written on it, everyone I knew got so tired of hearing about the "imminent" completion of *The People, Yes* that we had to hold a party. My colleague Marc Blitzstein hosted a gala Robinson evening at Town Hall on November 29, 1941. From California Norman sent a telegram:

I WISH I COULD BE THERE TONIGHT TO JOIN
    YOUR CELEBRATION
BECAUSE I YIELD MY DEEP RESPECT TO NO
    ONE IN THE NATION
BUT YOU SHOULD KNOW THERE ARE FIVE
    MEN WHO DONT LIKE EARL A BIT
THEY THINK HIS MUSIC STINKING AND
    THEIR NAMES ARE VIZ TO WIT
HITLER LINDBERGH MUSSOLINI COUGHLIN
    AND CIANO
WILL ROBINSON OR BLITZSTEIN KINDLY TRY
    THIS ON THE PIANO.[2]

Inwardly, I didn't feel so confident. The central characters and the storyline were still weak. Earlier that year Blitzstein staged his latest opera, and I wrote to Norman: "It seems very logical to everyone that *The People, Yes* should follow *No for an Answer*. And between you and me I think we have a better title. But we will have to go some to make it a better play."[3]

Just nine days after the gala came Pearl Harbor. The whole world situation changed. "The class struggle theme of the stuffed shirts versus Zeph isn't right for the times we are in," I wrote to my good old friend Jessie Lloyd O'Connor, heiress to the *Chicago Tribune* family fortune who nevertheless remained a solid, lifelong supporter of progressive causes.

It's sad, but when Marshall Field gives $25,000 to Russian War Relief and the *New York Herald Tribune* is the

> most consistent capitalist paper in defense of the all out
> effort, and in standing up for Russia, then I cannot see
> myself or Bill White attempting to put on a show
> which might contribute to disrupting some of this
> amazing unity that is being established. . . . Some day I
> feel confident *The People, Yes* as we have it will be perti-
> nent again, and maybe not so far off either.[4]

The People, Yes certainly became pertinent again, but sadly
I never finished it. For the duration I put it aside and started
what would become a stream of anti-fascist songs.

A nine-minute piece of dynamite, *In the Folded and Quiet
Yesterdays* remains one of my strongest pieces. It's had an up-
and-down history. One up certainly was the 1942 Keynote recording with Michael Loring and my American People's Chorus. The blacklist of the 1950s played a part in the down. But
Carl Sandburg and I became friends through the World War II
period. In New York he visited our apartment more than
once. For reasons I can well respect, Helen remained unmoved
by him and his entertaining. Did he talk too much? Pay no
attention to her? Take over the scene too completely? Come
always to be "entertained," not offering to contribute? Carl did
have a reputation in some circles as a tightwad. Whatever,
none of this affected me. He totally charmed me, and I loved
him. We even shared some programs as entertainers together.

Once in Chicago, at the somewhat left-wing Freedom
School, Carl came in from Harbert, not worrying about being
tarred with the red brush. Always "on," Sandburg hammed it
up in the great tradition. Speaking in barely a whisper, he
would suddenly rise to monumental volume when expressing
contempt for, say, Thomas Mann. Most impressive. Though I
had a tough time later when he adopted anti-Communism.

Things happening over there

Sometime in the mid-1950s, I got my first inkling of Carl
becoming anti-Soviet. He wrote a magazine article and was
quoted widely about his trip to the Soviet Union. He spoke of
the fear he encountered. Fear in the streets, fear of Stalin and

the higher-ups, fear among the people. Still in my pro-Soviet phase, I discounted most of it. I simply consigned Carl to the backsliders, those compliant ones giving in to the redbaiters.

Well, about this time a group of friends decided that Robinson and his music should be heard, that there should be a comeback concert, blacklist or no. My sister-in-law Helen Wortis (Joe's wife), producer Harold Leventhal, and Lee Hays—my "renaissance" committee—threw in suggestions. They discussed Carnegie Hall, and could we fill it? They drew up a list of honorary sponsors, and Carl Sandburg's name inevitably came up. We all had doubts about his accepting, but they decided I should call him. I learned that he was in town at his publishers, Harcourt Brace, and I wrote to him there. I told him about the concert, invited him to attend; and if too busy, would he allow his name to be used? I allowed two days for my letter to be received and digested, then called. The operator put me through, then a long silence followed after I announced my name. There began a strange conversation, every word loaded with meaning beyond meaning.

"I can't go along with you on this," he said. "There's things happening over there." (He never said where, but I surmised.) He went on not in direct criticism of me, but as if I were somehow responsible for the evils in the Soviet Union. Finally I got in a few words to the effect that I had always gone my own path and plowed my own field.

"Yes," he interrupted me, "but you haven't got what old Gene Debs had when he said, 'I won't take orders from the Moscow Vatican!'"

While I felt it immensely unfair of him, I had no answer. For while I had lived in my own way, I had also tried to follow party line and had from time to time "taken orders." Which I couldn't be proud of. So to an extent I knew he had a point.

Once Carl unburdened himself of this attack on me, he unbent and explained why he was in any case too busy to participate in the concert. "I have to reduce some million-plus words in my four Lincoln books *The War Years* to around 240,000. They're making one book out of that, and there's

chores, chores." He finished, saying, "Sometime over the next period we can perhaps get together, share a glass."

We had no contact for another few years. Toward the end of the '50s I suddenly found a publisher for *In the Folded and Quiet Yesterdays* and had to contact him for permission. I came back to my Brooklyn home one afternoon to discover that Sandburg had called and laid a trip on my teen-age son Perry. "He wants you to change the words," Perry said.

My subsequent conversation with old Carl, long distance to Asheville, North Carolina, where he and his family had moved, was weird, like walking down opposite sides of the street, talking but unable to hear each other. He didn't like the names of the martyrs that I'd added to his poetry. In particular he objected to the name of Tom Mooney, a framed labor leader from California who became a cause célèbre of the left for 23 years until his ultimate release from prison in 1939.

I intrude a contemporary joke, which depends on your knowing that freedom for Tom Mooney had for years been listed as a Communist Party demand. It seems that a band of neighbors under CP leadership were picketing a house where an eviction was occurring. They were so effective that the landlord finally came out and made a speech. "Look," he said, "I will restore this tenant to his apartment. I will give heat and hot water. I will reduce his rent by half. He can keep his dog and his cats. But I have to tell you, I can't free Tom Mooney!"

Sandburg said it like this: "To put in names like Mooney and leave out Lovejoy, the newspaper editor martyr, is pe-cyool-yur," implying that I had better stop pushing party line in anything that had his name on it. (He never objected to any names back in '39 when I visited him in Harbert.) So he instructed me to take out the names. "And if you make an elision, put three dots . . ." So befoozled by this conversation, I didn't think to ask him how to sing three dots.

I spent a rocky two months after that trying to figure out how to reach this man. I began a dozen letters and couldn't make them speak the healing words that I wanted to offer. Meantime I changed the names, taking out Tom Mooney and

adding names like Mohandas Gandhi, Miguel Hidalgo, Lovejoy, and others. And put my publisher on hold. My good
friend, the poet Walter Lowenfels, finally gave me the right
advice. "Don't write," he told me, "go down and see him."

I flew to Asheville, near the Connemara goat farm in Flat
Rock where the Sandburgs lived, and called from the hotel.
Carl sounded cool on the phone, but we made a date for three
o'clock the next day. I allowed a morning and part of the afternoon to hitchhike to the farm, but no one picked me up. I
finally caught a bus and arrived closer to five than three. In
trepidation I walked the long road from the bus stop up a hill
to a large white house. Not only was I late but I had no idea
what kind of lion would be waiting in the den.

Sandburg himself opened the door with a question. "How
is Foster doing these days?" (William Z. Foster, then head of
the Communist Party). In the old days, Sandburg knew and
respected him, but not now. As for me, I had "opened" for
him back in the 1940s; according to the FBI (quoting the
Daily Worker), I had even written a song honoring Foster in
1945 for his fifty years of service to labor (no doubt a mediocre
piece of which I have no recall). But by now, a decade later, I
was either out or on the way out of the Party and didn't have a
current answer. I just mumbled, "He's okay, I guess."

As before, after putting me on the spot, Sandburg began to
thaw, proving Lowenfels right. He couldn't carry on a grudge
in person. And in a perfect non sequitur to our whole previous
relationship he gave me an opening. "When are you going to
write some music to my words?" he asked.

"I have, I have," I answered. I practically jumped for the
grand piano, pulling out of my briefcase *In the Folded and
Quiet Yesterdays* and "The Tower of Babel," two pieces from
The People, Yes. The big living room served as his work space:
Loose papers and manuscripts lay scattered all around. I had to
move them to clear off the piano bench. So I gave him a concert, finishing off with "Black and White," an integration song
of mine, which he loved. I think I impressed him more as a
performer than as a composer.

They invited me to dinner. Could have stayed overnight except for a plane reservation that evening. Should have canceled, but I didn't. They arranged for me to catch the next bus to Asheville. My last conversation with Carl ran like this:

ME: Okay to publish *Folded and Quiet?*
HIM: Yep.
ME: Share royalties 50-50?
HIM: 50-50.

Shawnee Press published the cantata, appending a list of the martyrs to freedom mentioned in the text. The orchestra accompaniment is available from Shawnee on rental.

My visit to Connemara has been immortalized in a book by Carl's daughter Helga, *Sweet Music: A Book of Family Reminiscence and Song.*[5] Helga appeared at the farm not long after I had left. Her sister taught her "Black and White," which had so impressed the Sandburgs, and Helga has performed it ever since. One night she sang it to Soviet Ambassador Dobrynin and the poet Robert Frost, and she included it in her book, along with another favorite, "Joe Hill."

A final dip in the Sandburg well

Suppose, suppose, suppose they gave a war
And no—one—came. (Repeat)
Suppose the people said
We're standin' here in bed,
We're makin' love instead,
We like that mo-o-o-ore
And just suppose they gave a noble war
And no—one—came.

And suppose that people kept asking you to write an antiwar song and you remembered the little girl in *The People, Yes* who, seeing soldiers for the first time and asking what they were, came up with that beautiful line, "Sometime they'll give a war and no one will come."

Suppose they rave, and rant and even wave
The flag a-bout,
And then we say, About that war you gave,
Include—us—out.
Suppose in ev'ry land
They'd all understand
Instead of arms, a hand
Would reach their sho-o-ore,
Oh, what a time,
A time we'd all adore,
A time we're looking for,
That time they called a war
And no—one—came.

So in the 1960s I returned to Carl Sandburg's *The People, Yes* for further inspiration (on this I shared the lyrics with Bob Russell). I hesitate to say that "Suppose" is my last song based on old Carl's thoughts and words, for who can say when I might dip into his well again?

Notes

1. *The Letters of Carl Sandburg*, ed. Herbert Mitgang, New York: Harcourt, Brace & World, 1968, p. 404. See also Gregory d'Alessio, *Old Troubadour: Carl Sandburg with his Guitar Friends*, New York: Walker, 1987, p. 51.
2. See Joseph Foster, "People's Musician," *New Masses*, December 16, 1941.
3. Earl Robinson to Norman Corwin, January 16, 1941.
4. Earl Robinson to Jessie Lloyd O'Connor, December 18, 1941.
5. Helga Sandburg, *Sweet Music: A Book of Family Reminiscence and Song*, New York: Dial, 1963.

THE PHONY WAR

A repeat of World War I

People on the left referred to that period from September 1, 1939 (when the Germans invaded Poland), to June 1941 (when they attacked the Soviets) as the "phony war." England and France had declared war on Germany, but the U.S. had not yet entered the war. The Soviets and the Germans signed their (in)famous non-aggression pact in August 1939, which split Poland between them. That permitted the Germans peace on their eastern front while they tackled the West— Luxembourg, Belgium, the Netherlands, France. The Soviets took over the three Baltic states and tried to conquer Finland. We called the war phony at that stage because it looked like there wasn't much organized resistance to the Germans, except for England bearing the brunt of Nazi bombs.

The left justified its pro-peace stance because for the time being the U.S.S.R. looked safe, and we saw the conflict among the various powers as a repeat of the imperialist World War I. At the beginning of the period most Americans wanted to stay out, but over the course of the next couple of years the tide changed as we witnessed the Nazi juggernaut smash on relentlessly toward world domination.

Of course, our pro-Soviet peace policy wasn't the same as the right-wing peace policy. Whereas we proposed boycotting products from fascist countries (such as silk stockings from Japan), the big corporations continued trading with Germany and Japan in order to assist them, and the left pointed this out vociferously. Certain congressional and business leaders would gladly have welcomed fascism if it would mean total "law and order" at home—suppression of labor, the left, etc. Still, the left stood in a tricky position, having to defend the Soviet treaty with Hitler, and the Party lost members over this. We pointed out that Stalin had tried to get the Western nations to stop Hitler much earlier—in Spain, for instance. British Prime Minister Chamberlain's 1938 "peace in our time" pact with Hitler, handing Czechoslovakia to Germany, was just as indefensible, we said. And shockingly, in early 1939, as soon as Madrid fell, Roosevelt recognized the Franco government. But these actions didn't convey the same sense of betrayal and horror. The West preferred to appease the Nazis, hoping that they and the Soviets would kill each other off. Then, with the Nazi-Soviet pact, Stalin turned the tables on the West to avoid such a fate. Given our sympathy with the survival of the world's first and only socialist state, it was a surprise tactic we had to defend, but defend it we must.

In early 1941 some folks put on an Aid to Britain benefit, and asked Robbins Music for the rights to perform *Ballad for Americans*. I objected on principle. "Build up our own defenses and armaments by all means," I wrote to the publisher, "but stay away from foreign entanglements which may draw us into the war as they did in 1917." In the end I had little choice but to allow them to use the *Ballad*, for the publisher, not the composer, controls the rights; but I accepted no royalty and I demanded assurance that my name would not be used in any way to condone the performance.[1]

Perhaps the most enduring song I wrote during that period (in 1939) was "Spring Song." Harry Schachter wrote the lyric. Just one stanza of "Spring Song" will give you the idea:

> *When the fields are ripe for sowing, in the Spring,*
> *You can watch the children growing, in the Spring.*
> *We could have a celebration*
> *With folks from every nation,*
> *Must we destroy creation in the Spring?*
> *Oh, I'd just like an ordinary Spring,*
> *With people laughing just because it's Spring.*
> *And however he spells his name,*
> *I am sure he feels the same*
> *For it's great to be alive in the Spring.*

As it fit in with our anti-war policy, I sang this song around quite a bit—incidentally, the International Workers

Order (IWO) arranged most of my bookings out of their concert and lecture bureau. (I once conducted the IWO Chorus in a number that precisely expressed our "phony war" view: "The Yanks Are Not Coming.") American Peace Mobilization used "Spring Song" in an independent film called *Says Youth*, and Paul Robeson recorded it on Keynote. Later on, Edith Segal choreographed it up at Camp Kinderland.

Then on June 22nd of 1941, with the West tightly nailed down, the Nazis turned their attention eastward and invaded the Soviet Union. As of that moment we urged total support for the Soviets, encouraging the U.S. to enter the war and open up a second front against Hitler. For this was no longer a war among imperialist powers, but a war to save socialism in the U.S.S.R. and democracy at home. With the Soviets now bearing the brunt of the war, and the Nazis making advances every day, most Americans came to feel we should intervene.

I don't know what I might have felt in those complex times if I weren't in the Party. We know so much more now about what was going on behind the scenes. No one acted in full knowledge of the facts, and no one looking back can honestly say they did the right thing at all times. In history, as in the present, there is seldom a single right thing.

I certainly felt no pleasure at the way the Nazis ravaged the Soviet land, but I breathed a certain relief that we no longer had to soft-pedal our antifascism. We could be legitimate antifascists again.

"Spring Song" went out of my repertory during the war; Eric Bernay of Keynote recalled all copies of the Robeson recording that he could find, and destroyed his remaining stock. But as soon as the war ended, and it looked like the world was gearing up for another—a nuclear war this time—people demanded that song again. Many times I've offered to retire it permanently, if the threat of war became remote enough, but alas, it's been in my repertory ever since.

The afterglow from *Ballad for Americans* continued on CBS. The network brought together an imposing group of people to take part in a program called "Back Where I Come From." It ran 1940 to 1941. The folksongs, stories, and tall tales that made up this 15-minute Wednesday night show came from Alan Lomax, who with his father John had been collecting material for the Library of Congress for many years, and knew everything there was to know about a folk song. A quartet consisting of Burl Ives, Pete Seeger, Josh White, and me appeared regularly every week, and I emceed. Woody Guthrie and Richard Dyer-Bennett wandered in occasionally. Nik Ray directed. CBS paid this talent $17 a week. Such a group would cost considerably more today, to put it mildly. One time we did a program on war songs and sang "John Brown's Body." I expressed my phony war-period position of "a pox on both your houses" by announcing the song with great passion, "There was a man who *knew what he was fighting for!*" The show took me away from composing, though, so at the beginning of 1941 I quit.

Note

1. Earl Robinson to Abe Olman, February 6, 1941.

A VISIT TO THE WHITE HOUSE

Soup and fish

In December 1941, Pearl Harbor month, I was invited down to Washington, D.C., by my friend Adrian Dornbush, former head of the WPA Art Project and a friend of Mrs. Eleanor Roosevelt. It happens she was running a concert for the people in the Office of Civilian Defense (OCD), which she headed as part of her contribution to the war effort. The Roosevelts and their administration were unmistakably capitalist, but she was apparently happy to have this working-class Communist composer appear on her concert. In my former Thirties thinking, never the twain could meet in any kind of friendly manner, but the war changed everything. The Communists added their militancy to the antifascist cause, and the government welcomed all the help it could get.

My anti-Establishment posture reflected itself in dress as well as psychology. I had not worn a tie for some time. In fact, I didn't give much thought to how I dressed. Nevertheless, for this OCD event I bought a new blue serge suit, and brought it to D.C. with me the night before the performance, Saturday, December 27th. Olga Coelho, Brazilian guitarist-singer, an Argentine pianist, and a movie on national defense shared the program with me. We met together Saturday morning to case the hall, set up sound, and run through the program.

At this rehearsal, Adrian came to me with a striking question: "How would you like to go to the White House for dinner tonight?" I was amazed by the casualness of the invite: long as I'm in town, might as well drop in for dinner. He next asked, "Do you have a tux?" No, I said, but I have a blue serge suit, would that be all right? Adrian actually checked with Malvina Thompson, Mrs. R.'s secretary, and came back with the information, "I think you'll feel more comfortable with a tux. Mr. Churchill will be there." So I rented a "soup and fish"—what we called tuxedos in those days.

To the left of the President

My suspicions of the capitalistic White House proved unfounded. Adrian merely said, "Dornbush and Robinson," and we were waved through. Apparently the FBI had not advised the White House chief of protocol that only a year before I had signed a petition to the President protesting against the badgering of Communist leaders. The front of the White House was all lit up, not only like a Christmas tree but with one. Inside, except for certain special trappings, it was like a well fitted-out country home, relaxed and surprisingly democratic. No one checked me or my politics at the door, nobody frisked us for concealed weapons, and we hung up our own overcoats. I was approached almost immediately by a man with a seating plan for the dinner table. "You will sit to the left of the President," he said. I couldn't help noticing his plain blue suit, not even as fancy as the one I had just abandoned.

First on the program was cocktails. In a loud voice the man with the plan announced our names. Mrs. Roosevelt greeted me standing behind a large silver cocktail decanter. Sitting beside her, Winston Churchill reminded me of W. C. Fields, red nose and all. As she introduced us she asked him if he knew *Ballad for Americans*. He didn't. "You must hear it sometime," she said.

Fala scampered around underfoot. I was struck by Mrs. R.'s extraordinary grace as she bent down to pet and fondle the dog. She was taller than I am, at least in high heels; and she had a high laugh and a voice which cracked in and out of high and low register.

The President, late for cocktails, was pushed in briskly. Although I knew about his infirmity, it was something of a shock to see him in a wheelchair. FDR let himself be seen in the chair as little as possible. He always walked into the House and the Senate on somebody's arm, and you never saw the chair in press photos.

Eleanor greeted him with some small upset, "Well, Franklin, I went right ahead and poured. We didn't wait for you." He apologized profusely, though I found out later he had good reason. He had been with Ambassador Litvinov of the Soviet Union, fresh back in the U.S. for the forming of the Grand Alliance to fight fascism.

Conversational tidbits while we stood around with our cocktail glasses included Harry Hopkins observing that the Japanese followed well-established Axis custom by attacking Pearl Harbor on a Sunday, when good Christians are at their prayers. An atheist at that time, I murmured a half-hearted assent. Some tall gentleman—maybe he was with the State Department—related the story of his ride from Hyde Park to New York with an exceedingly stuffy bishop who prattled about nothing but the rich lords and ladies of the aristocracy that he knew. With her customary graciousness, Mrs. R. admitted it as one of his less laudable characteristics, but pointed out that he did a tremendous amount of good, raising money for the underprivileged. Apparently he talked so much about the rich because he was trying to get money from them to help the poor.

Mrs. R. introduced me, again as the writer of the *Ballad*, to the President. A friendly smile of recognition crossed his face as we shook hands, and he said, "Oh, yes." I didn't learn till later, when Mrs. R. revealed it to me, that he hadn't heard the piece yet. So I promised to send him a set of records, which I did.

When the dinner call came, the President led the way into the dining room, pushed in his wheelchair by a black attendant. (All the help—butlers, waiters—were black. It seemed to be an old White House tradition.) He sure traveled fast in that buggy. I wanted to notice how he would get out of his wheelchair into his seat at the table. And I missed it. Suddenly he was there, and I was sitting beside him, just as if I belonged.

To my left sat a British admiral, to whom I paid little attention. Across the table sat Mrs. R., with Churchill on her right and Hopkins on her left. To the President's right sat a woman, an old friend of the family, I gathered. Ten or twelve people in all.

I had thought even before getting to the White House that I should try to condense everything I wanted to ask into one sentence, because I figured that would be all the time I'd get with either Mrs. R. or the President. And now I found him so easy to talk to, and the atmosphere so much like home—with certain upper-class differences. One of the nicest things I could say about the White House couple is that they reminded me of my father and mother.

Getting another detail out of the way: What did we eat? We had a consommé with string beans cut into it and a dish of cooked tomatoes with a roasted crust. Also some kind of meat dish and potatoes. The waiters served everything in courses, coming around with each dish separately.

Good morality, good politics

A light-hearted affair, the dinner began with FDR and Churchill joshing each other. The latter opened with, "We made quite a few pep talks today, didn't we?" And FDR answered, "Yes, I was oozing inspiration all over the place myself." This after they had met with Litvinov to chart united action not just to defeat the Axis powers, but to frame the early drafts of a peaceful postwar world. And they kidded about it like a couple of schoolboys. Churchill didn't talk too much, but I was interested in what he had to offer. He impressed me as quite witty, and also more subtle than Roosevelt, probably natural in view of the longer time the English ruling class had had to work to keep its vast empire, as well as its own people, in line. Roosevelt was more forthright, though undoubtedly as smart in his own way.

Churchill told a story of Russia having captured a Polish general back in 1939 when the Nazis moved into western Poland and the Russians took over the eastern half. The Russians had put him in a concentration camp and treated him nastily, beating him about the ankles with a rubber truncheon. "Apparently this hurts quite badly," said Churchill. Then the Nazis invaded the Soviet Union in June 1941. "When the new situation came," the Prime Minister continued his story, "this general was sent for, resurrected out of prison, outfitted in his old uniform. . . ."

Now Roosevelt finished the story: "And they put him in charge of the Polish army fighting the Nazis." Everybody laughed. Except me. I was still laboring under the impression that all was right in the Soviet Union, so I could see nothing funny in that tale. On hearing this story from me, the labor journalist Mary Heaton Vorse said it didn't sound quite right, because if a man was that dangerous to the state, the Soviets would generally kill rather than torture him.

Meantime, the first result of their big day's work, the 26 Nations Agreement—not to be released to the press for another two weeks—sat between the President and me. I read the first two pages, and could have read more, about how the Allies had agreed not to sign a separate peace, and about their promises for the postwar era. I felt I was being let in on tremendously important political events, secrets even, as if I was one of the family.

Roosevelt had recently given a well-quoted speech about freedom of religion in Russia, pointing to guarantees in the Soviet Constitution. Not many in this country had approved his sentiments, but I did my best to reassure him of the importance of saying what he had said, even if he was attacked for it—my sole propaganda contribution of the evening.

FDR explained how at his suggestion they did not use the phrase "freedom of religion" in the 26 Nations Agreement, but rather "religious freedom." He turned to me directly to explain this was to allow Litvinov and the Russians to interpret it to mean freedom "not to have religion." This worried him. He made what I regarded as an astoundingly naïve statement. "I spent half an hour with Litvinov today, trying to get him to believe in God. And I still don't think he does!" Roosevelt then told about asking Litvinov about religion in Russia. Litvinov answered that many of the older people believed and practiced, but none of the younger. And with a real air of pulling off a fast one, the President leaned across the table and said to Churchill, "At that point I just wanted to use a good old

American expression—we use it often—but I didn't. It goes like this: *Oh yeah?*"

"Very expressive, very expressive indeed," said Mr. Churchill.

Here obviously was a religious man, upset at the Russians' atheism, but determined to let nothing stand in the way of agreement. From across the table, Mrs. R. asked him if he wanted to attend our concert later. "I can't," he answered. "I have to spend some time with Litvinov."

"You're seeing him *again?*" Churchill asked in disapproval.

"Yes," said FDR, "I want to make sure he understands that we are totally with him." Good morality, good politics, then and now. I felt reassured by Roosevelt's sincerity. But Churchill did not seem to agree. From this early warning, as the war progressed I could sense Churchill's resistance to opening up the Second Front against the Nazis. From his point of view, better to let the Nazis and the Soviets exhaust one another before unleashing the dogs of war on Western soil.

Singing for my supper

There came a time, after the politics had been somewhat covered, when husband and wife were able to get together across the table and catch up on the day's events. "Well, and what did you do today, my dear?" Franklin asked.

She answered with dignity, relating the activities she would write up in her "My Day" column. Discussion turned to the holiday just past. Eleanor leaned over and said, "Franklin, when *are* you going to open your Christmas presents?"

He answered, pointing at Churchill, "Well, with all due respect to the Prime Minister here, when *he* goes to Ottawa I may be able to open my Christmas presents." Everybody laughed.

Mrs. R. observed, "You did open the one I gave you, however."

"Why, I did not!"

"Yes, you did," she answered. "I saw you open it."

"Well, it didn't have your name on it," he countered.

"Oh, yes it did," said she. And she told him it was a picture, and then he remembered.

Recovering from his confusion gallantly, he said, "It was a very lovely picture, my dear."

Finally the moment seemed right to venture the one condensed question I had been saving: "What kind of music do you think should be done to help the war effort?"

The question may have been too abstract to be answered directly. Instead the President told a parable. "This American patrol was dug in under heavy fire in World War I. They had to be evacuated but were afraid to move. So this old soldier with a harmonica started playing 'Hinky Dinky Parlay Voo.' And they all marched back to safety."

This was the high spot of my relationship to FDR. A presence about that evening stays with me still. I cannot legitimately claim friendship with Franklin D. But with Mrs. R. (I never called her Eleanor) it was different.

After dinner we went to a hall in a big office building where Mrs. R. had arranged for more than four hundred of her people from the OCD to come and hear the concert.

I had done my homework. Being gung ho for this war, I had written a song called, "Brother, There's a Job to Do," and I'd collected some appropriate "home front" numbers from the Almanac Singers. Labor having taken a no-strike pledge, I prepared none of the old union songs. A Woody song about air raid shelters was the most humorous of the lot.

> *I'm takin' it easy,*
> *I'm a-takin' it slow,*
> *And I ain't a-gonna worry*
> *When the si-reens blow.* ©

I sang my numbers, to moderately good effect, ending with Pete Seeger's new song made popular by the Almanacs:

> *The butcher, the baker, the tinker and the tailor,*
> *We'll all work behind the soldier and the sailor.*

We're working in the city,
We're working in the woods,
And we'll all work together to deliver the goods.

But Mrs. R. crossed me up. I was totally unprepared when from her front seat in the audience she asked for "Joe Hill"! Which I had not been performing since the war began because it talked about strikes with great approval.

Well, a musician sings for his supper. How could I refuse? But I almost messed up a verse trying to avoid the word "strike." Turns out I was the only one worried. Sitting with her after singing, I apologized (believe it or not) for Joe Hill's pro-strike slant. Sincerely concerned, Mrs. R. started to mollify me. "Oh, I think they will understand." And before I knew it she'd leapt to her feet explaining to the entire audience, "Mr. Robinson was worried about his song giving the wrong impression. After all, we must remember, at the time 'Joe Hill' was written it was right and necessary for workers to strike."

An incredibly sensitive woman, and like all truly important people, she was a teacher, always teaching. I learned much from her in our relationship, which continued almost to the time of her passing in 1962.

Not only for one generation

FDR's State of the Union address to Congress and the nation less than two weeks after this White House gathering inspired me. I immediately adopted it as my project to set large chunks of the speech as a cantata for soloists and chorus:

We are fighting today for security,
For progress and for peace
Not only for ourselves
But for all men
Not only for one generation
But for all generations. . . .

The tune was pretty good, a bit of a rouser. In this unabashed endeavor to "sing the war effort," I included Roosevelt's call for 185,000 planes and 120,000 tanks, and I satirized Hirohito, Hitler, and Mussolini. John Latouche, writer of *Ballad for Americans*, was not around when I began work on *Battle Hymn*, and my adaptation was something less than immortal. I could place some blame on the President himself for not giving me longer stretches of uplifting, singable words. I strove to put him in a class with Lincoln and the writers of the Preamble to the Constitution and the Bill of Rights, and he didn't quite measure up. But John came around after I'd gotten into the writing some, and he helped fix the words, so we are both credited with the text.

Just as we saw music as a weapon in the class struggle of the Thirties, now again I strove to make my contribution to the war against fascism. After all, what's a man without a cause? Today I look back on *Battle Hymn* as a competently written topical piece that served its purpose at the time. In fact, it made quite an impression, at least with some people.

I got my old Seattle pal Jack DeMerchant to sing *Battle Hymn* with a chorus on a May 10th concert called "Music at Work" at the Alvin Theatre. A week later, on May 17th, CBS had Paul Robeson singing it on the Fred Allen Hour. Now I admit that Paul's wife Essie was hardly an unbiased listener to that broadcast, but I like to think that millions of people across the land might have shared her judgment:

> Man, that *Battle Hymn* is something! . . . The Sunday night performance, even with Paul's uncertainties, had a sweep and a magnificence that was very moving. . . . You know, the way good marches always make you feel like picking up a gun, and then when you think it over, you feel like a jackass—being "had" by the music? Well, now we can all be "had" by the music, and not feel dumb; because this time when we swing into the parade, we will be marching for something, and we'll pick up our guns for something—not just for a marching tune.[1]

And this reaction from Mrs. R.: " . . . the President heard the whole program on May 17th. We both think it was magnificent." Feeling particularly chummy, I responded:

> If you have any influence with that husband of yours tell him we are all behind him and to pay no attention to the appeaser element around Washington and that he should open up a second front tomorrow morning bright and early.[2]

After the broadcast, *Battle Hymn* ran in a show in Washington, D.C., for a couple of weeks, and Chappell published it. Horace Grenell conducted the American People's Chorus in a broadcast of it in February 1943, and I had the honor of conducting it myself with Mordecai Bauman, the Schola Cantorum, and the New York Philharmonic at Madison Square Garden on June 10, 1943. I won a citation from the U.S. Treasury Department for it.

Before the broadcast, Mrs. R. had actually wired for Paul and me to come down to the White House to perform *Battle Hymn*, but we couldn't make it. Then came her enthusiastic letter once they heard the piece. This was to be followed over the years by some thirty or more others I still have in my papers, and we met again many times, too. She always addressed me "Dear Mr. Robinson," except for once in 1956 (during the blacklist years) when she wrote to "My dear Earl." She asked for "command performances" from me several times, in New York and at the White House, whenever she hosted gatherings of students or anyone she felt needed to hear me. I complied whenever I could. I felt a real sense of privilege being able to help her out. "Could you come to Hyde Park on July 3rd and spend the night?" she wrote to me in June 1943. The Fourth of July at the President's private home? You bet I could!

> I want to have some sort of party for some of the soldiers stationed up there and I thought I would show the film of my British trip, talk a little about my experi-

ence, and then have you sing some of your songs and perhaps lead the men in singing.

We do not have a piano in the Roosevelt Library. I wonder if your banjo would be sufficient? I can hire a piano if you would rather have one.

Sincerely yours,
Eleanor Roosevelt

(very confidential)
The President will be there so if you can come will you bring the things you want him to hear?[3]

In Mrs. R.'s "My Day" column for July 6th, she writes about me and this library concert. Appreciatively, I might add.

Notes

1. Eslanda Robeson to Earl Robinson, May 19, 1942.

2. Eleanor Roosevelt to Earl Robinson, May 26, 1942; Earl Robinson to Eleanor Roosevelt, July 20, 1942.

3. Eleanor Roosevelt to Earl Robinson, June 17, 1943.

A PRETTY BIG MAN

People's hero for our times

Mark Warnow, conductor of *Ballad for Americans* and CBS's "Your Hit Parade," suggested my writing a Lincoln Requiem. Millard Lampell fortuitously happened to be present, and he undertook to write a text. Based on the last chapter of Carl Sandburg's biography of Lincoln, the libretto concerns the funeral train that carried the President's body from Washington back home to Illinois, and the responses of the people to the great leader. In a lot of ways this caring, common man's president resonated strongly with the New Deal of Franklin Roosevelt, making him a natural "people's hero" for our times.

Mill saved some bitter commentary for the "copperheads" —such as the cotton speculator who turned away from Lincoln's coffin to announce, "All right, boys, the drinks are on me!" or those who cheered the day he died:

> *A New York politician who didn't like Lincoln,*
> *An Ohio businessman who didn't like Negroes,*
> *A Chicago newspaper editor who didn't like people.*

By historical analogy we thus criticized the foes of progress today, those who would hold back the New Deal, and those who would weaken the fight against fascism:

> *For there were those who cursed the Union,*
> *Those who wanted the people apart;*
> *While the sound of the freedom guns still echoed,*
> *Copperheads struck at the people's heart!*

Mill came well recommended, being a singer and songwriter with the Almanac Singers, along with Pete Seeger, Lee Hays, and Woody Guthrie. His profound folk knowledge and understanding of the dynamite inherent in the simple rhyme proved ideal, and he wrote a brilliant text. The Lincoln quotes had humor, power, and timeless urgency. Mill's text would practically set itself to music.

That summer of '42, while in Washington, D.C., for the performance of *Battle Hymn*, I revisited Alan Lomax, supreme organizer of folk recordings at the Library of Congress, and responsible for recording me singing my songs on earlier occasions. Knowing of my upcoming Lincoln project, he sat me down and played hours' worth of unique recordings, especially of black revival meetings and preachers.

Back in New York, Helen and I leased a house out at Far Rockaway near the beach. To Mill's script I wrote a 27-minute cantata, *Abe Lincoln Comes Home Again*, in less than two months. On my second triumphant return to Seattle, the leftist Washington Commonwealth Federation and the newspaper *The Washington New Dealer* rented the Moore Theatre that 5th of September. We got a chorus together and created an impressive revue, with the Lincoln cantata and *Ballad for Americans* done on the same program for the first time. A beloved local balladeer, Ivar Haglund, sang in it; he later became a wealthy restaurateur, owner of Acres of Clams in Seattle.

How Seattle had changed! Everything was harnessed to the war effort, two large Boeing plants, shipbuilding yards, salmon canning, and the lumber industry all going full speed. Women had entered the work force in great numbers, and I could see them by the hundreds walking down the street in slacks and carrying lunch pails. From what I could imagine, this is what a Soviet town must have looked like—construction, fulltime devotion to the cause, a proud, free, energetic work force.

Nowadays it is said that the Old Left didn't do much except pay lip service to what we called "the Woman Question." In general, this is a useful criticism. I don't say I was any better than the rest, but I find an interesting letter I wrote to Mill Lampell August 31, 1942, just days before that first Seattle performance:

> One other thing I wanted to mention, and whether it is
> corrected here or not, it is something we should both

think about for future work. That is the tendency toward male chauvinism which expresses itself continuously in the progressive work that has been done, so
much so that almost no stirring songs have been written
for women soloists . . . ; the Lincoln piece . . . speak[s]
continuously in terms of free men, fathers, sons, "men
who watch him shoe a mare," "men who were not free
to speak," etc. What about the women? It is time that
we as progressive artists take the lead, first in developing
ways of including women both as singers, and to be
sung about. In fact one of my next big cantata jobs that
I want to do is a cantata or ballad for American women
or something of the kind.

I did actually begin a "Ballad of American Women" that
fall, and I mentioned it to Mrs. Roosevelt. She was all for it,
adding, "I am glad that you do not believe in the Equal Rights
amendment as a panacea for all ills."[1] In those days the Party
didn't support the ERA—and neither did Mrs. R.— because we
felt that business would use it to deprive women of hard-won
laws concerning loads women were allowed to lift, permissible
overtime hours, and pregnancy, child raising and sickness
leave. About the only people supporting the ERA then were
wealthy, single-issue women who didn't need to take workers'
rights into account. Anyway, Meridel Le Sueur was going to
write the text, but we never got very far, and I never did secure
another collaborator for the project. I honestly admit that in
my subsequent work I have not adequately responded to my
own criticism of progressive culture. In part from these failures
of the Old Left, and the 1960s New Left that followed, the
contemporary feminist movement emerged.

Speaking of criticism, I also find a wonderful letter from
Mill to me. After working on a radio play together, he takes
me to task for the way I would browbeat people. As a "cause"
man, sometimes I'd get carried away, especially when it came
to defending the latest twist in the party line:

Your criticism is usually just, and always sincere and
useful. But the offhand way in which you pass it out,

and the over-simplification which usually results, of-
fends people.

And what is more important, that goes for politics.
You must stop lecturing people as though they were all
political illiterates. . . . For example: in Corwin's office
that last day, when we happened to discuss the Grand
Coulee Dam, and you suddenly pulled me aside to
whisper, "That angle we had. That's out now, you
know. Everything's different now, you know. Teheran
and all that. Read the pamphlet."[2]

I look back on those days with some amusement, and chagrin.

Coming back to New York in the fall of 1942, I prepared
my American People's Chorus in the Lincoln cantata, the solos taken by Josh White, Richard Dyer-Bennett, Leadbelly, Sis
Cunningham, Woody Guthrie, and myself, and we gave it a
series of performances under the baton of Horace Grenell.
Josh's blues guitar was particularly effective in the black
church scene and the scenes of the people. On my next trip to
the White House in January of '43 I gave it a one-man performance. Among others, Mrs. R. had Secretary of the Treasury Henry Morgenthau and Vice President Henry Wallace
there.

> *Until all men are equal, and all are free*
> *There will be no peace.*
> *While there are whips and chains,*
> *And men to use them,*
> *There will be no peace;*
> *After the battles,*
> *After the blood and wounded,*
> *When the chains are smashed,*
> *And the whips are broken,*
> *And the men who held the whips are dead!*
> *When men are brothers and men are free,*
> *The killing will end, the war will cease,*
> *When free men have a free men's peace!*

And the cantata ends with the full chorus singing

Freedom's a thing that has no ending,
It needs to be cared for, it needs defending!
Free-dom!

A taste of Hollywood

Some have named this "Lincoln legend" the best thing I ever wrote, a confident, characteristically American dramatic cantata. It did not reach its full apotheosis, however, until Norman Corwin got hold of it a year and a half later.

Charles K. Feldman, a Hollywood agent and producer, met Mill and me. He had fallen hard for *Abe Lincoln Comes Home Again* and took me under his wing. In fact, that December he gave me a $1,000 commission as his "investment" in the work. He toured me around that spring of '43 to the New York offices of MGM, RKO, Columbia, and Warner Brothers, where I sang the entire work at the piano. All part of a Feldman plan to sell not only my music but me as a performer in Hollywood, which was all right with me, but barely. Performing was only a necessary adjunct to composing. I put my heart and passion into it because it was my work, my creation, not because I sought an acting career.

Charlie got me out to Hollywood. For a while it looked like Universal planned to put the Lincoln cantata in with a celebration of people's heroes from the principal Allied nations—Wat Tyler for England, Simón Bolívar for South America, Sun Yat Sen for China, and Lenin for Russia. As part of our plan, I asked Mrs. Roosevelt for her opinion and she responded promptly: "I think a film such as you describe would have great meaning, but would depend on its treatment for its real value. The Lincoln piece is very fine and would, I believe, make a fine film."[3]

The plan unraveled, but not long after I got out there, Charlie succeeded in getting Warner Brothers to take a seven-year option on *Abe Lincoln* for film. The $10,000 they paid was of course very welcome, but Mill Lampell and I feared for what they might do with the piece. For a time they considered using it in a cowboy picture. We were glad when it reverted to us, intact, at the end of the seven years. Warner's option stipulated that the work be kept off the air for a year. When the year ended in March 1944, I went back to New York, where Norman Corwin of CBS had been champing at the bit to get the piece for broadcast, thinking of it as a new *Ballad for Americans*.

Norman directed the entire production. It was a creative learning process to work with him. He is a master at finding the light, the satiric, the graceful way of handling every kind of content. He also wrote an opening narrative framework:

> The long war was over. The tall man with the sad eyes and the stooping shoulders was tired. So one night he did what anybody likes to do sometimes when they're tired. He went to a show. He went down to Ford's Theatre in Washington Town, and he sat in a box. And it was the number one box because he was a pretty big man. Well, the play went on, and along about the middle of the evening, something happened that wasn't on the program. I guess you all know what that was. The news spread pretty fast.

. . . and we're into the fast five-string banjo and the opening ballad singer. As with *Ballad for Americans*, Norman also renamed the piece. He simply called it by its rightful name, *The Lonesome Train*, and nobody saw any need to argue.

The conducting chores this time went to Lyn Murray, the choral director on *Ballad*, with Jeff Alexander handling the chorus. Raymond Massey, *the* Lincoln actor of that time, read the Lincoln lines. Two interesting choices had to be made for the Ballad Singer and the Black Preacher. Regarding the latter, we seriously considered Leadbelly. He spoke-sang the powerful Lampell lines (stolen as always from the best places, authentic church services recorded in the Library of Congress) with immense truth, conviction and intensity. We had only one problem: understanding the words. We eventually decided to go with a beautiful "5 x 5" black actor-singer, Richard Huey, who performed magnificently. My friend the alto Laura Duncan sang in the chorus of four. They made the Alabama church scene the most exciting part of the piece.

The choice for the Ballad Singer came down to a friendly contest between Burl Ives and Earl Robinson. I had no trouble with Burl doing the part. But because I had been singing the whole piece around so extensively, in Seattle, Los Angeles, New York and elsewhere, I had learned its nuances pretty well. My knowledge of the part, plus a strong voice when aroused, bulked large against Burl's natural sweetness. Davidson Taylor, executive producer of the Columbia series that programmed the work, finally made the choice for Burl. Not as if I was slighted. I shouted/sang the part of the square dance caller, and at Norman's urging spoke the narration for the whole piece—except for the opening, done by Lon Clark.

Incidentally, the Ballad Singer needed a five-string banjo accompaniment, which no professional banjo player in the New York area could even imitate. So we got CBS to spring Pete Seeger from an army boot camp in Alabama and fly him up for the job. I cannot tell you my immense joy when Pete was able to relieve the much weaker player we had been stuck with, and "frail" the hell out of the part.

The Lonesome Train did not have the whole-souled, spontaneous universal reception that *Ballad for Americans* inspired. It is two and a half times as long (27 minutes, to *Ballad's* 11), a much deeper work requiring a quieter, thoughtful response. People who listened did not jump to the phone immediately or even sit down and write a letter. And it was unquestionably a smaller audience (*Ballad* ran on a Sunday afternoon right after the New York Philharmonic broadcast, which had a huge special audience). We received some great reviews, however. *The New York Times*—"inspired and brilliant"; *Variety*—"a powerful work of great warmth and deep feeling"; *Newsweek*—"a magnificent performance, a moving drama."

Dave Kapp, head of Decca Records, called the next day proposing to record the entire work; in order to keep the cast together, we decided to record just a week after the broadcast. Pete Seeger had to return to the army right away, but we got him back a week later for the recording. There are a lot of fine banjo players around now, but at that time Pete was absolutely indispensable. Ray Massey was not available so Raymond Edward Johnson replaced him in the Lincoln part. Two writers of distinction, Louis Untermeyer and Howard Fast, wrote rave liner notes for the album.

Notes

1. Eleanor Roosevelt to Earl Robinson, February 23, 1944.
2. Millard Lampell to Earl Robinson, June 11, 1944.
3. Eleanor Roosevelt to Earl Robinson, February 25, 1943.

WOODY

His face lit up

I met Woodrow Wilson Guthrie in 1940 at a Theater Arts Center gathering in New York City. Into this group of distinguished progressive intellectuals wandered a nondescript westerner, not a cowboy exactly, dressed somewhat better than an Okie, though not distinctively. Immediately riveting and colorful, authenticity stamped his every gesture: The way he unslung his guitar, and his simple, no-nonsense driving rhythms. His pauses between verses, which did not seem planned for effect, yet were exactly right. His humor, sure and apparently unstudied. And when he stopped to clean his nails with the guitar pick, the action seemed perfect.

I looked forward to meeting him after he finished singing. I took a stroke from Woody that I've never forgotten: Some sizable names among the arts, sciences, and professions appeared at this affair, among them the well-known conductor and composer (and much later, president of ASCAP) Morton Gould. Woody had never heard of him and on introduction he dismissed him rather peremptorily. When I was introduced his face lit up (as much as that Oklahoma poker face could light). He pumped my hand, saying, "You wrote 'Joe Hill!'" Which did my ego no harm, though I felt a little bad for Morton.

Woody wrote up his meeting me in the *People's World*:

> Earl has always been liked a hell of a lot here. Always stayed in demand. Always kept busy. That was because every single thing he ever done, was for the hard working people, and the broke ones.
>
> If our gossipers up in the capital would learn to sing Earl's songs, and to make some laws like 'em, the war and the hard times would both end.
>
> Here's to more guys like old Earl!
> And less cops.[1]

I tried to get to know Woody the rest of his natural life, but never got close to him, really. He was an original, a great writer, a natural poetic genius with words, a songwriter but not a composer. He borrowed, stole, and expropriated tunes unashamedly. If the source was good, his words would make it into a good, or great song. He could be dull and longwinded, boring to distraction at times. And he could be most cooperative and creative with other folksingers, congenial listeners, and working people. But Woody was an excellent entertainer only when he felt good about himself and his audience. He'd take out his unhappiness on his public, especially if he thought them inattentive, or slick and upper-class. Depending on how he felt at that moment, he could be impossible to work with. I worked and sang with him in all these moods. I have been exhilarated, and frustrated.

On balance, I had more good times with Woody than bad. I remember fixing Woody up with the recording engineer and producer G. Robert Vincent for "Talkin Fishin Blues." It was pure joy, Woody's lines and his timing superb. Example:

> *I went out fishin' another time,*
> *Caught a pretty mermaid on my line,*
> *Little bit bony, little bit frail,*
> *But man alive, what a piece of tail!*

Then: "We wasn't married—but we had a fishin' license."

In Sophie Maslow's dance *Folksay*, Woody and I, as singer-talkers and joketellers, had a ball. I happily played the straight man and loved it. Example:

> WOODY: You know what they call people who ride
>   buses down in Mexico?
> ME: No, what do they call them?
> WOODY: Passengers.

We just look through 'em

In the fall of 1942 I returned to New York from Seattle, where I had tried out *Lonesome Train*. A leftwing entrepreneur wanted to present a grand evening of folk music in six or seven large auditoriums around town. We allowed ourselves to think of this as a pre-Broadway tryout. Mill Lampell wrote a script called *It's All Yours* about a bunch of folkies, appearing as themselves (Woody Guthrie, Josh White, Leadbelly, Richard Dyer-Bennett, me, and my American People's Chorus). In Mill's conception, we're all having a happy old time in our folk pad below ground level in Greenwich Village, when we are invaded by a nasty publisher who wants to *(horrors!)* commercialize and make money off us. Woody and I had a dialogue wherein we resisted the publisher's offers (in Mill's script, he never had a chance). I had the devil's own time getting Woody to show any emotion. I told Woody, "Look, this guy's trying to *steal* our music! Don't you ever get angry in Oklahoma?"

And Woody answered, "Down where I come from, if we're mad at someone, we just look through 'em." I couldn't explain to him that "looking" somehow wasn't very dramatic on stage.

Despite certain dramatic weaknesses, we all had impressive material, everyone singing their own tried and true songs, the chorus doing *Lonesome Train* as the first act finale.

Five days before opening night, I noted a sore throat. I ignored it at first, under the pressure of rehearsals, but it got steadily worse. The day before the first performance I had trouble being heard through the hoarseness.

On top of this, Woody disappeared. Nobody could locate him. On opening night I read Woody's lines, screamed his song "The Great Historical Bum" through a hurting voice, and we managed to get through the show.

I didn't see how I could force myself to do the show the following night, so a friend told me about a Dr. Mayer-Hermann who did wonders for actors with laryngitis. The doctor had a two-stage treatment. First, he got the patient to use his ration card for some quinine at the drug store—in short supply because of the war—which he injected in the buttock. The second phase was more useful. He instructed me I could not sing that night. He painted my neck with an ochre salve and wrapped it in a towel, and he applied drops of something on my vocal cords to shrink the swelling. I missed two performances. Mill Lampell had to go on in my place, reading Woody's part as well as mine. He was not very impressive but who could blame him? The audience forgave. When I got back, Dr. M-H came backstage and anointed my vocal cords again at the half. In the end, this "new revue featuring songs for the firing line" never made it to Broadway.

Kindly enough, Woody eventually dropped me a line:

> Your show was the best of its kind that's been throwed yet. I just spent five days flat on my back with the flu. I heard you had doctors grinding your valves backstage while the show was going on. This is just a quick note to hope that you're all better. I didn't miss myself nowhere on the program.[2]

In early 1943 I got "hired" by director Gadg Kazan to write songs for *It's Up to You*, a show scripted by Arthur Arent supporting food rationing in the homefront war effort. The U.S. Department of Agriculture, the American Theatre Wing, the Skouras Theatres, various food industry organizations, and the theatrical labor unions all backed the show. I say "hired" because everybody contributed their talents to this somewhat successful show. Howard Bay provided slide projections, and Peggy Clark did costumes. The film part of the show was photographed by Paul Strand and directed by Henwar Radakiewicz. Not too many name actors appeared on stage in the show, but my old Seattle pal Jack DeMerchant sang in it.

I worked with four different lyric writers on this. With Al Hayes I turned out "Porterhouse Lucy, the Black Market Steak" (Helen Tamiris danced it in the show, dressed in red satin, with the mask of a cow in back of her head). With Hy Zaret I did "Life Could Be Beautiful Without a Can Opener,"

"When You Gotta Grow," and the finale rouser "Victory Begins at Home." With Lewis Allan, a strong "We Can Take It!"
blues (sung by Laura Duncan of later *Lonesome Train* fame);
with Woody Guthrie, appropriately, "Plain Men in Dirty
Overalls"; and the title song with Lewis Allan and Woody.

The show opened in New York in late March. An un-
named reviewer for the *New York Times* cited Tamiris in the
hit song of the evening, predicting that "Crooners throughout
the country will probably be singing her 'torch' song,
'Porterhouse Lucy, the Black Market Steak.'"[3]

When *It's Up to You* began its ten-day run on June 22 at the
Department of Agriculture Auditorium in Washington, an FBI
agent, dispatched to see it on account of the "tainted" names
on the program, dutifully made notes. The agent recorded that
Roosevelt's Secretary of Agriculture Claude R. Wickard spoke
that night, praising the production and its message, and indicat-
ing that the show would be produced locally around the country with casts drawn from surrounding communities. D. M.
Ladd of the FBI wrote it all up in a two-page memorandum
dated July 15th that also cited Mrs. Roosevelt's recent "My
Day" column mentioning my Hyde Park appearance. Thrust
of memo being: Given Earl Robinson's background, doesn't
this prove that government money is going to support Communism? "It would appear that [*It's Up to You*] has been util-
ized as an outlet for some Communist Party propaganda with
respect to the Party line of 'rationing everything.'" In other
words, the *government*'s policy of rationing for the war effort
is accused of being subversive because Communists endorsed
it! The FBI and the repressive (one might say pro-fascist) mentality governing it obviously had no great love for either Roosevelt in the White House. I can't escape the impression that
the FBI directed its information-gathering as much at them and
their "Communist" sympathies as at me. If they'd only known
about my dinner at the White House—that woulda clinched it!

I got a fair amount of mileage out of "Porterhouse Lucy"
during those years of food rationing, and even recorded it on
the Alco label.

This is me. Woody

If you want to know more on Woody, read Joe Klein's biography, and Woody's own *Bound for Glory*. I still treasure the first edition, which Woody inscribed "To the Robinson Bunch":

> This book is brim full of the very people your good works are bound to help. They are poor and getting poorer, they're sore and getting sorer—not mad enough yet to go down to the meeting place and voting box and speak up for their selves in the right way. I don't know of one single solitary family that are doing any more to help my kind of folks than you, the Robinsons, all of you. Thanks for the flops and eats.
>
> Your Buddy,
> Woody Guthrie

To show you more of how Woody thought and expressed himself, I share part of a letter he sent to our son Perry (age almost seven) and incidentally to Helen and me, August 31, 1945, when he was stationed in the army at Scott Field, Illinois. In that period Helen and I were disturbed about the terrifying way Perry would make sick, monstrous creatures out of clay. But Woody totally identified with Perry's creativity.

Dear Perry
Dear Helen
Dear Earl
Dear West Coast from Vancouver down to Tia Guana: . . .

I sat down here at my desk to write to your dad and mom. They wrote me a letter. I have to write them one. But I wanted to write to you first because your work as a fixer and a maker and a mud and paint man really is what I recollect most about your house. I heard all of the music that you and mama made your daddy write and it sounded okay, but needs a lot of your clay and bullets and paint.

You climb up there on that piano stool and rub a handful of mud and colors across a sheet of your dad's music. He will cuss and holler some at me and your mama and yell at you too, but don't get scared of him. Just tell him that if he gets too loud you'll pound him back into the ball. He will tame down. Tell him that he's still got his best smearing to do yet in front of him. He might flip his lid and spew foam but he'll thank you because he would really be no good to his self if you let him think that his best work is in back of him . . .

Your dad and mama wrote to me and said something about some songs. Well I can't talk to you much about a song but I can tell you that the only good ones I ever saw or heard was dried out of dirt and some paint and a lot of guns and bullets . . .

Why don't you draw me some pictures? Draw me a picture and put it in an envelope and tell the mail man to take it way up high and bring it to me. I'll show it to all of the soldier boys.

42234634 Woody

The real Woody as I knew him was childlike, inventive, exuberant, brilliant, lovable, manic. He had an endless stream of poetry in him. No wonder he wrote such terrific songs for kids. He could observe and penetrate kids' minds, and he knew how to deflate swelled heads.

I guess we didn't answer that letter soon enough, or maybe a subsequent one: Here he is, still in the army, on a postcard, December 1945:

How are you this morning? This is me. I can really swing a dangerous pen and I'm gonna swing it on you or somebody just like you if you dont write to me once in a while I will kick your rear up so high you will have to take off your hat to use the toilet. Love. This is me. Woody.

See why I love that guy?

Woody had a daughter Cathy, and I suppose you know about Arlo. Another daughter Nora came along later. I'd like him, in one more short piece of writing, to introduce their son Joady Ben. Woody gave me a copy of this tender lyric, written Christmas Night 1948 at Brooklyn Jewish Hospital:

Joady Ben

My name is Joady Ben
I struck here Christmas night
I brung along my candle
And I'm looking for a light
My pounds were six ten
My fingers counted ten
My toes counted plenty
So they called me Joady Ben

Joady for the Joads
And poor folks on the roads
And Ben means I'm a son
So they looked around again
And they walked around again
And they eyed me up and down
And they called me Joady Ben

I'm the son of
All the poor folks
On the roads.

The reference to the Joads is, of course, the dustbowl family in *The Grapes of Wrath*. Early in his career Woody had written and recorded a song called "Tom Joad." And Ben means son in Hebrew, a recognition of Marjorie's Jewish background.

Marjorie

With some difficulty I can talk about Marjorie Mazia, dancer extraordinaire, Woody's mate, his lady lover, his guide adviser nurturer mother, his friend and wife. Because she turned out to be my friend also. I was there doing *Folksay* with him in the dance studio when they met. And this happily (though never faithfully) married man found himself jealous of Woody. She had already struck me as beautiful, but I saw that Woody had the inside track.

At some point Marjie got tired of Woody's philandering, plus his habit of just taking off without notice for the West Coast. He showed up twice on our doorstep there, greeted warmly the first time, not so warmly the second, wearing out his welcome with Helen after the first two weeks. Anyway, Marjie decided she needed something more than Woody was capable of giving. They divorced in the early 1950s, though remained close. "If you might have forgotten," she wrote me around that time, "you are one of the few people I can honestly say allow me to go easy and think and act like a good human being. So I guess you'd better come on out and lend your assistance where it is needed."[4]

We got together in L.A. when she was touring as a dancer with Martha Graham, and thereafter a special part of my New York trips would be to take her to a Broadway show and spend the night together. She supported me and my music solidly at a time when I was writing mainly film scores. And she danced to my "Good Morning," a singing square dance for children, which adults made more use of than the kids.

In New York, during the 1950s blacklist time, she was a source of strength for me, even while backing off physically because of other men in her life. In the summer of 1963, after my Helen passed on, I got with Marjie once again. Though we still loved each other, I made no effort to cleave wholly to her. Maybe I felt too much like a free man; maybe I felt guilt about appearing to abandon Helen's memory so soon. She noticed it, and let me know she felt hurt. Instead of creating a loving relationship with Marjorie Mazia Guthrie, I reached out for new women, and got myself into a marriage that in retrospect was a mistake. When that ended in the early '70s I tried again with Marjie, but by then she was involved with another man.

In the years since Woody got sick, she put enormous energy into the fight against Huntington's chorea, the gradually debilitating disease from which he died. In fact, it was I who drove Woody and Marjorie to Kings County Hospital on May 16, 1952, to enter Woody in an alcoholism treatment program, which we thought was the problem. In 1966, a year or so before he passed on, the Department of the Interior presented Woody with its Conservation Service Award for making the American people "aware of their heritage and the land."

On September 12, 1970, a capacity Hollywood Bowl tribute to Woody took place with a huge lineup of stars as a benefit for Huntington's research. Peter Fonda and Will Geer narrated, and Harold Leventhal produced. They raised $100,000, plus more from the record album and the folio with lyrics, script and photos that came out later. I sang "Mail Myself to You" and joined in on several ensembles. Attracted by such luminaries as Joan Baez, Richie Havens, Judy Collins, and Arlo Guthrie, the audience was mostly teenagers or folks in their twenties. It felt good to see them exposed to Woody and his work.

Notes

1. "Woody Sez:," *People's World*, March 19, 1940.
2. Woody Guthrie to Earl Robinson, October 1942.
3. *The New York Times*, April 1, 1943.
4. Marjorie Guthrie to Earl Robinson, n.d.

THE HOUSE I LIVE IN

To Lewis Allan (Abel Meeropol)'s beautiful words I composed "The House I Live In" in late 1942. The truth is, we didn't write it for Frank Sinatra. For my part it was a welcome chance to cover in a shorter song form than *Ballad for Americans* some of the same patriotic themes:

> *A name, a map, the flag I see,*
> *A certain word, "democracy,"*
> *What is America to me?*

A standard

Abel turned out lyrics unceasingly for the war, especially the home front war, some of which I set to music. These included "Kickin' the Panzer," "Look Out of the Window, Mama" (at your husband the air raid warden), "Get the Point, Mrs. Brown," "Brother, There's a Job to Do," "Fight, America!" (included in a 1942 show called *Sing for Victory*) and "That Man in the White House" (referring approvingly to FDR); also "We Can Take It" from *It's Up to You.*

I've mentioned that Abel sometimes preferred setting his own music to his lyrics. But Abel made no effort to set "The House I Live In," and turned it over to me in all its pristine beauty. I often felt free to change and rearrange a writer's lyrics. Deeply moved, I did not have that attitude on Abel's latest effort: I altered not a word or nuance. I struggled to get the best possible tune and for a long time spoke of the lyrics as better than the music.

> *The things I see about me, the big things and the small,*
> *The little corner newsstand and the house a mile tall;*
> *The wedding and the churchyard, the laughter*
> *   and the tears,*
> *The dream that's been a-growin' for a hundred*
> *   and fifty years.*

The town I live in, the street, the house, the room,
The pavement of the city, or a garden all in bloom,
The church, the school, the club house, the million
lights I see,
But especially the people, that's America to me.

I sang the song around at house parties, small bookings, unions, churches, even on the radio for more than two years without a splash. It earned "best song" mention by Brooks Atkinson of the *New York Times* when Mordecai Bauman sang it in the Youth Theatre's left-patriotic revue *Let Freedom Sing* at the Longacre.[1] My biggest success with it was a May Day rally in Union Square in 1943. Chappell published the song, and conductor Max Helfman and the People's Philharmonic Chorus performed an arrangement at Town Hall in January 1944. That year, Universal Films put it into a star-studded, rather self-congratulatory movie about USO camp shows called *Follow the Boys*, sung sweetly and simply by the Delta Rhythm Boys playing four soldiers in the South Seas. I used to go out on USO bookings with them. Seattle's Repertory Playhouse put on a musical revue, *Thumbs Up!* with music by Johnny Forrest and me, in which "House" was staged with six characters.

On May 30th of '44 the NBC network broadcast a radio play based around the song. Sometime after, I got a call on the phone. "Did you know that Frankie is singin' your song?" I never found out just how the "House" came to Frank's attention, maybe from the broadcast. But he began singing it and has continued to the present, much of the time giving me credit. Frankie knew my work, of course. In fact, to the tune of the "Saints," Woody Guthrie and I had written "When the Yanks Go Marching In," and Robbins published the sheet music with Frankie's picture on the cover.

Over the years "The House I Live In" became a standard, with at least a couple of dozen recordings by Paul Robeson and Josh White (if your thing is folk), and Mahalia Jackson doing a gospel version. For the classically inclined, Lauritz Melchior made a fine orchestral recording. On the jazz front, Sonny Rollins and Archie Shepp jammed the tune a bit. Popularly speaking, Eddie Fisher, Connie Francis, Sarah Vaughan and Ted Nealy, among others, took a crack at the song.

Fed up on division

Aunt Molly Jackson, the great Harlan County balladeer, was an authentic folksinger I got to know pretty well in the 1930s. She composed songs for the National Miners Union during the Depression, and when the musicologists as well as people on the left began delving into our American folk roots, she emerged as a revelation. She spent a decade in New York City on home relief, suffering from injuries she received in a bus accident, then got out to Sacramento in the late 1940s. She addressed a letter to me in October 1945, having heard "The House I Live In" over the radio, and couldn't help versifying her reaction. She was nearing her 65th birthday—October 30th, same as my wife Helen. Here is an original Aunt Molly Jackson poem, with its still relevant theme, just as I received it:

I hardly know how to start
First, I want to say you are a man after my own heart,
What I mean, you are just my kind
You are not afraid to speak up and tell the world your
     mind
And believe me you sure can put your feelings in a
     song
Which I think is the best way on earth to teach what is
     right and what is wrong.
That song you wrote "What America is to Me"
Is as powerful as any song can be
Please keep on composing songs, don't stop at all
For that is the best way on earth to bring around all
     for one and one for all.
That one big solid union that is so easy to understand
That Jesus Christ himself called "the brotherhood of
     man."

Yes Jesus told the people to love each other
like a father loves a son, and like a daughter loves her
*   mother,*
He said, "do unto others as you wanted them to do
*   unto you"*
He did not say for the Gentile to love the Gentile, and
*   the Jew to love the Jew,*
He did not say a thing about the black or the white
He just said for us to treat each other right
And that is just what I aim to do
I am fed up on division among races and colors, what
*   about you?*

To which I can only say, Amen, sister. That line about
Gentile and Jew really affected me and Helen.

I have a whole batch of strong, heartfelt letters from Aunt
Molly dating from 1942 or so to 1949. Desperate to get a book
out of her labor songs and poems, she sent me a long, beautiful
excerpt of her autobiography which tells how she was born
into a Kentucky culture that just loved passing on old songs
and making up new ones. These are the kinds of archival gems
residing among my papers.

In 1946, my alma mater, West Seattle High School, decided
to construct their annual senior magazine *Kimtah* around "The
House I Live In." They asked me to write something for it,
and could I get Sinatra to do the same? Well, Frank did not
have time, so he trusted me to write something "by him" for
the Annual. Which I did. Here's part of what "he" wrote:

> My folks were Italian-born and my being called a "wop"
> and "dago" early in life taught me a few things. I've
> learned since that if we let ourselves be divided by such
> silly and un-American ideas we are being made prize
> dopes. I know the young people of America are smarter
> than that. Our house can be a real home with all colors
> and religions living together in friendship and under-
> standing, and if we work together we will make it that
> way.

In 1945 Albert Maltz wrote the screenplay for a film short, giving Frankie a chance not just to sing the song but to speak words of wisdom to a gang of kids about to beat up a young Jewish boy. Frank Ross produced, and Mervyn LeRoy directed. *Time* called it "a worthy, heartfelt short." *Cue* wrote that the film "packs more power, punch and solid substance into its ten minutes of running time than most of the 500 full-length features ground each year out of Hollywood," naming Frankie "one of filmdom's leading and most vocal battlers for a democratic way of life."[2] In ceremonies at the Chinese Theatre, March 7, 1946, I received a Certificate of Special Award from the Academy of Motion Picture Arts and Sciences for *The House I Live In*. The honor tied Frank even closer to the song.

During those years, terrible gang fights broke out between warring black, Italian, and other ethnic student groups at high schools and in neighborhoods around the country. So they called Frankie in to sing our song, and things quieted down after that. In fact, he made a habit of visiting different cities to talk about tolerance and equality. He donated his services on the film, and RKO gave all the proceeds from it to the California Labor School in San Francisco and other organizations fighting discrimination. Between commercial showings and rentals, in the first couple of years it raised over $100,000.

You just never know where a song will lead
Time went by, and the "House" continued to be successful in ways I couldn't have foreseen in a million years. One year they used it in the Miss America Pageant. Another time, I orchestrated eight bars of it to accompany Frankie to the stage to receive an Academy Award. Some years back Frankie forwarded the following letter to me:

26 April 1973
Dear Mr. Sinatra,
    This perhaps will be an unusual letter of appreciation for you because of the unusual events prompting its being written.

I am an ex-POW; shot down 25 April 1967, released 4 March 1973. For 2 weeks during the initial period of captivity, I had a cellmate. I then entered my first stint in solitary which lasted about a year.

It was toward the end of that time that my marbles were getting loose. I had not dropped any; they were just starting to rattle.

The twice-a-day propaganda from that speaker in my cell was something I could not shut off and it was really frustrating! It was actually nauseating for me to be forced to listen to some North Vietnamese, usually a woman, who could not speak English too well, make such snide inferences about a country and a way of life of which she had not knowledge and could not even begin to comprehend.

Of course the 1/2 hour programs were "spiced up" with 2 or 3 songs, usually American songs. The anti-war songs were always "popular." Occasionally though they would play tunes with catchy little titles like "Are you lonesome tonight," "If I came home tonight, would you still be my Darling" or "Where have all the flowers gone."

Then one day in the winter-spring of 1968 to the amazement of all of us, we heard a new song, "What Is America to Me." (I had to stop writing the rough [draft] for this letter at this point because I started to cry like a damn baby.)

God it was great!!

I vowed then that I would give you a sincere and personal thank you for singing that song so very well.

Thank you, sir; thank you very much.

Most sincerely,

Charles D. Stackhouse, USN

You just never know where a song will lead.

At 75, Frank sang "The House I Live In" in support of the troops in the 1991 Persian Gulf War, his voice a raspy, almost tuneless shadow of its former glory. I opposed that war, appeared in concert against it. But if you are looking for an expose or an attack on Frank Sinatra, you need to go elsewhere.

His style and phrasing, his putting across the sense of a lyric, are unequaled. Apart from enjoying his singing over the years, I continue to like and respect the man. I listen to the put-downs, the revelations of his "Mafia connections," and they go in one ear and out the other. As far as I am concerned, the man is a lover and I forgive him his inconsistencies, his weaknesses. Incidentally, at the Sinatra compound in Rancho Mirage, near Palm Springs, each building is named for a different song by which he's identified. The main residence is—of course—"The House I Live In."

Notes

1. Brooks Atkinson, *The New York Times*, October 6, 1942.
2. *Time*, November 12, 1945; *Cue*, October 13, 1945.

HOLLYWOOD: TAKE 1

Budding starlets

The year 1943, encouraged by super agent Charles K. Feldman, I went to Hollywood. Charlie became interested in me not only for my composing but for my singing and acting. But my heart was only into presenting music and its message.

So I did not cooperate enthusiastically with Charlie's acting-singing plan. Ever the "cause man," I explained to myself and friends that I was merely attempting to enlarge my audience. I could sing for a few thousand people over a time in New York and around the East, whereas get a song into a movie and twenty to forty million would hear it.

A somewhat confused Earl climbed on the train with Betty (later Lauren) Perske (later Bacall) in April of 1943. She was also a budding Feldman protégé, unknown as yet, and I had no idea who she was. Her mother saw her off; I think she saw me as Betty's guardian on the trip. The presence of my wife Helen at the train station apparently made me "safe" for Betty. We didn't turn each other on, and I expressed this in a reassuring letter to Helen, after a day stuck in Chicago:

> The trip has been completely uneventful and uninteresting so far. I walked around town with this girl Betty Bacall, bought Perry a toy at Marshall Fields, and when she didn't want to go to a movie, I went by myself. This girl is a very immature young thing with apparently not a thought in her head beyond a high school girl's conception of Hollywood and what it means. Actually I am bored and finding ways to dodge being with her and being a father guardian. I paid for the first meal without receiving any protest from her so I promptly suggested that Dutch treat might be in order because I have a family to support, and she is probably making as much as I am.

I had second thoughts about B. Bacall after being thrown together at the Claremont Hotel in Westwood, separate rooms. A bed, a shower, and an adjoining towel, not much else. We were budding "starlets," her for real, me just along for the ride, both waiting for a screen test. Charlie would parade us around Hollywood, me to sing, Betty to be seen, and in the process we became friends. I gradually came to appreciate her as a charming person with some sense in her head. She even learned a couple of my songs, "Porterhouse Lucy, the Black Market Steak," and "Life Could Be Beautiful Without a Can Opener."

Our screen tests were directed by Howard Hawks, who later directed her first picture with Bogart, *To Have and to Have Not*. Howard and Charlie Feldman got me a scene from a John Garfield picture where he played the piano. I felt pretty good about my test, but it was too understated, and I didn't get called back. So I created in Charlie what I wanted him to be, the agent for my musical works rather than for me the actor. I was mildly amazed when Betty became Lauren and made it so big—and moved out of my space so fast.

Not long after the screen test, Helen and Perry came west to join me. We found a house just on the edge of Beverly Hills, on Oakhurst Drive. My big excitement around that time came from visiting the set where the Lillian Hellman film *North Star* was being shot (with Aaron Copland's music). In this film that celebrates our Russian ally, I felt for a few hours like I was really on a Soviet collective farm.

While I was supposedly looking for film work, a New York writer and teacher named Lou Lerman got together with me for *That Freedom Plow*, a cantata for narrator and singer with violin and piano, which cast Thomas Jefferson more or less in the role of a Paul Bunyan. The conceit of this number was that Jefferson, having bought the Louisiana Territory, needed to populate it, so he invented a fabulous plow

> *A mile high, ten miles wide,*
> *Crossed eighteen rivers in one big stride,*

A mile high, ten engines long,
Plowed the earth with a giant song.

This revolutionary instrument would plant Liberty Trees in the furrows it created, overcoming the skepticism of Ebenezer, the ramrod New Hampshire farmer who preferred his old inefficient ways. This 1943 composition received a performance at a Jefferson evening where John Howard Lawson, Alvah Bessie and the California State Attorney General all spoke. I wonder what to make of the FBI, which wrote up the event for my dossier, calling the work "Freedom Pillow," at the same time mentioning I had also sung my song "Paterhouse Lucy." Their special agent needed glasses! *That Freedom Plow* received a couple of East Coast performances, one a benefit for the Jefferson School in New York, then quietly crept away.

Becoming established as a composer in Hollywood, my reason for going there, wasn't easy. My first employment came through Carlton Moss, a solid new friend then producing *The Negro Soldier* for the War Department. This 1944 film, supervised by Col. Frank Capra, met a host of problems and objections. Southern congressmen held up its release for some time, because it portrayed black soldiers too positively. Then an independent producer filed suit against the government because he was making a similar film himself that the War Department film would be competing against. Finally, as a number of published reviews made clear, the 40-minute film gave no hint whatsoever of race problems in America, nor of race discrimination in the armed forces. Despite these limitations, *The Negro Soldier* is quite touching, even inspiring.

Originally Carlton wanted me to do the score for the whole film, but I speedily got whittled down to one long segment about the Negro soldier's place in American history. I used the opening of *Ballad for Americans* under the Crispus Attucks scene (Attucks, a black man, was the first soldier killed in the Revolution), moved on to the Spanish-American War with the Negro soldiers at San Juan Hill, and worked in the folk song "John Henry"—his epic struggle versus the steam drill—as a fitting background for the westward trek. William Grant Still, the noted black composer, orchestrated for me.

Dmitri Tiomkin, head composer for the series, prevented my scoring the entire film, for he wanted to do the film himself. David Tamkin, orchestrator for Tiomkin, was apparently instructed to undercut my contribution to the picture in every way possible. He not only pooh-poohed my musical ideas wholesale, but made the startling statement, "You take out 'John Henry' and what do you have? Nothing, nothing at all."

I felt considerably abashed by this attack. I seemed to have no friend within the music department, and had little heart for a battle against such unified opposition. I talked with Carlton about resigning, but he bucked me up and insisted that I stick it out. My name did not appear on the film, Tiomkin getting the entire credit. I would experience this kind of back-knifing more than once in my film composing career.

I've talked about the impact that *The Lonesome Train* made in Norman Corwin's CBS production. Well, MGM, which had not been able to find my Beverly Hills phone number for nine months, called me in New York after the broadcast with an offer of a contract at $500 a week. Everything I wrote while in MGM's employ would belong to them. I contracted to be hired as a writer-composer, not under any illusion of being a writer, but to insure that I would be brought into the production of a film early on. The typical Hollywood practice was to get the film shot and rough-edited, or even in the can, before calling in the composer. I worked with writers on two films, but no scores, during the MGM year, *Valley of Decision*, Eddie Knopf producing, being one.

On August 25, 1944, *Lonesome Train* was produced at the Hollywood Bowl, Franz Waxman conducting the Philharmonic Orchestra of Los Angeles and the Los Angeles War Industries Chorus, with Raymond Massey again as an excellently dry-witted Lincoln. John Garfield narrated, and I renewed a sort of friendship with him—or Julie, as I knew him from Group Theatre days. Alfred Drake sang in the production as well. I shouted the square dances as I had on CBS and the subsequent Decca record, and took bows after the show. At midnight, from his home on South Clark Drive in Beverly Hills, an eminent composer colleague wrote me his reaction:

> My dear Earl,
>   I was absolutely *convinced* by your Lincoln Cantata: it is simple, it is moving, it is direct! I didn't have the slightest feeling of being too long (as I was afraid of). Therefore I want to repeat you, not only that *I was wrong*, but that *I am glad I was wrong!*
>   With all best wishes and congratulations, and with my sincerest friendship, I am
>   Most cordially yours,
>   Mario Castelnuovo-Tedesco

The L.A. *Times* liked it pretty well, too. "So reverent and so free was this music and the words that inspired it that it is probable the 'legend' will become another *Ballad for Americans*. This is a work which should be repeated in the Hollywood Bowl for several times 20,000."

Composer Percy Grainger didn't attend that night at the Bowl, but a couple of years later, after coming to (in his words) "an evening of genius" that I gave, he wrote to me:

> I am deeply impressed with the score of *The Lonesome Train* which you were so generous to give me. It is clear, even on paper, how thrilling and touching this inspired work must be in performance, and I long to hear it![1]

That "evening of genius," by the way, was a little house concert at our place on North Kenmore Avenue. I forget what I played, except for Grainger showing up with a new folksong arrangement for piano four-hands (possibly "Molly on the Shore"), and propping it up for me to sightread with him! We negotiated his lovely setting with flying colors, to our joy and the fun of those present.

The text of *The Lonesome Train* was published in a collection of mostly wartime-inspired pieces called *Radio Drama in*

Action. Curiously, this also included Arch Oboler's *The House I Live In*, a character study of a man whose son and daughter are off fighting. My song figures into the plot significantly, thus the title.[2]

Just a little walk

The first complete A picture I worked on in Hollywood came while I was still under contract to MGM. Before getting to MGM, I had agreed to write the songs for Lewis Milestone's *A Walk in the Sun* at United Artists, an adaptation of Sgt. Harry Brown's novel, and occasion for George Tyne's first major screen role. When I signed with MGM I had been properly advised to retain my copyright on a whole series of individual numbers, including the *Walk in the Sun* titles, which could not be claimed by MGM. My contract with MGM thus made it impossible for me to do the background score for a United Artists picture, opening the way for another attempted back-stabbing.

As a writer of a ballad—*for Americans*—I was welcomed onto this war film early in the conception by Milestone, veteran producer-director who had attained his elegant stature from, among others, the landmark *All Quiet on the Western Front*. Milestone (Millie) had the idea of my writing a ballad not only to open and close but punctuate the film throughout. He made this picture the way a film should be made, the composer brought in early for a complete exploration of what the ballad should say and where it should go. Then Millie shot it in such a way as to make ample room for the music to be sung, not just as background but integral to the picture. I appreciated the opportunity not to use massed strings and screaming brasses under the opening title, but instead a simple ballad with guitar gently drawing the audience into the story. Mill Lampell, who had done such a superb job on *The Lonesome Train*, was obviously the lyric man for this. When the director had spotted all the songs, I shipped the script to Mill in New York. In less than two weeks he sent back nine ballad lyrics. Here are some examples.

From the opening intro:

> *Gather round all you people,*
> *While I tell you a tale.*
> *It began in September '43*
> *When the lead platoon, the Texas Division,*
> *Hit the beach at Salerno, Italy.*
>
> *(Refrain) It was just a little walk*
> *In the warm Italian sun,*
> *But it was not an easy thing,*
> *And poets are writing*
> *The tale of that fight*
> *And songs for children to sing.*
>
> *Let them sing of the men of a fighting platoon,*
> *Let them sing of the jobs they've done.*
> *How they came across the sea*
> *To sunny Italy*
> *To take a little walk in the sun, Great God,*
> *They took a little walk in the sun.*

After the landing, the troops move up the beach and have to dig in and wait. And wait. Over the faces of the men we hear the narrator-singer, "Seems like this war is nothing but waiting."

> *I think of a girl I've never seen,*
> *Her hair is black, her eyes are green.*
> *Her name is Helen, or maybe Irene,*
> *It's a long, long time a-waiting.*
> *I think of the things I have not done,*
> *All of the women I have not won,*
> *It seems like my life ain't really begun,*
> *It's a long, long time a-waiting.*

Many variations on the refrain follow; then at the end:

Oh the road that they walked
Was a mighty long road,
Round the world from Chungking to Rome,
It's the same road they had
Comin' out of Stalingrad,
It's that old Lincoln Highway back home,
It's wherever men fight to be free. (Repeat)

It's not inspired poetry, but with the music it works. You can see the film and judge for yourself. I also recorded the entire score with guitar, along with nine other numbers, on a still available album originally put out in 1957 by Moe Asch and Folkways Records, currently obtainable from the Smithsonian.

Now about the "knife in the back" attempt on me with this film. The villain in this case was Freddie Rich, on staff at United Artists, who composed the background score, since I couldn't get released from MGM for that purpose. Freddie (Fredric Efrem Rich) was diabolically clever in his quietly waged undercover campaign *to remove the ballad from the picture* and substitute his own score, particularly at the end of the film.

For the first sneak preview, with Freddie's score roughly complete, it was decided that I should record the ballads, to be temporarily laid in to the film, leaving for later who should sing them in the final version and how. Well, Freddie comes up to me to ask a favor on the final ballad. Would I mind moving the song down from E to E-flat? The implication being that the lower key would fit his score better. At first I worried. The key of E is a great guitar key and I can't play in E-flat. But I saw a way of doing this by tuning the whole guitar down a half tone, *playing* still in E but *sounding* E-flat. Get it? Good.

At preview time, the ballad comes off presentably enough. Until the end sequence, when Freddie's full singing-strings orchestration builds magnificently up to a soaring high E. Then the audience hears—slightly off, down a half tone—just an amateur voice and guitar, a real let-down for such a noble finale. Freddie designed this for Milestone's ears to make the ballad seem unnecessary. Fortunately Millie did not fall for the trick. Justice and integrity triumphed. The song was reorchestrated in a different, non-conflicting key. They got a good bass singer, Kenneth Spencer (who sounded a lot like Paul Robeson), and our ballad resumed its natural place . . . in the sun.

A Walk in the Sun supported a necessary war (if any war is truly necessary). And warmly, humorously, showed that war is still hell. Shortly after I'd completed the movie but before it was released, Mrs. Roosevelt invited me to her apartment off Washington Square in New York to play for her guests, who included Senator Tom Connally from Texas. I sang the *Walk in the Sun* numbers and when I finished, the Senator gave a whoop and spoke out proudly, "Those are my boys!" The *Daily Worker* film critic wrote, "It has humanity, humor, reality and is quite the finest soldier film that Hollywood has made." The pic had a successful run, became a staple on TV, and is still shown occasionally on the late late show. A recently published guide says, "One of the best WW II dramas. Realistic, well acted." A London-based magazine wrote about the ballads that they "[crystallize] into poetry the moments of fatigue and suspense."[3]

An interesting addendum: You may wonder why MGM paid me $500 a week to do nothing for a year. Well, I wondered, too. I learned only later that they had optioned *Remembrance Rock*, a new book by Carl Sandburg, which they planned to make into a movie. And they wanted me to be available for the music. But old Carl was four years late with his manuscript, and MGM never filmed it.

Segregation and contradictions

During the famous Hollywood film strike of 1945, I joined a group protesting the conduct of police officers in connection with the studio picketing, pledging to appear before Warner Brothers in Burbank on October 9th to observe the goings-on. The following day, several papers carried the story that I'd been arrested there for alleged violation of the Riot Law. This clipping, no author or source, probably dates from the 11th:

When Mr. Robinson was being hustled off with the rest
of the sign-carriers, he protested.

"This segregation is disgraceful. Disgraceful."

"But we're not segregating the Negroes and the
Whites," an arresting officer explained.

"I don't mean color segregation," replied the distinguished composer. "I mean men and women."

"Jailbird Earl Robinson," reported the *People's World* on
October 13th, "led the crowd in singing 'Which Side Are You
On?' and 'The House I Live In.'" Of my three arrests in life,
this one I am proud of. We put up bail and got out that day.
The case was dismissed in June of 1946, by which time I was
on the Committee for Motion Picture Strikers, and working
for MGM.

So many contradictions marked this period in Hollywood.
How did making more money than I had ever made before
stack up against wanting most sincerely to remain a leftie?
Helen and I somehow managed to spend the money ($13,000
in 1943, $23,000 in 1944) without going in for any fancy material things. I never did understand where the money went—I
had a business manager who took care of all that.

We had a very ordinary house with four small bedrooms.
Helen's only indulgence was she'd keep fixing over the house,
always artistically, and pretty economically, too, from what I
could tell. But basically, she never altered her lifestyle a bit.
She never stopped organizing for the Communist Party, and
she went out faithfully to sell the *Daily Worker*. In the summer
and fall of 1944 she took charge of a whole precinct to get out
the vote for FDR and other win-the-war candidates.

But Helen never went out of her way to meet the "name"
Hollywood people. Though we happily accepted Woody
Guthrie for a time—until he wore out his welcome—we never
made a point of inviting film industry people to the house.
The one time we had a producer to dinner, he dropped some
food on the floor. Perry jumped down from his chair, picked it
up and said, "It's all right, we're not sanitary!"

Helen left it to me to be the public representative, which I did for quite a time by ignoring the contradictions. I would go to MGM in the daytime, making my contribution toward what would today be a ten- or fifteen-million-dollar film. Then at night I would take delight in appearing at a packed Shrine Auditorium for Ben Davis, a New York City Communist Councilman on tour, and raising money for the left. On the NBC Blue Network one Sunday in November 1943 Arch Oboler had put together a dramatization of the "Writer's Credo," a progressive statement about the responsibilities of writers under present conditions. Eight well-known public figures participated, and Arch had me playing piano and talking about how music, too, formed a part of the struggle. In between appearances like that I would sing for school assemblies and labor unions. In my papers today I still have my picket card for the asparagus workers' strike.

Always, I placed my name on petitions, appeals, open letters, as a sponsor, endorser or whatever they wanted. The proper state and Congressional committees on un-American activities took note, and not just in California, as I appeared so often in other states. *The Shield*, publication of the New Jersey State Civil Service Commission, identified me in July 1947 as "one of the most active Communists in Hollywood," and went on to list my progressive résumé at great length.

I did some work on a film for the Office of War Information that would follow our boys into Europe and elsewhere and tell the local populations about American music. But during the years 1944 to 1946 I did not work on films steadily, so I had time for other activities. The Musicians Congress took up some of my time. This group did all we could for the war effort and a variety of progressive causes. Digging down into the ethnic sections of L.A., I emceed and helped to produce several large-scale folk festivals. A Pan-American Festival was followed by Songs of the Firing Lines, then at Hollywood High a black-oriented Spirituals to Swing program where a black church chorus sang not only "Accentuate the Positive" but the first performance I ever heard of "Amazing Grace." Later came an

All-Slavic Festival, a History of California, and an Oriental Festival.[4]

In the days when the Communist movement represented a force in American society, practically any time you saw a mixed gathering, political or social, guaranteed you were among Communists or fellow travelers at the least. That's how far apart white society stood from any communities of color. So it's hardly surprising that the FBI would dog not only the political left but any and all movements and organizations, like the NAACP, committed to redressing the grievance of race. If Communists understood their concerns and reached out a hand of solidarity, that automatically "tainted" such people and made them enemies of the state. The government thought it more useful to put its energies into keeping people apart, then redbaiting them, than do anything about the problem of racism.

Thus the FBI cited Helen and me as sponsors of an NAACP cocktail party for fair employment in January 1946 that drew over 500 people. Because of our names they titled the report "Foreign Inspired Agitation Among American Negroes in L.A." As if the "natives" were too dumb to recognize unfair practices on the job unless they had been "agitated" and "inspired" by "foreigners" (like Helen and me!). The feds also kept tabs on a project I helped initiate in 1944: The Little Theatre Guild of Los Angeles set up an Inter-Racial Film and Radio Guild, which offered a complete course of instruction in all phases of theatrical life, coupled with underwriting shows which would train black people for positions in movies, radio, and theatre. This venture never made the impact we had hoped for, but a few months later, in May 1945, I did receive the Guild's Unity Award given to "those who have made outstanding contributions to international harmony and universal understanding through the medium of motion pictures and radio." Fellow recipients that year included Orson Welles, Bette Davis, and Lena Horne.

Racism infected every area of public life, including housing. Do you recall that brief moment when the Democrats raised the issue against Presidential candidate Ronald Reagan that he had once signed a restrictive covenant on his home in Los Angeles? That meant that if he decided to sell his property, he wouldn't sell to Blacks or Jews. Thus neighborhoods were kept lily-white. Well, folks were organizing against this kind of discrimination back then. One rally I attended at Independent Church in May of 1946 featured victims of both restrictive covenants and KKK cross burnings. Speakers included Lena Horne, Gus Hawkins, William Bidner "and other known Communists" (according to the FBI), plus Robinson with (naturally) "The House I Live In." Charlotta Bass, a truly great American, chaired the meeting: She edited the *California Eagle*, an African-American newspaper, and six years later ran for vice-president on the Progressive Party ticket.

All of these associations, like my closeness with Paul Robeson, must have rubbed off on me in the inscrutable G-man mind, for an FBI report from Chicago in 1948 states with some assurance, "It should be noted that Robinson was a colored concert pianist." Which reminds me of an old Yiddish proverb about a none-too-smart fellow: "He spells NOAH with five mistakes."

Robinson's war

As the war progressed, I wondered if making music was the best and only contribution I could make. I contemplated joining the armed forces, but on the advice of my draft board, as well as that of many soldiers I came to know, I was persuaded that I could do more musically outside the army than in. At the Writers Congress that met at UCLA in October 1943 I led a seminar called "Song Writing in War." Like many other musicians and entertainers, I did my share performing for factory workers at war plants, for servicemen both at training camps and on the special services' radio division show which went out to soldiers all over the world. And for a gigantic Madison Square rally in New York, with Senator Claude Pepper speaking, I wrote new lyrics to "Joshua Fit the Battle of Jericho," saying:

Open up that second front, second front, second front,
Open up that second front
And beat those fascists down

the point being that an Allied invasion of Europe would help
defend and save the vast resources of the Soviet Union, where
the Germans were making daily advances. I brought this song
home to Seattle the summer of 1942 for a rally of 5,000 people
at the County-City Building, where I also got to conduct a
coast artillery army band in the national anthem. Because D-
Day took so long in coming, I had plenty of opportunity to
hammer away at the second front message.

A little cantata I wrote with film writer Bernard Schoenfeld, *Song of a Free People*, appeared on a November 16, 1943,
Shrine Auditorium program in L.A. celebrating the tenth anniversary of U.S.-Soviet diplomatic relations. More than 6,000
people attended. The whole town celebrated Friendship Day
between the two powers—being strategic allies at the time—
with a Soviet ship in port, declarations from the mayor, and
the Soviet flag flown all day at City Hall. A U.S. army band
played "The Star Spangled Banner" and "The Internationale,"
and speakers brought greetings from the military, the film industry, unions, the Urban League, and from the Red Navy and
the Soviet consulate. The spirits of five million Red Army
casualties filled the hall.

Our cantata, dedicated to Vice President Henry A. Wallace, featured a mixed chorus with soloists Albert Dekker as
narrator, Edward G. Robinson, Olivia de Havilland, J. Edward
Bromberg, and Minerva Pius. Dooley Wilson sang a "Freedom
Blues" in it, which I shortly recorded myself on the Alco label:

Freedom, it ain't a silver dollar,
Shinin' oh so bright.
Freedom, it ain't a silver dollar,
But folks what seen it
Say it has a holy light.

The reviewer from the *People's World* wrote that the cantata "brought the house down. People applauded and stamped their feet in enthusiastic comment on the hard-hitting rhymic [*sic*] drama-music of this new work."[5]

But music alone didn't satisfy all my urges to help the war effort. For a year or so, beginning November 1943, I worked on the swing shift in a small machine shop making aircraft precision parts. The tiredness I felt after eight hours there I found a thousand times more restful than the kind that comes from entertaining, meeting, and talking. I wrote to a friend, "When I finished yesterday my first 'cooky cutter' (a precision tool for cutting out perfect circles of steel with every measurement having to be within five-thousandths of an inch) and it turned out all right I felt better than I have about some songs I've written."[6] One day at the lathe a twisting splinter curled up into my forehead, the only casualty in Robinson's war.

Notes

1. Percy Grainger to Earl Robinson, March 1, 1946.

2. Erik Barnouw, ed., *Radio Drama in Action: Twenty-Five Plays of a Changing World*, New York: Rinehart, 1945.

3. Steven H. Scheuer, ed., *Movies on TV*, New York: Bantam, 1985, p. 716; Gavin Lambert, *Sight and Sound*, April 1951. One actor in this film, Norman Lloyd, talks at length about it in his autobiography, *Stages of Life in Theatre, Film and Television*, New York: Limelight Editions, 1993.

4. Don Christlieb, once a member of the Musicians Congress, testified April 20, 1956, before HUAC, concentrating on our ineffectiveness, naming me and several others as known Communists. His 16 pages of testimony appear in "Investigation of Communist Activities in the Los Angeles, California, Area," Part 10.

5. Ed Robbin, "Soviet-American Friendship Hailed," *People's World*, November 20, 1943.

6. Earl Robinson to Jack Shapiro, December 27, 1944.

SAN FRANCISCO MEETIN'

An important name to be exalted with abiding friendship is that of E. Y. (Yip) Harburg, already famous for his lyrics to "Brother, Can You Spare a Dime," perhaps the greatest song to emerge out of the Depression. He added to his renown the wonderful songs to *The Wizard of Oz*: "Over the Rainbow" won him and composer Harold Arlen an Academy Award. Yip first called me in autumntime of 1943, suggesting we might get together on some songs, but we were in friendly disalignment from the moment we started working together. I was accustomed to finding words or ideas, or some kind of written or dramatic inspiration to get me fired up. Yip was exactly the opposite. He became galvanized first and always by a good tune. And now he proposed to work with someone who had no scrapbook full of spare melodies. Determined to work together, however, because we both wanted to say the same things about equality, about labor's struggle to organize, about the antifascist war, we searched out a way to move closer. We found it first in "Free and Equal Blues."

Scientific talk-talk
It is often easy to measure the effect of society on a song. It is more difficult to assess the effect of a song on society. "Free and Equal Blues" came out of a definite need posed by World War II. It was possible in those antifascist days for a white-skinned U.S. soldier to demand, if he got wounded, that he receive blood from another white-skinned person. Though contrary to all scientific knowledge, this nonsense was perpetuated by the United States Army, Navy, and Air Force. Despite the fact that blood from a black-skinned person could save a life, while "white" blood of the wrong type could kill, this potentially hurtful idiocy was supported even by the Red Cross, which should have known better. So Yippur and I decided to handle this problem with a song.

We made the main body a glorified talking blues, the lines written to a rhythm without a tune. I contributed to the lyrics a section from Sandburg's *The People, Yes* on taking the human body apart, which Yippur found very congenial.

> *So I stayed at that St. James Infirmary,*
> *I wasn't going to leave that place.*
> *This was too interesting. I said, Doc,*
> *Give me some more of that scientific talk-talk.*
> *And he did. He said, Melt yourself down*
> *Into a crucible, son. Pour yourself out*
> *Into a test tube, and what have you got?*
> *3500 cubic feet of gas,*
> *The same for the upper and the lower class.*
> *Well, we'll let that pass.*
> *Carbon, 22 lbs., 10 ounces.*
> *You mean that goes for Princes, Dukeses, and Countses?*
> *Whatever you are, that's what the amounts is.*
> *Carbon, 22 lbs., 10 ounces,*
> *Iron, 57 grains,*
> *Not enough to keep a man in chains.*
> *50 ounces of phosphorous,*
> *Whether you're poor or prosperous . . .*
> *Buddy, can you spare a match?*

Yip then moved my way slightly by tossing off a refrain—doggerel he called it—which I amplified into a rousing chorus that people join in on:

> *And that was news. Yes, that was news,*
> *That was very, very, very special news,*
> *'Cause ever since that day*
> *I've got those free and equal blues.*

Dooley Wilson, of "As Time Goes By" fame in *Casablanca*, performed and recorded it with me. The Hollywood Democratic Committee issued the record, and they sold a lot

of them. Josh White later recorded "Free and Equal" commer-
cially—he also sang it on Broadway at the Belasco, along with
"The House I Live In," as part of a black revue called *Blue
Holiday*. Yip and I made quite a humorous splash in America,
which might have come to the attention of the military and
the Red Cross. It is hard to tell the effect of a song, but by the
end of the war, they were no longer segregating blood according to race. It's still among the most popular songs in my active repertoire.

Our next song, "Same Boat, Brother," was a verse-and-
chorus effort where I supplied Yip with a tune for the verses,
he then contributed some lines to which I set a tune, and we
worked on the refrain together.

> *Oh, the Lord looked down from his holy place,*
> *Said, "Lordy me, what a sea of space,*
> *What a spot to launch the human race."*
> *So He built Him a boat with a mixed-up crew,*
> *With eyes of black and brown and blue,*
> *And that's how come that you and I*
> *Got just one world, with just one sky.*
>
> *(Chorus) And it's the same boat, brother (repeat)*
> *And if you shake one end*
> *You're gonna (clap) rock the other,*
> *It's the same boat, brother.*

People immediately joined in on the chorus, but the verse
form was a little more complicated. I felt highly honored when
my friend Leadbelly picked up the song and started singing it.
We soon became aware that this song of peace had a destina-
tion—nothing less than the United Nations. Along with a second Robinson-Harburg song, "Have You Heard About the
Meeting?" they were to grace the founding of the U.N. in San
Francisco, April of 1945.

"Same Boat, Brother" joined three other songs—"Tower of
Babel" from *The People, Yes*, "Freedom Blues" from *Song of a*

Free People, and "Porterhouse Lucy"—on a *Songs by Earl Robin-son* album on Alco that came out toward the end of the war, me doing the honors on vocals. Another album, on Keynote, shortly followed this one: *Americana*, on three 10-inch records. This included two by me, "The House I Live In" and "A Man's a Man for A' That," my setting of a Robert Burns poem, plus "The Frozen Logger," "Jefferson and Liberty," "Sweet Betsy from Pike," "Dirty Miner," and "Drill Ye Tarriers Drill."

Yippur and I were meshing our songwriting skills more comfortably. As a plug for FDR's fourth term we were "commissioned"—for no salary, but high honor—to score *Hell Bent for Election*, a cartoon short put together by some of the leading animators of the time, Chuck Jones, John Hubley, and others. Long after John's passing I remain friendly with his wife Faith Hubley, and with Chuck Jones. Who commissioned it? Industrial Films, Inc., for the United Auto, Aircraft and Agricultural Implement Workers Union, CIO, aka United Auto Workers, to distribute to union locals and other appropriate pre-election venues. Why? To make sure that complacency among FDR's working-class supporters didn't keep them from the polls. The film also got shown at the Democratic National Convention.

For the theme song of this project, "Gotta Get Out and Vote," I was able to give Yip almost a complete tune! Which in turn became the musical theme of a "commercial" directed by Norman Corwin on CBS—the Democratic Party's salute to FDR the night before his victory against Gov. Thomas Dewey. It was sung by Judy Garland and backgrounded a lineup of stars, all of whom were there just to lend their names—"Linda Darnell for FDR," "Joe Cotten for the old man," Groucho Marx, James Cagney, Danny Kaye, etc.—all to the rhythm of "Gotta Get Out and Vote." Averill Harriman spoke—so did FDR himself for ten minutes at the end—and Dooley Wilson and I sang "Free and Equal Blues." A recent biography calls this broadcast "clearly a high point in Yip's career as the bard of left liberalism."[1]

I don't know how much the history books have ever dwelled on this, but I can share with you the views of FDR's wife regarding this election. "The President is well," E. Roosevelt wrote to E. Robinson in February 1944,

> but I hope very much that he will not have to run again. I recognize the fact that he may be in a position where it is his obligation but I would give a great deal if that position did not come about.[2]

Yip not only proved adept at getting good tunes out of me, but he taught me much about work. We'd labor on a song for days at the piano, until it seemed just right. And Yip would inevitably say, "Let's try it again." He had an original sense of humor, with an inexhaustible energy for perfection. I respected and loved him in equal measure. In all I wrote nine songs with him.

Paradoxes

FDR's death in April 1945 struck a powerful and eerie downbeat. Would he have lived longer if he hadn't run for that fourth term, as Mrs. R. hoped? Still, the event provided a strange lift for me, in two ways. For two days afterward, no commercials or light music aired on the radio, and broadcasters played *The Lonesome Train* over and over again. A unique poignancy that never approached mawkishness tied in the people's mood at Lincoln's death with that of Franklin Roosevelt. Mrs. R. wrote about it in her "My Day" column, quoting, "A lonesome train on a lonesome track/Seven coaches painted black." These words and my music reverberated in her mind as she rode with her own husband back home on the train to his final resting place at Hyde Park, New York.

The other way FDR's death paradoxically uplifted me had to do with San Francisco. This town and the Bay area have always been special for me. It is romantic on more than one level. My first singing experience there took place over a closed radio hookup to 80,000 shipyard workers in World War II. In this war there was an incredible heady spirit of togetherness with the Soviets, the Chinese, the English, the underground fighters in occupied Europe, yes even in Germany, which was nowhere more compellingly symbolized than in San Francisco. The representatives of the winning fighters gathered in that city in April 1945 to form the United Nations. Though the war with Japan still continued, Hitler had been defeated: On the very day of the U.N. founding, April 25, Soviet and American soldiers had joined forces—from the East and from the West—at the little town of Torgau on the Elbe. So we permitted ourselves a look at the peaceful world ahead. Franklin Roosevelt's dream, which he was not destined to witness, was coming together.

I was there, with Yip Harburg's and my music, to help CBS celebrate the budding U.N. on radio. Even if this had not been in the works, I would surely have gone up to answer Mrs. Roosevelt's call, for on March 31st, just days before the fatal stroke, she wrote to me:

> I expect to be in San Francisco for the day on April 25th, with the President. If you are to be there let me know. I am sure the boys at Oakland Hospital would love your songs.

"Same Boat, Brother" and "Have You Heard About the Meeting?," both sung by Alfred Drake of *Oklahoma!* fame, backed by a chorus of Army and Navy men and women, were right on target, and an integral part of the proceedings. Norman Corwin, still the fair-haired boy of CBS, directed the whole program superbly from the control room, reputedly the first round-the-world radio hookup. I got to throw in a few deathless lines with Drake:

> DRAKE: Gonna have a big orchestry.
> ROBINSON: Thirty-seven musicians!
> DRAKE: International orchestry!
> ROBINSON: Blondes, brunettes, and clarinets!

And when it was noted it was too bad FDR couldn't make it, I affirmed, "He'll *be* there." (Still pushing this "no death" message that Al Hayes and I began with "Joe Hill.")

I remember a beautiful moment with some friends up at the top of Mt. Tamalpais, listening to the radio broadcast of the U. N. proceedings, gazing across at the Cow Palace where it was happening. Ah, euphoria, *euphoria!* We could see clearly a world of peace everlasting.

In his acclaimed radio special *On a Note of Triumph*, Norman Corwin spelled out in some detail the kind of world available to us if we wanted it enough and were willing to learn some lessons. My part in *Note* was small, but I was there: I helped Pete Seeger and the Almanac Singers sing "Round and Round Hitler's Grave."

The fact that this lovely vision became tarnished with the coming of the Cold War, the fact that "Same Boat, Brother" and the "Meeting" song were revived again so rarely, and the fact that the vision has been forgotten by many—was never even known by later generations—all this does not take away from the basic fact of San Francisco 1945 as the cradle of peace. The dream lives on.

Now, with all the top-level summit meetings in Moscow and Washington, it appears that despite the naysayers, the put-downers, the whatiffers, the doom and gloomers, we *are* making progress. Nation will yet line up with nation, brothers and sisters together. Justice and peace will win.

Notes

1. Harold Meyerson and Ernie Harburg, *Who Put the Rainbow in The Wizard of Oz?: Yip Harburg, Lyricist*, Ann Arbor: University of Michigan Press, 1993, p. 217.

2. Eleanor Roosevelt to Earl Robinson, February 23, 1944.

NAME DROPPING

Lee Hays, eventually of the Weavers fame, became very close with me. Our friendship survived nine years of living together, then some miscommunication (we weren't even talking for a while), and a reconciliation shortly before Lee "changed his address."

I must not have been very impressed with him when he first came over to see me in Brooklyn sometime in 1940, because he said later I told him he should study more piano. I don't remember being so teacherly, because soon after I was full of admiration for him and his excellent bass singing on the Almanac albums *Songs for John Doe* and *Talking Union*. And I listened very carefully, as did Millard Lampell, to his sharp suggestions on *The Lonesome Train*. He pushed for more working-class content, which Mill and I met by inserting Lincoln's quote, "The strongest bond of human sympathy, outside your family of course, should be the one uniting all working people, of all Nations, Tongues, and Kindreds."

Lee and Mill did not get on any too well at that time. Lee thought of Mill as opportunistic for presenting Lincoln in the typical romantic manner of the Great Man theory of history, so as to appeal to the broadest—and lowest—common denominator. Why, even Republicans might like Mill's Lincoln! He wanted more emphasis on the villains of the period, those who killed Lincoln, and those who stood to profit from cutting off the leader of national unity. In that way, listeners would derive an active, fresh and usable truth about our own times. In the narrowest sense he was probably correct. Interestingly, Mill turned around and called me an opportunist when I first went to Hollywood in 1943, when all I insisted I was doing was "opportunistically" reaching for the wider audience that films could offer. Then two or three years later Mill "opportunely" made the same move.

This was a sample of the arguments we had on the left through the years. And Lee partook fully. He didn't so much

argue as quote approvingly, or satirically, the various pundits
in American society. Lee was an expert at uplifting, mostly,
but also at putdowns by citing someone else's negative opinion. In any case, his singing and songwriting exerted a positive,
powerful force for good his whole life. And his Southern
Methodist biblical and hymnal church background, together
with his trenchant sense of humor, helped make the Weavers
the important and inspiring group they became from the late
1940s on.

Another collaboration I enjoyed with Mill came just after
the war, in 1946. The Detroit Automotive Golden Jubilee
commissioned us to write "Pioneer City," an upbeat number
that might still give a little lift to that town that today suffers
so many of the contemporary urban ills.

> Oh, the pioneer, the pioneer,
> Breaking the trail to the new frontier.
> Now old man Cadillac came down the river
> With an axe and a pelt and an old French horn.
> The Indians said, "Don't walk any more,
> Just squat right down by the Lake Erie shore."
> He squat right down and dreamed up a city,
> Sweet as a woman and twice as pretty,
> And that's how Detroit was born.

A 150-voice chorus sang "Pioneer City" at the jubilee celebration, and Fred Waring programmed it on NBC.

Eisler and Ettl

For six months or so I took advantage of Hanns Eisler's
presence on the Hollywood scene and studied with him. I
didn't have formal lessons; mostly I came in every week and
showed him what I was working on, and he gave me comments and criticism. "Ettl," he told me in his strong German
accent, rolling the r in "Earl" like timber tumbling down a ra-
vine and rhyming my name with *kettle*, "Ettl, every morning
you should write a fugue." While I was absorbing that counsel,

I must have had a puzzled look on my face. So pudgy Hanns, seated at the piano, demonstrated what he meant. Rapidly, repeatedly, he thrust his arms into the air with astonishing violence. "Like setting-up exercises," he puffed. "Every day!"

Now a fugue is a musical device not often encountered in Hollywood film scores. But occasionally Eisler used one. A movie he scored opened with a man coming into a room. He falls dead. Then, in succession, three other people enter and walk past, and with each entry Eisler's fugue theme recapitulated. Studio musicians are usually pretty bored by their work. But when they recorded this scene, they tapped their horns and violins, applauding Eisler's remarkable musical invention.

I heard about it and complimented him. "It was just a fugue," Eisler said. "That's all, just a fugue."

Hanns Eisler and I both served on the Music Advisory Committee of *Hollywood Quarterly*, which came out under the joint sponsorship of the Hollywood Writers Mobilization and the University of California. We formally launched the magazine in November 1945 at the home of UCLA Provost, Dr. Clarence Dykstra. Our editorial staff included John Howard Lawson, Abraham Polonsky, Abe Burrows, and Sylvia Jarrico, all well-known names in the film community. This handsome, erudite review—not particularly left-wing, just serious—came out in issues of 100-plus pages packed with trenchant criticism and commentary that still hold up. After 1951 it became *Film Quarterly*, which is still being published.

Trivia buffs may recall that Eisler's score for director Fritz Lang's 1943 film *Hangmen Also Die* won him an Oscar award. And in 1947 Eisler published a valuable book, *Composing for the Films*, under a substantial grant from the Rockefeller Foundation. None of which discouraged HUAC from calling the composer before its august tribunal. On September 24th of 1947, Chief Investigator Robert E. Stripling interrogated Eisler, and in the process brought forth a copy of *America Sings*. This songbook, to which I had written the foreword, contained some of Eisler's songs. Within weeks, Eisler returned to Europe, where he wrote the national anthem of the new Ger-

man Democratic Republic. How curious, that fascism in the
Old World gave us the extraordinary talents of its exiled intellectuals; and that now—how soon afterwards!—some of them,
playwright Bertolt Brecht among them, could find no peace
here in the land of thought-control.

Only in July of that year I had attended a five-day conference on just that subject, "Thought Control in the U.S.A.,"
held at the Beverly Hills Hotel, with my old friend Norman
Corwin as keynote speaker. The sponsor, the Arts, Sciences
and Professions Council of the Progressive Citizens of America (PCA), published the proceedings. After a panel addressing
music and the arts I am quoted as saying:

> One aspect of the discussion that can stand a little more
> emphasis is that the best defense against thought-control
> is a counter-attack. Join PCA. Counter-attack with our
> art. There will be a strong tendency on the part of art-
> ists to be afraid, but this is the time to put our feeling
> into our art in strong terms and attack the Tenneys and
> Rankins through our art. . . . The PCA audience is
> looking not only for speeches, but for art."[1]

People's politicians

Two good friends, people's politicians, deserve special
mention. Vito Marcantonio was a good working-class New
York City Italian boy, who came to lead the radical American
Labor Party, in whose ranks I registered. Representing East
Harlem for fourteen years, he was the only person in the 1950
Congress who voted against a war appropriation for Korea. He
used to maintain an open office right in the center of his district where folks could come in at any time, day or night, to
ask him questions, and get his help on their problems. I was
proud to know him.

One time in New York I got off the express subway to
change for the local and I heard the *Ballad for Americans* blaring out of a loudspeaker up on the street. I went upstairs to
see, and my music was being used to draw crowds to a street
meeting. I was thrilled, until I learned it was an anti-

Marcantonio rally—very poorly attended, I must say. I don't know how I suppressed my rage. Helen said I shouldn't have let them get away with it. Vito died prematurely, at 52. The epitaph on his tombstone in Woodlawn Cemetery reads, "Vito Marcantonio: A Fighting Congressman."

I met Hugh DeLacy in the backyard of my folks' home in Seattle in 1940, the first time I came back home, famous from the *Ballad for Americans*. He came with his wife Betty and four kids. A great family man, then. He had been elected to the Seattle City Council in 1937, a moribund and mostly reactionary body if there ever was one. Well, he started raising all kinds of resolutions about labor, old age pensions, and selling scrap iron to Japan, which was a big issue on the West Coast. He forced the newspapers to take notice, and the City Council for a while became a hot news item. After his two-year term, the redbaiters, armed with a $50,000 campaign chest, booted him off the Council, which reverted to its old ways, making an inside page of the local papers about once every two weeks.

Well, Hugh got into the ship scalers' union and started working several days a week painting ships, scraping off barnacles, and organizing for pro-New Deal politics which the mainstream Democrats had abandoned. On the strength of his broad base among the people he got voted to Congress in 1944. Hugh was always gay, ebullient, interested in everything, a brilliant raconteur, a teller of jokes dirty and clean, in short a scintillating person. A sample of Hugh's wonderfully outrageous method of operation comes from his tour of Congress. He would walk up to Hugh Rankin in the cloak room, a reactionary "nigger-hatin'" Mississippi Congressman, and slap him on the back. Then, with every reason to despise this bastard, DeLacy would let fly with, "Well, fellow worker, let's get together and see how we can cheat the people a little today, shall we?"

He lasted just one term in Congress, being dumped in 1946 by a gangup of big business and reactionaries who didn't like his progressive voting slant. My mother never forgave him when he left his wife in this congressional period for his secretary, a woman of great beauty, who only stuck by Hugh till he lost his congressional job, then left him. He became a carpenter and building contractor again, and stayed pretty close to the left from then on till he finally settled in Santa Cruz Soquel with a new wife, Dorothy. Over those Cold War McCarthy years we had some small karmic problems. Thinking I was too easy on the bad ones, he put out for a while that I had written a song called "I Like Nixon," which was not true. I only said to my progressive friends, "Look, I've got news for you. Maybe this is upsetting, but Nixon is a human being."

I won him over, though. Every time I visited Santa Cruz, I read him and Dorothy whole operas and music dramas I was writing. I wanted to read my *Listen for the Dolphin*, but he had a stroke and was unable to hear it.

A floor-length gown

I got along especially well with Katharine Hepburn, and through her with Spencer Tracy. One of the perks associated with being under contract at a studio is the ability to invite friends onto the set while shooting is in progress. So I impressed a few folks in 1944 with *Dragon Seed*, an MGM picture where Hepburn played a Chinese woman of importance.

We got friendly enough for her to invite me over to her house one evening. Only thing is, I didn't know it was a dinner engagement, the time being eight o'clock. So I ate my usual dinner at home before going. And arrived to be sat down, unhungry, to a sumptuous meal with Katharine and Spencer. She asked me if I wasn't feeling well, since I was sort of picking at the food. Always one for honesty, I told them the truth, which amused them no end.

In 1948, the mass media went to town attacking Henry Wallace and his Progressive Party bid for the presidency, on the grounds that the campaign had been captured by the Communists. Katharine Hepburn made it a point to show up at a big fundraiser in a gorgeous *red* floor-length gown. You couldn't fail to notice. She had a lot of spunk, and still has.

The guy doing most of the fundraising that night had a running gag. Whenever anyone asked him a question on Progressive Party positions, he'd answer, "Wallace takes care of the politics, I take care of the money." I gave a contribution, and when he read my name, he said, "All that music—and money, too!" Though by then there wasn't much of that. The blacklist had struck.

Note

1. Arts, Sciences and Professions Council of the Progressive Citizens of America, *Thought Control in the U.S.A.*, Hollywood, 1947, p. 247.

HOLLYWOOD: TAKE 2

Here's where I set down

In early 1945 I wrote songs for the Paramount film *California*, directed by John Farrow, starring Ray Milland, Barbara Stanwyck, Barry Fitzgerald, and Anthony Quinn. This happened soon after I finished that first year with MGM. We parted company and the $500 a week amiably. Yip Harburg, being the "name" person, was hired first, at $30,000, to write the lyrics and routine the score, and I came in at $10,000 for several weeks' work, a significant raise over the MGM wage.

Yip being in the driver's seat, I had to really work to produce a tune that could turn him on. I faced the almost impossible task of doing a noble tune for Yip, without any noble words to inspire me. I struggled at the piano unsuccessfully. But Yippur the old (young then) master, was totally equal to the occasion. He got me to improvising square-dancy tunes, light and meaningless as far as I was concerned. He stopped me at one point and said, "There, that one, play that slow." Lo and behold, it turned out to be a fine, noble song which formed our title number, a tour de force, singing and soaring with room for tall story jokes.

> *Oh the sun keeps rolling to the west,*
> *'Cause its home is California*
> *(Yep, that's where the sun likes to take his shoes*
> *off, put his feet up on the High Sierras,*
> *and say, "Here's where I set down!")*

and

> *When you see a mountain split the sky,*
> *Brother, you're in California*
> *(Some of them hills are so high it takes two men*
> *and a boy to see over the top of one of*

*'em. . . . Yeah, a lady eagle tried to fly
over, she got her tail caught, couldn't lay
an egg for a week!)*

This became a production number under the opening titles
depicting a long line of covered wagons, and led into a rousing
dance tune, "California or Bust."

Yippur got excited by a folksong that the Almanac Singers
used to satirize right-wing New York Rep. Hamilton Fish, and
this became "Lilly Aye Lady O," a gambling song that Barbara
Stanwyck sang. We produced a bunch of good show numbers,
in a sense too good for the film, which turned out to be a glorified western with higher aspirations. The music credit on the
film went to conductor Victor Young, who only composed a
little fragmentary bridgework here and there. (Incidental intelligence: He had led the Ken Darby Singers and the Decca Concert Orchestra in Bing Crosby's *Ballad for Americans*.)*

The Romance of Rosy Ridge was written by Lester Cole, of
later Hollywood Ten fame, based on a *Saturday Evening Post*
story by MacKinlay Kantor, with a nice peace theme of post-
Civil War blue and gray soldiers needing to live together again
after having fought and killed. A sort of "Allegheny Mountain" western, now referred to as a "well made, charming
drama." It starred Van Johnson as an itinerant school teacher,
billed as his first character role. As his leading lady, *Romance*
introduced the 19-year-old Janet Leigh—"as fresh and pretty as
a daisy in the spring," said *The New York Times*.[1]

The rest of the cast, including child actor Dean Stockwell,
came from the MGM stable, but the other leading performer
was the scenery: They shot way up in the rugged High Sierras
near the magisterial Sonora Pass, and in the wilderness around
Angels Camp in gold mining country. *Variety* thought well of

---

* In 1995, the movie *Something to Talk About* included a clip
from *California* lasting a few seconds, earning the songwriters an on-
screen credit.

the pic—"good screen entertainment," they said, and Van
Johnson's "best role to date." They liked "femme newcomer,
Janet Leigh, whose work indicates a bright future."[2]
I found myself back at MGM again, working at $800 a
week during the shooting period, and I helped score. I got my
old friend Lewis Allan/Abel Meeropol to do the lyrics, and he
did a good job. Van Johnson learned to play banjo and harmonica for the film, and sang six of our songs in a mediocre
way, including "I Come from Missouri," a rouser that naturally brought Harry S Truman to mind, and that Robbins published, along with "Far from My Darling." *Time* said, "The
songs are pretty."[3] Janet Leigh had to learn how to milk a cow.
Roy Rowland directed, and Jack Cummings produced. Regarding music with a message, he used to say, "The only message I
recognize comes from Western Union."
This movie confirmed me—typecast me—as a "folksong"
composer. George Bassman, on MGM contract, wrote the
background score. He got into some trouble paraphrasing or
directly copying some Aaron Copland in one section, which
someone noticed. He wasn't removed from the film, but his
Copland section was.
The film did get into political trouble insofar as Louis B.
Mayer had just named Lester Cole as a Communist when the
Oscar committee started to make its nominations. In his autobiography, Cole believes he might have won for best screenplay that year.[4] Getting wind of the controversy surrounding
the picture, the *New Yorker*'s "Talk of the Town" column
came up with a truly hilarious commentary that I wish I had
space to reprint in its entirety. It's written, anonymously, from
the point of view of a critic scribbling notes while viewing the
film in a dark theatre.

> Possible current allusion when Van says, "The war's
> over, but some people, 'stead o' lookin' for friends,
> are lookin' for trouble." Crack at somebody here?
> . . . Van says of dead soldier buddy & himself, "We
> both wanted to make this country a free country,

for folks—all folks—to live in." Pinko sentiment,
maybe? Noticed one thing. Communists supposed
to be exploiting plight of Negroes in South nowadays. Well, this about Civil War issues & not a single Negro in it, not even one in background
strummin' on ol' banjo. I'd give it a clean bill of
health but wouldn't want anyone to think I recommend seeing it.[5]

My first major film score

I went back to New York City in October of 1946 to score
The Roosevelt Story, my most important film, a documentary of
our late and great President written by Lawrence Klee, di-
rected/edited by his brother Walter (Wally) Klee. Eleanor
Roosevelt had recommended me to the producers Martin
Levine and Oscar Unger. Unger came to my home in Hollywood to put the proposition. I took a cut in fee, but the opportunity to break out of the songwriter status and be responsible for an entire score was too good to miss. I worked five
months, with a Christmas break back in L.A., for a $5,000 flat
fee. I wrote a good song with Lewis Allan, "Toward the Sun,"
recorded on the sound track by the Robert Shaw Chorale, and
generally poured out my heart's blood for that film.

Facing my first major scoring, I became aware of an unexpected weakness in my knowledge and ability. Supposed to
write strong noble music for the exciting, progressive 1930s, I
came up with much more powerful scoring for the Hitler-Nazi
buildup leading into the war. Using Wagner's *Götterdäm-
merung* theme, satirically I thought, I misplaced the satire and
the music soared. One of the sound men said, "It's a shame the
Nazis get all the good music." My attempt to steal from Wagner didn't misfire, it fired all too well. I achieved greater success in the D-Day prayer scene; Mrs. R. invited Helen and me
to her apartment at 29 Washington Square West after the premiere (August 21, 1947), and told me she cried when she saw
it. Ads for the pic quoted Walter Winchell: "You have to see
'The Roosevelt Story' twice. Your orbs are crowded with tears
the first time."

A larger problem related to the script for the picture, by and large one long praise narration by a taxi driver who loved FDR. Anxious to restore some balance, I made strong efforts to include some clarity about FDR's position on Spain. The United States, along with England and France, had adopted a "neutrality" position there which had the effect of encouraging Hitler and Mussolini, not at all neutral in their support of Franco. My efforts were not wholly successful: The writer felt committed to his monochromatic treatment, and the film emerged with a sameness which contributed to a lack of popularity. The *New York Times* review—which failed to mention the score at all—said, "the whole tone is unmistakably eulogistic," "it lacks perspective," "an interesting, compelling document. But it does not cast any more light upon its subject than a campaign brochure would."[6]

The narrator does, however, say that FDR was sorry he had signed the Neutrality Act. (Mrs. R. wrote me an interesting letter on this, saying that the President had definitely been for the Loyalist side and wanted to help, but was deterred because the League of Nations requested no intervention.) As my private salute to progressive culture, I slipped a piece of the Russian song "Meadowland" into the score, and in another place used a hunk of "Rúmbala Rúmbala," a Spanish Civil War song. Of course, Roosevelt's positions on equality and peace and cooperation with the Soviet Union were under attack with the onset of the Cold War. Besides which, any film made independently of Hollywood had rather rough going.

Much as I tried to concentrate on the film job in New York, word shortly got out that I was in town. Every progressive organization wanted me to appear at its rally or banquet. In the lulls between spurts of work, I accepted a few bookings both in and out of town.

In February 1947 I flew out to Minneapolis and Chicago to sing. On the way back, in Detroit, I bought a newspaper at the airport, and read the horrifying news about the fire at Woody and Marjorie Guthrie's apartment that burned their daughter Cathy. I got back to New York and called immediately. Cathy lived for five hours in the hospital, Marjie told me, then died. I wrote to Helen: "They say she was burned so badly that she couldn't ever have recovered either her looks or her faculties. The fire came evidently from an electric plug, defective, caught the blankets, and they think Cathy tried to put it out. Marjie was just gone 5 minutes." I had met Cathy several times, a beautiful and talented little girl. Marjie's pregnancy with their next child may have given her other things to think about at the time, but I know that the pain and remorse over Cathy's death never entirely left her.

While working on the score, I accepted an invitation to sing in New York's Madison Square Garden at a 23rd Anniversary Lenin Memorial sponsored by the Communist Party. They paid me $100, but mostly I wanted to do something to answer the Cold War frenzy the Hearst syndicate was pushing. The performance was "reviewed" by *Time* magazine (February 3, 1947), which particularly noted my singing of Vern Partlow's "Old Man Atom" (aka "Talking Atomic Blues"):

> *We hold this truth to be self-evident*
> *That all men must be cremated equal. . . .*
> *Atoms to atoms and dust to dust,*
> *If you listen to the moneybags*
> *Something's bound to bust. . . .*
> *Listen, folks! Here's my thesis:*
> *Peace in the world, or the world in pieces.*
> *Whooooosh!*

The song did not fall in line with the Cold War and the Hiroshima approach of keeping the atom bomb secrets to ourselves. So *Time*, which in December 1940 had praised Paul Robeson and me for the *Ballad for Americans*, now pursued a different tack. Their report described me as, "Tall, talented [at least they gave me that], leftist Earl Robinson, crooning close to the Party line."

My appearance, together with doing the music for that "Red" Roosevelt, inspired a former Communist to whip up an expose in the Hearst *Daily Mirror* where he was working. That in turn alerted my producers, who called me in. Without denying my left connections, I said that it had no bearing on the score for their film. Which they accepted. I guess they reasoned that Mrs. R. would not have recommended anyone dangerous. But this and the Lenin Memorial appearance had unpleasant repercussions later.

After a New York farewell party held in my honor as a benefit for People's Artists, I went back to Hollywood, where some of us in the film industry worked at salvaging pieces of FDR's New Deal legacy. I sang the official world premiere of "Toward the Sun" at an April Shrine Auditorium meeting honoring Roosevelt that also featured Ava Gardner and Burl Ives.

The film debuted in Washington, D.C., at the National Archives Building, August 11, 1947, an affair packed with the capital's press corps and a host of prominent New Dealers. That day's *New York Journal American* carried a story about the opening, which breezily confirmed Robinson's 25 citations for Communist front connections helpfully supplied to the press from HUAC files. Two days later the same paper published an article, "Red-Led Unions Back FDR Film," exposing the heinous treachery involved in the hotel workers and other unions offering group rates to see the movie. Worst of all, those who put together the biggest theatre parties received a "decidedly pro-Russian as well as pro-New Deal" prize—a copy of Elliott Roosevelt's book, *As He Saw It.* Other fine upstanding Republican paragons of our free press churned out equally damning critiques.

Whatever the reasons—some lukewarm reviews, people in major cities not getting a chance to see it—*The Roosevelt Story* soon faded away, along with the 16-page study guide written by Allan Nevins, with surprisingly few re-releases. It did, however, win an award in the 1947 Brussels World Film Festival as "The Picture That Does the Most for World Peace and World Neighborliness."

Next on deck, a full score—songs and music—to a United Artists film, *Man from Texas*, with Wally Ford, Una Merkel, Sara Allgood, Bert Conway, and others, directed by Leigh Jason. Another western, this time about Jesse James, it involved writing songs, with Joseph Fields, to be shot with the movie, the score added after. I had fun during one of the chases "mickey mousing" the rise and fall of the two groups of horsemen, moving the music up in pitch as they topped a rise, then descending with them as they moved down the other side. The sound editor noticed this approvingly, but I wonder if anyone else ever got it. I was learning to get my strokes where I could. With "stars" James Craig and Johnny Johnston singing "My Darlin'," "El Paso Kid," "Sunday Song" and "Wedding Song," this was what could be a called a B picture, I fear, and not top-drawer Robinson either. It's a shame that just as I had finally made a claim for myself as a film composer, with this and *The Roosevelt Story*, the time came to start feeling the effect of the blacklist.

Notes

1. Steven H. Scheuer, ed., *Movies on TV*, New York: Bantam, 1985, p. 552; *The New York Times*, September 12, 1947.

2. *Variety*, July 2, 1947.

3. *Time*, September 29, 1947.

4. Lester Cole, *Hollywood Red*, Palo Alto: Ramparts Press, 1981, p. 253.

5. *New Yorker*, November 1, 1947.

6. T. M. P., *The New York Times*, August 22, 1947.

SECTION FOUR
1947-1957

THE GRAYLIST

The left in the immediate post-war years wasn't nearly so isolated as it soon became. In some people's minds a wholly Communist Party-dominated front, but in my judgment much wider in its liberal appeal was the Hollywood Independent Citizens Committee of the Arts, Sciences and Professions, on whose Executive Council I served. Yip Harburg was our secretary, Danny Kaye treasurer; Johnny Green chaired our music division. We had broad support for the September 2, 1946, Hollywood Bowl concert that again featured *The Lonesome Train*, plus nothing less than Artur Rubinstein playing the Tchaikovsky Piano Concerto and Larry Adler with a solo harmonica rendition of *Rhapsody in Blue*. Frank Sinatra sang a couple of songs. Florida Senator Claude Pepper spoke: "Small and half-seeing men at home and abroad are hurtling us, mistake by mistake, toward the certain horror of war."

Franz Waxman conducted the Hugo Strelitzer chorus of 100 and the Hollywood Bowl Symphony Orchestra, Gregory Peck acted as Narrator, Vincent Price did Lincoln, Alfred Drake was the Ballad Singer, and yours truly the Caller. We had 15,000 in attendance that Labor Day. Tickets ran from $1.20 to a $5 top.

Over time *The Lonesome Train* didn't exactly stall at the station, but definitely slowed down. Two years later I wrote to the publisher asking them to revise their way of doing business on the piece:

> Lower prices, larger volume. Henry Ford, Sears Roebuck, and a few others apply this principle and successfully. Why the hell can't Sun and Decca do likewise? Besides, I am getting sick and tired of having my indebtedness reduced by $23.36 or some such sum every three months. At this rate I will have a grey beard and grandchildren before I get a royalty check on what is probably the best composition I have ever written.[1]

My letter produced mixed results: Sun reduced the $2.50 price for the vocal score down to $1.50, but our royalties got cut accordingly.

How much of freedom must I give back?

Shortly after ABC Radio was formed in 1946, they commissioned me to write a celebration piece for broadcast. I went right to Abel Meeropol, who turned out a workmanlike text for a cantata which he named *The Town Crier*, appropriately using this historical figure and his cry of "Hear ye" to hail and salute the new network. I wrote good music for this; it received a splurge production, and I was unclear as to why it was aired only once, then dropped.

Town Crier's theme of freedom of information started to come under attack with the Cold War and the incipient Hollywood Ten blacklist. It's possible that Abel's and my left orientation came to the attention of the network after the broadcast. In any case, with the onset of television, radio got put on the back burner, and TV had little room for longer musical works, especially ones with a message. Neither the words nor the music moved the listener with the same kind of power as *Ballad* or *Lonesome Train*. A labor-oriented cantata, *The Big Ol' Tree*, commissioned for radio by the AFL-CIO a year later, also received a single broadcast on NBC.

In this period I made some half-hearted attempts at "serious" composing. I remember spending a lot of time with a piece in 7/4 time. I succeeded with a couple of songs with lyrics by Harry Schachter, "Good Morning" and "Come Along," which we conceived as song-and-dance numbers for children. "Come Along" took a trip around the world in versions of the "Varsovienne." But it was actually danced and sung not by children but by adults in Seattle, New York, Chicago, Los Angeles, and around. Which just goes to show, you can't trust the generation gap.

Jack Shapiro and I came up with "Quilting Bee" in about 1948. As a young boy I remembered how a family that needed a big job done, like painting a house or digging a basement or putting up a barn, would gather all the relations, friends, and neighbors for a day-long "bee." The women would prepare a big meal, while the kids would run around underfoot, trying to be helpful and sometimes being. Couple of weeks later, another family would have a bee and get their job done. So it seemed a natural thing to move the bee onto the international scene. If it worked so well for us little folks, why couldn't it work for all the people around the world?

> Oh, the world is all in pieces like a crazy quilt
> That's lying all apart, that's lying all apart.
> Each a different color and a different form,
> But put them all together and it keeps you warm.
> Pick up the pieces, let's do it right,
> Let's sew them all together, make 'em good and tight.
> Let's have a quilting (twice)
> Let's have a great big quilting bee.

The Weavers, who became rather famous shortly, recorded this tune in their usual boisterous, upbeat fashion on Decca, their picture gracing the cover of the sheet music.

With the coming of the blacklist, Abel and I collaborated congenially on a powerful song on racial discrimination, "If I Am Free":

> I am free and I am black,
> How much of freedom must I give back?
> Why do I stop at the halfway note
> With the freedom song stickin' in my throat?

This song, however, never had a chance to be heard. I even censored myself, choosing not to perform it too often for fear of getting myself into even deeper, hotter water.

I personally began to experience the blacklist when my agent let me know that the film composing jobs were drying up, blowing away. There didn't seem to be enough to go around. He advanced such reasons as: The industry was in a

mess economically; Hollywood was facing competition from
the burgeoning film companies in Europe; the Cold War was
affecting the market, etc. Whatever the reasons, my audience
began dwindling, then disappearing. After I appeared at the
1947 Lenin memorial program, I noticed a sharp drop in my
school bookings. Union bookings became rare; even black organizations became fearful.

I must mention a pleasant surprise when the International
Mine, Mill and Smelter Workers invited me to sing for their
46th convention over four days in September 1950. I knew
that union people had taken up my song "Joe Hill," but here at
this Denver hotel I found the panels of the hall decorated with
Al Hayes's verses. "Our official song," they proclaimed, and
the whole union rose to their feet and sang it with me. The
same thing happened in Canada, where working people even
more quickly adopted the song as their own.

In early 1948 newspapers bristled with the scandalous story
"House Gets Data on YWCA Reds," detailing how Communists had infiltrated that worthy organization over a twenty-
year period. Chief evidence consisted of the official songbook,
Sing Along the Way, which included "Joe Hill!"

Now, the reason I use "graylist" instead of "blacklist" for
this chapter is that I did not actually lose jobs that I already
had, as the Hollywood Ten did. Discrimination against me was
more subtle. I just didn't get any more offers. But the result
was no less effective: I couldn't work.

An important exception, John Houseman's L.A. stage
production of Howard Richardson and William Berney's play-
in-music, Dark of the Moon, brought me back into the theatre
world in 1947. The authors had adapted the traditional ballad
of "Barbara Allen" into a folk drama for a huge cast, with
Carol Stone as the protagonist. I wrote the musical score,
bringing in Pete Seeger and his five-string banjo as a singing
narrator. The show played the Coronet Theatre for a sold-out
month. Superb reviews brought in crowds we had to turn
away at the door.

A lovely singing movement

Not that we didn't fight back well and effectively. We did. The Henry Wallace for President movement was the big news of 1948. On February 24th of that year, I joined a delegation that delivered 278,619 signatures on petitions from Los Angeles County alone demanding the placement of a third party on the ballot. A celebration followed at our Progressive Citizens of America headquarters, where I entertained, as I did in July at the founding convention of the Progressive Party in Philadelphia. This right away landed me a rich citation in an article in the red-baiting magazine *Counterattack*, helpfully recording "Who's Who in Communists' Third Party."

Whatever the weaknesses of this new Progressive Party, which showed up in force with the Truman victory over Tom Dewey that November, this was a lovely singing movement, and in a way, the left's last gasp in the post-war years. Really it was the New Deal's last gasp, for Wallace had been FDR's Vice President before Truman, and he stuck with New Deal policies and values. He did not want to see our country embroiled in a war—hot or cold—with the Soviets. Aside from a song I wrote for Wallace, I scored (for piano), played, and narrated a film-strip called "Whose Century?" that contains perhaps my most dissonant music; and joined with Paul Robeson, Pete Seeger, Lee Hays, Michael Loring, the Singing Mechau Family, and countless folkies in singing our hearts out.

The campaign sent me traveling around the country, with appearances in the Twin Cities, New York (with Wallace's running mate, Idaho Senator Glen Taylor), and dozens of other places. Closer to home I sang at the home of Burl Ives in Van Nuys in support of a Progressive Party candidate for Congress, and a group of Korean-Americans for Wallace featured me at an election rally. Several times on the West Coast I warmed up the crowd for Wallace himself. The powers-that-be sabotaged our campaign in subtle ways. The Boise *Idaho-Statesman* placed the paid ad for our rally in a very prominent place—and gave the wrong date! They corrected it the next

day, but stuck the ad on the next-to-the-last page in with the
local grocery ads.

Still close to Eleanor Roosevelt, I told her I thought she
was wrong in saying that only the Communists would put up
a good fight for Wallace. All kinds of people liked him, I assured her. "It makes me feel bad to find myself so often lately
on the opposite side from you," I wrote her.[2] More than forty
years later I appreciate that basically she saw the situation correctly; but at the time I regretted that as a committed Democrat she felt forced to support Truman, when her real sympathies seemed closer to Wallace's New Deal-type program. (We
referred to Truman's administration as the Stacked Deal.)[3]

I also knew the Roosevelt children from various family
dinner parties over the years. I shared the program with Jimmy
Roosevelt for Russian War Relief and elsewhere. In February
1948 I attended a family dinner the day after a special election
in which the leftwing American Labor Party candidate Leo
Isaacson got elected to Congress from the South Bronx. None
of the Roosevelts had supported him. Thinking ahead to the
Presidential election in November, Franklin, Jr., said, "It looks
like we'll have to vote for Truman and hold our noses." For
one thing, the Roosevelt clan had not liked Truman's dropping
the A-bomb on Japan.

When Elliott was married to Faye Emerson, she confided
to me her impression that Mrs. R. loved Elliott the best of her
four boys. Elliott and Faye left early that night to attend the
opening of *Mr. Roberts* with Henry Fonda. On his way out, he
winked at me, remarking, "I'm phoning my review in to the
Daily Worker!" Just a joke, of course; but I think it meant that
I was welcome among the Roosevelts, not just for my songs or
my personality, but as a congenial representative of a point of
view they wanted to hear. After they divorced, Faye said her
big regret was losing Eleanor as her mother-in-law. Politically,
the Roosevelt children held widely differing views, but I remained on friendly terms with the whole tribe.

In 1949 or so Mrs. R. came to L.A., and I was feeling the
hurt of her sticking solidly with the Democrats, and (so it ap-

peared to me) lending herself to attacks on the Russians. Painting myself into a smaller and smaller left-wing corner, I didn't
call her. I was out of the house when *she called me*. When I got
home, Helen relayed Mrs. R.'s message. "I heard you were
sick," she said. It took me many years, until well into the
McCarthy period, to understand what she meant, and that she
was right. I must have been "sick" to have allowed a political
difference to come between me and this extraordinary, loving,
faithful woman.

It wasn't our fault that Wallace got only a million and
some votes. It turned out that his One World-Sixty Million
Jobs dream was a little out of date. Higher on the agenda stood
the anti-Soviet Cold War, the suspicion of the Russians discovering our atomic bomb secrets, the anti-Communist line at
home, and the blacklist. With the indictment of the Hollywood Ten, HUAC began riding high. The main thing that
upset me about HUAC was their success in creating fear, not
only in Hollywood, but among working people and professionals, which took away my natural audience.

Taking a crack at the Klan

Another way we musical people fought back was through
People's Songs, founded after the war. I served on its Board of
Directors. Again, just as music and theatre of the 1930s had
thrown their weight behind the workers' struggles, we committed our talents to helping common people take their rightful place in the democracy their blood had saved. People's
Songs really leapt into action in the 1946 National Maritime
Union strike on the east coast. We still felt that "art is a
weapon."

"Would you like to take a crack at Bilbo, Hearst, Rankin,
Hoover, and the Ku Kluxers in song or cantata?" I asked in an
article for the *People's World* (August 23, 1946).

> Would you like to work along with fellow song writers
> and singers, union folk and housewives, students and
> chorus leaders, organizing the business of making music

do a job that many and many a speech is unable to do? If you can say yes to the above and mean it, you are invited to join People's Songs.

We also encourage and give help on more general subjects, control of atomic power, Spain, the fight for peace.

Almost in direct answer, right-wing columnist George Sokolsky warned readers

to be vigilant when they see or hear a song issued by the People's Song, Inc., or by the Almanac Singers, a related outfit, that here is propaganda designed to destroy the American form of government by every means usable, including songs.[4]

Some of these songwriting workshops I taught at the Los Angeles branch of the California Labor School, a substantial independent educational institute founded in 1946 in San Francisco. Within a year or two, red-hunting California State Senator Jack Tenney and his Joint Fact-Finding Committee on Un-American Activities had branded the school subversive. When the federal government withdrew its non-profit tax status and charged it retroactively for back taxes—a common tactic to force struggling left organizations out of business—the school had to fold. While it lasted, a decade at most, it gave students a real grounding in economics, social sciences, and the arts, and always in an interracial setting.

People's Songs also acted as a booking agency for me and many others in that first post-war generation of folk and topical music that led to the Bob Dylans and Joan Baezes of a decade later. I sang at hundreds of rallies and meetings, as well as full Robinson concerts, so much so that the FBI clearly believed that when Robinson sang you could tell it was a Communist front organization. Well, without in any way diminishing all those good causes so right and necessary for their time, it usually was! I put in some time occasionally for the American-Russian Institute of Southern California, which sponsored a series of musical discussions in people's homes. One time I played Russian and American folk tunes and asked the audience to name which country they came from. They couldn't do it. I guess I was trying to prove something.

It was People's Songs in the late '40s that really spread the concept of the hootenanny, those musical potpourris where the distinction between audience and performers became blissfully blurred. Long before official "multiculturalism," we proudly presented musicians from various folk traditions on the same concert stage, and our audiences ate it up. By the way, do you know Woody Guthrie's explanation of the origin of that word? It seems a gal in Oklahoma had a well developed pair of lungs. She'd get to singing at a party and people would come from miles around, drawn by the wonderful sound of Hootin' Annie's voice. Pete Seeger discounted this story, however, tracing the word to my own home town of Seattle in the summer of 1941, where he (and Woody) of the Almanac Singers were sponsored by the Washington Commonwealth Federation, and that's what they called their monthly fundraising parties.

If you look into the 1940s and '50s you'll find so many "People's" organizations: People's Songs, *People's World*, People's Peace Crusade, People's Radio Foundation, etc.—all of which I supported, natch. How to account for this? In the post-war world, the left wanted to de-emphasize the word "worker" and the concept of class as too sectarian. After all, *everyone* wanted to be spared atomic destruction! The fascists had used the same term—*das Volk, il popolo*—but in their mouths it became a racist, xenophobic slogan of exclusion. So our use of the term helped to counter that image and restore a sense of universality.

And I think we were trying to capture a little glory from the new "people's republics" in Eastern Europe, countries under the Soviet system that had been freed from fascism and backward feudalism. Whatever their limitations—very severe in retrospect—to us these lands looked like beacons of culture and progress. The Communists in control there, many of them veterans of wartime resistance movements, within a few years had accomplished so much to bring industry, housing, and education back up to and surpassing prewar levels. Economic integration of the Soviet Union and Eastern Europe looked like a sample on one continent of what could be done in the rest of the world to equalize the terrible disparities between rich and poor. Plus, those countries actively encouraged Africa and Asia in their struggles for independence. So our "people's" culture aimed for justice, for humanity, for equality; in short, eventually for socialism—*American-style*, I would emphasize, because to us the Bill of Rights, starting with the First Amendment, meant everything. Perhaps we were naïve, but I believe our intentions were decent.

One issue of *People's Songs*, our publication, printed my lyrics to "The Unfriendly 19" (the original number of the Hollywood Ten), to the tune of "Tam Pierce," also known as "Widdecombe Fair":

SPOKEN: *Gather round me you lovers of the Silver Screen*
And I'll tell you a fantastic thing I have seen,
I'll sing you the song of the Unfriendly 19:

Parnell Thomas, Parnell Thomas, he tried a red smear,
All along Washington, Washington town,
And he called on 19 men to appear:
Albert Maltz, Lester Cole, Edward Dmytryk,
Sam Ornitz, Ring Lardner, Dalton Trumbo,
Herbert Biberman, Alvah Bessie, Adrian Scott,
And John Howard Lawson and all,
Old Uncle Jack Lawson and all.

To censor the movies was clearly his aim,
All along Washington, Washington town.
He thought he could do it by sland'ring the name
Of Albert Maltz . . . etc.

He just didn't figure these boys would fight back,
All along Washington, Washington town.
With klieg lights and headlines he thought he could
          crack
Albert Maltz . . . etc.

He tried to divide them, he treated them rough,
But they all stood together when the going was tough,
And Rankin and Thomas, they soon had enough
Of Albert Maltz . . . etc.

The big shot producers did Thomas fear
All along Washington, Washington town,
They groveled before him, they used his red smear
Of Albert Maltz . . . etc.

If we don't stand together and fight this wrong,
All along Washington, Washington town,
You may discover your name in this song
With Albert Maltz . . . etc.

Many times I sang to defend the Hollywood Ten. For if they could be persecuted, any of us could be.

I felt very close to Albert Maltz, my screenwriter for the *House I Live In* film. In 1946 he published an article in *New Masses* questioning the slogan "Art is a weapon," saying there could be good art with bad politics. I sent him a five-page letter admonishing him that he was drifting perilously close to approving of "art for art's sake." And that, for us dialectical materialists, was strictly *verboten.* You know how sometimes you state a strong position on something, because you need to be convinced of it yourself? Well, my change of heart came gradually, but come it did.

Maltz wound up going to prison in 1950 and '51. At that time Congress had established a system of concentration camps in this country, to be used whenever it should be decided to round up all the dangerous radicals. Major newspapers, like the *Los Angeles Times*, had stories about it, and we'd had the precedent of the Japanese-American incarcerations. Perhaps at no time in our history did a home-grown fascism appear so imminent. In prison, Maltz worried that he would be released from his sentence, only to be placed in a detention camp.

> And I remember on a bleak day in February, Lincoln's Birthday is the 12th, I was in the hospital, which was where I worked, and on came *The Lonesome Train*. And I listened to that with such excitement, I can't tell you. It was as though someone was saying, "Look, it's going to be all right. Things are not so bad." That piece of music and the personal link with Earl was for me a very high experience.[5]

One effort that People's Songs threw itself into was the Veterans' Motorcade to Sacramento, which took place in the Spring of 1947. At the end of the war veterans had been promised lots of housing and low rents, but two years later somehow it hadn't happened. With others from our singing organization I traveled with the caravan, pausing frequently en route to make our point, and composing original songs along the way, so our demand would be heard. With Sandy Arkin, Bea and Dave's son, we put some new words to a song by Yip and me from the movie *California*:

> *Kilroy was here and didn't like it,*
> *He's got a powerful lust,*
> *He wants a place to hang his toothbrush,*
> *He wants some housing or bust.*

In early 1948 I helped edit the *People's Songbook*, which sold well among our branches around the country. In part it answered my criticisms of songs submitted to us for publication. "Better music needed," I said, "real tunes that sing and have a higher musical value, twists and turns and beauty and strength to occasionally go beyond the extra simple folk song. And yet be very singable."[6]

Under pressure of the anti-Communist campaign, People's Songs folded in 1949, shortly replaced by People's Artists. In 1950 they started the magazine *Sing Out!*, which continues to this day. My name appeared on the masthead, and I contributed songs, lyrics, and musings on the passing scene over the course of its first few years. It remains a vital vehicle for getting songs out that address social issues.

From the start, however, I objected to the sectarianism, the holier-than-thou leftism in *Sing Out!*'s pages. They came out critically, for instance, against the Weavers' commercial compromises, not seeing that the times called for a different approach than the Almanacs had used ten years earlier. The main force behind this attitude was Irwin Silber, writer, editor, ideological theorist, a commissar-of-the-arts type, and our business manager. Twenty years later, and for the same reasons, he gave a rather sour review to Pete Seeger's fine, wholesome book *The Incompleat Folksinger*. I still considered Silber a friend, even collaborated with him on a book. But gradually I strayed far from his ultracorrect Marxist line, coming to feel ultimately that the theory of class struggle fails to account for everything in life.[7]

After the 1948 election I wrote to Truman enclosing my song from the movie *Romance of Rosy Ridge*, "I Come from Missouri." People kidded me, thinking I'd written it about Truman and his anticipated defeat, because in the last line the singer says, "And I'm a-going back to Missouri again some day." I assured the President that I'd written the song much earlier. But then I implored him

as a fellow American and fellow musician, not to renege on those noble promises made in the heat of the election battle. Implement your Civil Rights program, call off this Hitler-like red-hunt, abolish the Taft-Hartley Act, get together with Stalin or whatever is necessary to lighten the danger of a world war which will thrust civilization back centuries into barbarism. . . . Nobody but the people will be with you if you move ahead.[8]

No psalm-singing, please

The blacklist posed an impossible set of problems. On the one hand, I wanted to continue singing for causes which interested me, and not give in to pressures. I music-directed the first L.A. production of Blitzstein's *The Cradle Will Rock*, with Will Geer repeating his Mister Mister role from the original New York staging. On the other hand, perhaps it was wiser to recognize these pressures as real, and live with them if I wanted to support my family. I might have fought harder to stay in the film industry, but the tide rose against me.

I tried going back to my '30s working-class roots. I went to the L.A. CIO Council to talk with Slim Connelly about starting a labor chorus. He was all for it. We got a place with a piano and sent out the call. The national CIO had been bitten by the redbaiting bug, giving in to the Un-American Committee and the Taft-Hartley anti-Communist provisions, so the chorus hadn't been in existence much more than a month when Slim got removed from his position as local head of the CIO because of Communist sympathies. (He was married to Dorothy Healey, leader of the Communist Party in L.A.)

The chorus had too good a start to fold, however, and it continued, thirty strong, with a true poly-cultural membership and even a be-bop subgroup. Still under the CIO name we made one of our first public appearances in L.A.'s Embassy Auditorium at a meeting sponsored by the *People's World* to hear veteran Communist journalists Al Richmond and Joseph Starobin. When CIO sponsorship fell away we regrouped in 1949 as the California Labor School Chorus, and in 1950 as the Earl Robinson Chorus, singing for good causes. We did an impressive Leadbelly Memorial Hootenanny at Symphony Hall in March 1950. Another time, we had a big festival of labor choruses in L.A. Always we did a May Day program and included my "May Day" song.

Paul Robeson sang with us more than once, *Ballad for Americans* and other favorites. Not long after the infamous Peekskill Riot in upstate New York, Robeson came out to the West Coast to sing in a rally at the old Wrigley Field. A large human ring of trade unionists and veterans surrounded the podium to protect him, and no trouble resulted. We later learned that the police group on hand to keep order included Officer Tom Bradley, later Mayor of Los Angeles and an official sponsor of the Friends of Earl Robinson.

A delegation from the chorus drove out to the airport the day the Hollywood Ten flew off to Washington for sentencing on contempt charges, and we sang as part of the program before 1,000 well-wishers. Their kids clinging to their fathers' arms, these American prisoners of conscience walked out through the crowd to the plane that would take them away, and I admired them profoundly for their dedication.

Two more choruses warrant mention: one at the Dance Center, where I also had a youth orchestra. I programmed folk and ethnic songs a lot, wrote a couple of original songs for them, and we had guest singers like Pete Seeger, Odetta, and Ernie Lieberman when we performed at UCLA's Royce Hall. Anne Lief Barlin directed the Center; she's now living in Israel, teaching dance teachers how to teach.

In the fall of 1950, at the behest of Rev. Steve Fritchman, friend and minister, I started a choir at his First Unitarian Church of L.A. In this democratic church, Steve put the idea of a choir to a vote. The congregation voted it down, not wanting any psalm singing in their radical sanctuary. But (he later told me) Rev. Steve falsified the vote, knowing well the kind of chorus an Earl Robinson would produce. We programmed not only Bach and Handel, but folk and labor and progressive works by modern composers, at every Sunday morning service from then on. The choir became a fixture at First Unitarian for years. Which, by the way, the FBI knew all about—they had an SA (Special Agent) on the mailing list!

The Earl Robinson Chorus thrived for a couple of years. After I left for New York with Waldo Salt in 1951 to write *Sandhog*, it hung on two or three years before it folded.

Lending my name and talents

In 1950 a couple of ex-FBI agents calling themselves American Business Consultants, who had been issuing a newsletter *Counterattack*, put out a 213-page book, *Red Channels: The Report of Communist Influence in Radio and Television*. With research no doubt supplied by the FBI, it listed 151 people and their left-wing dossiers, culled from *Daily Worker* articles, open letters to public officials, letterhead endorsements and appearances for radical causes and organizations. The book clearly aimed to get producers and studios not to hire anyone listed. Those who resisted could be sure to get the American Legion and other "patriotic" groups on their necks with powerful weapons such as letters of protest, charges of pro-Communist sympathies, pickets and boycotts. About the earliest of my affiliations that *Red Channels* recorded dated from 1940, and the latest came from just a couple of months before it went to press. My entry ran a full two pages. For your amusement, here are the organizations they cited, to which I lent my name and talents—by no means an exhaustive list, I might add:

> People's Songs
> Joint Anti-Fascist Refugee Committee
> Congress of American Women
> National Council of the Arts, Sciences and Professions
> American Committee to Save Refugees
> American Peace Mobilization
> American Rescue Ship Mission
> Artists' Front to Win the War
> Hollywood Democratic Committee
> League of American Writers
> Hollywood Writers Mobilization
> International Workers Order
> School for Democracy
> National Federation for Constitutional Liberties
> Schappes Defense Committee
> Protest Against "Badgering of Communist Leaders"
> National Council of American-Soviet Friendship

The only one of these outfits that survived was the last named, though now that the Soviets have gone out of business they're probably defunct, too. I can't say which of these organizations you'd remember, but there's not a one I wouldn't fully endorse today.

For a while I actually debated changing my name. I didn't, but one thing I knew for sure. My income of $25,000 a year in 1945 and '46 dropped to $8-9,000 by 1950. *Red Channels* gave me a gentle push back East. If being listed effectively closed off work for me in film, radio, or television, maybe the New York live theatre world would be a better place to earn a living. There, among stage people, anxiety over past political loyalties didn't run so high: Actors' Equity protected its own better than the other unions.

Notes

1. Earl Robinson to Bill Downer, September 9, 1948.

2. Earl Robinson to Eleanor Roosevelt, February 2, 1948.

3. The classic study of the Wallace campaign is Curtis D. MacDougall, *Gideon's Army*, New York: Marzani & Munsell, 1965, 3 vols.

4. George Sokolsky, *New York Sun*, September 13, 1946.

5. Interview with Gwen Gunderson, May 30, 1982.

6. *People's Songs*, February/March 1948.

7. See the exchange of letters between me and Irwin Silber in *Sing Out!*, April 1952.

8. Earl Robinson to Harry S Truman, November 17, 1948.

MORE PAUL ROBESON

From the time that Big Paul sang *Ballad for Americans*, our paths tended to converge. Of course, his contributions, both home and abroad, were much more dramatic. As we both supported the antifascist character of World War II, we shared gigs at USO *and* Russian War Relief benefits. We both supported FDR's successful run for a fourth term. And we both shared the same vision of a better postwar world.

My connection with the White House and Mrs. Roosevelt was stronger than his. Mrs. R. once mentioned to me that she would like to invite him to the White House. And the President admired him. But he never went. I criticize myself for not taking responsibility for making this happen. I see now I could and should have. Both parties had a right to know each other better. But I lacked the confidence to take advantage of my position. I have always known instinctively that I brought people together with my music. Why didn't I feel free enough to take that additional step?

Robeson and I supported and celebrated Henry Wallace's bid for the presidency in 1948. And we shared a temporary heartsickness when the American people supported Harry Truman, who stole much of the Wallace program and became the "lesser evil" against Tom Dewey. (Seems like we've been voting for nothing but lesser evils ever since.) Paul's attempt to reach Truman for help on the slow path toward equality, and his lack of success in winning the President to a strong antilynching stand, were signs of the time. Another was Victor Records deleting his *Ballad for Americans* from their catalogue.

How a black man can operate

As the Cold War developed into the McCarthy red scare, Paul became politically ever more forthright, choosing more and more to challenge those in power. One experience I had with him profoundly thrilled me.

I got a call in March 1948 from Lou Gottlieb of the International Longshoremen's and Warehousemen's Union, offering me a free ten-day trip to Hawaii if I would accompany Big Paul on a series of concerts. It seems that Larry Brown, Paul's regular accompanist, had backed out because he hated to fly. And the only way to get around the islands was flying. I jumped at the chance, sharing the stage as soloist and accompanist for Paul. Those ten days were the most exciting, the most educational, the most fulfilling time of my life. When I returned I asked Larry Brown about him and flying. He told me, "I'd rather die in bed, surrounded by my grandchildren. And I haven't even begun yet!"

Consider that we were sponsored not by a regular concert agency, but by the union, which hired the halls, schoolhouses, and the usual entertainment venues. We weren't paid, but it didn't matter: We both felt so happy in this budding blacklist time to be singing for the union movement. The union sent concert proceeds to the families of two labor leaders, one Cuban and one Filipino, who had recently been assassinated for organizing.

Paul and I often roomed together, had many talks, and meshed artistically, politically, personally. He was one of the few people who ever called me "Earlie," and I savor to this day the caress of his voice as he pronounced that name.

We traveled by plane and car on six of the islands, presenting a total of twenty-seven concerts (fifteen of them public), averaging three a day, talking, listening, and learning from that marvelous polyglot people that make up Hawaii. Though only a U.S. territory then, the islands were totally and irrepressibly American in their enthusiasms and their healthy zeal for freedom. For instance, the Hawaiians loved baseball. Every child, it seemed, began swinging a bat at an early age. Passionate Yankees and Brooklyn Dodgers fans cropped up throughout our tour among all ages, sexes, and colors.

On the first day, in preparation for a concert in Honolulu, Big Paul learned four new songs—in Chinese, Japanese, Filipino, and Hawaiian. I was with him when this Filipino fellow

came up with a song for him. Paul listened carefully, memorized the tune, wrote down the words, and sang it on his program that night and thereafter. He was a master linguist. He
once explained to me why he was studying Chinese (quite a
few Chinese lived on the islands). "I want the Big Five—Dole
Pineapple and the others who own and run Hawaii—to notice
how a black man can operate."

At that time, racists argued against the evils of mixing
races: Offspring of interracial couples would tend to be sickly.
There were "scientific" attempts to prove this. Well, Paul and I
could not remember seeing more beautiful children anywhere
than those of Hawaii, young combinations of Japanese and
Filipino, white and Chinese, black and Hawaiian. "It would be
a tremendous impact on the United States if Hawaii is admitted as a state," he told the *Honolulu Star-Bulletin*. "Americans
wouldn't believe the racial harmony that exists here. It could
speed democracy in the United States."

In Hawaii, Paul tested and confirmed his wholly intelligent
theories about the similarity and crossovers of folk music.
Driving in the car one day between bookings, we noticed on
the radio a tune that we both thought might be Scottish. We
asked the driver: The song was Korean! The pentatonic scale
was almost exactly the same.

Paul made such a splash, I think the islands have not been
the same since. The leading paper in Honolulu had a full page
of letters every day we were there, one writer from the American Legion charging that both Paul and I had been cited as
Communists in a 1947 Congressional report. But the letters
ran about six to one in favor of Robeson, in spite of his never
pulling any punches. From a speech he gave at McKinley High
School, his final Honolulu concert, before 1500 people:

> I take no back steps, have no reservations to my love
> and support for the common folk, for the working
> people. But to those who run things, those higher-ups
> symbolized as the Big Five, from them I ask, and give,
> no quarter.

Now this was frightening stuff. I could never have said it, though it thrilled me to hear him say it. He stuck his neck out continually, and there were those who tried to chop it off. But plenty extended their hand as well: At that concert, the Hawaii Civil Liberties Committee granted honorary membership to us both. We sang for the Leper Settlement at Kalaupappa, where they joined in the singing better than anywhere else. To hear them sing "Aloha-oe" after we finished our concert moved us both almost to tears.

Paul had a light and winsome sense of humor. And he was a consummate singer of love songs. There is nothing on earth more tender than Paul singing "lulla lulla lulla lulla bye bye." His voice was more naturally a lyric instrument. Which is not to take anything away from the immense militant power he could bring to "Ol' Man River," the song he rewrote because it was too defeatist and reminiscent of slavery. The fact is, Paul Robeson could sing anything that appealed to him, including the classics. Anything with a tune at all memorable. A man for all seasons.

During the 1950s, the government tried to silence him. The State Department withdrew his passport, restricting him to the then forty-eight states, and a campaign was instituted to deny him any "respectable" concert halls. Paul answered, "They can't shut me up. How can they? I'll sing on street corners for two bits or whatever they can pay." And the big black Baptist churches opened their doors and their hearts to him. Two to three thousand people would turn out for him. I accompanied him on some of these concerts, sharing the singing on "Free and Equal Blues" as we did in Hawaii. Still, in those years, Paul saw his income drop from some $100,000 a year to about $6,000. In his own way he also managed to defy the big record companies that no longer issued his singing voice. He started up his own Othello Records and released several recordings; on *Let Freedom Sing!* he included "Joe Hill."

Bridge over the ocean

For some time in the late 1950s I had been in touch with a friend, George Alexan in East Berlin, who translated my opera *Sandhog*. (I jump ahead of myself now.) At one point he wrote to me asking how much it would cost to shoot a film with and about Paul Robeson for distribution in the German Democratic Republic (East Germany). Since Paul couldn't leave the country, the East Germans would pay for it to be shot here. I couldn't believe Alex at first. This was American dollars he was talking, from an East-bloc nation that "we" weren't even speaking to, without easy access to convertible currency. But he followed up the letter with a phone call insisting on a budget. I contacted some progressive film friends who put together a production team. Transferred to my bank, through a third party, came $10,000, and the same to Paul's, the total the producers required to shoot a union film. Big Paul and I, plus the directors, worked for nothing, and we turned out a good half-hour concert film for Deutscher Fernsehfunk called *Brücke über den Ozean*, which premiered at a 60th birthday festival for Robeson in East Berlin in 1958. It played for a number of years in the GDR and around socialist Europe. Paul looks grand and sings beautifully. I didn't do so bad myself. What at first seemed an impossibility turned into a small victory in those arid "un-American" years.

The next major togetherness with Paul came in socialist Prague, 1959. Robeson had finally got his passport back; in effect, he had been "sprung" by the British Actors Union which demanded that he be freed to come to Stratford and play Othello. I was in Europe, in the GDR to assist in and conduct *The Lonesome Train*. From there Helen and I traveled to attend the Prague Spring, an important annual music festival, and also to sing at the famous Czech spas. And in between *Othello* performances, who shows up in Prague but Big Paul, in need of an accompanist. We performed for a huge audience that included high government officials. This massive socialist audience loved him so. In fact, it's always been my sense that the tremendous responsibility he felt to meet the demand their love created may have contributed to his health problems which began to surface in the '60s.

On the way home from that trip, Helen and I stopped in London for a week. There we visited Paul and Essie in their apartment, and I saw an aspect of him that I had never sensed before. He wanted very much to come back to America, back to his homeland. Yet he feared that if he came home he might be shoved back into the "house arrest" that he had endured for eight years. And I saw this great strong man weep.

His monumental anger had always been directed at those who ruled the country, never at the land itself. And he loved the people, with tremendous, abiding affection. This all came out in his music.

SAN CRISTOBAL VALLEY RANCH

Meanwhile, back at the ranch

In the early blacklist years, I spent summers, 1949, 1950, and parts of '51 and '52, at the San Cristobal Valley Ranch, a recreational retreat eighteen miles north of Taos. Craig and Jenny Vincent hired me as a sort of social director, concentrating on music. These two beautiful lefty people, with Irving Bazer, manager of the ranch, gave sanctuary to me and Helen, Perry, and Jimmy. Craig was a true people's politician. He made his way into the Colorado legislature for one term. Then, the Depression being on, he became the director of the Colorado State Employment Service. And went from there to the U.S. Employment Service in Washington, D.C., where he became secretary of the CIO Council for two years. With the onset of World War II he transferred to the War Shipping Administration in New York, where they named him head of recruitment and manning of Liberty ships in the Atlantic Coast Office. Here he found himself happily carrying out presidential orders to eliminate racism aboard all American vessels. Craig was justifiably proud of his paving the way for minorities, resulting in Hugh Mulzac becoming the first black captain of a merchant marine ship, the *Booker T. Washington.*

A people's fighter his entire life, Craig was also a charming raconteur and storyteller. Here's one of his jokes: A farmer had a red cow and a white cow to be serviced, so he rented a prize bull for that purpose. He put the three of them in a yard, and the bull just stood around. Having city folks coming down for a fancy Sunday dinner, he told his hired man to watch and report. Well, just after the soup, the hired man burst excitedly into the dining room, with the news, "The bull fucked the red cow!" Embarrassed in front of his guests, the farmer took him aside, saying, "Look, you're doing fine, but these city people aren't used to such language. Suppose we find another word. If anything happens, just say 'surprised.'"

Right before dessert the hired hand burst in again, his face all flushed, and he stopped short. It looked like he'd forgotten the word. The farmer, thinking to help, asked, "Did the bull surprise the white cow?"

"Darn right he surprised her," answered the hired man. "He fucked the red cow again!"

So this is only some of Craig. Jenny, who married him after the war, fought the good fight her own way. A musician through and through, Jenny plays piano and also accompanies her lovely singing voice with a small accordion. I refer to her still as the "Rocky Mountain Thrush."

She and Craig had bought and established this San Cristobal Valley Ranch. There they welcomed, as had Camp Unity back East, progressives of all colors and persuasions from North America and the Caribbean, and Europe and Asia, too, in addition to members of the Taos Indian pueblo and Spanish speakers from the Sangre de Cristo mountains of New Mexico.

Sound subversive? Well, the Albuquerque office of the FBI thought so: They considered the ranch the "headquarters for the Communist Party" in New Mexico. I never saw any conspiracies there, though they reported me as the "west coast representative" of the ranch. All news to me, but maybe the FBI knew better. I can't say as I remember him, but the well-known professional anti-Communist star witness Harvey Matusow, who had infiltrated a number of organizations so as to finger Reds for HUAC, claims he visited the ranch in 1950, and somehow knew I was a Communist. Incidentally, 1950 is the last year the FBI had any supposedly definitive ID on me as a Party member.

From this rainbow crew at the ranch I would organize choruses and ensembles to produce mostly Robinson songs and cantatas for Saturday night performances. I did sections from *The People, Yes, Ballad for Americans*, and the entire *Lonesome Train*. The programs would be leavened by folk dancing to "La Raspa" and other Mexican-American tunes Jenny and I played on accordion and piano. And of course Israeli and other international dances as well. While in the area I'd do an occasional gig at the University of New Mexico.

The ranch was an ideal place to research Mexican-American and Indian folklore, and I took full advantage. Listening to the young Indians sing at night, from a spot within the Taos pueblo forbidden to most whites, I was astounded and thrilled. The autumn after my second summer at San Cristobal I composed in Los Angeles a trumpet-violin duet based on a Mexican dance tune, which became a Lester Horton ballet score called *Bouquet for Molly*. I expanded the scoring to trumpet, accordion, violin, and guitar, recording it for the dance. For a long time I considered this new composition a reach in the direction of serious music. George Antheil, with whom I studied a while in 1949 and 1950, wanted me to make a suite out of it, which I never could see my way clear to doing. Though I wrote this mainly for a celebration dance (an Anglo versus a Mexican cowboy after the same woman, danced by Bella Lewitzky), Lester Horton used the word "tragic" to describe the music. Music hits people in different, often unaccountable ways. Increasingly, Lester Horton's reputation grows as the West Coast's equivalent of Martha Graham, but he remained less eminent because of his progressive politics.

Our children

One day our young son Jimmy, age three, wandered off and we couldn't find him. His crib had been placed on an incline alongside a stream, and somehow he got free and disappeared. I reasoned that he would walk down hill, taking the path of least resistance, and I followed the stream down, my heart in my mouth, expecting to find his drowned body somewhere near. Well, Jimmy was discovered *up the hill* a good ways from where he had been left, hale and happy and not even crying. He chose to climb rather than take the easy path. Which confirmed the strong leanings we'd begun observing in him, and foreshadowed somewhat his subsequent career. The day of his birth, July 23, 1947, a Mine, Mill and Smelter Workers Union organizer named Jim Robinson died, and we named Jimmy for him. It seemed in the cards for Jimmy to be a working man, a fixer. Jimmy never used any toy tools. He was playing with a real chisel and hammer at the age of two. Our older son Perry's music stand was always falling down and he had no idea how to fix it. One day Jimmy went at it on his own. He simply inserted a small dowel in the bottom and made the stand stand up. This was about the age of five and we were all amazed.

Graduating from a New York City high school that sent its students to the best colleges in the country, Jimmy never even applied for college. He went to work in a law office, and we had visions of his going on to become a lawyer. We should have known better. He listened instead to a union organizer who told him he should ship out as a seaman before doing anything. So before we knew it, Jimmy joined the National Maritime Union and waited his turn for a job on a boat. He worked on the Great Lakes, then made his way to the West Coast, where freighters were heading for Viet Nam. I saw him off on one loaded with napalm. He was a seaman first: It would have done no good to advise him to skip ship and join the picket line of young folks opposing the war.

Jimmy became an organizer and president of a union local. He organized a young Puerto Rican woman on a picket line and that's how I'm a grandfather. That marriage lasted seven years. He speaks Spanish fluently. He has taken up photography in an effort to supplement his organizer's wage. For the last couple of years I've been using a very expressive picture by him as my press photo. As close to me as Perry, he is a perfect joy.

As for our older son, I mentioned the touch-and-go circumstances of his birth. Quiet rebel that he is, Perry survived his chancey beginnings. At first, I knew consciously very little about what being a father meant. Trying to be a good one, I spanked him once—he had broken a vase—and I regretted it ever since. We started him on piano lessons early and he would trick the teacher into playing a piece for him so that once he heard it he didn't need to learn to read the music. He struggled

My beautiful mother and me. From the Special Collections Division, University of Washington Libraries.

Warm, *heymish* Helen. From the collection of Jim Robinson.

A sample of Helen's work. Her message is always in season.

The multi-talented me. On guitar. From the collection of Jim Robinson.

And on piano. From the Special Collections Division, University of Washington Libraries.

Rehearsing for a 1944 Broadway for Roosevelt program at the Hotel Astor, sponsored by the Independent Voters Committee of the Arts and Sciences. Ethel Merman, seated; L-R: Charles Friedman, Moss Hart, Beatrice Kaufman, Frank Sinatra, Yip Harburg, and me. Check out my profile in the mirror behind Frankie.

And down below, that's Woody Guthrie and me, teaching boxing champion Joe Louis how to play the guitar. From the Special Collections Division, University of Washington Libraries.

The Lonesome Train
(A Musical Legend)

Text
MILLARD LAMPELL

Music
EARL ROBINSON

They were his people, he was their man.
You couldn't quite tell where the people left off,
And where Abe Lincoln began.

The vocal score published by Sun Music Co. in 1945.

In this glorified western with high aspirations and production numbers, Barbara Stanwyck sang my "Lilly Aye Lady O." I started hitting my stride as a film composer just when the blacklist struck.

Paul Robeson and me. We were friends from the time he sang *Ballad for Americans* in 1939 until he left us in 1976. He was one of the few people who ever called me "Earlie," and I savor to this day the caress of his voice as he pronounced my name. He also performed my "Spring Song," "Joe Hill," and "The House I Live In." From the Special Collections Division, University of Washington Libraries.

New Jersey Governor Thomas H. Kean recited "The House I Live In" at the Republican National Convention of 1988. We later met at his office in Trenton. "I'm a fan of Paul Robeson," he said. "He's a Jersey man, you know. I have every one of his records."

My two sons—Perry the musician and Jim the labor organizer. I love them both in equal measure. From the collection of Jim Robinson.

"I never died," said Joe Hill. Seventy-five years later, we came together in Salt Lake City to celebrate his memory. L-R: Ken Shaw, Mark Ross, me, Pete Seeger, Faith Petric, Joe Glazer, Utah Phillips. Photo by Andrew Connors for the Joe Hill Organizing Committee.

Looking ahead. Photo by Jim Robinson.

Eric Gordon with me at a Jesse Jackson rally, April 1988. Photo by Rick Barnett.

Think of me and I'll be present. From the collection of Jim Robinson.

with a clarinet his grandfather Pop Wortis gave him, and in time this became his instrument. He has become a master jazzman and improviser par excellence. He later took up flute and saxophone—necessary adjuncts for a clarinet player to make a living—but dropped them both. He has a lifelong problem with creating and holding onto money, though he has overcome this partly with the help of friends, of whom he has a tremendous number. Loaded with talent, he continues to win *Downbeat* polls, and shows unexpected ability organizing unusual concerts around New York and northern New Jersey. I love him deeply and wish for him only to realize that he has already made it, that he is great regardless.

Three by three by ten

My brave Helen never stopped our attempts to have another baby. She underwent five miscarriages between delivering Perry and our adopting Jimmy. The thought of having a girl child had a deep hold on me ever since Perry. Once, the hospital in Los Angeles called me to ask what kind of burial did we want to give the miscarried child? I tried to avoid the decision, saying, "It doesn't matter, cremation, whatever."

"That will cost you $25," they said. "It's the mortuary law." So I paid.

The doctors had told Helen that she might as well give up having another child. She had been menstruating irregularly, so it was a surprise in San Cristobal that first summer when she began having abdominal pains. Her stomach was nicely rounded, but neither of us had any thought of what was to happen. I started clocking the pains, and when the timing got down to seven minutes, I called the doctor at the local Taos hospital. He told me to bring her in, and less than an hour later Helen delivered a baby too small to live.

We didn't expect to have anything to do with this fetus, but one of the nurses, bound not by any mortuary rules, but by her human empathy, approached me. "I can give the baby to you," she said. "You can take care of it any way you like." This being no big-city hospital, they charged no fee for burial.

So she presented me with this little box, three inches wide and three deep, by about ten inches long. An indescribable moment came as I opened the box in my car, alone. There lay a tiny, but perfectly formed girl baby. Helen didn't want to see her. With her permission I took it over to the Rio Grande, where I found a recessed hole among the rocks above the river. I kissed the little lady, placed her in the hole, and filled rocks in over the box. A decent burial, I thought.

Just one concluding fact. The next summer I went back to the burial spot and pulled the rocks away. The box was gone!

A final story about San Cristobal. In a moment of pique, Helen told me straight out that she had slept with another man. It was the first and (I believe) only time it happened. And I could do absolutely nothing about it: I had been sleeping with other women since early in our marriage. At the time, in fact, I had an affair going with one of the guests at the ranch. So I could only accept her action as justified reciprocation. I even kept on friendly terms with the guy for a time—till I realized after a couple of weeks that nothing required me to do so. I grew colder and he caught on immediately. It blew over after a while, and it came to make no difference in our relationship, though I carried a quiet chip for years. The "chips" on Helen's shoulders, I realize now, could have weighed a ton! Not an easy burden for her to have borne. Only recently could I totally forgive the guy at San Cristobal, Helen . . . and myself. Forgiving is a wonderful thing, very healing.

WALDO AND ME

Hollywood eleventh
"Maybe the blacklist is the best thing that ever happened
to us. It might break us of our lazy habits, because we've been
relying on the film industry, whereas we should be getting out
and doing what we really want to do." The speaker finished
with a flurry, throwing his challenge out to the crowd, then sat
down next to me on a platform we shared in 1951.

He was Waldo Salt, screenwriter for *Rachel and the
Stranger*, *The Shopworn Angel*, and many more. He survived
the first indictments of the Hollywood Ten. There had been
nineteen slated to be called, but Albert Maltz, John Howard
Lawson, Ring Lardner, Jr., and the others who took the First
Amendment fought back so strongly and well that HUAC
could only take ten at first. Scheduled to appear, he wasn't
called, so Waldo used to refer to himself as "the Hollywood
Eleventh." For the time being, Waldo and eight others were
still free to work, and he continued at his salary of upwards of
a thousand a week for a year until new calls from the Committee came along. Meantime the Supreme Court ruled the First
Amendment defense of the Ten invalid, and they went to jail
for contempt of Congress. The new line became—if you didn't
want to go to jail—take the Fifth. Which Waldo did and
promptly found himself out of a job.

I thought his speech rather cavalier—"we should be getting
out and doing what we really want to do." So I said, "Do you
really mean that? How would you like to do something
worthwhile with me?" One unexpectedly good thing about the
blacklist: It produced collaborators—writers—with time to
work with me.

We decided on a musical. From the first we saw eye to eye,
both of us excited about a Theodore Dreiser story, "St. Co-
lumba and the River." In February 1908 Dreiser published a
feature article in *Munsey's Daily News* celebrating the completion of the first great tunnel under the Hudson River, which

231

had been begun in 1874. Richard Creedon, a worker employed on the tunnel being cut under the East River to Brooklyn, served as the prototype of our musical hero, Irish immigrant Johnny O'Sullivan. On March 27, 1905, the force of compressed air blew Creedon through the roof of the tunnel and through the silt and mud of the river bed, shooting him up over the river practically unhurt. Dreiser wove this event into his story.

Twice Waldo got RKO Pictures to take an option on the story, and twice they dropped it when he was called before the Committee. So we saw no problem getting the rights for a musical.

Alvin Manuel, agent for the Dreiser estate, didn't want to give us the rights for two reasons: One, the blacklisting of Waldo. All the papers had reported it, and Manuel was frightened. Two, an even bigger reason, was that Manuel thought he had a hot property here, due entirely to Waldo's persuading RKO to option the story for a picture that only he would work on. For a time we thought that my position of not yet having been called before HUAC could be used to get the rights, but it turned out that my graylisted status was scarcely better than that of the unemployed writers.

Facing an intransigent Alvin Manuel, we went over his head to talk with Helen Dreiser, Theodore's widow. We found her kind and receptive. She pulled in a cousin of the family who was also open to our request, and together they instructed Manuel to grant us the rights. Manuel made a further effort to screw us. He wrote an impossible contract requiring us not only to complete the musical but get it produced on Broadway *within a year* from the signing. This being clearly too burdensome, we went back to Helen Dreiser to get better terms. She and her cousin again instructed Manuel, and this time we signed an option—for no money, we had none—to deliver a completed musical for Manuel's perusal a year from date.

A very beautiful period followed. A year seemed like a good long time. In June 1951, stopping at San Cristobal on the way, we moved our families cross-country to Brooklyn, and we became totally enamored with the Irish. Where Dreiser had treated his hero with somewhat humorous disdain, satirizing his fear of water, we researched Irish folktales and songs in detail and gave our hero Johnny a mate, Katie. It took six months and the whole first act to bring them together in Ireland. The main story of building the tunnel under the Hudson River, connecting Hoboken and Manhattan at Morton Street, and Johnny's getting blown up through it, we began to write only in the last three months of the year. What with the complications of our move East, finding apartments, and our bohemian pace of work, we woke up in the twelfth month with the entire third act to be finished. I could improvise the music if necessary, but words and lyrics had to be put down on paper in a recognizable play script. This was essentially Waldo's job; he put in longer and longer hours those last weeks, until we decided it didn't really matter what he put down, just so we made the deadline. The last two nights, neither of us slept.

A little after midnight of the last day of our contract year, I got to the central Brooklyn post office. The postman knew me by then, was sympathetic, and agreed to postmark our package to Alvin Manuel with that day's date. As I left, he expressed a heartfelt wish. "I sure hope you win that contest!"

So passed the first of three years spent writing *Sandhog*. In between, Waldo and I turned out some other work together. The Union of Electrical Workers commissioned a song from us, and we wrote "The Power of U.E." (published in the January 1952 issue of *Sing Out!*). I also scored *End of Summer* for accordion, guitar, and voice. A short film by Al Mozell, it's a gentle, nostalgic tone poem on the waning of summer, with a lovely song, "My Fisherman, My Laddy-O," to Waldo's lyric. Bina Mozell, Al's wife, sang it in the film. It was published in *Travelin' On with the Weavers* (Harper & Row, 1966), for they recorded it nicely; I also recorded it later on. Capitalizing on its modest popularity, Sanga Music published a choral version.

A workers' opera

When we got around to looking at the carbon copy of the *Sandhog* script, we realized some important things. Many of the songs scrawled out in such a hurry would have to be dumped. We needed more living with Irish sandhogs to communicate the flavor of their lives. Most important, we cut the whole first act and began with Johnny and Katie in New York, married and looking for a home. And we incorporated the horns and whistles, the whole atmosphere of river sounds, that we heard from the back porch of our house on Cranberry Street in Brooklyn Heights.

We began our real sandhog research by joining the James Connolly Society. This true Irish revolutionary had deep roots in the working class. And the society in New York named for him included some of the noblest, most humorously alive people I have ever met, such as the Irish American Joe Kehoe, organizer and secretary-treasurer of the Communications Union, and adviser extraordinaire to Waldo and me on our musical. There was Sean Cronin, full of good thoughts and advice on the Irish "troubles." And the Irish subway workers from Mike Quill's union, who loved our musical, especially the tender parts, and Tim Murphy, president of the sandhogs. Tim Murphy became the inspiration and prototype for Tim Cavanaugh, Johnny's friend and adviser. We characterized Tim as having learned tunneling the hard way—tunneling his way out of a British prison. Tim advised Johnny, as Tim Murphy advised us, that a worker becoming a foreman while still representing the sandhogs decently would be "contrary to fact." Tim and I shared boilermakers together—whisky with a beer chaser. His congeniality somewhat concealed a native shrewdness that did not become clear till much later.

With *Sandhog*, the path to production did not come easy. This was the McCarthy period, remember. Both the professional redbaiters' organ *Counterattack* and the American Legion's aptly named *The Firing Line* denounced Waldo and me as Communists as soon as word of our project went out. And no production outfits were hanging around with money to

back two blacklisted writers with a dream of a workers' opera
in their heads. As we kept working on the piece, Waldo and I
developed a presentation superb in its clarity, humor, and
strength, and we toured it around to our friends' living rooms.
They may all have been sympathetic to our folk opera, which
is what we began to call it, but though New York was considerably freer of fear than Hollywood, we couldn't raise much
money. One time Waldo assured me that he was *not* prepared
to produce *Sandhog* "underground"!

We did, however, work well with the sandhogs. At first.
There were no tunnel jobs at that time, but we talked with
them extensively on how exactly the bends felt. "You have a
toothache? It's ten times as bad. You wouldn't wish it on your
worst enemy." All of that went into our "Song of the Bends."
The theme of pride in their work found magnificent expression when we drove through the Brooklyn-Battery Tunnel
with two black sandhogs. They described a scene just after finishing that tunnel where they both turned to each other at the
same time and screamed, "We made this!!" Waldo and I followed our Marxian impulses in wanting to make our opera a
blow for the working class—to give them pride in themselves
and their labor. Not to move them toward socialism necessarily, but if you encourage a worker's pride in a good job well
done, you've helped a long way. So the sandhogs' approval of
our opera became very important.

The entire sandhogs union executive committee came over
to my apartment in Brooklyn Heights to hear Waldo and me
sing and talk through the show. Most of them liked it. I remember the little Italian secretary-treasurer saying, "When I
first heard about this show, I didn't think much of the idea.
But you know, that music brightens things up a lot." Only
Tim Murphy expressed disapproval. He was covering his bets
for something he foresaw might happen later.

We finally got real production interest from two blacklisted people, Arnold Perl and Howard da Silva of Rachel Productions, who had made a hit off-Broadway with *The World of
Sholem Aleichem*. They loved the piece and brought us to the

Phoenix Theatre, down on Second Avenue and 12th Street. There T. Edward Hambleton and Norris Houghton had just scored a hit with *The Golden Apple* (John Latouche's words and Jerry Moross's music), and they agreed to coproduce *Sandhog* with Rachel Productions. *Counterattack* countered by reminding its readers that the Phoenix had—according to them— steadily employed known pro-Communist actors in pro-Communist plays.

The production of what we finally called "a ballad in three acts" was a mixed blessing, with emphasis on the positive. Jack Cassidy was perfectly cast in the part of the volatile and vulnerable Johnny O'Sullivan, his excellent tenor voice with a well realized young Irish timbre. Alice Ghostley sang well the hardbitten wife of Tim Cavanaugh but did not come across as hardbitten enough. David Brooks, the other "name" in the cast, and more of a romantic lead, had a superb voice but did not quite realize Tim's irascible, revolutionary pungency. In a by and large fine cast I give high marks to Gordon Dilworth as Sharkey the Tammany politician, Paul Ukena, Mordecai Bauman, Michael Kermoyan, and Leon Bibb, who created so well his role of Sam on the Stick that I incorporated his variations into the published version. The children's chorus, exuberantly choreographed by Sophie Maslow with rope skipping and ball bouncing, was a continuous joy, as they both deepened the mood and lightened the heavier parts. They included the young Eliot Feld, now a recognized ballet master. Hershy Kay supplied high-level orchestrations, and Ben Steinberg conducted. Bob De Cormier, besides singing the role of a policeman, did a fine job with the chorus, which is basic to any production of *Sandhog*. Bernard Gersten, now head of the theatre at Lincoln Center, was stage manager.

Coming now to the "mixed" part of the blessing, Waldo and I felt that the huge stationary set by Howard Bay—around which he created a variety of playing areas—though it drew oohs and ahs and some good notices, was too big for the production. It dwarfed and belittled the more personal scenes in the Cavanaugh flat, positioned some thirty feet in the air and reached by ladders. Nor were we totally happy with Howard da Silva's direction. He just didn't know how to handle a production of this complexity—the mass scenes, the chorus of sidewalk supervisers, the sandhogs in the tunnel and on the picket line. He was better with the individual scenes.

Before opening night our producer T. Edward Hambleton called me and Waldo in to question us about our politics. The FBI had obviously visited him; though in any case neither Waldo nor I hid our views very well—the *Daily Worker* publicly promoted my appearance at a meeting to "Defend the Bill of Rights and Repeal the Smith Act" put on by the Citizens Emergency Defense Conference, which Waldo served as treasurer. ("On February 17, 1954, Special Agents of the FBI observed EARL ROBINSON entertain with songs at the above mentioned affair.") But our producer had no intention of backing out.

The sandhogs union was something else. The feds scared them out of supporting us and our show. They asked questions like, "Do you fellas know that those two writers, Salt and Robinson, are Communist?" And the bold and sturdy sandhogs—some of them—folded. Tim Murphy was able to keep his presidency because he reminded them that *he* didn't like the show, and had never cared for the script since we first showed it to them. Remember I said the man was shrewd. The sandhogs' position, however, aside from perhaps losing us a small part of our audience, did not shorten the run or affect the production. The Connolly Society continued to support the show, and some other redbaiting efforts only had the effect of uniting the cast behind da Silva and Waldo and me. It was a typical example of the FBI butting in once all the money had been invested and trying to destroy a work of people's culture.

To complete the picture of this production: It ran six weeks, the time allotted for actors to be paid an off-Broadway basic scale, at the end of the year 1954. They considered transferring it to Broadway but refrained because they had lost their shirts attempting to do that with *The Golden Apple*. The reviews ran the gamut from lukewarm to generally good, and some excellent. In some people's opinion *Sandhog* is my best work.

"It conveys the sounds and the flavor of street scenes, of everyday city byplay, more convincingly than any other musical show I can remember," said John Lardner in *The New Yorker*. Brooks Atkinson in *The New York Times* wrote, "Another original musical has come to Second Avenue. *Sandhog* is enterprising and versatile . . . a beguiling piece of work . . . embellished with saucy sidewalk dancing."[1]

By Broadway standards not a successful show, *Sandhog* commanded not a cast album but a very good "composer's album" on Vanguard Records. With their recording magic, they made it possible for me to sing not only the "Johnny-O, Katie-O" duet, but the entire four-voice "Fugue on a Hot Afternoon in a Small Flat." Those sessions at the Brooklyn Masonic Temple on Lafayette Avenue had a rare intensity. Out of sheer desire Waldo and I made up for the absence of an orchestra, transforming a composer's run-through into a fully-staged performance, at least in our imagination. We sold 1,600 records, one to Eleanor Roosevelt. Another copy excited the Soviet composer Dmitri Kabalevsky, who told me in New York once that his sons loved it. Chappell, the publisher of Broadway music, put out the entire vocal score and a few individual songs as sheet music. "Katie-O" showed Vince Martin on the cover—he had crooned the number on Glory Records.

The *High Fidelity* review appreciated *Sandhog* well. It alludes to *Kismet*, which was a hit in 1955:

> One comes away from this recorded synthesis with the feeling that the American theatre is seriously sick when a musical of such obvious quality is left to languish in a downtown alley while every theatrical and promotional opulence is lavished upon the burglarized melodies of Borodin who, being dead, is unable either to collect royalties or protect his good name.[2]

Sandhog received a production by San Francisco's Opera Ring, another in Sydney, and it was filmed, broadcast, and produced on several stages in Czechoslovakia and East Germany (as *Sandhog* and as *Die Maulwürfe von Manhattan*—literally, "The Moles of Manhattan"). This latter production, March 1960, by the Landesbuhnen Sachsen, the State Opera at Radebeul, had no less than Klaus Tennstedt at the podium. The most convincing case that a huge Howard Bay-type set was not needed came from the Speech Department at Northwestern University. Robert Schneideman had been directing Brecht often and well in the Midwest, and he readily understood what *Sandhog* was all about. In February and March 1959, in a small theatre seating 200, using just lights and sound, he created a more exciting production than the Phoenix. The oppressiveness of the tunnel so pervaded the theatre, I remember a woman running out before the end of Act I crying, "I've got to get out of this damn tunnel!"

The famed Komische Oper in East Berlin produced *Sandhog* in 1960, and Kabalevsky happened to see it. "The production could have been livelier and more dynamic," he wrote to me, "but even in this production, many scenes of the spectacle made a very strong impression."[3] Kabalevsky told me the opera had already been translated into Russian, and that he wanted to stage it at home, but I can't say if this ever came about—in those days the Russians weren't into paying royalties.

I have never before or since worked in such a perfect and satisfying collaboration as I enjoyed with Waldo Salt. Our relationship was characterized by total love and respect. Lacking his experience with words, I sometimes had trouble expressing criticism. He would pursue my half-spoken thoughts, dig my meaning, and go rewrite the scene even more beautifully.

After *Sandhog*, we contemplated other projects together—a light musical about the American Revolution and a ballet based on the *Song of Songs*, but neither came off. Waldo worked "under the table" on films for a while. See Woody Allen's movie *The Front* for a demonstration of how people had to work in those times. When the blacklist broke, Waldo came back to write two Oscar-winning scripts, *Midnight Cowboy* and *Coming Home*. He also wrote *Day of the Locust* and *Serpico*. It makes you wonder what great works were lost to our American culture with so many artists prevented from creating during those years. We always treasured the idea of rewriting *Sandhog*, simplifying it to reduce production costs, making it more available for smaller theatres. In 1987, under the pressure of a debilitating emphysema, and some strong production interest, Waldo cut down on his film writing and got together with me to fix our piece. But after just two sessions he became too sick to continue.

Notes

1. Brooks Atkinson, *The New York Times*, November 24, 1954.
2. *High Fidelity*, August 1955.
3. Dmitri Kabalevsky to Earl Robinson, November 16, 1960.

"BLACK AND WHITE":
AN UNFINISHED CELEBRATION

The ink is black

The historic 1954 Supreme Court decision outlawing segregation in the public schools of our land naturally inspired me to song. Even before that, in October 1952, *Sing Out!* magazine had me on the cover, and inside ran my seven-page choral number "If I Am Free," text by Matthew Hall (aka Lewis Allan, aka Abel Meeropol), on the theme of equality. In 1954, with Lee Hays, I wrote "Side by Side" (or "Study and Learn Together"), a singalong "spiritual" which went

> *We will study and learn together side by side* (repeat)
> *For a new day's begun*
> *In the light of the rising sun*
> *We will study and learn together side by side.*

To present this song properly, Lee organized a quartet consisting of him and me, Marian, our beautiful spiritual-singing housekeeper, and little Jimmy Robinson, scarcely seven years old at the time. We'd perform it at churches, meetings and wherever we could. "Side by Side" never went anywhere; maybe the tune just wasn't memorable.

Another song from 1954 did not take on any commercial importance for almost another twenty years, but eventually took off like a rocket to the moon. David Arkin, an artist and my brother-in-law (married to Helen's sister Bea), decided independently of me to celebrate the nine justices' decision. He wrote a deliciously simple lyric:

> *The ink is black,*
> *The page is white,*
> *Together we learn*
> *To read and write* (repeat).

For now a child
Can understand,
This is the law
Of all the land (repeat).

Bill Oliver, drama critic for the *Los Angeles Herald Tribune* before he was blacklisted, composed a classical-type setting, which Dave didn't care for. So Dave gave the lyric to me and I took it to the state of Washington the summer of '54. There, during raspberry season, in the Grapeview schoolhouse near my folks' home, I created the song "Black and White."

It didn't do much right away. Instead, it acted like a folk song, finding its own way, in its own time, to its audience. *Sing Out!* magazine published it (with "Side by Side") on May 1, 1956, as did Alec Templeton (later bought out by Fred Waring and the Shawnee Press). Somehow it came to the attention of Sammy Davis, Jr. A curious thing comes from Sammy having embraced Judaism—"the only Jewish Mau Mau," he would say. The B'nai B'rith Anti-Defamation League asked him to cut a record for their members, and in October '57 he put "The House I Live In" and "Black and White" back to back on a 45. In 1960 I got a call from CBS, the first occasion in many years that CBS had been in contact with me. They wanted to clear the song for national broadcast. Edward R. Murrow's crew had filmed a group of Peace Corps-type volunteers for a show called "Crossroads Africa." The Americans were helping the locals build a recreation hall, using "Black and White" to teach English, while focusing on the problem of desegregation in America.

In England, the song picked up speed. A church song book reprinted it. The Spinners recorded it and it crept up the British pop charts in 1971. Another version by Greyhound reached the British Top Ten. In America the song lay in a quiet sleep.

The three dogs

One day in early 1975 I got a call from a friend. "Did you know that Three Dog Night is singing your song?" At the time I didn't know who the three dogs were.

Well, I found out: a highly successful folk-rock group who had recorded my song a couple of months before. (The only time you have control of your song is before the first recording. After that the song may be recorded by anyone. All they have to do is pay royalties to the copyright owner. So Three Dog Night was already paying my publisher before I met them.)

They told me they first heard the song in England, broadcast on the radio from Holland. They knew immediately it would be a hit. It made the charts several weeks in a row, ending up number one. Sold over a million singles that first year, and $1 million sales on the album *Seven Separate Fools*. And the Robinson family ate—though I shared a percentage with Bill Oliver, who had persuaded Dave Arkin to cut him in on the royalties thanks to his having written the first tune to Dave's lyrics. I felt upset about this for a while, but the amount of money the song made—probably more than from any other number—soothed me. The 28-year royalty period came due a few years ago and I am no longer paying money to Bill Oliver's widow. Bea Arkin and I go on sharing, however.

Dave also created a lovely illustrated children's book using the lyrics to the song, which the Ward Ritchie Press brought out in 1966. Our U.S. government bought up quite a few of these and distributed them in seventeen countries, saying it exemplified American democracy at its best—while both lyricist and composer were blacklisted! During the civil rights era, black people all over the South used the song in literacy tests to prepare voters for the polls. I'd like to see this beautiful book back in print: Unfortunately, racism is still very much with us.

I sing "Black and White" to this day—not exactly the way Three Dog Night does it, but with all the verses. From the horse's mouth.

Run of the house

Returning to Lee Hays: He was always a family man. When I moved the Robinson family from Hollywood back to Brooklyn Heights to write *Sandhog*, Lee happily shared the rent with us in our two-floor apartment at 11 Cranberry Street. Lee had the back two rooms on the second floor, and shared a bathroom with Perry and Jimmy. At the time he moved in, he was singing with the Weavers. But the blacklist soon caught up with them too: By 1953 they were about finished. They liked to think of it as a "sabbatical," but Lee commented that it "turned into a Mondayical and Tuesdayical." With time on his hands, Lee sat around watching a lot of television. His income derived mostly from his Weavers royalties. He had written that great song "If I Had a Hammer," which brought in some bucks in its day.

Early on in the nine years Lee stayed with us, we held a family meeting at which we faced together the fact that I could not support all of us. Recognizing that I had to be free to compose, and teach children's choruses and guitar classes, we agreed that Helen would go out and get a job. She reactivated her cartooning ability in the animation industry, which was thriving in the '50s and '60s, and joined the union. Take a deep breath for this one: the Motion Picture Screen Cartoonists Local 841 of the International Alliance of Theatrical Stage Employees and Moving Picture Machine Operators of the United States and Canada, AFL-CIO. I did the shopping and helped to supervise the boys. Perry and Jimmy did the dishes and agreed to clean their own rooms. Lee volunteered to cook, and did so excellently. For the most part. Once Helen asked him, "Lee, how long are you going to cook that spaghetti?" With that devastating deadpan face he often assumed, he replied, "Till I cook all the vitamins out of it."

Having the run of the house—the boys in school and Helen at work—made it possible for me to invite women in from time to time. Which I did, with Lee sleeping or keeping to himself upstairs. I never did talk with Lee about this, but he considered it none of his business. Though he loved gossip of

every juicy kind, he never mentioned this, and I am eternally
grateful. As I reflect on his discretion, I realize he may well
have had his reasons. Though in essence a loner, he did enjoy
the company of young men, and occasionally one would stay
overnight with him. We Robinsons never paid much attention
at the time, but it does seem to me now that Lee was probably
homosexual.

He was a contrary cuss. Sometimes when he didn't feel
good about himself his self-inflicted humor could be painful. A
full-fledged hypochondriac, he could always be depended on to
perceive the most negative aspects of a situation, personal or
political. But he rebounded soon enough. His quick, subtle
appreciation of the light and ridiculous side of things gave constant joy.

He and Helen enjoyed playing Scrabble. Helen once asked
if there was a word "dod." Lee chuckled, "Yes, it's a 'bumb'
what didn't go off." Another time he returned from a trip to
L.A. on the same airline that had just suffered a massive crash
the day before. We greeted Lee at the door. He lifted Jimmy
up ponderously, Jimmy supplying the unintentional humor,
saying, "Gee, Lee, but you're heavy." We asked him how was
the flight? "Well," Lee said thoughtfully, "it was all right. But I
didn't put my full weight down the whole trip." Which took
some doing because Lee weighed quite a lot in those days.

At his best Lee and his humor could be very nurturing.
When one of us couldn't turn someone around who persisted
in doing their own thing regardless, Lee would admonish us,
pronouncing, "If it don't fit, don't fuss it."

My parents came visiting from Seattle. My mother asked
him what he thought about the fair going on at Flushing
Meadows. He began quoting, as he often did: "Well, they do
say as how the fair ain't all it used to be; in fact it never was."
And he proceeded with more and more outrageous "quotes"
until he had her in stitches. Up to his final peroration: "The
kind of people that like that kind of thing, that's just the kind
of thing they're going to love."

Lee could also be a good listener. My old man loved to tell stories, was really pretty good at it, and Lee unfailingly appreciated them. He would laugh uproariously at my father's collection of jokes, dirty and otherwise—though Lee would say, "If it's not dirty, why waste our time?"

When a scene called for solemnity, such as the death of a loved one, Lee lifted the gloom with his positive storytelling, recalling the warmth and humor of the departed. I can never forget his emceeing a memorial to Bob Reed, an actor important to the left wing and the progressive struggle within Actors' Equity. Lee is the first one I remember approaching the subject of "death" saying, "We have come here to *celebrate* the grand and glorious life of Bob Reed." A way of looking at mortality in a refreshingly unmorbid fashion that has since become more widespread. Similarly, he lent his loving strength on the passing of Pop Wortis and my Helen.

Though we lived together fairly intimately, we wrote only three songs together. The first was a science fiction song:

> *My true love's an ordinary thing,*
> *You'd know her anywhere*
> *By her pink antenna and her polka-dot skin*
> *And the hydrogen sulphide of her hair.*

Perhaps a little shamefaced at writing a song with no social content, we decided to remain anonymous and act as ghostwriters for the well-known Martian lyricist XTRPL8. Freddy Hellerman of the Weavers sang and recorded this song, as I did on my second Folkways album, but it never became a hit. The second song, "Side by Side," I discussed in connection with "Black and White." The third I'll talk about later.

Time came when I had to ask Lee to leave 11 Cranberry Street. After nine years of sharing our lives, this was a heavy occasion. Helen's father, Pop Wortis, was getting old and confused, a sad situation. His wife Selena had died a few months before. He would imagine the "FB and I" coming for him at the front door, and we'd have to restrain him from leaving the house with them. He needed a place to stay, with a live-in nurse, and Lee's two rooms seemed to be the only ones available. Lee took this move well, saying, "I'm glad it wasn't anything less than Helen's father," and moved to uptown Manhattan. Helen took care of Pop—mothered him—with a constant, fierce tenderness, until he passed on two years later.

Imprimatur of sincerity and truth

While finishing *Sandhog*, I got involved with children's choruses, as in Los Angeles. This glad, upbeat time right in the middle of the blacklist brought in a bit of income. One of these groups, at the Church of the Holy Trinity, the progressive Episcopal church in Brooklyn Heights ministered by William Howard Melish, held regular concerts. Holy Trinity truly practiced integration, with black people at every level of participation and leadership, quite rare for those days. The church also invested heavily in resolving gang problems, holding regular dances, swims, and picnics for Puerto Rican, black, white, and other teenagers. One time I brought Leonard Bernstein over to a dance so he could meet and study these young people, research that contributed to his *West Side Story*.

In 1952 the church sponsored our children's film, *When We Grow Up*, based on a cantata that I had worked out with the kids and performed a few times. Words by Roslyn Rosen of Chicago, this 11-minute piece had a format of solos singing, talking, and acting what they wanted to be when they grew up. My son Perry, 14 and already a maven on the clarinet, said, "I want to be a musician," and I scored a jazz riff for him to play. Waldo Salt wrote the film script, and Irving Fajans and Carl Lerner shot it. I raised $1,300 for expenses ($100 came from Arthur Miller, whose kid appeared in the film), and the church distributed it. The first showing took place at the Episcopal General Convention in Boston, September 1952.

It allowed us to present a solid pro-peace, anti-nuclear message. One effective scene has a child saying he wants to be a soldier when he grows up; the others take this up enthusiastically, and they end up all lying dead on the floor; in another scene they hide under their desks to avoid the Bomb. The film never reached movie houses, but got a lot of church screenings. From a review in *The Churchman*, a liberal religious magazine: "It is not always the slick and subsidized commercial films that touch our emotions. Now and again there comes along some simple, unpretentious little movie, made on a shoestring budget but bearing the imprimatur of sincerity and truth. . . . Such is the film, *When We Grow Up*." Chappell published the score, which received performances in Chicago, Toronto, and L.A. that I know of.

If *When We Grow Up* never crossed your path, another film short that I scored might have. Irving Lerner and Joseph Strick made a non-political documentary film in 1952 called *Muscle Beach*, about the bodybuilders of Venice, California, for which I wrote the singing/talking blues "It's a Clear Day." Poet Edwin Rolfe wrote the lyric. The film has just guitar and voice accompaniment. This doc won the Cannes Film Festival prize. Lee Hays saw it in New York on a bill with a "horrid Cocteau film." The audience "only muttered sad comments after the feature but *applauded* the short," he wrote me. We had a running gag throughout the film, where the camera returns to a guy straining his massive biceps to lift a weight, while the lyric on the soundtrack counterpoints with the languid phrase "Come on and ta-ake it easy."

The other children's chorus for ages 7-11 was at the Metropolitan Music School on West 74th Street in Manhattan, successor to the Downtown Music School which had given me my Aaron Copland scholarship twenty years earlier. The school still defined itself as "a non-profit cooperative, progressive both in teaching methods and social outlook." This indirectly resulted in my being called before HUAC, for in 1954 *Counterattack* had thrown its spotlight on the school as a CP front with *tax-free status* (always that cruel twist of the knife to get the citizenry in a rage).

Both of my choruses got together in Carnegie Hall to sing "The World We Live In," new words to "House" by Waldo Salt, on a program sponsored by the American-Soviet Friendship Council or some such dangerous subversive group. Honoring Paul Robeson who, denied a passport, was under a form of "house arrest," the program packed the house. I remember Waldo's beautiful refrain, which the kids sang with sweet enthusiasm,

The land we live in, its people great and small,
The folks who fought in slavery to free the bonds of all,
The folks who give their freedom to keep our nation free,
Like Paul and Essie Robeson, that's America to me.

Speaking up

The Sixties are thought of as the noisy, activist years, while the Fifties were supposedly "the silent generation," something like the Dark Ages when *nothing happened!* But please remember, some of us spoke up. Not everyone was silent. From this distance it might appear that we just hunkered down with our remaining comrades, our wagons all in a circle, our voices never heard beyond a tight ring of fellow travelers. But during the Fifties we had ideas, people, committees, meetings, demonstrations; we had a myriad of professional organizations, publications both local and national.

Most important, we knew that in a certain way we had history on our side, for all around the world we saw whole nations and continents rising up and declaring independence, we saw the old colonial powers in steep decline. And when it looked like the United States was stepping in as the neocolonial power, well, that spurred us on even more to keep up our activism at home. We felt pretty vulnerable on the Korean War because we'd been so marginalized by that time, but we even dared to question America's role: In 1952, under the sponsorship of the New York Peace Institute, I led a group of Christmas carolers in front of President-elect Eisenhower's residence at 60 Morningside Drive.

We didn't have the hundreds of thousands any more, but at least our few thousands would valiantly stage a May Day festival every year at Union Square. We had petitions and protests and lawyers to free our imprisoned leaders—which came about later in the decade because we relentlessly pursued these cases all the way to the Supreme Court. The justices ruled that Communists had, after all, the same rights to free speech as other Americans, and that the government was persecuting us unconstitutionally. These holdings, and cases involving full political rights for the foreign-born, and other suits seeking to secure our rights to a passport and to travel abroad (I was denied a passport 1952-58)—all of our victories in this "silent" era benefited not just Communists but every American.

People's Artists ran anniversary concerts for Joe Hill, released records, like one in 1954 with my song "Varsovienne" about children around the world in a dance of brotherhood and peace. I traveled out many times during the Fifties to encourage activists in Pittsburgh, Milwaukee, Chicago, Seattle, and elsewhere. And by no means was I the only one doing this kind of work. The point is, we didn't give up on America's promise, though our faith cost us dearly.

The Fifties need a revised history: Far from cowering in repression and terror, the left managed to create a culture in many ways vibrant, resourceful, and fulfilling.

THE $64 QUESTION

We hardly needed censorship laws

In 1955, the blacklist was still going strong. One prolonged fight over censorship in the new housing development of Levittown, New York, involved *The Lonesome Train*. It started when a Catholic newspaper published an attack on Millard Lampell and me, purporting to find in every line of the work some insidious Communist propaganda. Lincoln as we portrayed him had too much love of the common man and not enough for men of property. There were meetings, protests pro and con, an avalanche of letters to the editor, confrontations with the school district superintendent, formal requests for rulings from the New York State Education Department, and a polarization of the town into staunchly anti-Communist and supposedly "soft on Communism" factions, all over the question Should the *Lonesome Train* recording remain in the school library? (It served at most as an annual Lincoln's birthday tribute if some teacher decided to play it for a class.)

The saga dragged out over nearly two years, with our cantata as the centerpiece. The issue of anti-Communism led to a hotly contested school board election, which the antis won. They promptly banned the recording. I sometimes wonder what they actually did with it. Broke it? Burned it? Buried it? And I wonder if *The Lonesome Train* has ever been heard in Levittown since.

Ballad for Americans underwent similar travails. The Catholic War Veterans protested to the Marine Corps about a planned performance on July 4th, 1957 at the Monument Grounds in Washington, D.C., with the University of Maryland chorus. It was to be the grand finale preceding the fireworks display. (Earlier, the chorus had sung *Ballad* not only for President Truman but for a week's run at the Capitol Theatre.) The CWV mentioned my troubles with HUAC. The American Legion's *Firing Line* got into the act with a two-page exposé, making sure that readers all over the country would know what to expect should they ever want to perform a work of mine. The same effective ban applied to network radio: What disk jockey wanted to lose a job for airing my music? In such an atmosphere we hardly needed censorship laws.

I began singing concerts again in 1955, with the help of Paul Endicott, a resourceful agent in Detroit who had undertaken to confront the blacklist and represent Pete Seeger. He proposed to be my agent also, with quite astonishing results. My first bookings came suddenly as a result of Pete being laid up with laryngitis. Paul called me two days before a performance scheduled for twelve noon on a Tuesday in Galesburg, Illinois—birthplace and early home of Carl Sandburg.

I drove into town at 11 a.m., an hour early. A 6'4" professor with a Norwegian name met me, leading me into a room where several other individuals were waiting. For what, I couldn't be sure, but they wanted some kind of conference before I sang my concert. I was introduced to professors and graduate students from the chemistry department, the history department, sociology, etc. Introductions completed, we settled down, and my Norwegian professor got right to the point.

"Mr. Robinson," he began, "we want to ask you the $64 question."

!!!!!

I could only hope that my face did not show any of the inner turmoil I experienced. Are you now or have you ever been a member of the Communist Party? This question you tried to avoid even being asked, much less tried to avoid answering, because of the repercussions engineered by the Un-American Committee. My friends of the Hollywood Ten had gone to jail for refusing to answer that question, relying on the First Amendment. Countless others had "taken the Fifth" and lost their jobs. And here was some professor asking it.

"We want to ask you the $64 question."

So he asked. The professors wanted to know:

"Is there an indigenous Illinois folk music?"

Well, I took off on that for seven minutes, never relying once on the First or the Fifth Amendment. I absolutely

streaked. Where I didn't know or wasn't sure, I made up songs
and answers. I had recently been in touch with a progressive,
labor-oriented Illinois songwriter, whom I quoted extensively.
The concert I gave at noon went successfully, I believe. But
I don't remember a thing about it. My mind was still in shock
from The Question.

Arise, ye prisoners of starvation
My next booking took place at the University of Kansas,
and again, the extracurricular proceedings are what I remember. A student met my train in Lawrence, and his research zeal
was to embarrass me again. He brought me to his room at the
fraternity house, sat me down amid a clutter of clothes and
papers, and got out his guitar. He began strumming some
Leadbelly songs and with his friends made a not-so-subtle effort to get me singing. But I was not about to give my concert
then and there, preferring to save it for that evening. I approved of their interest in folk music, but refused to perform
for them. When out of left field—literally—my young friend
asked me a different kind of $64 question.

"Do you know 'The Internationale'?"

I hadn't sung that song since the late '30s, and most particularly not during the blacklist period. Temporizing, I said,
"Well, I used to know it."

"Would you sing it for us, *please?*"

This was too much. How could I deny these young folks a
chance to hear Pierre Degeyter's stirring revolutionary anthem
from struggles past, right in the middle of this present repressive period? I took up the guitar and began:

Arise, ye prisoners of starvation,
Arise, ye wretched of the earth,
For justice thunders condemnation,
A better world's in birth.

As I sang, I realized that in the version I had learned in the
Thirties, the word "soviet" appeared prominently in the last

line, and somehow I had to get that dangerous word out of the
song. Such was the fear of the blacklisters that permeated most
of us on the left. So when I reached that last line, I sang it with
the original French word, "The In-ter-na-tion-a-le" instead. But
the line repeats. With some fear and trembling I threw caution
to the winds and sang

The International Soviet shall be the human race.

The students reacted marvelously. "What a noble song,"
one said. And before I knew it, they were discussing what the
word "soviet" actually meant. "That was when the Mensheviks
broke off from the Bolsheviks," said another, "because the Bolsheviks were insisting on using the soviets as a more revolutionary instrument to advance the revolution."

I broke in to ask, "Do they teach you that here in this college?"

"Oh, yes," they answered. "But the professor is a little cut
and dried about it, and we wanted to experience the real stuff,
from you."

So I was a teacher again, learning more than I could teach.
These young folks in the Midwest couldn't care less about the
blacklist. For them it didn't exist.

At a house party after the concert that evening, a New
Yorker somewhat out of his element on the Kansas faculty
glommed onto me like an old friend just discovered. To him,
my leftist program was a breath of fresh air. He told me that
during my singing of "Free and Equal Blues" he heard from the
couple seated in back of him, "He's a Communist. Doesn't he
sing well." So I casually began accepting that in these people's
eyes, there was nothing wrong—with either fact.

The last place I sang on this trip was a black college in
Asheville, N.C. As I walked through the campus, white and
black people greeted me with unfailing warmth, respect, and a
desire to help this stranger with whatever I needed. I rode the
plane home to New York with a new black friend who impressed me with his depth of understanding, his wisdom and

incredible presence for such a young man. Only years later I realized who he was: James Baldwin.

I believe that essentially I create everything that happens to me. The blacklist was real all right, but mostly to the extent that we tended to give power to the blacklisters, endowing them with a strength that was illusory. It vanished when they were confronted wholly, intelligently, with vigor and purpose. This is not a popular viewpoint among the victims, however, with whom I have deep sympathy.

Timber!

In the year 1956, while struggling against the blacklist, I took time out to compose a piece for the University of Washington symphonic band, *A Country They Call Puget Sound*. This work turned out to be valuable for me on several counts. It opened up my classical, "pure music" self in ways I didn't expect. It gave me a chance to stop being just a songwriter, and begin flying a little, symphonically. With my old friend Jack DeMerchant's help, I even got to recover some high C's I had developed while at the university. For of course I protected myself by building the whole piece around a folksong, "Acres of Clams," sung by tenor voice. My friend Ivar Haglund revived it as his theme song on the radio, and when he went into the restaurant business, he reprinted the song on the paper placemats. So folks in Seattle knew the song well. (An incidental note: As an old progressive, Ivar organized his restaurants along the lines of a pension and profit-sharing plan for his more than 200 employees—unheard of in the eatery business— which accounted for the tremendous personal and company loyalty he earned from his workers.)

The piece started out safely anchored in the song, a series of verses with accompaniment, but as it progressed the orchestra began to take over. The great logging industry of the Northwest became a fugue, wherein I developed a theme based on the sound of the old crosscut saw that I'd been on one end of many a time with my father. The fugue led into a whole movement punctuated by the sound of the doublebladed axe,

culminating with the cry of "Timber!" and the felling of a huge
Douglas fir. The music has no words there, and doesn't say
"Douglas fir," but to a Northwest audience that is understood.
We get back to the verse words which lead this time into a
long, slow "Lonesome Section," informed by Puget Sound
tugboat chuggings made with the horns blowing only through
their mouthpieces. It didn't exactly turn out to be "pure music," but I was finally reaching in that direction. For the climax
I used a Swedish schottische we used to dance to.

This composition has been "premiered" in several different
ways. The UW symphonic band played it in Meany Hall in
July 1957, with me guest conducting, and Tommy Goleeke as
tenor soloist. I reorchestrated *Puget Sound* for small symphonic
ensemble, performed in Vancouver over CBC by the Chamber
Symphony. When they played it in East Berlin, they cut the
schottische because it sounded too much like a German popular song. The Long Island Community Orchestra and Chorus
premiered it in 1959 as a choral work, still with tenor solo.
And Robert McGrath sang solo when Milton Katims and the
Seattle Symphony Orchestra gave this "American folksong
tone poem" its full orchestra premiere in 1963. Shawnee pub-
lishes this work. I haven't heard of any performances lately,
but it has always been well received.

Also in 1956 I got to write a film score, a freak happening,
considering the Hollywood blacklist. A New York independent commercial film company had a contract from General
Motors for an industrial film on diesel engines, called *Giants in
the Land*. The biggest folk giant of them all, Paul Bunyan,
served as the integral force in the film. Scriptwriter Joseph
Moncure March and the producer saw folk music expert Robinson as a necessary part of this combo. *Giants* was mostly
high-level fun to work on. Joe March turned out excellent lyrics on the huge earthmoving equipment, a diesel truck topping
Pike's Peak, a beautiful streamlined diesel electric train, and
the tugboats in the harbor, with a "Floodwater Blues" thrown
in to dramatize what can happen when the engines are not
available to dam up a river. They shot a large part of the film

from a helicopter, symbolizing the viewpoint of Paul Bunyan, who kept looking down from his immense height, in wonder at the ability of the machines. We used talking blues, Woody Guthrie's "900 Miles from Home" train music, a professional chorus, and Pete Seeger on the soundtrack with his banjo. I wrote to Helen about my progress with the score:

> It's such an exacting job making notes meet feet and frames on the beam and still be emotional and exciting and advertise diesels besides. Will people run right down and buy a diesel, I wonder, after seeing this film?!??

Not the slightest echo of redbaiting occurred until the film was shown at a GM Motorama in Chicago. An FBI man caught my name in the credits and went to the film department at General Motors to point out that Robinson was a Communist. The film man refused to concern himself. "The man's a good composer, that's all we know." Which pointed up a difficulty the FBI had not considered: You can't hardly redbait GM.

I thought I could never forgive him

Sometime back in 1939 this big folk singer with the sweetest, most natural voice came to New York. He had a collection of numbers superb for their originality, artfulness and humor, and he found my "Joe Hill" song worthy of adding to his repertoire. We became friends, Burl Ives and I, and he graced our parties and hootenannies for some time. He joined me on "Back Where I Come From" on CBS in 1940, where he acquitted himself admirably.

Burl was drafted into the army but it didn't take. He didn't malinger, but had kind of a rough time in basic training. A singer, not a fighter. Helen and I had moved West and our home in Hollywood was a welcome place for him on furloughs and after he got out. Once, when Helen had delivered his breakfast in bed, he said with heartfelt emotion, "I sure do know who my friends are."

Our paths diverged after the war. One time we met, he said, "I'm doing a lot of singing for the Jews these days," a remark to which I could see no significance beyond gratitude for paid bookings. Then the McCarthy period hit, and Burl "sang" (and not his folksongs) to HUAC. This friendly witness named names, presumably including mine, in camera (in a private session). We on the left were shocked. Burl had gone bad. It hit me harder than some. Most of us blacklisted had particular friends we trusted and thought a lot of, and I found it tough to see him turn into a songbird. So Burl became Earl's *bête noir*, and I thought I could never forgive him.

Comes 1956, Woody Guthrie is sick with Huntington's chorea, and the left folksingers (or should I say the folksingers left?) decided to run a concert of his songs to help him. Pete Seeger, Lee Hays, Ed McCurdy, Richard Dyer-Bennett, Josh White, and I got a script by Mill Lampell, and Harold Leventhal managed the benefit. Burl had gotten a lot from Woody, as we all had, and it occurred to us to give him a chance to participate, perhaps exonerate himself. We planned this carefully: Harold would make contact with him backstage where he was playing on Broadway in *Cat on a Hot Tin Roof*. We had three choices for Burl. One, he could attend and sing for Woody. Two, if this was difficult for him, he could attend and contribute. Or three, he could just send a greeting to Woody and some cash if he liked.

Well, Harold never could get an answer. Some people said Burl's then-wife was responsible. In any case, we felt we had to write Burl off. He went on to become a star of stage and screen, and was (apparently happily) lost to the left.

One day, a dozen years ago, I woke up to discover that Burl was living in Santa Barbara, right around the corner, so to speak. I'd been uncomfortable with this estrangement for a long time. It got to be less and less important to "punish" Burl for something that maybe he had good reasons for doing. I harked back to a sage saying of Waldo Salt, "Never blacklist the blacklisters, never redbait the redbaiters."

I found Burl's address and sent him a note inviting him to a 66th birthday celebration. I got no answer, but I didn't give up. I saw Burl was giving a concert at the Arlington Theatre in 1984 as a local benefit for something. I attended, went backstage after, and Burl (and his second wife) greeted me with a warm hug. Someday it would be nice to be able to discuss the blacklist times with him, but I swear it is not necessary. I'm not even that interested. More important is that we stay friends of a sort, not uncommunicating enemies. As Carl Sandburg, in *The People, Yes*, has a former convict say, "In my case it pays to have a good forgettery."

ME AND THE UN-AMERICANS

You may want to refer back to "A Moment Out of Time," which begins this book, for a couple of choice exchanges from my April 11, 1957, hearing with the House Committee on Un-American Activities, 85th Congress, First Session. As to more on this subject, I feel split between two opposing temptations. First, I would love for you to read my entire testimony, to show what kind of know-nothings felt themselves qualified to delve into an artist's relationship to ideas. And to show—all modesty aside—how some of us were able to withstand Congressional meddling in the arts. Which is by no means a dead issue, the recent Jesse Helms-inspired controversy over the National Endowment for the Arts being a case in point. My other temptation is to skip this section entirely, for to dwell here might suggest that my confrontation with HUAC represents a Very Important Watershed in my career, and I don't see it as that. It had significance, to be sure, but I have tried not to view people's behavior in front of HUAC as the determining moment of their lives, and I include myself. I choose not to adopt this single-minded way of seeing things.

So I will compromise. You can read the testimony complete in every important detail in Eric Bentley, ed., *Thirty Years of Treason: Excerpts from Hearings Before the House Committee on Un-American Activities, 1938-1968* (New York: The Viking Press, 1971). In case you have trouble finding that book, I will offer a few short passages from the hearing and make some comments.

Taking the Fifth . . .

This round of HUAC hearings on supposed Communist influence in the music field began on Tuesday, April 9th. People interrogated in these four days included the composer Wallingford Riegger, president emeritus of the Metropolitan Music School, and Lilly Popper, director of the school, plus a number of other teachers there, including myself. These hearings also included Max Goberman, conductor; David Walter, former chairman of the Symphony of the Air board; Johnny Mehegan, jazz pianist; and Sidney Finkelstein, a Party writer on music and art. Among those who "sang" were Max Marlin, a theatre orchestra conductor, and Abram Chasins, author and WQXR radio station music director.

These being public hearings, I attended the entire session to lend my support. I watched friends of mine being forced to "take the Fifth" with barely a chance to fight back. Soon after they identified themselves, the Committee's staff attorney simply asked The $64 Question, Are you now or have you ever been . . . ? If you tried to avoid answering, they would keep asking, saying, Do you mean to say that if you spoke freely here you would be supplying information which might be used against you in a criminal proceeding? You'd have to say Yes.

Do you then claim the protection of the First and Fifth Amendments in declining to answer? And as soon as you'd answer Yes again, thereby taking the Fifth, you at once branded yourself a "Fifth-Amendment Communist." Whatever else you may have said in testimony—the brilliant repartee, the slashing broadsides you leveled, the dignity you somehow maintained—the media picked up none of it. That wasn't their role in this theatre. They simply and dutifully reported that you had taken the Fifth. (If you cooperated to the extent of saying, No, I never joined the Party, or I did and I got out of it, we called that the "diminished Fifth.")

What did "taking the Fifth" mean in the context of the witchhunt? For those of independent means, for the rare person working for a sympathetic employer, or for someone whose employability had already been nixed by the blacklist, not much resulted from having their name in the paper. Most of the rest would show up for work the next day to find themselves fired.

How did one prepare for an engagement with HUAC? In part, by studying other people's experiences. The testimony of Jay Gorney helped me, the guy who wrote (with Yip Harburg) the classic Depression song, "Brother, Can You Spare a Dime?" Every time they asked him a question, he'd say, "Well, I've expressed that in my music," and he broke out into the song "Congress shall make no law respecting an establishment of religion . . ." that he'd composed out of the words of the First Amendment.

. . . and all the amendments

Martin Popper served as my lawyer. A regular counselor to the Communist Party, he had also represented East German and Soviet interests in the U.S. He would be present for my hearing, he told me, but I would have to work out my own approach toward HUAC—how "friendly" I would be, and which constitutional privileges I wished to claim. At a number of points the transcript indicates that I conferred with counsel. And then I say, "I am sorry, I will have to decline to answer this." To the naked eye it looks on the page as though I depended on Martin very substantially. I feel some chagrin over this today, wishing it might appear that I could stand more on my own two feet. But the Committee had a lot of practice in tripping up their witnesses. Though I expanded rather liberally on certain questions, I needed caution on others.

Staff Attorney Richard Arens did most of the questioning, a slimy character, expert at trying to trap you into taking the Fifth. For a long time, half an hour or so into the interrogation, I avoided getting snared. With my whole soul, I wanted to deny the Committee and the press the ability to list me as a "Fifth-Amendment Communist." I concentrated on all my positive contributions to American music, such as setting parts of the Declaration of Independence and the Constitution to music. Such repeated questions as "Why did you, then, join an organization that was dedicated to the overthrow of the Constitution?" I refused to answer.

"You decline to answer that, claiming your privilege under the First and Fifth Amendments of the Constitution?" asked Morgan M. Moulder of Missouri, trying to speed me right to the point.

"All the amendments," I replied. That confounded them for a while. I also confounded them by launching into a speech on my hallowed Constitution.

> MR. ROBINSON: When a time like this comes, when I am called before an un-American Committee—pardon me, before a Committee on Un-American Activities—I not only rely on my American rights under the Constitution, but when I see, when I feel I see, any of this Constitution threatened, and I believe no matter how sincere you gentlemen are and feel you are, you are deeply wrong with this kind of activity, calling up people and destroying in many, many—

> MR. DOYLE: Mr. Chairman, I think that this gentleman has had plenty of time to read us a lecture, and then calling this committee an un-American Committee, which he deliberately did. He didn't get by me with that.

Since I had appeared at many Party and other progressive functions over the years, my name frequently appeared in the *Daily Worker*. These mentions, studiously documented by the FBI, provided the Committee with ample fodder. Did I write such and such a song? Did I have any connection to the National Council of American-Soviet Friendship? Did I affix my signature to an appeal to the President requesting amnesty for Communist Party leaders convicted under the Smith Act? Did I sponsor publication of a brochure called "Thought Control in U.S.A."? And so forth.

Attorney Arens asked how music is used politically.

> MR. ROBINSON: "John Brown's Body" is one of the most famous songs which helped to produce the Civil War and was sung by the soldiers during the war. There are dozens of examples. In the American Revolution, if you will pardon the expression, tremendous songs came out: "The Bennington Riflemen," the story of our forefathers that shot at the Redcoats from behind trees. . . .

MR. ARENS: Is music an effective weapon in political action?

MR. ROBINSON: I am not sure how effective it is, but it has been used a lot.

Of course, I did not fail to make mention of the *Ballad for Americans* being performed at the Republican National Convention of 1940. Nor about singing at the White House. I proudly confirmed that my songs had helped to fight fascism in Spain. I found myself agreeing with my inquisitors that music has the power to persuade, but I also emphasized that music often supersedes ideology.

MR. ARENS: Tell us, in view of your statement here about counterattacking with art: Is art a potent weapon in the ideological differences between, say, the East and the West? Is art a potent weapon?

MR. ROBINSON: I think art is a potent weapon for understanding, for making this a better world. I think it is a potent weapon to help [people] to get along with each other.

MR. ARENS: Would art be a potent weapon, say, in the hands of the Soviet Union, in undertaking to propagate its ideology?

MR. ROBINSON: Well, I suppose Shostakovich's Fifth Symphony or Seventh Symphony, which was performed over here in wartime when we were fighting together, I suppose this was propaganda for the Soviet Union. It is pretty good. I don't think that he was trying to subvert the United States with the Seventh Symphony. I think he was trying to help his own country, but that symphony was played here in Carnegie Hall, and it was played in all the major symphony orchestras in the country, and it was good.

At one point Arens referred to the 1953 Stalin memorial meeting, reviewed in the *Daily Worker*, where supposed words of mine were quoted, "Sleep well, beloved comrade; we pledge our bodies now. The fight will go on; the fight will go on until we win." The song "Beloved Comrade" is not by me, rather by Abel Meeropol. I didn't name him, but did remind Arens that I wasn't a lyricist, and that I never wrote such words. The dialogue degenerated into farce.

> MR. ARENS: Now look at this article, if you please, Mr. Robeson—
>
> MR. ROBINSON: Robinson is the name.
>
> MR. ARENS: Robinson?
>
> MR. ROBINSON: R-o-b-i-n-s-o-n.
>
> MR. ARENS: Robeson recited. I am in error. Robeson recited Earl Robinson's words, and you are Earl Robinson, are you not?
>
> MR. ROBINSON: That is right.

California's Clyde Doyle took off on a tack involving a songbook called *America Sings*, to which I'd written an introduction some twenty years before. He made a big point that with a title like that, the introduction mentioned no American songs, only Soviet and German revolutionary songs.

> MR. DOYLE: And yet they call it *America Sings*. And that is the kind of Soviet propaganda that is infiltrating our country. I have one thing more, Mr. Robinson. Can you show me in your writings—and I ask you in good faith—one single song upholding and promoting loyalty to the Stars and Stripes, to the American flag?
>
> MR. ROBINSON: Everything I have written does this.

At that point, with his splendid prodding, I quoted several lines of "The House I Live In."

The fact is that my introduction did refer to American songs, but not having read it for years, I hadn't remembered. It took another Committee member, Morgan M. Moulder, to correct Doyle on this point, and to his Honorable credit, he did so.

In the end they got me to claim the protection of the First and Fifth. After a few more minutes of harassing interrogation, I exploded.

> MR. ROBINSON: Do I make my speech about the Constitution again, how much it means to me? I am not going to let you destroy either the First or Fifth Amendment with this kind of insinuation. Somehow I am made out to be subversive, and I refuse to be. I am not.

> MR. MOULDER: You claim the protection of the First and Fifth Amendments in declining to answer?

> MR. ROBINSON: Yes.

In almost any context, Yes is a beautiful word. In this one, a simple Yes did me in. All the newspapers named me the next day, including Ralph Chapman in the *Herald-Tribune*, the only one to perceive any grace or humor in the sorry affair. Graylisted for a decade already, I had no regular job to lose, so I didn't suffer as others did. In fact, curiously enough, I was offered a steady teaching job in part because of the way I spoke to HUAC.

You'll recall from "A Moment in Time" that while I sat on the stand testifying, Rep. Doyle asked for a copy of "The House I Live In." After the proceedings had concluded, Doyle met me in the lobby and said, "I grew up in Seattle myself. Went to University Heights grade school."

"Heaven's sake," I answered, "I went to West Seattle High."

And now he earnestly repeated his request. "How much is that song?"

"Fifty cents."

"Here's a dollar—will you send me one?" said Mr. Doyle. He handed me a bill right then and there and we closed the deal.

"My latest composition is called *A Country They Call Puget Sound*," I added, but the Congressman's interest had peaked. I sent him the song and never heard from him again.

Helen attended the session, and I felt strengthened by her presence. For if by that time my political allegiances had begun to dwindle, and I did not feel such intense commitment to the Party, I couldn't let Helen down by doing less than my best. Waldo Salt, having already been blacklisted, was enormously helpful. He felt very proud of me, and let me know. In my testimony, I had called HUAC "sincere gentlemen," and Waldo told everyone he knew, "It's some time since the Committee has been called sincere!" Corliss Lamont, a wealthy supporter of good causes, often emceed at Emergency Civil Liberties Committee functions. I sang at their dinner not long after, and he introduced me, saying, "Here's Earl Robinson, who told the Un-American Committee to go to hell."

The judgment of people and time

After the hearing, any friends I lost who feared associating with me, I never missed. They were losable. Except Carl Sandburg, I lost him for a while. He was scared of the Red thing. Langston Hughes handled himself embarrassingly before HUAC; also Josh White talked, though he never stopped singing "Free and Equal Blues" or "The House I Live In." I used to classify my friends on the basis of how they handled themselves in front of HUAC, but I have long ceased judging people by that standard. Time and circumstance take a different toll on everyone. I prefer to ponder the words of Jesus, "Judge not, lest ye be judged."

Only three or four years after my testimony, a new '60s generation of political activists came along. What a difference their whole attitude made! They considered it perfectly OK to be a commie revolutionary—Cuba and Ché Guevara, and later Vietnam, served as their models—and when HUAC asked The $64 Question, they declared proudly, Yes, yes! They didn't squirm and evade as we had, and it made the Committee look like fools. Like the Wizard of Oz, HUAC had power to the extent that people ceded it to them. Of course, a great sea change came over American society in the 1960s, beginning with the election of John F. Kennedy over Richard Nixon, which we earlier activists couldn't foresee. God bless those kids. Maybe they defended their ideals so boldly because being so much younger, few of them had jobs to lose and families to support. But for whatever reasons, they helped to preserve the vital centerpiece of our democracy, the right to speak out.

It's a shame that the Party had become so namby-pamby, so secretive and protective, and so dependent on the Soviet Union for political guidance. Part of this comes from the war period. I now believe our peace policy from 1939 until June 22, 1941, when the Nazis attacked the Soviet Union, was wrong. We should have joined the Western democracies—however badly they had behaved during Hitler's rise to power—right from the beginning, and not waited until the Soviets came into the war. And I think we lost ground when the left tried to melt into the great American-Soviet alliance, when we submerged working-class interests under the all-class purpose of winning the war. Remember? No strikes, please! Accustomed to adapting to events instead of creating history, we allowed the redbaiters and the right wing to dictate the agenda.

In addition, as I should have known from my experiences performing out in the heartland, large sectors of the population, maybe an overwhelming majority, had no use for the blacklist. Nor did they regard the blacklisters as having any genuine authority. "He's a Communist," they said of me. "Doesn't he sing well."

SECTION FIVE
1957-1972

NORMAL TEACHING AT LAST

A detour?

When I graduated from the University of Washington with a normal teaching diploma I made a commitment to composing rather than the classroom. The independent Elisabeth Irwin High School, the high school of the Little Red School House in New York's Greenwich Village, offered me a job in 1957. I would be taking the place and building on the work of Bob De Cormier, who left to do arranging for Harry Belafonte, for which I envied him. I didn't know if I wanted it or not. Would this be just a detour away from composing?

But they truly wanted me at Elisabeth Irwin. My blacklisting and my HUAC appearance, far from being a hindrance to Rank Smith, head of the school, or to the democratic faculty who ran the school, represented a badge of honor. For all they knew, I might well have been an active Communist Party member. Indeed I was, though an increasingly restive one: I drifted out a year or two later.

Khrushchev's 1956 report on Stalin's excesses opened my eyes. Horrified by the untruths they had defended for so long, and by the Soviet invasion of Hungary that year, many Party members left in its wake. While I considered myself a friend of the Soviet Union, I hadn't defended every one of its policies. So the Khrushchev revelations alone did not separate me from the Party, because I owed my allegiance to America and its working people, and to the positive work of the U.S. Communist Party in defending American liberties.

I had my problems with the Party along the way. There were times I'd work with other artists to prepare new material for a rally, and in the excitement of introducing the speaker, an Elizabeth Gurley Flynn or a William Z. Foster, the emcee would "forget" to bring on the "entertainment." In the 1930s the Party had produced spectacular pageants in Madison Square Garden, with only one speaker of the evening—maybe Earl Browder; clearly, those huge audiences came for the cul-

273

tural uplift. By the early 1950s, with the Party in sad decline, an Earl Robinson or a Leon Bibb or a Laura Duncan was reduced to leading a few songs as the afterthought to a program. Other members of People's Artists could tell many similar stories of the disparagement of our talents by just about the only organization left in America that rightfully should have held our contributions on a high plane. I happily find a statement in the FBI file: An informant (name blacked out) "advised that in August 1948 subject made certain suggestions toward the improvement of Communist Party leadership in New York." Comradely, I'm sure; but firm, I hope.

Still, if I entertained my doubts, the FBI knew better. From a 1957 report:

> The following reasons are set forth to justify subject's retention on the Security Index: During the period 1955-1957 subject has in some way been connected with the following groups: American Committee for Protection of Foreign Born, California Labor School, California Emergency Defense Committee, Civil Rights Congress, National Committee for Freedom of the Press, International Publishers, Jefferson School of Social Science, Labor Youth League, National Committee to Win Amnesty for the Smith Act Victims, National Council of the Arts, Sciences and Professions, *New World Review*, People's Artists, American Labor Party. He refused to be interviewed by the FBI in 1954 and invoked 5th Amendment before House Committee in 1957. Previous to the above activity, subject identified as a member of the CP as recently as 1950 and as early as 1935. He has entertained as a singer and guitarist before numerous front groups and has written music especially for certain of these groups. Although subject has not held a leadership position in any one specific front group, he has been so associated with the entire subversive movement in such a way that he continues to qualify for inclusion in the security index.[1]

The situation with the American Federation of Musicians, my union, started me thinking seriously about my connection to the Party. The union instituted an anti-Communist loyalty oath which members had to sign to stay in. Our Party lawyer advised us C.P. musicians to sign (enough of us existed to form our own group within the union). Now I felt confronted. With poignant reflection on more than two decades of Party affiliation, I asked myself, What am I doing? What am I lying for? What am I defending? And the answer came: Not much.

By then the Party was falling apart under such heavy government attack that the overwhelming bulk of Party work consisted of raising money to defend our leaders in court. The time barely existed, nor the forces, to do any other political or organizing work. I had already stopped attending meetings, and had also stopped paying dues. But I still thought of myself as a member. Until this Musicians' Union question came up, which forced me to decide. So without fanfare I quietly dropped out. Helen's feelings coincided with mine. And seemingly no one ever missed either of us. In no way, though, did I join the redbaiters and begin attacking the Party. Others have made that their specialty; I didn't care to add my "singing" voice.

If I regret any aspect of my Party years, it's that I followed the dictates of authority over my own conscience. The example that weighs on me more than any other is what happened to the respected writer and journalist Anna Louise Strong, friend of the Soviet Union and of China for long years, and often quoted authoritatively in the *Daily Worker*. I knew her— we had shared the speakers' platform on at least one occasion during the war—and she had given compliments on my work. In 1948 and '49 the USSR suddenly denounced her as a spy. Instructions came down to have nothing to do with her. I asked a reporter for the *People's World*, the West Coast Communist paper, what he knew about the case. In his sublime ignorance he said, "It's very simple. She's a spy, that's all." Others on the independent left, the *National Guardian*, or my friend the Rev. Steve Fritchman, defended her, continued to see her, reassuring her that she still had friends. Then the news came from Moscow that she'd been rehabilitated. When I reminded the reporter of what he'd claimed so self-importantly, he said, "I don't remember that. But if I said so, I was wrong." Fine. Good to start thinking about accepting a line and turning off your brain. But I don't like turning off my brain. This is my whole theory about government: Good people get into the machine, shut off their powers of thinking, and become part of the machine themselves. It happens in every system.

I considered myself then and now an intense American patriot. But when America went to war against the people of Korea, then Cuba, then Vietnam, while regretting bitterly the loss of so many American lives, I saw more justice on the other side. We must take responsibility for peace. My country right or wrong, but when it's wrong, help to set it right.

I have come to believe that there may be a peaceful road to a more democratic future, and that class struggle is not the only definition of how to get there. In that sense I have found Communist theory too limiting.

My built-in chorus

My work at Elisabeth Irwin, producing music for an audience, had a powerful attraction. I had a built-in chorus: The entire 10th, 11th, and 12th grades were assigned to chorus twice a week, a hundred captive voices mine to do with as I wished. Then I had an orchestra to organize before school hours on Tuesdays and Thursdays, the days I taught. Also a Special Music Group and a ninth grade music class which each met once a week. I liked it as a part-time job, and I made it even more part-time, refusing to accept the 7th- and 8th-grade music classes. To get me they had to hire another teacher who would teach elementary music skills to those two classes. I became the "production boy" and never let them forget it. I began teaching in the fall of 1957—at twice the age I had been in 1933 when I got my diploma—and stayed with it until 1966.

The orchestra built itself up to thirty pieces, out of a student body of two hundred. We played symphonic repertoire,

Bach, Beethoven, Schubert, even Copland. And pieces arranged for school orchestra such as Richard Rodgers's *Victory at Sea*. Either in the pit or on stage, we shared the regular Thursday assembly with the Drama Department.

I encouraged young geniuses like Paul Levin, who accompanied the chorus and once played the Schumann piano concerto first movement, which he had arranged specifically for our orchestra. Bob Fishko did a similar thing with a saxophone concerto, arranging it for our little band. Just a few weeks before I wrote this chapter, I was approached at a Chinese restaurant on New York's Upper West Side by a fortyish fellow, David Lulow, who is now a top studio musician and composer—he spotted me and came over to my table to thank me for inspiring him at E. I. some thirty years before. Other students I had there included Kathy Boudin, daughter of Jean and civil rights lawyer Leonard Boudin (she played the oboe), Nora and Joady Guthrie, whose birth I recorded several chapters back.

I have spoken of my numerous collaborations with Abel Meeropol—Lewis Allan—but I wonder how many people are familiar with another, less public, aspect of his life. The story of Ethel and Julius Rosenberg, that noble couple framed and executed as "atomic spies," has been often told. Thousands of sympathizers and friends filled 17th Street in Manhattan between Union Square and Fifth Avenue that June 19, 1953. The hope that we had clung to up to the last possible minute, that President Eisenhower would commute their sentence, was not to be realized. When the news of their electrocution reached us, an indescribable wave of moaning moved through that vast throng. Ethel and Julius took the rap for something no one ever proved they did. That day lives in infamy. The question immediately arose, What about their two sons, Robbie and Michael? Well, Abel and Anne Meeropol were ready: They adopted them. Not without some opposition from conservative members of the family, who succeeded in removing the children from Abel and Anne for a short time. But the Meeropols' struggle to retain the boys won out. I never felt prouder of Abel when he expressed his undying determination to "fight for these kids."

As a crazy kind of footnote to this story, the FBI reports that "in connection with the Julius Rosenberg espionage work" a certain Alfred Epaminondas Sarant (never heard of him) had been interviewed on July 19, 1950, and that during that session a search was made of his home in Ithaca, New York. This search revealed a photograph of Earl Robinson. Diligent experts at cross-referencing placed that significant gem of incidental intelligence in my file. At taxpayers' expense.

Michael and Robbie attended E.I. and studied music with me. Michael, particularly talented, developed as a good solo folksinger for a while. He went on to become a professor of economics. Robbie is a practicing attorney today. Both are working hard to exonerate their mother and father.

Permit me now a fast-forward, this time to February 2, 1975. I was back on the West Coast then, and the Meeropol brothers were traveling around the country making appearances on behalf of the Rosenberg cause. At the Santa Monica Civic Auditorium I took part in a big rally, with my old friend Michael Loring (by then a cantor at Temple Beth Israel in Fresno), Henry Fonda, Herschel Bernardi, Lee Grant, Roscoe Lee Browne, and Martin Sheen. Just as my piece "In the Folded and Quiet Yesterdays" from *The People, Yes* had begun, a fantastic crash landed on the stage. We thought maybe a spotlight had fallen. Then we smelled gas, which started burning our eyes and skin. We evacuated the hall, which was packed with close to 3,000 people—in fact, we had to turn people away at the door—and everyone stood outside in the rain, half of them retching from the stink, until police cleared out the gas. A man from some neo-Nazi group called "the provisional wing of the National Socialist Liberation Front" telephoned a news office claiming responsibility. The bomb squad said it was "the type of bomb used to get the Viet gooks out of their tunnels," something not commonly available to anyone but law enforcement or military. In those closing weeks of the war in Vietnam, I guess some of the fans of that horrible misadventure were feeling their oats. The show went on after an hour or so, though my piece had to be sacrificed. The crowd reacted to the attack by really opening their pockets to the Rosenberg cause, and the case got a lot of renewed national publicity. So the bombers got the opposite of what they intended.

With the chorus at Elisabeth Irwin I would prepare two major concerts a year. At Christmastime, we usually did a Bach cantata, one year Handel's Hallelujah Chorus. At the spring concert I took shameless advantage of my position and programmed mainly Robinson, new and old cantatas. The old included *Ballad for Americans, The Lonesome Train* (with Michael Meeropol as a Ballad Singer), and "Tower of Babel" (from *The People, Yes*). My first spring concert in 1958 I did the choral score from *Giants in the Land*, the General Motors film. In fact, it was not as a result of the film, but of this performance that E. B. Marks published the piece.

Twice in later years we also did my *Preamble to Peace*, a half-hour work based on the United Nations Charter. I had written it, for a small commission, for a Trenton, New Jersey, celebration of the U.N. After I had struggled some with the text, I asked Lewis Allan to lend a hand. Mainly, he contributed a powerful lyric about the Four Horsemen of the Apocalypse. Time pressure forced me to hire an orchestrator and a copyist, both of whom consumed enough in wages to put me into debt for months—an experience probably many idealistic composers have when they accept well-meant but inadequate commissions.

The Greater Trenton Symphony Orchestra played the first performance, under Nicholas Harsanyi, with a semi-pro chorus, on October 23, 1960. Mrs. Roosevelt gave a speech, and Melvyn Douglas narrated. Before the performance, Helen and I, and Lewis and Anne Allan, dined at the executive mansion in Trenton with Governor and Mrs. Robert B. Meyner and Mrs. R. All were very friendly, and it felt almost like 1942 again. The audience seemed to like the piece—they called me to the podium half a dozen times. Eleanor Roosevelt lived only a couple of more years after that. My last meeting with her occurred when she invited Helen and me and Jimmy to a luncheon. I had always wanted my sons to meet her.

After one of the Elisabeth Irwin performances, a *Village Voice* critic noted, "Although it's not *great* music, its emotional impact of an important theme should make it an international repertory piece in these troubled times."[2] On balance, I consider *Preamble to Peace* only a moderately successful work. The reason may be the text. As in the Roosevelt *Battle Hymn*, the Preamble to the U. N. Charter kept striking me like the words of lawyers trying hard to say the right and noble thing, and not quite making it. They just didn't have the poetic content to make them sing. Too bad a Jefferson or a Lincoln doesn't come along oftener.

A more conclusive critical success in 1960 was the reissuance of *Ballad for Americans* on record. Vanguard released a new version with Odetta as the solo, the Robert De Cormier Chorale and Symphony of the Air. "The whole work takes on its old excitement and exuberance," wrote Herbert Kupferberg in the *Herald Tribune*. It still had "the stirring qualities of good folk music. It addresses itself to the heart."[3] I performed the solo myself that May of 1960 at a rather belated (by four years!) memorial for my librettist, John Latouche. He had died of a heart attack in August 1956 at the all-too-early age of forty-two, and for a few of those later productive years under the spell of a listing in *Red Channels*. Aside from the *Ballad*, we have his lyrics for *Cabin in the Sky*, *The Golden Apple*, and the opera *Ballad of Baby Doe* by which he is remembered. He had also worked with Lillian Hellman and Leonard Bernstein on *Candide*.[4]

As "captive voices" most of the E.I. chorus enjoyed their singing potential. But a few either didn't like to sing, or were moved to rebel. I found myself shouting more and more to get attention. One day I came into rehearsal with bronchitis and couldn't speak above a whisper. Well, the entire chorus not only listened closely to the whisper, they remained proper angels the whole rehearsal. We accomplished more than at the two previous rehearsals. This taught me a lesson and I seldom yelled again. I had no discipline problems with my Special Music Group. Ten to sixteen people each year freely elected this class, and I produced with them a number of folksong and Robinson arrangements that made successful assembly fare, and contributed to our annual concerts as well.

So Elisabeth Irwin did not detract from my composing, as I had feared. Rather, teaching turned out to be a useful, fun experience, because right away I got to try out everything I wrote—a luxury not every composer enjoys.

My years at E.I. coincided with some momentous times. As in 1945, in 1963, after JFK was killed, *The Lonesome Train* again found an audience seeking an outlet for its grief. It was programmed a number of times. In 1965 Mill Lampell revised it for a successful theatrical presentation by the Arena Stage in Washington, D.C. Itche Goldberg even wrote a Yiddish translation of it.

These years also coincided with the civil rights movement. Some of the music we programmed related to the burning issues on the front pages. Back in the days of writing *Sandhog*, Waldo and I had become friendly with Bob and Carolyn Goodman. Bob was an engineer involved with tunnel work; aside from giving us information for our folk opera, he invested in the production. With awful grief I learned that their son Andrew was one of the three boys killed by the Ku Klux Klan in Philadelphia, Mississippi, the summer of 1964. I wrote to Bob and Carolyn expressing my feelings, and received this reply:

July 24, 1964
Earl dear,
Your note and offer of help were beautiful and so like you. Perhaps in the near future when we learn more of the fate of Andy and his friends, we will call on you.
Somehow as I write you, who in my mind and heart stand for all that is good and true in our land, Paine's words keep ringing in my ear—for this truly is the time that tries men's souls. These past weeks of ter-

ror and pain have tried us—yet we feel strong in the knowledge that our son with his companions went forth to fight for their belief in dignity and freedom. History tells us that this is an unending struggle, yet it is the bravery and determination of young people like those in Mississippi today which make justice and equality possible.

While we may have lost a son in this struggle, we shall always have his beauty and love for humanity to make us strong.

Our love to you and hopes that we meet soon.

Bob and Carolyn

In response to Bob and Carolyn, and to the demands of the movement, I performed a number of benefits for SNCC, the Student Non-Violent Coordinating Committee, over the next couple of years, in Los Angeles, Berkeley, Cleveland, and Portland, Oregon.

My bibliography

Since the 1930s, my songs had been anthologized in any number of labor songbooks, World War II song collections, People's Songs bulletins, and *Sing Out!* magazine. But I was directly involved in the production of several books issued by mainstream publishers.

In 1963 Simon and Schuster published the *Young Folk Song Book*, with an introduction by Pete Seeger. The editor had chosen Joan Baez, Bob Dylan, Jack Elliott, Peggy Seeger, the Greenbriar Boys, and the New Lost City Ramblers (with Mike Seeger) to represent the new generation. They each sent us five of their most popular numbers. I arranged these both in guitar (and banjo and mandolin) tablature, the way they were performed—Ethel Raim helped on this—and for piano. In most cases this was the first time these songs had appeared in musical print, and I felt intimately connected to this group of talented young people. Dylan's songs included "Masters of War" and a "Song to Woody," which personally meant a lot to me. Plus we dedicated the book to Woody. Peggy Seeger and Ewan

MacColl's "First Time Ever I Saw Your Face," first published here, went on to become Roberta Flack's big hit.

Macmillan published a book completely of my own authorship, *Folk Guitar in 10 Sessions*. This compressed all that I had learned from teaching folk guitar classes, which for certain stretches during the blacklist was one way I had to make a living. In print for ten years or so, this book did better than any other I ever published. After a while the publishers gave it a new lease on life by calling it *Play Guitar in 10 Sessions*, so you may find it under that title.

Also published by Macmillan in 1967 was a book called *Songs of the Great American West*, a sizable volume compiled and edited by Irwin Silber. I served as music annotator, editor and arranger. Most of these simple folksongs had guitar settings, but on a few I felt particularly happy with my piano arrangements.

In 1967 as well, *The Brecht-Eisler Song Book* came out, from Oak Publications. (It may also be listed as *Songs of Bertolt Brecht and Hanns Eisler*.) Eric Bentley rendered Brecht's texts into an English that truthfully I found awkward in places, as I had known some of Eisler's songs in more idiomatic translations from the '30s. I edited the music. I preserved Eisler's original piano, though as he had so often observed, "Workers don't carry a piano around with them." So I also provided some more portable guitar chords. Not all the forty-two songs included are for solo voice: Some are for chorus, which is unusual for a book of this kind. I can't express sufficiently my satisfaction at being able to bring before an American public these wonderful songs of my teacher, songs that have meant so much to the whole progressive movement the world over. This book, incidentally, is still available.

The following year, Oak released the last book I worked on: *German Folk Songs*, compiled and edited by Arthur Kevess. I was music editor, and also supplied some lyrics in English. Of all these books, only the folk guitar paid off at all well, though the *Young Folk Song Book* sold 30,000 copies in the first six months and went into a second printing.

For the truly esoteric bibliophiles among you, I mention one further publication, *Erl Robinson Pyesni*. That's *Earl Robinson Songs*, which the Soviet publishing house Muzgiz put out in 1963. This 35-page collection included "The House I Live In," "Black and White," "Joe Hill," "I Come from Missouri" and "Far from My Darling" from *Romance of Rosy Ridge*, "Katie O'Sullivan" and "Katie-O, Johnny-O" from *Sandhog*, and "Spring Song." The Soviets priced this lovely book at only 45 kopecks. I'm still waiting for an *Earl Robinson Songbook* made in the U.S.A.

Notes

1. Group 3 (of my FBI file), pp. 177-78.
2. Nancy K. Siff, *Village Voice*, May 7, 1961.
3. Herbert Kupferberg, *New York Herald Tribune*, April 15, 1960.
4. See Earl Robinson, "Balladier for Americans," *The Nation*, August 25, 1956; also Richard Merkin, "The Holy Beast of Song," *GQ*, January 1991.

ETTL IN EASTERN EUROPE

Now this will be a little bit of history. Die Deutsche Demokratische Republik is a whole country that doesn't even exist any more. In English that's the German Democratic Republic (GDR), which is what they called themselves, rather than East Germany. It is interesting to note how they combined both Democratic and Republican in their title. I leave it open just what those words mean, but it is considerably different than in America.

There never was a Cold War for me

George Alexan first contacted me about going to the GDR. He had commissioned the Paul Robeson film and was translating *Sandhog* for production there. A complex of circumstances made this a very interesting trip, the first to Europe for both Helen and myself. I was coming out of the blacklist time: I had appeared before the Committee with some honor, also some scars. Paul Robeson had at last won his right to a passport, and here I was planning to travel not just to a socialist country, but to one which the U.S. didn't even formally recognize. My fears were balanced by a genuine sympathy and interest in socialism which persisted strongly through those years. Though my allegiance to the Party drew to an end in the late 1950s, I've decided I am too old to become anti-Soviet. I continue to honor Russia and the Russian people, and plan to work and play in peace with them forever, and that goes for the other socialist countries as well—or what's left of them. Of course, I am writing this in the era of *glasnost* and *perestroika* and arms control treaties. So if the Cold War is finally over, well, there never was one for me. They could have done without it and we'd all be a helluva lot better off today. But some people are just slow learners.

Another reason I wanted to visit East Berlin: That's where my friend and teacher Hanns Eisler lived. By this time he had become the country's leading composer.

In 1952 the State Department denied me a passport, but now it came through all right. I learn from my FBI file that our embassies abroad received a photo of me and appropriate background data in case I engaged in any public activity. I hadn't mentioned going to East Berlin in my request, and the GDR cooperated by not stamping our passports during the three weeks we spent there in May 1959.

Large preparations had been made to welcome me in the GDR. I had come to sing a concert and to conduct *Lonesome Train* on an all-American program that included works by Gardner Read, Norman Curtis, Robert Kurka, and a *Robert Burns Rhapsody* by Serge Hovey. My piece had been magnificently translated into German by Eva Lippold, survivor of eleven years in Nazi concentration camps, as *Lincolns letzte Reise (Lincoln's Last Ride)*. I had come, in their eyes, as a part of the *"andere Amerika"*—the "other" America—the America of the left, the friend of the workers and the blacklisted.

Helen and I were feted, wined and dined, all expenses paid the whole time we stayed there. We occupied the "Oistrakh Suite" at the Neva Hotel. I had only to express a wish to visit the town where Johann Sebastian Bach worked, and our hosts arranged a trip to Leipzig. I went with Helen and George Alexan to the Saint Thomaskirche rather late in the afternoon. The church had closed, but Alex persuaded the guard to open the doors for us. "Mr. Robinson came 3,000 miles to see the Bach cathedral," Alex said. While inside, I paused reverently in the choirloft where Bach conducted, and I bent down and kissed the floor under which his bones are still now resting.

Following our visit to the Thomaskirche, we met with the directors of the Leipzig Opera. It happens they were producing *Sandhog* and felt honored to meet the composer. Almost the first question they asked, the question every creative person welcomes: "What's new? What are you working on that we can consider doing next?" The importance of that question contrasted sharply with my own U.S., where in the blacklist period nobody seemed at all interested in "what's new." The main interest at home centered around The $64 Question.

Eisler, an esteemed national medalist, practically worshipped in his homeland, offered me a home in the country with a piano: I should come, live, and compose. I didn't take him up on this, however, feeling my place remained in America, blacklist or no. But I met several Americans who had made their homes there and felt reasonably happy.

At the Berliner Ensemble, the company Bertolt Brecht had founded and led until his death three years before, I met his widow Helene Weigel and saw his *Private Life of the Master Race*, which he had directed and which featured Weigel. I understood about a quarter of the dialogue, but through the genius of his production I got the entire story most excitingly.

The East Germans made good use of me, and kept me on a hectic schedule. This had some negative aspects, but I managed to take them in stride. I was interviewed several times for newspapers, magazines, and radio. They made a TV film of me singing eight songs, and I set up deals with two separate music publishers. One time they asked my opinion about some new economic policy they were pushing in the papers. I had no idea what it was all about, but I said something like, "It sounds all right to me, I guess." The headline on next day's paper read, ROBINSON IS ALL FOR NEW ECONOMIC PLAN. I was upset, but didn't protest; after all, I was a guest. Maybe I was going by the old P.R. axiom, Say anything you want about me, just spell my name right.

One time, a gathering of a small group of internationalists included a man from Vietnam. They asked for the song "Joe Hill." In order to make the song understandable to this fellow, I sang a verse in English, which they translated into German. Then into French, finally into Vietnamese. Verse by verse, the song made its way into the ears of four nations.

Struggle continues under socialism

Now the main reason I had traveled to the GDR was to help produce and conduct *The Lonesome Train*. I took the orchestral score to Hanns Eisler. Practice-conducting it himself, he came to a one-beat bar which had bothered me. He came to a stop, as I had, then immediately came up with a solution. "Ettl"—he rolled the "r" trippingly when he pronounced my name—"you must be *bold*. Conduct it *boldly*."

Our refrain lines

> *A lonesome train on a lonesome track,*
> *Seven coaches painted black.*

came out very powerfully in German:

> *Zug der Trauer, still gelenkt*
> *Sieben Wagen schwarz verhängt.*

Eva Lippold's translation went off-track in places. I spent hours trying to get her to understand the meaning. She re-worded the script but most of her changes came out not as good as the first version. They never did get "copperheads." She came up with *Verräter*—traitor—which wasn't quite right. Alex suggested *Reaktionär*. At the first rehearsal, Hanns Eisler quite properly said, "Ettl, dis iss no gut. *Reaktionär* cliché. Nein. Use *Bankier*—banker." We stuck with the original *Verräter*.

I saw mine as not only a conducting job but one of direct-ing, coaching the soloists and the chorus, especially since the material was foreign to them. A rehearsal schedule had been set up where I met and rehearsed the Ballad Singer, the Narrator, the Abe Lincoln character, the Square Dance Caller, the "black chorus," and the main chorus. But before I had a chance to meet with any of them I was called to an orchestra rehearsal. The conductor of the Grosser Chor und Grosses Orchester des Berliner Rundfunks, Adolf Fritz Guhl, needed to complain about the use of voices under the symphonic fabric in the *Robert Burns Rhapsody* by my old friend Serge Hovey. Serge had the voices singing a Burns song in their lowest range with the orchestra above them, which worried Guhl. I couldn't hear anything wrong. At that point Guhl laid the baton down and said, "You take over."

My score hadn't arrived yet; the music copyists were doing some last minute work. I hesitated at first to conduct without a score. But I thought to myself, I've conducted this dozens of times, I've sung it a thousand times at the piano, I'll give it a try. Well, I simply forgot the varying time signatures in the piece. I'd be conducting 1-2, 1-2, two beats to a bar, unprepared when suddenly a 3/4 bar would show. So I messed up the third beat, to the confusion of the orchestra. German musicians are among the best, but all musicians expect a downbeat at the beginning of the bar, not elsewhere. So uncertainty shadowed our communication in addition to the language difficulty.

I found myself ignoring time signatures even more because of what was happening in the speaking parts. The opening narration, a quiet storytelling statement, "The long war was over . . . ," came out of the Narrator's mouth like a dramatic Sermon on the Mount. He began at high-pitch intensity in what was German gibberish, to me anyway, and proceeded to wax even more heroic. I could do nothing but promise myself to tone him down in our private rehearsal. The Ballad Singer also sounded overblown but at least sang the notes as written. That first rehearsal, a near-complete shambles, was shortly suspended while Alex went into the control room to converse with the brass. They came up with a score and the second half went better. But damage had been done. Alex came out with a sad look, saying that perhaps they should have the regular conductor lead the piece. It seems that Herr Guhl had wanted to conduct from the beginning, before I ever got there. Now he saw a chance to advance his cause at the expense of this "amateur" from the States. I never got all the dialogue from the control room but it's easy to imagine how it went:

"Look, Robinson is a nice fellow and a good composer. He just doesn't know how to conduct. I will be happy to step in and help."

A somber Robinson returned to his hotel that evening for dinner with Helen and a very welcome friend Joris Ivens, just arrived in town. Dutch-born, Joris (pronounced Yoris) was one of the world's leading documentary filmmakers, a strong leftist whom I had met in Hollywood about 1944, when agent Charlie Feldman tried unsuccessfully to put him to work making commercial films. I told them my story, wondering if I should continue with all the crucial rehearsal work, or allow Guhl to conduct. Maybe he would give a better performance, I said. Helen showed sympathy, but Joris delivered himself of the right message that I needed to hear.

"Earl," he said, "you were brought here to conduct. You must conduct. Do not be afraid of a little conflict. Struggle continues under socialism."

With this fine support and stiffening of my backbone, I went into the coaching sessions with the soloists and decided to write a letter to the orchestra. At the next rehearsal Alex translated my statement line by line as I read it: I have traveled 3,000 miles to come here to your beautiful land and conduct my *Letzte Reise*. I now have the score here, and it is right that I conduct it. *Herr* Guhl (I had the idea that emphasizing *Herr* was like overemphasizing "Mister" to exaggerate respect for a person, demanding more than he deserved), *Herr* Guhl is a good conductor. He will do fine with the other American numbers of the program.

The GDR singers—I found out that half of them came over from West Berlin (this was before the Wall)—cooperated extraordinarily well, and gave me as close as they livingly could to what I wanted. The Narrator and the Lincoln character toned down their readings to a warm, conversational sound. The Ballad Singer, Hermann Hahnel, became a good friend. (He also performed Lewis Allan's "Strange Fruit [*Fruchte des Zorns*]" and Oscar Brown's "To Be Free [*Frei sein*]" on the program.) We shared Eisler and Brecht songs in our spare time. The Square Dance Caller and the entire chorus unbent during that scene to give some modest whoopees and celebration. The biggest problem I faced was getting a quartet of milk-white, classically trained singers to make like the free black, untrammeled, orgiastic Alabama church. It sounds obvious, but there was just no way I could make these white singers black, and once I recognized their limits, things went pretty well.

In any case, taking responsibility now for my stupidity in initially trying to conduct without a score, I helped create that scene to force me to take charge. The rest of the ten-day rehearsal period was almost a ball. I still worried too much about the translation of this complicated but essentially simple American folk legend into formal, constrained German.

Between two of the other works on the program, the concert promoters at the Staatsoper wanted me to perform a few solo songs. Afterward, I learned how it upset the decorum of the whole evening when I helped the stagehands move the piano out in front of the orchestra. *Lincolns letzte Reise* finished the evening. I had changed into a rented tux, and I did conduct my piece boldly. The performance went well, though I was deeply amused by the intensity of the Alabama church scene, with the original "Lord, Lord," "Praise the Lord," "Sure 'nough" and "yeah yeah" coming out as "*grosser Gott*," "*Gott in Himmel*," and "*ja, ja*," my private humor entirely hidden to the German audience. To me it sounded more like a cantorial service. But they seemed to regard it as all very exotic. A prolonged standing ovation followed. I must have been called out ten times. The next Sunday they rebroadcast the performance on radio and TV.

A day or two after the concert, I learned almost by accident that they were recording the whole piece, with Guhl conducting! This didn't bother me somehow. I had made my point, and I "second conducted" the instruments and choruses in little crescendos of celebration that he might be too busy to properly emphasize. He didn't seem to mind this either. We ended up collaborating acquaintances, if not friends. Struggle, continuing under socialism, is indeed not all bad.

Joining hands around the world

To recuperate from three fantastically busy weeks in Berlin, we proceeded to the beautiful city of Prague and their annual Spring Music Festival. It's a place I'd always wanted to visit. In the 1940s and early '50s, when things got rough politically in the States, I thought of living there for a while, maybe writing a Czech-American musical. The Czechs invited me to participate in the 1955 Spring Festival, but I couldn't get a passport. In such ways, our government prevented the world from knowing about American artists and our work.

I mentioned that besides being a composer-conductor, I also sang; this news met respectful silence. Helen and I enjoyed the festival, and met many engaging people from all over the world. One night we organized a fine impromptu hootenanny in an after-hours night club. Tossing in songs were two Romanians, a Bulgarian conductor, a Finnish music critic, three Vietnamese musicians, some assorted Czechs and Slovaks, a West German and four stray Americans.

We returned to our hotel at three a.m. to discover messages from the Ministry of Culture and the State Concert Agency, that I had been booked for three appearances out in the hinterland, beginning the next evening.

Our first and immediate problem was to make sure the songs would be understood. This is always nice. Our interpreter, Eva Obermaierova, worked all day making translations of my hit numbers. Taken so by "Casey Jones," she rendered that in rhyme. Numbers like "Study War No More," "Oleanna," "Joe Hill," and "Joshua" would be introduced with only a sentence of explanation. I also managed to get a translation into Czech of "Take This Hammer" and Wade Hemsworth's "Wild Goose."

On the way out to our first gig we paused in Plzen for some real Plzen beer (that's Pilsen to you). When we got to Mariánské-Lázné (Marienbad) we encountered one of the thorniest communication problems I have ever faced. Nobody at this rest home could speak or understand a word of English. A charming young lady read the translation and introductions before each song, with some feeling, I could tell. Then I sang. But each number seemed like a dud. In this big barn of a place with almost a thousand seats, about 400 attended and politely applauded. I couldn't get them singing along on anything. When I came back for the second part, more than half of the audience had left. I really couldn't blame them. I later learned that this was neither disrespect nor dislike, but only that many of them were patients who had to be in bed early. Those who remained said afterward they just weren't used to joining in. I was assured the next night's concert at Karlovy Vary (Karlsbad), a more cosmopolitan spa where people spoke English, would go better.

Besides, we folksingers learn by experience. On the train I dropped a couple of the longer, wordier numbers, moved "Everybody Loves Saturday Night" and some of the "mass precipitation" songs up nearer the beginning, replaced "Joshua" (which I had been told everyone in Czechoslovakia knew but which nobody did) with "Ti Yi Yippy" and the "Banana Boat Song." Also I worked hard on my pronunciation and even succeeded in getting some words in Czech to Woody's "So Long, It's Been Good to Know You" to finish the program.

A young fellow named Viktor met us. He spoke a bit of English. They gave us a fantastic suite of two rooms, each the size of a tennis court, and a wonderful sun deck with a view of the mountains. Only one minor problem. As I went over the program with Viktor, he informed me that 80 percent of the occupants of this particular rest home were Russian. And though many words are similar, Russians really don't understand Czech. They just think they do. And vice versa. So I said, with some shock, "Viktor, you mean every song has to be translated into Czech *and* Russian before I sing it?"

"Yes," said Viktor, searching for the proper English words. "It will be—uh—heavy."

Despite all the extra problems, that evening was a sensational improvement over the night before. The same number of people crowded into a much smaller hall; many of them stood. They joined in on all the songs. They enthusiastically sang "Take This Hammer" first in Czech as follows (please do not rely on me to teach you Czech spelling—this is written only something like it sounds):

Vez mee klah-*dee-vuh, Huh!*
Day ho kap-i-tan-*o-vee, Huh!* (repeat twice)

Ya ook too, Huh!
Nek tsee beet, Huh!

Now you want to know what happens to it in Russian?

Vez mee mah-*lu-talk, Huh!*
*Ah-de-dye kap-i-*tan-oo, *Huh!* (repeat twice)
Ya nee ha-choo, Huh!
Zdyess zhee-tuh.

This lovely audience even applauded the introductions, especially on numbers like "Spring Song" and "Quilting Bee," which speak of peace. They asked for copies of some songs, especially "So Long," in which I translated the last part of the chorus into words of friendship (the Folk Process at work).

The next night at Constantinova Spa, where again everybody spoke only Czech, was almost too easy. By then I could use expressions like *"Spevavta semino, proseem*—join in singing, please." The only problem this time was that without an automobile it took ten hours to get the sixty miles from Karlovy Vary. Three trains, and long waits. As the saying goes, "You can't get there from here."

The three-day tour turned out well. I returned to Prague just in time to accompany Paul Robeson in a hastily scheduled concert at the Cultural Conference taking place in conjunction with the music festival.

How many times have we said, Folk music speaks across the borders? Well, it's true. So I reported in an article in *Sing Out!* magazine about my adventures.

Of course, I'm not above poking a little fun at all my benevolent internationalism either. Just think, if we all joined hands around the world . . . three quarters of us would be under water!

A YIDDISHE COWBOY ON A WOODEN HORSE

The high point of my collaboration with Abel Meeropol was a full-scale musical based on two books by Yuri Suhl, *One Foot in America* (which gave its name to the show), and *Cowboy on a Wooden Horse*. Out of the blue, Abel sent me story and lyrics for Act One, and I set to work immediately. As an out-and-out musical with a story format, and without topical songs, it recalled *Sandhog*. But it required a Yiddish approach.

At the time it didn't seem strange, just the continuation of our long-time collaboration, for Abel to approach me as the composer for such a musical. Thinking about it now, it does seem anomalous that, passing over all the great Jewish composers for Broadway—and most composers for Broadway have been Jewish—Abel came back to me. I am a devoted reader of the magazine *Biblical Archeology*. Once, years later, after I'd gotten into more mystical soul exploration, I asked my spirit guide Dr. Peebles about this. He called it perfectly natural: I had a lot of incarnations from those Middle Eastern parts.

Changing minors to majors

Portraying first-generation Jewish young people and their folks fresh over from Europe, I had to deal once again with the Americanization process—the show is set in the 1920s—in ethnic as well as Broadway musical terms. So in more than one way I felt ready for this new assignment. It helped that at that time, from our house on Cranberry Street in Brooklyn, I could see the Manhattan skyline and the great Lady of the Harbor.

Not that these titles will be familiar, but just to give an idea of the flavor of the show, the songs included "Siegel Street," "Anything Can Happen to a Feller," "Why?," "Shloimele Helped a Little," "He's Not a Greenhorn Any More," "It's Never Too Late to Marry," "It's a Very Nice Day," "I Love a Girl Named Shirley," and "Rose of Sharon," perhaps the most moving love song I've ever written. In a minor key with a pulsing Near Eastern rhythm, only this song from the show found a publisher. One other song, "Cowboy on a Wooden Horse," is a Yiddish Western number with a loping cantorial yodel halfway between Hank Williams and Yossl Rosenblatt. With Anne Allan directing and me on piano, we put on a concert-reading as a benefit for *Jewish Currents* magazine in 1959 with as big a cast as would ever perform this material: Alan Arkin, John Randolph, Sarah Cunningham, Martin Wolfson, and others. This secular monthly is still being published.

I've told of how well Northwestern University produced *Sandhog*. Well, *One Foot in America* received its world premiere production there in 1961, also directed by Bob Schneideman. Multi-talented David Seltzer played the tenor lead, later heading out to the West Coast to write for TV and film. He wrote *The Omen*. Other films he wrote and/or directed include *Green Eyes*, *Lucas*, and *Punchline* with Sally Field.

One Foot attracted a Broadway-oriented producer and former assistant to Cheryl Crawford, Hope Abelson, who came to New York with sunny prospects. She hired Lehman Engel as director, and at his suggestion changed the title to *Siegel Street*. Hope set a budget of $300,000, and began the audition and money-raising process. Lehman went after me to brighten up the score—a salutary experience for me, because he had me changing my minors to majors. I found, while protesting a little, that they could be in major just as well, and come off with more pizzazz.

Hope got Abel rewriting—adding and cutting—but he had trouble meeting her more commercial requirements, principally a big, glamorous starring part for the likes of a Theodore Bikel, Morris Carnovsky or Howard da Silva. Abel preferred to keep the show a neat balance between the father Chaim and the son Sol, and proposed that instead of putting a star into the show, a star might come out of it. But with our not being able to announce a name star, and the auditions therefore not turning on prospective angels, our essentially off-Broadway ensemble musical had no real chance of making it with Hope's Broadway approach. We had created a work of huge proportions, with fourteen characters, two children, and at least six in the chorus. When inquiries came in from colleges or local Jewish community centers, the size of it scared them off.

By 1963 we were still trying to do something with the show, but by then *Milk and Honey* was playing and *Fiddler on the Roof* had been announced. We put our work to one side, and waited to see if the *Fiddler* would play. *Fiddler* played, all right, and the Broadway wisdom we received told us there just wasn't room for yet another show with a similar *tam* (Yiddish for flavor). Abel and I both took the demise of *One Foot in America* philosophically. But there's no inherent reason why the show shouldn't work: It had, after all, been well received at Northwestern. It has a youthful naïveté, a simplicity, that a lot of people would find appealing.

Liberty Bell blues

Sadly I record that Abel's and my friendship began a gradual deterioration. Already with *One Foot in America* problems had arisen. Abel guarded his role as writer like a mother lion. Apparently his solo working pattern had served him okay on Elie Siegmeister's *Darling Corie* and on Robert Kurka's *Good Soldier Schweik*, but for my taste he set far too sharp a delineation between writer and composer.

The real breakdown began in 1974, when he received an NEA grant to write a half-hour Bicentennial cantata, "Song of the Liberty Bell, 1776-1976," which treated the way we've dealt with minorities, starting with the Indians. As he wrote them, he mailed me his lyrics and scenes. But they held minimal appeal for me. Aside from the fact that I had already served our history well with *Ballad* and *Lonesome Train*, Abel's lyrics said little new and had no lift or power. By the time I received the entire work, I saw that it added up to not much. Also, more and more I had started writing my own words. I knew I would have to explain my eventual rejection to Abel. I wrote him as nice a letter as I could, taking responsibility for this job not being for me, and urging him to try another composer.

This did not sit well with Abel. He began telling me, in letter after letter, how poor a collaborator I had always been, taking undue credit and so forth. Almost systematically he seemed to be breaking off the relationship. I could only stand helplessly by, unable to level with him on his lyrics because of my tremendous respect for him, his relationship with his adopted sons Robbie and Michael, and our whole past history. Sometime later I won him back partly, by negotiating with Chappell a renewal on "The House I Live In." The second 28-year period had come due, and I succeeded in getting $15,000 for the rights, of which half went to Abel.

Why did he act this way? I finally found an answer. Abel began showing signs of Alzheimer's disease, from which he finally passed on in 1986. This could be the reason that his writing depreciated and that he attempted to cover this up by lashing out at me. I hold nothing against him for his actions during that time, and prefer to concentrate on the best period of our relationship.

One creation of mine is still done quite a bit since its first 1965 production. Probably no one over the age of ten ever gets to hear it, but I'm not complaining. It's a piece of children's theatre, a musical fantasy something like *Hansel and Gretel*, called *The Gingerbread Boy*. Elsa Rael wrote the libretto. John Ahearn continues to produce it in New York.

During these years I organized a high-level quartet consisting of me and Martha Schlamme, Liz Knight, and Leon Bibb. We sang around a bit—the usual church halls and progressive rallies. A much bigger impact came from a couple of Town Hall concerts the producer Harold Leventhal organized in my honor, designed to remember and recover Robinson from the obscurity of the blacklist. In 1962 we presented *The Lonesome Train* with Leon Bibb, Bob De Cormier conducting, and in 1963, *Giants in the Land* with a 40-voice chorus under David Labovitz. This second concert lost money and Harold never tried again with Robinson.

FARE THEE WELL, MY HELEN

In 1960 our beautiful Cranberry Street apartment got sold out from under us. We moved to Willoughby Walk, out in Brooklyn a ways, nothing being available at our price in the Heights (our price being not much). In the new apartment, we had fun at Christmastime. For three years running I organized a chorus to sing carols in the lobbies of the three Willoughby Walk buildings, something I still miss at Christmas out West.

Still sickily

The summer of 1962, Helen and I made what turned out to be her last cross-country trip, and just about her last trip anywhere. I had a booking in Saskatchewan, where the doctors had launched a strike against the new provincial medical care plan slated to go into effect on July 1st. Helen hadn't written lyrics before, but the theme, and maybe her own health troubles, inspired her. So we wrote "The Ballad of Dr. Dearjohn" together, and I performed it to the tune of "Cod Liver Oil" that Burl Ives used to sing. It starts off about a poor man wed to a "sickily" wife, paying out some strong doctor's bills. Then he hears about a government medical plan.

> *I ran out to tell it to my friend the doc.*
> *He grew purple and green and went into shock.*
> *"Don't believe all this garbage that you have been fed,*
> *It's socialist, communist, and also it's red!!"*
>
> *"A patient's and doctor's relationship*
> *Would be spoiled by a government dictatorship.*
> *The rights of us both must always be free."*
> *Says I, "That's the truth, but what about the fee?"*
>
> *I went home and I thought out the whole matter through.*
> *My wife was still sickily and what should I do?*
> *Must I work my whole life here in Saskatchewan*
> *Just to pay for the freedom of Dr. Dearjohn?*

299

Oh doctor, oh doctor, oh doctor, dear sir,
I hope there's a way that we both can concur.
Perhaps we can find us a compromise plan
To heal my sick wife here in Saskatchewan.

Well, I hear that the doctors and government met
With the help of Lord Taylor from Great Britain yet.
Yes the government sat down with Dr. Dearjohn
And the world will be praising of Saskatchewan!

The doctors lost the strike after the provincial government brought in "scab" doctors from Britain—maybe the only time I ever found myself opposing a strike. But these doctors were regressive souls trying to stop the force of history. Studies proved that universal, single-payer healthcare was cheaper than government subsidizing poor people only. By 1966 all of Canada had a health plan that people are by and large happy with—doctors included. When will the American people rise up—go on strike ourselves if that's what it takes—to get one here? We seem to be inching toward it ever so slowly, but so much time, and so many lives, have been wasted already.

I mentioned that when Helen gave birth to Perry she went into toxemic shock. All through the '40s and '50s there followed the damnedest string of problems—miscarriages, convulsions, phlebitis, nervous stomach, and an enlarged spleen—so we knew of her fragile health. Over a long eight years she developed a rare blood disease akin to leukemia called myoplasia, characterized by the bone marrow being unable to create red blood corpuscles. Trying with all her might to fight off the hopeless inevitability, Helen took a number of challenging college courses during that last year of her life, hoping to complete a degree, and also created some lively watercolors.

Helen entered Sloan Kettering on April 10, 1963, with kidney trouble. The next two months gave her a kind of torture that only medical science could devise. Maybe now, with the technological advances since then, her life—or her agony—

could be extended by many months or years even. People who
have gone through similar times will know what I mean.

Helen conducted a noble struggle. On May 14th, about to
face the knife, she said, "I can't do anything else than look to
the future," which meant spending the summer relaxing and
recuperating out at our home off the tip of Long Island on
Shelter Island, a real sanctuary for us, something like Puget
Sound had been in my childhood.

Before she was done, Helen went through three operations
and 124 pints of plasma and whole blood, suffering incredible
ups and downs. Word got around, and beginning with my own
donations of blood, many of our friends gave a good deal of
help along the way. "Her battle to live became more than a
mere struggle for survival," brother-in-law Dave Arkin wrote.
"It became a people's battle, a symbol of the tremendous value
of a single life."

Those weeks showed me a lot about myself, and I didn't
always like what I saw. How tempting I found it to revert to
familiar habits when it seemed for a day or two that Helen was
out of danger. A sweet-faced black lady worked in the lunch
room at the hospital, and I would light up when I saw her.
Even during this crisis, as the life of my dearest daily oozed
away, I could smile at a pretty girl. I questioned what kind of a
shit I'd become, feeling even more rotten if for a moment I
forgot about my worry and dark despair. It all seemed to con-
firm how hurtful I'd been, considering all my unfaithfulness to
Helen, all the different women there had been and, mostly, all
the times I had failed to communicate honestly with my devoted wife. I hated to think it had taken a final illness to fully
engage my attention on Helen and her needs. I couldn't pray;
it felt too hypocritical. Though if I thought Helen believed in
it, I would have tried.

After a while, Helen's mind began to wander, almost exactly like Pop in his latter years. "Shouldn't you get ready?"
she asked me of nothing in particular. "Can you write down
the message to them? Will the Soviet Union go for this?"

"Did I have a bad operation?" she wrote on a notepad, unable to speak with the tube in her throat.

"Three," I told her, to her surprise. The seizures she suffered had fortunately erased her memory. She talked of conspiracy. "Take me home," she said. "I want to go home. There's things going on here that aren't right." At the same time, shafts of brilliant recall pierced through. She referred to a Mrs. Brown from Tanglewood, where we'd stayed overnight years before.

Most days I spent with tears in my eyes. I forced myself to switch gears for an obligatory appearance down at Elisabeth Irwin, where the kids were rehearsing *H.M.S. Pinafore*. Sometimes I brought my guitar to the hospital and sang for the other patients, but I did it all with a lump in my throat.

When I could be useful I tried, giving Helen a backrub, massaging her scalp the way she liked. She had become so unbearably emaciated, the veins protruding across her bluish forehead. Often she had an oxygen mask on, or tubes connected up here and there. But she was still my beautiful Helen. I loved holding onto her hand, and touching her wavy brown hair flecked with the shining grays. One of her smiles sufficed to give me some wisp of new hope to cling to.

"Hope?" I'd ask myself. I hadn't realized that I'd already given up.

The time of Helen's last illness also taught me something about other people. "How is Helen?" someone would ask.

Not caring to launch into the whole medical prognosis, I'd say, "Fair, improving a little."

"Wonderful," says she.

"It's not wonderful at all," I'd answer. "Just a little better than last week."

"Wonderful," she says again. People ask questions and very often hear only what they want to hear.

One time when Perry came to visit, on extended leave from the army, he fainted when he saw her condition. By then the doctors were telling me, "She has her ups and downs, blood pressure and so forth. But each up is a little lower now. It's hard to be positive."

"I've had a good life," Helen said, preparing for the end. "Take care of the boys."

On Wednesday morning, June 19th, the call came to me at school. I left a meeting and drove to the hospital. Rachmaninoff's Second Piano Concerto came on the car radio. The shameless sentimentality helped me, and I cried. I went in to look at her once more. Her hair. I wanted to go back and see it.

Helen, warm Helen, no more.

Keep on living

I organized a memorial at the Melish church in Brooklyn—home of the Piscopalians, as Lee Hays called them—on October 30th, her 52nd birthday. I didn't say or sing a word, only invited as many of Helen's friends as I could reach. Alan Arkin emceed. The whole Wortis clan came, and some of Helen's co-workers from the animated cartoon field. Helen's union contributed a death benefit, very helpful to the struggling Robinsons at that time. A hundred or more condolence letters came to me, from the famous and the unknown, all citing Helen's gentle forbearing spirit. In the end, perhaps it was her ancient Aunt Faga, almost a second mother to Helen, who, deeply grieving herself, comforted me the most. "Living peopple have to live," she wrote in her idiomatic style. "This is my belive. So try to make the best of it. Keep on living." Helen's pictures I gave away to friends, and the beautiful pearls she inherited from her mother went to her sister Bea.

In the year that Helen passed, Perry, at 24, was in the Armed Forces Special Services, playing his clarinet. He'd already played all over Europe; in the military he played a lot while stationed in Panama. Back in New York he cut his first record and soon began to make a name for himself. At 17, Jimmy's only interest in tunes was tuning motors—early on, he developed extraordinary technical skills that make him one of the handiest guys you'd ever want to know. He has almost a compulsion to know how things work. The summer that Helen died, he spent with me out on Shelter Island, working at Jack's Marina on boats and engines. Even on that remote speck of land, with all my supportive and sympathetic neighbors, I now learn that one of them—unknown to me—kept the FBI informed as to my comings and goings.

Both our boys have gone through some rough periods figuring out what to do with themselves, working out their personal lives. For a long time, and still some, I felt I could have been a stronger parent, providing more structure and discipline. Kids have these needs, and too often I didn't feel confident enough to provide the firm guidance I should have. But they're grown men now and whatever my failings, they'll have to lead their own lives.

I plunged into my composing work with some relief after the long time away from it. I sang to myself

> *Fare thee well, my dear, I must be gone*
> *And leave you for a while.*
> *Though I roam far away, I'll come back again,*
> *Though I roam ten million mile, my dear. . . .*

I thought often of basing a farewell piece on this old and still fresh folksong. But I couldn't do it. Many times that summer, I wept.

By the time my old friend Hugh DeLacy heard the news of Helen's passing and got around to writing me (December 7, 1963), the nation had gone through the shock of John F. Kennedy's assassination. Perhaps that experience lent extra color and righteousness to his letter: "God damn it all!" he wrote . . .

> You know something? I have come to think that if any of us can pry out even a few years of rational companionship and even a small measure of personal happiness, we have damn near circumvented the whole system. It is not organized right, my friend. The premium is on discord, gigantic, repeated, and unresolved discord, a perpetual blue-ribbon cacophony.

Those who could sing are made dumb, and the tone-deaf are loose upon the land with jack-hammers and violin bows.

So here's my salute to a gallant and fine woman and a gallant and fine musician whose dedication is to bringing cacophony under rational control, for the everlasting good of all of us.

And I say, Amen.

ILLINOIS POLICE RELAY

Strangely, Helen's passing had the effect of freeing me to open up in fresh directions. I started composing with a new writer, Josef Berger—message songs like "The People Painter," and one about putting away childish toys like the atom bomb. We also did some love songs, such as "Janie in the Rain" and "All the Words are New." Only the latter is still in my active repertoire, and it gets a good reaction.

I moved to an apartment on Willow Street in Brooklyn Heights after Helen died. I resented Helen's absence when it came to setting up and furnishing the place. I held on to the Elisabeth Irwin job until Jimmy graduated, as he had free tuition. Lonesome myself, I had trouble being a good parent for him. Perry had gone out on his own completely by then.

Weave me tomorrow

In 1964, some internal instinct pointed to Hollywood again. This prospect gave me my first hit since *Ballad* and "House I Live In." As usual, it didn't happen immediately. I had fallen in love with the novel *Hurry Sundown*, and sought out the authors, Katya and Burt Gilden, a lovely wife and husband team. We got along famously, discussed a musical, an opera even. But Otto Preminger bought the film rights, so Lou Harris, a progressive friend from the Forties who was doing trailers at Paramount, put me in touch with him.

My gung-ho attitude about the book only heightened when I found out that Preminger was looking to get a song—for no money—to advertise the film. The prospect of going back to Hollywood and scoring the movie, dangled before me. "If we have anything to do with the film," Katya Gilden wrote me, "the musical direction has to be yours. It's still open and we're still hoping somehow to develop a situation in which our word will count."[1] With this kind of encouragement, I turned out words and music to a rousing song, which Preminger didn't like. So I went for the best, to Yip Harburg, to see if he'd be interested in writing the lyrics. Yip was quite favorable at first, until he learned that Preminger wasn't paying. He backed off, calling Otto a "cheap bastard" among other choice names. Well, I didn't give up. I wooed Yip by continuing to visit him and play him tunes, until he got turned on and eventually yielded.

I first played him parts of slave songs, black songs of protest, moderately engaging to him. But we struck fire with a song I had composed for an aborted sequel to *Dark of the Moon*, planned for a New York production which never came off. The main tune, which Yip enthusiastically latched onto, became the base of "Hurry Sundown," and we added a refrain:

> *My seed is sown now, my field is plowed,*
> *My flesh is bone now, my back is bowed,*
> *Then hurry sundown, be on your way,*
> *And hurry me a sun-up*
> *From this beat-up sundown day.*
>
> *(Refrain) Hurry down sundown,*
> *Don't stop to pray,*
> *Weave me tomorrow, out of today.*

We created a fine outstanding song. But Otto Preminger turned this one down, too. There's no accounting for some people's taste.

There were pitfalls yet to come, but a final retribution. I had played the song for Milt Okun, music director for Peter, Paul and Mary, and he liked it. Next thing I knew, he told me how much Peter and Paul were enjoying working out a guitar arrangement. Then he says they're planning to record it. And here's where a nice thing happened. I had lost touch with Preminger after the turndown, but in the meantime he had contacted PP&M about singing *his* song under the opening titles of the picture. He had gone ahead and got another composer, Hugo Montenegro, for the song and the picture, but his was an inferior song. PP&M confirmed this by rejecting it in favor of recording Yip's and mine. In a conversation on the phone between Otto P. and me, he tried attacking, then pulled back. In short, he could do nothing about it. PP&M had made a choice, and the title which he had bought for the film was not legally copyrightable as a song.

The trio recorded "Hurry Sundown" with an arrangement I added for brass quartet. It went on to make the charts, sold quite a few records, was published as a solo (a choral version also exists), and the following year won a Grammy nomination.

Addendum: I take no delight in the fact that the movie was not good, despite the presence of Jane Fonda, Michael Caine, Burgess Meredith, Faye Dunaway, and Diahann Carroll. *Halliwell's Film Guide* (4th edition, 1983) calls it an "incredibly cliché-ridden epic melodrama . . . [that] long outstays its welcome even for unintentional hilarity." "To criticize it would be like tripping a dwarf," said Wilfrid Sheed. Katya and Burt Gilden deserved better. Don't bother seeing it. Buy the book, if you can find a copy. It remains one of the best examples of 20th-century American literature.

Linking events, bookings, and love

The year 1965 spelled growth and change. The growth didn't always seem obvious, but change there was. I grew into a relationship with Ruth Martin, widow of Peter Martin, writer for the Workers Laboratory Theatre, subsequently for NBC and ABC television and Universal Pictures, and old friend and collaborator of mine. Toward the end of his life, Little, Brown published two novels in his projected Jewish family-saga trilogy, *The Landsmen* and *The Building*. Ruth wrote me a condolence when Helen died, and we met in early 1964. She came back east from her home in Los Angeles to visit my place on Shelter Island that summer. The result was our marriage on May 5, 1965.

We started out with a lot working for us. I had been invited to Salem, Illinois for a presentation of *Lonesome Train* and a Lincoln celebration that first weekend in May. And the governor in Springfield invited me for dinner—I happily sang a few songs for my supper. Linking up events, bookings, and love—a favorite activity of mine—we decided to get married the next day at the home of my brother Duane and his wife Marjory, in the little George Williams College town of York Center, near Chicago.

Ruth came in from the West Coast, and I thought I could easily get up from Springfield in time for the wedding, which became the subject of discussion at Governor Otto Koerner's mansion, where they wined and dined me. "How you gonna get up there?," someone asked.

"Is there a plane tonight?" I returned. Governor Otto offered that I shouldn't fly, but should go by "police relay," whatever that was. I found out, and thus occurred a dramatic trip which eclipses in my memory both the marriage and Mr. Lincoln's celebration.

The Governor arranged for a policeman to come to the door for me. Telling him of my Lincoln activities, *The Lonesome Train* and so forth, I felt some surprised at his lack of interest. As we traveled north in his cruiser, he revealed his own original thoughts about how our sixteenth president could be exploited better. I listened astonished as this cop outlined his P.R. plan.

"The trouble is," he began, "people come into Salem in the morning, see the statue, the park, read the sayings of Lincoln, get through all there is to see about him, and are out by nightfall. There's nothing to hold them there, see? But what if you throw a little dam across the Sangamon River, the water backs up and you get a lake, see? And what happens when you have a lake? You get motels, people stick around for swimming, see? They have a place to spend their money, really appreciate the place. That way, you get some value from Lincoln. The way things are, you get no damn good out of Lincoln whatsoever!"

With all the thinking and research I had done on Abraham Lincoln—the Great Emancipator, the man who put saving the Union ahead of freeing the slaves, the consummate politician, the man of war as well as peace—I had never grasped this particular commercial angle on him.

The way the relay works is the cops communicate with each other over their car radios, and arrange where to meet to transfer their cargo. The first cop turned me over to another policeman in the next county on the way to Chicago. The second policeman was not so talkative, but he developed a mission that I felt privileged to be part of. We were cruising along at 60 conversing (not about Lincoln), when a car passed us going close to 80 miles an hour. My friend at the wheel apologized for the interruption in the conversation. "Mr. Robinson, will you pardon me? I'm going to have to take out after this fella."

"By all means," I said, "go ahead and do your job" (being extremely happy it wasn't me he was chasing). It was a thrill to be on the inside of the law for a change, to go as fast as you wanted with never a fear. He caught up with this speedster, left me in the car while he went over and relieved him of his license (that's what cops in Illinois do, or used to do), to insure that he show up in court the next day.

"We've been after this fella for some time now," my friend explained.

The next cop in the relay had been something of an athletic star in high school. So the conversation wasn't quite as dramatic as the first two. But he delivered me to the door of my brother's house a hundred and forty miles from Springfield in record time, exceeding the speed limit several times that night, and all within the law. Who's going to arrest a cop?

Postscript: Governor Otto Koerner was later indicted and removed from office for some money shenanigans. Guess he didn't cover his tracks well enough. I was sorry to hear it; he had been generous to me.

Note

1. Katya Gilden to Earl Robinson, February 27, 1971.

HOLLYWOOD: TAKE 3

Ruth and I married in May 1965. In retrospect I am unable to say why I chose her. We struggled for seven years trying to figure out how to be good for each other, but never could pull it together. It's still painful. In part I married Ruth relying on her to manage all the money and practical matters that Helen used to do. I expected too much. My fault more than hers.

Ruth introduced me to psychologists and psychiatrists who gave me some ongoing help. She also introduced me to Transactional Analysis and to books like *Games People Play* and *I'm OK, You're OK*. I in turn told Abigail Van Buren about the latter book. Dear Abby wrote to me, "I am in your debt. And by the way, you might be interested in knowing that I've been okay for a long time, and I think you're okay, too."[1] But in the end, marriage as therapy, I don't recommend it.

Ruth served as the most important catalyst in turning my life toward Hollywood again. It became ever more important to get back out there, to up my moderate standard of living, to reach again for the larger audience, and to test if the blacklist had truly passed. As one sure sign, Camera Three televised an interview with me in July 1965. Another good reason for moving back involved Ruth's son Mike and my Jimmy, who'd been squeezed together tightly with us in our Brooklyn apartment. Ruth's older son Howard was in college and on his own already, likewise Perry. Our newly patched-together family didn't always function copacetically, so once Jimmy graduated from Elisabeth Irwin, we felt freer to pick up stakes.

Promising a new creation

My classical composing career received an unexpected boost the moment we moved west. Just after arriving back in Hollywood the summer of '66, I received a commission to compose a Concerto for Five-String Banjo. No one had ever written such a work, though I am told that Samuel Orchard Carr wrote a Concerto for Tenor Banjo around 1940. The

313

commission came through with the help of Manny Greenhill, representative for a number of folk artists, including Joan Baez and Pete Seeger. As a young man attending vaudeville in the '20s I got a kick out of Eddie Peabody and his "brassy" plectrum four-string banjo. Only in the late '30s, when I started digging deeper into folk music, did I hear the remarkable five-stringer with its drone string and amazing contrapuntal sound. I first used it in *The Lonesome Train*, asking Pete Seeger to play the CBS broadcast and record it. Once, after the war, I heard Pete in the middle of a concert knock off eight or ten seconds of scintillating cadenza on his instrument, then pull back apologetically and say something like, "Let's all join in on this civil rights song, shall we?" I wrote Pete about it at the time:

> Pete, could I make a deep and sincere suggestion to you? This is personal. In addition to whatever picket line and organizing activities you engage in in the coming period, bind yourself down to at least two hours a day on your instrument. Get to be the best goddamned five string banjo player in the country, or the world for that matter. In other words, increase your technique to the point where you will be respected as an artist as well as a singer and organizer. I will write you a couple of compositions for banjo and orchestra, or banjo and voices.[2]

So for a long time I'd felt determined to persuade Pete to allow his hands to really do the symphonic magic that he clearly could pull off. When this $2,000 commission came from the Boston Pops, I went to work.

I bought me a Seeger-type five-stringer and learned to play, slowly, everything I put down on paper. I figured if I could play what I wrote, Pete could, too. I cringe admitting that my working title for this concerto was "Pete Suite." I put in folk tricks like frailing, blues picking, audible tuning as part of a cadenza, and left a section where the banjoist could create his own bluegrass-style cadenza. People tell me that the unusual crossover of such a strongly folk-identified instrument into

Symphony Land recalls the way some Asian composers have integrated Eastern and Western instruments. In places the banjo sounds like an Indian sitar or a Japanese koto. Which wasn't my intention with this originally African and now quintessentially American instrument, but that's okay.

The concerto starts with the suggestion that the soloist is working out an original melody. One by one, other instruments join in—flute, oboe, clarinet, then the orchestra. The second movement opens with a banjo cadenza, followed by strings playing pizzicato. Then it proceeds on the idea of audience participation, with the orchestra as audience. The third movement has the spirit of a scherzo, taking its basic form from the square dance, to which I added a jazz quality.

The fourth movement is a song. It seemed as if after playing more banjo than had ever been attempted before, the picker might feel ready to sing. If the banjoist can't sing, another singer, preferably with a clear, high yodel, can do it, or even a quartet. I also imagine that some day a conductor might ask the whole orchestra to join in on the last round. The emergence of the voice at that point has ample precedent: Beethoven's Ninth, or Mahler's Fourth, or the Busoni Piano Concerto with male chorus, where pure music alone can no longer express all the composer needs to say, and he must resort to words. I harked back to an old Shaker hymn, "How Can I Keep from Singing," and Lee Hays helped me with new words. (Notice there is no question mark here: It's always a positive statement.) I had a long, flowing, lyrical melody to stimulate him, and Lee, with his church singing background, together with his love for Walt Whitman, met the challenge well.

> *Over the sound of Earth's sad lamentation,*
> *Through all the tumult I hear music ringing,*
> *Hearing the voices that promise a new creation,*
> *How can I keep from singing.*
>
> *Life is an endless song of joy and sorrow,*
> *Singing each day of defeat and victory,*

> *But I know that love is the hope of all Earth and Heaven,*
> *How can I keep from singing.*

For the record: Yip Harburg liked this tune a lot, and without my encouragement wrote new words to it. We named that song "One Sweet Morning."

> *Out of the fallen leaves the autumn world over,*
> *Out of the shattered rose that will smile no more,*
> *Out of the embers of blossoms and ashes of clover,*
> *Spring will bloom one sweet morning.*
>
> *Out of the fallen lads the summer world over,*
> *Out of their flags plowed under a distant shore,*
> *Out of the dreams in their bones buried under the clover,*
> *Spring will bloom one sweet morning.*

Yip's is a very beautiful lyric, but I never pushed it because I felt committed to Lee's.

I sent the score to Pete, and a few days later received a troubled phone call. He wanted me to come to Beacon (on Hudson) at his expense, to go over the concerto. Pete had convinced himself that he couldn't play it. He considered himself too slow at reading and picking up new material. We worked for three days, but finally I had to accept that he had decided it wasn't for him. Totally used to singing for masses of people, Pete and his flying fingers automatically found the right notes and chords. Here he had to relate to all those musicians waiting on him for carefully written-out notes. "I could see myself just standing there, doing nothing," he said.

We agreed to get Juilliard-trained Eric Weissberg for the performance a month and a half off in Boston. Pete volunteered to give an illustrated talk on banjos at the concert, and since Eric was to singing as Pete was to concertos, we arranged for Pete and me to sing the fourth-movement song.

Arthur Fiedler conducted the concerto in February 1967, and Robert Gustafson in the Boston *Globe* reviewed it nicely:

"the highlight of the evening," he said, "most successful." The concerto is

> a piece of Americana with brashness, impudence, wit, tenderness, and charm, and is unabashedly romantic.
> Mr. Weissberg, aware of his pioneering role, was equal to his task, both in the area of technique and sensitivity. It is a difficult work for any banjo player, and Mr. Weissberg obviously is one of great skill.
> Mr. Robinson and Mr. Weissberg made an otherwise pleasant evening an exciting one, and the capacity audience responded appreciatively and enthusiastically.[3]

In the *Record American* Rolfe Boswell called the concerto "modishly American as pumpkin pie with whipped cream." "Musically," he added, "its influences, apart from the vocal balladry, are early Copland, Dixieland jazz and a smattering of Gershwin."[4]

The concerto has had a number of good performances, but has not been recorded. Eric played it in Corpus Christi, with Maurice Peress conducting, also with the Omaha Symphony under Joseph Levine (with the Symphonairs, a mixed vocal quartet, on the song). Elmer Bernstein conducted it twice, in Long Beach and Inglewood (yours truly singing), with a new young banjo man Mike De Temple (a prize-winning fiddler as well), who couldn't read music, so I tutored him on the score. He invented some great flourishes on his own. He also played two movements one Saturday at a Los Angeles Philharmonic children's concert.

The person who has learned and truly mastered the concerto is Michael Martin, my stepson. Very much present in our home while I was writing the piece, Mike absorbed it by osmosis. He initially learned to play it when his college orchestra at Cal State Sonoma scheduled it in May 1970. But because of Nixon's bombing of Cambodia just then, half the orchestra refused to play unless the concert was dedicated as a political statement; and the other half wouldn't play unless it was just another orchestra concert. Five days before the performance date, they canceled the concert. Mike has since performed the piece with symphonies in Ventura, California, and Palm Beach, Florida. Mike later went into computers, and music became not the substance but the spice of his life. Piano became his main instrument. Still, he kept the concerto in his fingers, and in 1990, in connection with celebrations of my 80th birthday, he played it in Freiburg, Germany, and Ventura again. So I cannot claim that it hasn't had good, high-level performances. But I'm still patiently waiting for this "piece of Americana with brashness, impudence, wit" to be recorded.

Starting at the bottom

I pursued employment opportunities in Hollywood with an organized determination. I studied the film schedules in *Variety* and the *Hollywood Reporter*. I would clip anything that might mean a Robinson job. I got my agent Al Bart to take an ad in *Variety* plugging the Boston Pops Banjo Concerto premiere and the nomination of "Hurry Sundown" for a Grammy. I tried to get the Hollywood Bowl to bring out Fiedler with the concerto, which might have led to a recording besides placing my name in plain sight for film-scoring jobs. All with minimal payoff.

Having encouraged me so forcefully to get back in the mainstream with a revived Hollywood career, Ruth put a lot of energy into promoting me. She created résumés, hustled on the phone, entertained people in the industry, and came up with ideas. As the widow of a writer, and now the wife of a composer, she liked being attached to celebrity. This had a stifling effect, of course—the classic thing of the woman supporting the husband's career and subjugating herself—but there is no denying how hard she worked. And not only for me, but in her volunteer-spirited way also for Women's Strike for Peace, the Democratic Party and other causes.

I slowly learned to start at the bottom. I introduced myself to the music departments and extension divisions at the various universities around town, hoping at least to keep my foot in the Hollywood door by teaching. Some of the courses I conducted, at UCLA and elsewhere, included Choral Master-works, and Sound and Music for Film and Theatre.

I tried putting myself into the mind of the movie producer or director, agent, actor or writer, and coming up with a useful thought, whereby he would see that I could be appropriately involved. An exponent of the "glass is half empty" school might conclude that these years were moderately unsuccessful. Being a "glass is half full" type, I will ac-cen-chu-ate the positive, merely noting a few of the defeats along the way. In the end, with a deep nod of acknowledgment to Ruth, who lifted me out of my New York City guitar-teaching, high-school doldrums, it felt good to have the blood rushing in my veins again.

The first defeat occurred with *Cool Hand Luke*, where the banjo in Paul Newman's hands could form the basis for the whole score. I had been recommended by no less than Alex North, old friend from my Composers' Collective days and a premier Hollywood composer. I hadn't gotten far into my concerto by then, so when I talked with Gordon Carroll, producer for Warner, I didn't bring my banjo. I may thereby have lost the chance to do the score, which Lalo Schifrin eventually composed.

An old friendship with Marty Ritt also didn't help when he needed a composer for *The Mollie Maguires*, a fine working-class film for which it seemed I'd be a natural. I attended shootings, got to know Sean Connery and the other lead actor, Richard Harris. But the folklike tune I'd written on spec wasn't forceful enough. That score went to Henry Mancini.

I note another defeat—for a powerful tune I got from Pop Wortis, Helen's father, that he remembered from his genius father Wolf Wortis. I heard it as a perfect theme song for *The Fixer*, directed by John Frankenheimer, with Eddie Lewis producing. I talked to Eddie at a party about the song, won his interest, but somehow couldn't nail it into a job.

In '68 my old pal Jules Dassin came back to the States for the first time in twenty years, to produce a black version of *The Informer*, called *Up Tight*, which takes place in Cleveland in the aftermath of Martin Luther King, Jr.'s, assassination. It starred Raymond St. Jacques, Ruby Dee, Julian Mayfield, and Roscoe Lee Browne. Julie had appropriately picked a young (23) black folk-rockman, Booker T. Jones, for the score. I suggested that since Booker T. had never made a film before and since he and his band members couldn't write out what they played, Julie might like to have old pro Robinson on the set and in the scoring chamber, to bring out the band's best creative profile. Which Julie bought. And took me, with Booker and his soul rhythm group, to Paris, where he felt more comfortable scoring the picture than in Hollywood. By and large I remained a good boy for those five weeks, wrote some underscoring and bridges but did not thrust myself forward too much, and only once got Booker mildly irritated at me. As music coordinator representing the Paramount music department in Paris, I helped him produce a good, useful score for *Up Tight*—my first commercial film credit in twenty years. Out of this experience I wrote an original twelve-minute band piece called *Soul Rhythms*, which Herbert Haufrecht helped me publish in 1972 at Mills Music. It never made any big splash, but helped establish me as a composer of band material. Ever attentive to duty, the FBI played its part in trying to squash the film by releasing Jules Dassin's HUAC files to the press.

Most people don't think about it, but much of the music in our culture never gets celebrated at the Academy Awards, on the top forty charts, or in the concert hall. Hardly anyone notices a lot of workaday, functional, and totally unglamorous music that's there making its contribution. Many composers piece out their income with such occasional jobs, and some specialize in it. Actually, the amount of music written out of the composer's purely esthetic impulse, with no commercial motivation, is minimal compared to what's written for hire.

John Sutherland got me a job of composing an 18-minute score for a series of Intensive Coronary Care Nurses' Training films. That brought in $2,000. I did TV commercials too: nurse recruitment ads for the U.S. Public Health Service, frozen turkey dinners for Ralston Purina, BankAmericard for Bank of

America (three high tenors singing a jazzy "I Want to Be Happy"), Wells Fargo Bank, and an ad for a flying Billy Blast-off Space Toy for the Eldon Toy Co. For Pan American World Airways I composed the score to a film about communication, *Speaking of Words*. I also scored a New Zealand promotional film called *Something New Under the Sun*, in which I had recordings of Maori singing as the background, and me singing new words on top. John and I got together in 1967 on "Ballad of a Jazzman," written for TV from an idea of mine with Gil Melle. Eventually unrealized, we based this 60-minute animation with live action film on the life of John Coltrane, using him to symbolize the development of the jazz art form.

Still striving to complete that half-full glass, I talked myself onto *September Country*, a Tennessee mountain film, Eddie Lewis producing, John Frankenheimer directing, starring Gregory Peck. They scheduled Johnny Cash for the score. I saw a good chance for an experienced composer to give a hand to Cash, who as far as I knew did not write movie scores. Frankenheimer and Lewis bought this concept, and hired me at a decent $10,000 salary. I accompanied Frankenheimer to Nashville to meet with Johnny and his wife June Carter, whom I knew about from Woody Guthrie's love for the Carter Family and their recordings.

Everything felt so hunky-dory that I neglected to look clearly at where Johnny might be, and to check carefully on where I stood in relation to him. Johnny had been on TV every week with his railroad theme song, so I brought along a record of *Lonesome Train* for him. I allowed myself overblown ideas on my importance: Johnny could be so impressed he would choose *Lonesome Train* as his new theme song, he could choose me to be his trusted adviser, his mentor, even. Without thinking it through, I began acting as if it were accomplished fact. I never really heard Frankenheimer say, "Look, Johnny Cash doesn't need us, *we* need *him*."

We went to see the film in a theatre, and Johnny showed up with a Nashville producer, who proceeded to take over the spotting of the music. Every time I opened my mouth Frank

322   Section Five: 1957-1972

shushed me fiercely. None of my good and important ideas on music were asked for or even allowed.

At Cash's home for lunch, he asked Frankenheimer, "What is he doing here?" pointing his head at me. And Frankenheimer hastened (indecently, I thought) to assure him, "Nothing, nothing at all. He's just here to help—if any is needed."

On the plane home to L.A. I drank deep from my cup of gall and wormwood. Frankenheimer sat across the aisle from me with the Nashville producer, hanging on every word, and ignoring Robinson. Before we parted I gave Frankenheimer my second copy of *Lonesome Train*. To this day I don't know if Johnny Cash or Frankenheimer ever listened to it.

I told Ruth the story, smiling all through the tale, as if something good had happened. The next afternoon a call came from Eddie Lewis: Cash had decided to do the score and they had no need for my services. Lewis paid me off with $2,000.

Thomas Harris, writer of *I'm OK, You're OK*, analyzed all this at a transactional analysis session. I had been operating with a "losing script," acting in such a way as to *create* the losing. I felt so comfortable in this scene that I could smile and laugh about it. I might have changed this into being on the film as Johnny Cash's quiet and willing helper, gaining valuable experience in film scoring, if I had been able to operate with a winning script. (Might not have either.) Instead I chose to learn the hard way. I dumped that losing script and got a tremendous discovering experience.

A procession of discomforting gadflies

Illinois celebrated its sesquicentennial in 1968. As I had already made my name known in the state for my Lincolniana, Verlyn Sprague of the Sesquicentennial Committee asked me and Carl Haverlin, another Lincoln buff, to write a cantata. With *Chicago Tribune* money, radio station WGN commissioned a half-hour work. As usual, I attempted too much. *Illinois People* ran over an hour, calling for chorus and soloists, Indians, jazz men and children, speaking voices, and overall a dramatic interpretation. It had a huge "Names and Places" section, a Lincoln section, and a soliloquy to be trumpeted by a good voice. We spoke of the 1909 mine disaster in which 268 men died, and we reminded our listeners of the Haymarket bombing and the martyrs to the eight-hour day.

All rather formidable, perhaps too much so for the WGN committee who heard me present it. They turned it down, and I never did get all the why. They said it was too long, even when I offered them the second half hour for free. Maybe what one reporter referred to as the "procession of discomforting gadflies" had something to do with it: The Haymarket affair is still not talked about in certain sections of Chicago. Whatever, I was left with a cantata on my hands.

The Francis Parker School, a progressive institution in Chicago with children up through high school, had previously performed *Sandhog*, and even made a record of it. So they readily turned on to a new Robinson opus, and presented it in November 1968. According to the *Tribune* review: "Like *Ballad*, the new work is part history, part travelog, and part amiable corn. . . . Few history lessons are as candid and tuneful."[5]

Still yearning for a more professional production, I got one at Southern Illinois University in Edwardsville in 1974. There the exceptionally talented choral director Leonard Van Camp not only conducted but sang the soliloquy, which had been cut from the Chicago production. I accompanied at the piano. But that was the last performance of the cantata. Did WGN put a curse on it?

That performance in Edwardsville came about in part because a couple of years earlier I had donated a dozen or more boxes of my papers to the SIUE library. Originally I had hoped to be paid for these materials, but that never came about. Later on I gave another huge batch of papers to the Southern California Library for Social Studies and Research in Los Angeles, an excellent repository for all kinds of "movement" history. Recently, having moved back to Seattle, I've arranged to gather my complete archive together in one place, the University of Washington.

Rocketing

One "topical" success here. In a fantastically hurry-up job in July 1969, to take advantage of its commercial timeliness, we agreed to put out on Bell Records (a division of Columbia) a "Flight to the Moon" album, just days after the successful Apollo moon flight splashdown in the Pacific. Norman Corwin wrote the narration, spoken by astronaut Wally Shirra, with score by Robinson. A press release said, "Side Two written during a lunch break between recording sessions"—a slight exaggeration, showing, however, the time pressures. We put that side together as the taped voices came in from the moon. I scored the album for trumpet (with electric trombone attachment), guitar, two woodwinds, organ, percussion, and Moog synthesizer. Despite being so rushed to completion, the album sold 8,629 copies by the end of the year—the only documentary-type album to stay on the charts for five weeks.

Finally in 1970 came a breakthrough. My first film with a complete score and song came from Joseph Sargent, who produced and directed *Maybe I'll Come Home in the Spring* for ABC television. It starred Sally Field as a runaway hippie who returns to her dysfunctional family only to endure the same situation she had run away from. Eleanor Parker and Jackie Cooper played her parents, Lane Bradbury her younger sister, and David Carradine her irresponsible boyfriend. This was the first Hollywood film where I composed, arranged, and conducted the entire score. I got to work with Linda Ronstadt, who sang on the soundtrack scriptwriter Bruce Feldman's and my song "Different Day." Linda had attended the Hollywood Bowl benefit for Huntington's research and liked my singing of a Woody Guthrie song. I visited her home several times, both to rehearse the song and later, but this almost-friendship faltered after a time.

Reviews came in solidly for the picture. The *L.A. Times* called it "an engrossing drama of real people about whom it is possible to care." *Daily Variety* said, "Superior work all around. . . . Music by Earl Robinson contributes enormously to overall beauty of pic. Pair of songs . . . add yet another dimension." *The Hollywood Reporter* chimed in, "Music by Earl Robinson is some of the best to come out of the Movie of the Week series, especially his and Feldman's 'A Different Day,' which is lovely."[6]

The movie could have become important for my career. With that in mind, I bought a half-page ad in *Variety* to thank all concerned for putting me and my music back on the map. For by that time, aside from those rave quotes, I was able to include the full commercial flowering of two of my songs—the first being "Joe Hill," both on the Joan Baez Woodstock album and in Bo Widerberg's film *Joe Hill* that formed part of the 1970s revived interest in the man and the legend. At the time Joanie sang the song, her husband David Harris was in jail as a conscientious objector against the Vietnam War, and he organized the guys there—with the help of Joe Hill. She and I shared some personal time in the recording sessions for the film, and she told me that David and she had separated. "You know, he was wonderful as long as he was in jail," she said. "But the kid and the closeness we can't handle." The song continues as one of Joanie's most requested numbers, so I expect she'll be singing it for many years to come. Widerberg's film won the Jury Prize at the Cannes Film Festival; the nationally distributed newspaper ad featured the first stanza of Al Hayes's lyric. Phil Ochs also recorded the song on his *Tape from California* album.

The other song, "Black and White" with Three Dog Night, rocketed up the charts.

Strange unusual evening

In the '60s and '70s I rejoiced with our emergence out of the Red scare, with the "black is beautiful" movement, and with the struggle against the Vietnam War. But the attitude of the young radicals somewhat frustrated my efforts to help, to place my music on the line in this period. They didn't trust anyone over thirty! With the exception of Arlo Guthrie, with whom I renewed a childhood (his) friendship. I had him in a guitar class in his early teens, a short-lived apprenticeship because he rapidly advanced way beyond what I could teach him.

I loved and supported the Beatles, sang "Give Peace a Chance" with the young folks at demonstrations. And I would advise whoever of my serious-music colleagues would listen, that they study the Beatles, listen to their striking phrasing, their original ways of uniting music with exactly the right words. I know I learned much from them.

In between the Hollywood hustle, the political Earl kept moving on. The war was beginning to wind down in Vietnam. Then all of a sudden "we" were in Cambodia with Nixon. More and more young people felt outraged. On campuses students declared moratoriums. In Santa Barbara someone burned a Bank of America building. The plane accident death of the United Auto Workers President Walter Reuther led to a well-run memorial meeting sponsored, remarkably enough, by students from the University of California at Santa Barbara.

Just ten days before the memorial took place, an appalling action happened in New York City: Hardhats beat up on young peace demonstrators, a terrible, unholy conflict between labor and their natural allies. The students, who for the most part acted maturely, sanely, lovingly, attempted to heal this breach. It couldn't go on without untold harm to both sides.

In deciding to program "Joe Hill," one of Reuther's favorite songs (he had sung it publicly at the 1955 CIO convention), one knowledgeable member of the student committee asked, "How would you like to invite the composer?" So that is how I got to Santa Barbara, to sing on a Sunday in May of 1970, ending the program with "Joe Hill" and, by audience demand, a repeat of "Solidarity Forever." The most moving portion of the ceremony came with a Chemical Workers Union officer who traveled all the way from Pennsylvania to speak. He had lost two sons to the carnage in Vietnam, and before the spellbound crowd, he unfolded the two flags that had draped his sons' coffins. This bona fide hardhat said, "I don't trust the men in Washington with these flags. I don't like what they're doing, and I don't like the direction they're going. I'd like to give them to you."

A year and a half later I produced a record entitled *Strange Unusual Evening* (subtitled "A Santa Barbara Story"), a collage of my songs, some traditional union songs, and a selection of Wobbly numbers, unified by a narrative I wrote myself. In my liner notes I free-associated on "the growing realization that labor was losing its commitment, deep human values altering— changing, its history traduced, the *meaning* of the struggle— forgotten. And American labor, big sections, supporting the war in Viet Nam, ending up in the nest of the Hawks." The UAW, under Western Region 6 Director Paul Schrade, sponsored the recording with $10,000, and issued 5,000 copies. These are true collector's items now, so I am told, for the UAW got cold feet later on, and buried most of them in deep storage.

Musically, this record production has significance because as a "talking blues" cantata, it was the first major words-*and*-music creation of mine: Up to this time, most of my songs and cantatas had been written to other people's words. This whole Santa Barbara episode helped make my 1975 move there a natural thing. I lived there until 1989.

I spent a trying time in the late 1960s with a niece of mine who got involved with the Progressive Labor Party, one of the far-left factions that flourished then and is still around. In their supermilitancy, this group put itself at ideological loggerheads with every other radical and revolutionary movement. They criticized the Cubans and the Vietnamese, as well as the Black Panthers, all of them bearing the heavy brunt of American power. She actually spent some time in jail for refusing to co-operate with a grand jury fishing for information. I supported her completely insofar as her idealism went, and helped raise some money for her defense. I also had to tell her how disheartening I found all this divisiveness on the left, but I could do little about it.

In line with my habit dating back to FDR's fourth term election in 1944 and the Henry Wallace campaign in '48, I contributed a song to George McGovern in 1972. As cited in *Time*, September 4th, McGovern quoted lines from "The House I Live In" before the American Legion convention in Chicago during his campaign. I did house concerts and rallies for him, and rewrote Woody's "Roll On, Columbia" as "Roll On, McGovern." A gracious letter from him acknowledged my contributions. My niece must have wondered what was so revolutionary about preferring government by McGovern, as opposed to Nixon. But the way I see it, people must act on all levels, seeking out the most potential from every opportunity. Liberal action on the electoral front does not preclude more radical direct action on another.

Abe Lincoln again

The momentum from *Maybe I'll Come Home in the Spring*, and from my *Variety* ad, helped me onto a score and songs for a Lincoln's birthday film on NBC. *Great Man's Whiskers* was a natural for me in many ways. I collaborated with Adrian Scott, one of the Hollywood Ten, on his first job since coming back to America from England, where he had gone to live out the blacklist. Adrian had authored a story about the little girl who wrote Lincoln a letter urging him to grow a beard so the ladies would get their husbands to vote for him. Being an expert on Lincoln, and coming out of the blacklist myself, I logically became an integral part of this project. I made suggestions on story and characters, and brought in Yip Harburg to help create "Things That Go Bump in the Night," a "Wilderness Man" song, and a troubadour to comment on the action.

Harve Presnell played the Troubadour and a heavily made-up Dennis Weaver made a warm and attractive Lincoln. The cast also included Beth Brickell, Ann Sothern, John McGiver and, as the little girl, Cindy Eilbacher. Stanley Wilson, head of music at Universal Studios, conducted. Why NBC doesn't pull *Great Man's Whiskers* out of the can and show it more often is a mystery to me. It is excellent. Listen to this rave:

In view of the fact that so little was made of the anniversary on TV this year, this could not have come at a
timelier moment. . . . It ought to become an annual
classic, like "Wizard of Oz" or "Charlie Brown."

I hope Universal will forgive me if I say that it
looked very much like a Walt Disney feature—except
that it wasn't done by Disney. It had all the earmarks—
humor, inspiration, imagination, aptness, a feeling of
wholesome goodness, and even one of his favorite leads,
Dean Jones, as the widower-schoolteacher whose inventive child started the whole business.[7]

I finished up this film scoring period with a job I did in the
winter of '75. I came back to Hollywood from six months up
in Spokane, Washington, to work on a retelling of *Huckleberry
Finn* on TV. Alex North's son Steve produced for ABC, and
Bob Totten directed. With Steve's lyrics I wrote a theme song,
"Said the River, I'm Your Friend," designed for opening and
closing titles and for underscoring throughout.

In December 1974 it looked like we had time for proper
planning. But once the steamroller of shooting and editing got
underway, creative values began to suffer. The film had to be
scored in less than two weeks before its March broadcast. I met
the deadline, then conducted and recorded the entire score in
one three-hour session, with two hours overtime. The theme
song would have come off better if I had had more time to
work with country-western man Roy Clarke. He sang the song
just adequately.

Still potentially dangerous

I end this section on a strangely nostalgic note. After my
1966 move back to Los Angeles, it took the FBI just a few
months to locate me by means of the usual pretext telephone
calls, both to my home and to the Composers and Lyricists
Guild of America. Through the early 1970s the Feds continued
surveillance of my activities, not ignoring my current marital
status, though in time with gradually less attention to detail.
No longer did they clip newspapers looking for my name, or

send agents to my concerts; and seemingly none of their informants watched TV or listened to pop recordings.

Right up until February 1974 the FBI was sharing their files with the United States Secret Service, marking me "potentially dangerous because of background, emotional instability or activity in groups engaged in activities inimical to U.S." (I wonder which!) The last business the FBI conducted on my behalf, so to speak, involved a check on my most recent passport application in 1973. And then, with a memo about that dated March 29, 1974, the file suddenly ends. At least that's all the pages the FBI sent me in 1991.

I know that with finite resources—yes, even the FBI, I suppose, had only so many agents to go around—the young antiwar activists in the Vietnam Era must have seemed a lot more threatening than a 64-year-old composer. And it's true that the latest report of my being a Party member dated back to 1950—amazingly, they weren't so well informed on the last seven years or so. But I sigh with a certain sadness nonetheless, like at the end of a torrid love affair, that I no longer held the FBI's interest after thirty-five devoted years.

I like to think the FBI still had reason to pay me some attention. But I'm afraid that the end of this affair can be attributed to other factors. You see, old J. Edgar Hoover finally died in 1972, which led to a re-examination of FBI priorities. The Frank Church senatorial committee that looked into this found some amazing information. For example, in one ten-year period in the '60s and '70s, the FBI had 5,145 paid *political* informants in Chicago alone, who produced some 7,700,000 pages of files. All the while, Chicago witnessed a thousand gangland murders, and the FBI never solved a single one. So between these revelations, Nixon's Watergate troubles and his 1974 resignation, the new Attorney General Edward Levi appointed by President Ford, and new guidelines that came down reminding the FBI to go after criminal activity exclusively, the whole internal security field went through big changes. Of course, not knowing how extensively I'd been snooped on in the past, none of this made my life much different.

A final update: By a secret executive order which the Freedom of Information Act is not strong enough to make public, Ronald Reagan reinstated the FBI's old privileges in 1981—now to prevent "terrorism" instead of Communism. So U.S. citizens are once again being spied upon and all the rest. *The Lonesome Train* said it well in back in 1942:

Freedom's a thing that has no ending,
It needs to be cared for, it needs defending!

Notes

1. Abigail Van Buren to Earl Robinson, January 2, 1970.
2. Earl Robinson to Pete Seeger, April 12, 1949.
3. Robert Gustafson, "Banjo Goes Symphonic for Winterfest," *Boston Globe*, February 21, 1967.
4. Rolfe Boswell, *Record American*, February 21, 1967.
5. Thomas Willis, "'Illinois' Cantata Enjoyable," *Chicago Tribune*, November 27, 1968.
6. Kevin Thomas, *Los Angeles Times*, February 16, 1971; *Daily Variety*, February 17, 1971; John Goff, *The Hollywood Reporter*, February 17, 1971.
7. Percy Shain, "Great Birthday Gift for Lincoln," *Boston Globe*, February 14, 1973.

SECTION SIX
1972-1981

HEAD TRIPS

For a time in the early 1970s I looked into a series of personal growth psychologies in an attempt at "getting my shit together." Transactional Analysis reflects the thinking of Thomas Harris in his best-selling book *I'm OK, You're OK*, of which I gave away half a dozen copies. I tend to go for things hook, line, and sinker, and as a budding evangelist I would ask friends for a half hour of their time to listen while I expounded TA. However useful and mentally stimulating, TA turned out to be a "head trip" for me, an intellectual system which never hit me in the gut. This only became clear when I got into Re-evaluation Counseling, or co-counseling.

RC bypasses the experts, and sets up groups for listening and being listened to. A profound thought. None of us gets listened to enough. Harvey Jackins of my home town Seattle discovered and developed this truth. Harvey came to my attention in a highly recommended way. I listened to a tape of his singing. The first song spoke vaguely about a better world, but he introduced it as "a song the YCL used to sing." This galvanized me because I had not heard the Young Communist League referred to so freely since before the McCarthy period. A brave man as well as a lefty, I reasoned. The second song was "A Horse with a Union Label," a funny pro-union number by Mike Stratton and Sol Arons whom I knew from Cabaret TAC days. Harvey's third song brought a haunting sense of déjà vu; the tune wasn't familiar, but the words were, increasingly so:

> *On dark Republic's bloody ground,*
> *The 30th day of May,*
> *Oh workers, hear that mournful sound*
> *Of the men that died that day.*

At the end of the singing I exclaimed, "That's a song of mine!" Alfred Hayes and I had written it two years after "Joe

Hill," to remember and celebrate the workers struck down in the 1937 Republic Steel massacre by Tom Girdler's gun thugs. I had completely forgotten it, till it showed up like a folk song with a new tune, but the words intact.

The goal in RC is to *discharge* so as to reach inside and uncover hurtful behavior patterns. The counselor's whole job is to encourage animated, free-associative talk, yawning, trembling, laughing, and especially crying. Sweating is a fairly sure sign that discharge is taking place.

RC allowed me to first accept myself, then place me out in the world, in front of God and everybody, as a *lover*. Surely I had felt love, for those immediately around me, and in a more diffuse sense for the whole world, but in my lamentable state of emotional blockage, I had seldom expressed this love, plainly, openly, affirmingly. I became a good listener, learning with organized compassion to assist my co-counselor's discharge. Approaching my own discharge took longer. These Robinson eyes had almost never known tears. Crying was something a boy, or a man, just didn't do. I had never seen my mother or my father cry, nor as adults either my brother or sister. As a kid I had internalized the message, "Shut up or I'll give you something to cry about."

I intrude here a theory about why women outlive men in our society: They are allowed, if not encouraged, to cry.

In August 1972, at an RC seminar north of Santa Barbara, the tears started to come. One early morning I took a long walk up a mountain and came back with a song, which I sang with Harvey Jackins and the counselors after breakfast, it definitely being a "mass precipitation" number:

Appreciate, appreciate, appreciate me (repeat),
For I am so fine, right down the line,
This power of mine can be yours all the time,
Appreciate, yes and validate,
Please appreciate, appreciate, appreciate—ME.
I love me with no reservation,
I understand I'm a sensation,

Man, I'm just brilliant, I'm really neat,
I am so sweet I don't have to compete,
Appreciate, etc.

Counseling became a way of life. Ever the evangelist, I'd ask for only ten minutes to explain it to my friends. One time I tried talking to Pete Seeger and his wife Toshi about *what they really wanted.* I expected some big concept, but Pete surprised me by saying, "I want Toshi." Lovely relationship they've had for more than fifty years. Another time I ran up to Pete after a performance, gave him a big hug, and he said, "Easy, easy does it." He's not your gushy type.

For a time I thought RC might save my rocky marriage. Occasionally Ruth and I discharged, and we took a temporary turn for the better. But seldom could we be objective counselors: We ended up raging at each other, neither of us able to just listen.

Meantime, counseling with a number of attractive, listening women, I let my naturally loving self expand, despite the Counseling Manual, which forbade "socializing" with anyone you met in counseling. These Blue Pages protected people who allowed themselves great vulnerability during counseling. But in the light of the new sexual freedom espoused by the young, I came to a higher understanding: that, as a general principle, we are here on earth to say Yes to each other, not to say No. If communication, warmth, and love are available, what is achieved by suppressing a natural sexual expression? This attitude served in no way to draw Ruth and me closer; in fact, just the opposite. Was this just the old womanizing Earl in trendy new clothing? Maybe so. But I liked the way younger people had happily shed the old guilt-ridden morality. The slogan "If you're not with the one you love, love the one you're with" sums it up. Should I, because of age or marriage, be entitled to less?

In 1973 I met my ongoing friend Joanne Ver Straten through counseling. Still married to Ruth but looking for a way out, I drove to Santa Cruz to sing at Greenwood Lodge, a somewhat left-oriented camp in Soquel where Hugh DeLacy hung out. As usual in those days, I'd seek out trained counselors wherever I found myself, and in Santa Cruz I learned about an excellent woman newly moved there. We co-counseled in the form of one long wooing, and I proposed getting together that very night. She didn't immediately say yes, but agreed to attend my performance at the Lodge and give her answer then.

After the concert she followed me back to where I was staying, but just inside the door expressed her hesitation. "Listen," she said, "I've never slept with a celebrity before." Once I eased her mind on celebrities, I carried her into the bedroom and we busted the Blue Pages wide open.

I've especially delighted in Joanne because we've never stopped loving each other. We've just never figured out how to live with each other steady, which is a lot my fault. Dammit, but didn't I repeat my old behavior with Helen, setting up dates with other women, especially when traveling out of town, never wholly cleaving to the one woman whose love I had in my hand if only I would fully accept it. I see more clearly now that despite the probing into the deeper recesses that my new psychological explorations offered me, ancient patterns found ways of reasserting themselves. They can be summed up in a simple phrase: A fear of intimacy. I always had to have that escape route: If getting too close might bring me pain, I can find relief in someone else's bed.

Having said which, I'm eternally grateful to Joanne for understanding my need to leave my marriage, for hanging in despite my foolishness, and continuing to love me. She even moved to Santa Barbara to be with me, and later, for a time, to Seattle.

As the musical climax of my RC experience, I composed a song based on a slogan of Harvey Jackins, "Four Hugs a Day." This song is a winner. It supports a very basic human need with a catchy tune and clever words:

> *It's not sex, that's not where it's at,*
> *Might be far out deeper than that,*

Nevertheless, it lights a fuse,
Puts a hex on the person you choose—to use,
You can't lose with
Four hugs a day—that's the minimum,
Four hugs a day—not the maximum. (Repeat last
two lines feelingly)

"Four Hugs a Day" has become a staple in my concerts. I sing it to introduce the "New Age" Robinson. It hasn't really taken off yet, but the song is a join-in hit. I continue to have high hopes for it. Recently Charlotte Diamond recorded a kids' version of it on Hug Bug Records, a Canadian label, with "Four Hugs" (*"Embrasse Quatre Fois"*) singled out on the cover. It won the Juno Award for Best Canadian Children's Album.

Be here now

Shortly after meeting Joanne I learned about est—as presented to me, a faster way of uncovering old patterns. I especially appreciated learning that *we choose everything that happens to us.* Maybe not literally in every instance, but on some level a lot more than most people will admit. In other words, est helps keep the focus on *you,* so you don't go through life blaming other people or Fate for your situation.

Werner Erhard was my first trainer in June of 1973, and I came to love him, respect him and call him my friend. Est stands for Erhard Seminar Training, but since the chief idea behind it is *Be Here Now,* it's appropriate that *est* in Latin means "is." I did a song for him which I got to sing in San Francisco for about 7,000 esties at a huge Werner-directed seminar.

(Refrain) Where it is, is where it is,
And it's where I want to be
Where it is, is where it is
And it's there I long to be.
Here it is, here it is,
Here's the cheese and the jam,

Where it is, is where it is
And it's right where I am.

(Verse) You can blow—cold or hot,
Take the blues, lose or not,
Still if you'd move off that spot,
Just choose—what you got.
And that's—

Where it is, etc.

Trust me, this song sounds better than it looks.

John Denver, an est graduate, agreed to come with his band to a giant seminar of 8,000 people at the Cow Palace in San Francisco. That many people would always turn out for an affair with Werner, and with John Denver added, a high time was anticipated by all. Shortly after eight, out comes Werner, greets everyone and casually makes an upsetting announcement. "An interesting thing happened today. John Denver will not be here." Imagine a statement like that with an ordinary rock crowd: There would be a wave of moans, cries, and deep disappointment. This est audience made not a sound, merely sat waiting for Werner's further explanation.

> John called me ten o'clock this morning from Aspen, where it was snowing, so his arrival time would be a little delayed. But "I'm coming," he said. An hour later, it was still snowing and he was driving to Grand Junction to catch a plane from there. "I'm coming," he said. 12:30 he calls, "We're getting on the plane in Grand Junction, be into San Francisco airport around 2:30." A half hour later John calls with the news that a wheel fell off during the takeoff. This was the only plane going to San Francisco today. "It looks like we're not going to make it." (Still not a sound from the audience.) One last call came half an hour later. John said, "I just wanted you to know, Werner, I chose not to come!"

Finally the audience broke out into applause and laughter. We listened to some substitute performers, and everybody had a wonderful time.

Est and Werner Erhard were exciting and good for me. Mostly I took from it a commitment to personal responsibility and the truth of living fully in the here and now.

BACK IN THE GDR

A proper liberated musician

The idea of my writing a piano concerto came almost by accident. This requires a little backtracking. My stepson Michael Martin, already a budding talent at age 15 when I married Ruth, shortly blossomed into an accomplished all-around musician. He played guitar, banjo, piano and harmonica, and even in high school got gigs with a number of bands. When Ruth and I were married, I never tried to play the heavy with Mike, nor tried to take over the father role. We enjoyed a relationship of friend to friend, and increasingly as musical collaborators. If he learned something from me about composing music, I can also state that I learned much from him, for he exposed me to newer musical styles, in the pop field especially. And as much recording as I had done over the years, Mike showed me some sounds you can get out of a modern studio by mixing in different tracks and so forth. Even in my composing, Mike never put me on a pedestal and praised every note I wrote. He could be critical, and he helped me edit myself when I wasn't at my best. I might add that Mike and his friends teased me away from my square old crew-cut, inducing me to grow my hair out to a proper liberated musician's shoulder-length.

After Mike's college had canceled the banjo concerto he had prepared to play, he still wanted to perform the piece. A couple of years later, 1972 or so, after many concerts and recording sessions together, he said to me, "We ought to work up an act, do a tour. How about Europe? Where could we go?"

So I began negotiating with the German Democratic Republic again, this time to come as conductor of my *Concerto for Five-String Banjo* and other American works. I had studied closely both Arthur Fiedler of the Boston Pops and Maurice Peress of Corpus Christi when they conducted the concerto. I learned from Stanley Wilson, who led my score for *Great Man's Whiskers* at Universal Pictures. And I conducted entirely my score for *Maybe I'll Come Home in the Spring*. So I had done my homework since the first East German experience and felt ready to be the compleat composer-conductor.

The GDR impresarios, represented by Gustav Watzinger of Kunstler Agentur (the Artists Agency), saw me in a different light, however. From the very beginning they strongly countered that a German maestro should lead half the program, and I would have the other half. They asked, What other American work, besides the *Banjo Concerto*, would I wish to conduct?

It took me six seconds to answer that question. What other American work indeed? Robinson, of course! I wrote them back that I would be happy to conduct my *Piano Concerto*. Not a note of which existed on paper. But I felt supremely confident that I could write it. Piano was my instrument. I had been composing on the piano since my mother first sat me down to it at the age of six. Without a doubt, I set to work. First I needed to find an overall theme, a story if possible. Program, not pure music, is what I wrote, and I liked it that way.

The program I worked out followed a child from birth to maturity, a "Symphony for a New Kid." This idea had been with me ever since I baby-sat my son Jimmy. I marveled at his developing changes. Everything was a struggle. Rolling over from front to back, and back to front again, pushing up into a crawling position. Then came the effort to stand up, wobbly at first, and the striving to take a few steps. Never once did he pull back and say, Why do I have to go through all this? He took the struggle totally for granted. Perhaps "struggle" is the wrong word. Maybe it should be "realizing life."

The first movement would be in four parts, beginning with a long piano section "To Be Born." Too big to be called merely a piano cadenza, it would enunciate the opening struggle of the new human. The second section would be "Cry Baby Cry"; the third, "Grow Up!" would begin with a lullaby I had created back in 1947; and the fourth would be a fugue under the title "Let's Get Organized, Mother."

I researched the first two movements spending hours at a maternity hospital in Los Angeles. Not to see but to hear. I positioned myself back of the young mothers in labor, listening intently. The sounds I heard included the baby's first soft cry, similar to a fluttertongue flute (I researched this with Louise DiTullio, studio and symphony flutist extraordinaire); and Ellington muted trumpets for the more explosive baby cries.

I worked through March and into April 1973 on my orchestral sketch, with an end of June deadline so the piece could be ready for rehearsal and performance in September. Then I started worrying about German trumpet players: Where would they get Ellington mutes? It seems hard to believe after all these years, but my worry developed into an obsession. When I got to transferring the sketch to the actual orchestra score page, I found myself stymied by that "Cry Baby Cry" section. There on my card table by the piano lay my orchestra paper and I couldn't figure out how to write the trumpets so those unimaginative Germans could play what I wanted.

A self-created obstacle entirely. But I was stuck, increasingly haunted by the fear of not finishing by the June deadline.

Getting experimental

Into this agonizing, blocked situation came the est training in early June. The second day of my first est weekend, I took a good look at what was bothering me. We had been instructed to find an item—they never used the word "problem"—that we could take up in the Truth Process coming up Sunday afternoon. Most people picked something physically wrong with them. Being in practically perfect health, I took up my empty orchestration paper and the approaching deadline.

Masterfully, the trainer led all 250 of us down, back, and inside to where the "item" lay festering. He encouraged me to go to the bottom of it, with questions like, What does your head tell you about this? What does your heart say about it? What do your friends think? What do your parents feel? And so on, pulling me ever deeper into the miasma of guilt and frustration where I was stuck. Until I reached the lowest possible point of my ego, where I stayed, hanging in with it to savor, to *feel* the "defeat." The room increasingly filled with cries and moans, screams even, as people went through and into their "items." Being in it together with so many others helped. In my case I looked at not being able to finish the concerto. After I wallowed in this bottom position for a while, the trainer asked profoundly releasing questions: How important is this item to you *now*? How long do you *want* to stay there? And, How much are you able to *let go*?

The minute I opened up in this way, I was able to examine my scene and say, I don't want this, I don't need it. I became free to climb up and out. Feeling so alone before, I began to feel for and love everyone in the room. What liberation!

I went back to my orchestration the next day, transcribing my sketch onto paper. I assumed I was dealing with intelligent musicians, instead of "moronic" Germans, and wrote out in detail exactly what I needed to musically render the cry of a newborn child. The "Cry Baby Cry" section practically wrote itself. The lullaby gave a much needed respite from the crying-birthing struggle, and with the fugue in the fourth section I ate up the paper with exhilaration. I reported this wondrous progress to my fellow esties the following Saturday and received prolonged applause.

Originally projecting the concerto "To the New Human" in three movements, I reduced it to one and finished it by July 2nd, my birthday, in time to mail it to East Berlin for extraction of parts, preparation, and rehearsal. Listening to a tape of the concerto—the only way anyone in America so far has heard it—people have said that in this work I reached the farthest away from folk in the direction of dissonance. For some reason I never got that experimental again.

I suggested they get a German pianist, though I could play and conduct if necessary. This they did. But my troubles with the concerto hadn't ended yet. For I was not allowed to forget that I had gone to the GDR as singer-entertainer as well as conductor. Herr Watzinger had scheduled no fewer than eight *Soloabende* concerts in Berlin, Leipzig, Erfurt, Dresden, Cottbus, Suhl, and Eisenhüttenstadt, during their Oktoberfest, and only three Halle Philharmonic concerts, in Berlin, Halle, and Zeitz. Preparing for these eight appearances represented a new kind of challenge, for with Mike Martin on electric bass, harmonica and five-string banjo, and his pal Jeffrey Landau on electric guitar, I had thereby (and not without some trepidation) changed my image, developed over thirty-five years, from solo performer on piano to member of a performing ensemble, as in the old days with the Blue Knights. Both young men also assisted with vocals, Mike himself writing a number of our musical arrangements. Not only did all of this require extra rehearsal, but the electrical instruments needed amplification, which had to be supplied by our German impresario.

Communication-wise, we thought it necessary to pick a program that relied on music more than words for effect. I dropped pieces like "Free and Equal Blues"—too much dialogue and jokes to translate. A German audience dictated more American folk songs, and an uncomplicated presentation.

Mike acquitted himself remarkably in the *Banjo Concerto*. From a base of self-taught guitar he went at all the musical complications of another instrument, and emerged with the piece triumphantly in his hands, head and heart. (Before leaving for the GDR, I arranged him a performance in Ventura with Frank Salazar conducting.) That concerto was a hit, more so than the piano concerto, which suffered from a pianist, Rolph Dieter Ahrens, not taking his job seriously. It rankled the hell out of me when I'd come into rehearsal and this young "genius" would be practicing Mozart instead of my piece. His cavalier attitude resulted in a less than perfect rendition.

However, the *Piano Concerto* was appreciated well enough. I remember particularly the reception afterward in Zeitz. I sat next to the mayor's wife. "I felt very moved," she said. "I'm a mother." A workers' city newly built by the GDR after Hitler's defeat, Zeitz represented just the kind of place, antifascist in character, where I loved to have my music performed. And what more appropriate piece there than "The New Human"?

Mike was a joy. Besides making up his own cadenza—he used more of my theme than Eric Weissberg had—he sang the fourth movement song, "How Can I Keep from Singing," that it took both Pete Seeger and me to do in the premiere. The spirit he conveyed at these three performances in the GDR made it hugely successful, and he has continued to play it.

Besides this primary job he was a tower of strength to me on the eight *Soloabende*. His own composition, a "Sonoma County Hoedown" on banjo, opened our show. His unfailing humor and seriousness, both constantly needed, and his ability with German, proved valuable. I think we made quite an impression on the East Germans, these three long-haired, laid-back California musicians, a weird, exotic species indeed. Many people had never seen anyone play a banjo before.

We stayed an extra three days in Berlin to make an album, not of the concertos, but of the solo performance. For the record, since copies cannot be obtained from the no longer existing GDR, these are the numbers on the album:

Seite 1:
1. *Sonoma County Hoedown* (Michael Martin)
2. *The House I Live In* (E.R./Lewis Allan)
3. *Same Boat, Brother* (E.R./Yip Harburg)
4. *Big Rock Candy Mountain* (Mac McClintock, folk song)
5. *Joe Hill* (E.R./Alfred Hayes)
6. *Pie in the Sky* (Joe Hill)
7. *Old Abe Lincoln* (E.R./Lincoln & Alfred Hayes)

Seite 2:
1. *Animal Kingdom* (E.R./Mel Leven)
2. *The Turtle Dove* (English folk song)
3. *Suppose* (E.R./Bob Russell)
4. *Shenandoah* (American folk song)
5. *Old Paint* (Cowboy song)
6. *Logan's Lament* (E.R./Logan—American Indian)
7. *Black and White** (E.R./David Arkin)

---

*As "Schwarz und Weiss" this song came to be known and sung all over the GDR and Europe.

MY NORTHWEST:
LONG SUMMER IN SPOKANE

There were no film jobs for me in '73 or '74. In retrospect this could have been my creation, allowing me to expand as my marriage came to an end. Putting the whole Hollywood system behind me, for better or for worse I tried being more of myself. I opened up in many ways, including conducting and singing, and I moved back—and forward—to a singing appreciation of my home state of Washington.

I had been there early in 1974 for a month, wandering around, asking people, What is Washington to you? and researching a musical eventually to be called *Washington Love Story*. Then I got invited to Expo '74 in Spokane, which featured the environment as its theme. Beginning in June, I was folklorist in residence at the Folklife Festival on the Expo Fairground. Never one to think small, I put out four major projects to be accomplished that long summer in Spokane.

From Pleistocene to present

Washington Love Story was a labor of love, a panorama of Washington state themes, music and lyrics by Earl Robinson. These included a bright and snappy "I'm a Sockeye Salmon (You Can Call Me Red)," a moving "Harvest Time in Eastern Washington," a "Sailing on Puget Sound" (a song for Seattle with words by Malvina Reynolds). The first and second acts climaxed with "Ride the Wind" (based on William O. Douglas) and "Building of the Grand Coulee Dam." This latter is an immense production number with a Magic Lady, Pokine, representing the River Columbia. Pokine's tears hollowed out the Columbia River gorge in an ages-long geological construction, and her monumental weeping is finally harnessed by the Grand Coulee Dam to reclaim the desert and furnish e-lec-a-tri-ci-ty to the people. Woody Guthrie's song, one of twenty-six he wrote in two weeks he spent in Washington in 1940 for the

Bonneville Power Administration, formed the entrance to the
cantata:

> *Oh the world has seven wonders,*
> *That the travelers always tell,*
> *Some gardens and some towers,*
> *I guess you know them well.*
> *But now the greatest wonder is*
> *In Uncle Sam's fair land,*
> *It's the King Columbia River*
> *And the Big Grand Coulee Dam.* ©

The cantata then moves from the Pleistocene Age to the
present dam in full operation. If there is a theme to it all, perhaps it's summed up in this line: "Washington is a restless,
stubborn, optimistic people."

As my first job in Spokane, I had to get *Washington Love
Story* finished and produced at the fair. I determined to use the
chorus at my old Alma Mammy, West Seattle High. The chorus director agreed and we set a week of rehearsals for a presentation just after Expo opened. Though well conceived, the
piece did not quite jell with the choir. It was underrehearsed,
done outdoors, and poorly miked. Our audience dwindled
away throughout the evening.

Indiansong of friendship and peace

I had no time to feel bad, however, because I had just six
weeks, during this centennial year of the city, to compose a
major work for the Spokane Symphony to perform at the Opera House in Spokane in September. I called this musical legend *To the Northwest Indians: A Symphonic Narrative,* and for
its composition I received a $2,000 grant in the jazz/folk/
ethnic category from the National Endowment for the Arts.
Expo '74 gave me another $2,500, but most of that went for
copying orchestra parts. I wrote it on the shores of Loon Lake,
fifty miles north of Spokane. I had a lot of heart-searching fun
with this. Working with a good orchestra, an excellent conduc-

tor, Donald Thulean, I early on established a narrator-singer as
The Messenger, which

1) permitted me to fully state my feelings about the American Indian, to face the exploitation and oppression we had delivered to them over the years, and to allow the Indians to express their position and balance out the conflict;

2) restated my thinking about Washington being a half-step
ahead of the rest of the country, through its forward position
on Indian fishing rights, plus the tremendous number of Indian
place names for rivers, lakes, and towns. In other words, I
could be as patriotic as I wanted about my homeland;

3) got me to talk simultaneously in the language of the
symphony, the flute, the rattle, and the drum. I wanted to
open with the land as it was before the coming of white settlers. How better to do this than with the sounds of the birds,
squirrels, and chipmunks, who chanted and sang so joyously at
Loon Lake, long before breakfast every morning in July of
1974.

We hear of man's inhumanity to man, white to Indian, Indian back to white. We hear the healing words of Chief Joseph
and Chief Sealth (Seattle). And the fallen drum is resurrected,
brought forth for dancing again. The piece finishes with the
Messenger inviting the audience to join in chanting the Indian-
song of friendship and peace. "Hey-yo. Hey-yo-wa. Hey-yo."

I had suggested they try to get old Spokane boy Bing
Crosby to narrate the Messenger. He couldn't do it, so I did
the honors myself. On the same program Thulean offered my
teacher Aaron Copland's *Appalachian Spring* and the Brahms
Violin Concerto with Itzhak Perlman. From the reviews:

> The work is loosely structured and episodic. At times
> the orchestral accompaniment is highly atmospheric,
> with dissonances and transmuted "primitive" rhythmic
> configurations. Other passages have a more familiar
> "soundtrack" quality, and even echo incongruous jazz
> rhythms.
>
> Robinson is an effective narrator. He progressed
> from opening understatement through a crescendo of

dramatic intensity to an invitation which underscored his sincere convictions: In the work's final pages, he invites his auditors to join him in a brief, ascending chant which both expresses and engenders a sense of human community. The work thus ends with what may be the only audience-participation finale in symphonic literature.

The composition was a pleasant surprise—dignified, dramatic and the narrative did not in the least bit seem phony or particularly simplistic. . . . Robinson has composed a work which has meaning for both Indian and white man.
    To paraphrase the closing, "we (the Indians) don't trust you, yet come and dance with us."[1]

Most people agreed that Expo's Folklife section was its liveliest part, and I held court as its elder statesman. As such I made myself available for concerts and communication of all kinds throughout the six months Expo lasted—a heartwarming position to be in, in contrast to the constant struggle in Hollywood to be accepted. After Expo wound up, I spent a week as composer-in-residence at Western Washington State College at Fairhaven. The duties weren't onerous—a lecture or two, an evening at the local coffeehouse, and informal meetings with students.

The fourth project I had in mind that summer, a Christmas opera for the Seattle Opera Company, never got off the ground. Perhaps the idea was too grandiose, but it was the only one of my '74 Spokane projects that did not materialize in some way.

The only incorruptible man

I first got involved with William O. Douglas, Associate Justice of the Supreme Court, on reading his book *Of Men and Mountains* in early 1974. It triggered a lot of "school spirit" about my homeland—the plants, trees, lakes, mountains of the great Northwest. I felt refreshed not only by his extraordinary feel for nature, but by his indomitable spirit. As part of my Northwest rediscovery, I determined to tell his story, become his musical "biographer." The cantata I wrote based on him found its way into *Washington Love Story*.

Douglas responded to my first overture nicely enough, encouraging me to go ahead and write what I wanted. But then my letters went unanswered. I began to worry, because being his self-appointed biographer, I needed more access to this "commie lecher who loved all these young women" (the reactionary view of him) vs. "the only incorruptible man in the U.S. Government for 37 years" (the true and progressive view). My experience with Sandburg came to mind, and I thought, This can't be the same, this judge is not afraid of "reds": We are on the same side. After all, this is a man who had said, "The Fifth Amendment is an old friend and a good friend. It is one of the great landmarks in man's struggle to be free of tyranny, to be decent and civilized."

Still he didn't answer my letters. I decided to go visit him in Washington, D.C., finding there an almost hyperactive man with little time to spend on me. I left a copy of his new book *Go East, Young Man* for him to sign, and retrieved it later in the day with a scrawled dedication.

Nevertheless, I didn't leave him. I started rewriting the cantata, which I called *Ride the Wind*, realizing I had loaded it with too high praise; his words just didn't sing, as Lincoln's did, and even Roosevelt's to an extent.

> *Oh, come with me and please attend*
> *To a scene I have to send,*
> *For I need to sing of a friend.*
> *His name is Douglas, Bill for short,*
> *I call him William O.*
> *He works up there in the Supreme Court*
> *And he's helping me to grow.*
>
> *To know how to say "Full speed ahead,"*
> *And just when to holler "WHOA!"*

And how to accept the wind and rain
And reach on through the sometime pain,
Look at the Chinook and spot the rain—bow.

"William O.," I said, "this state's so great,
But the people are thin-skinned."
He said, "Underneath they're all one piece,
Together we can ride the wind."

Good ol' boy from Goose Prairie

After my summer as Expo '74 folklorist, I returned to Spokane from Seattle via Mt. Rainier, and Douglas surfaced unexpectedly. Figuring out the best way to cross the Cascades to reach the eastern Washington prairie and Spokane, I saw that the best of seven routes appeared to be the southern, winding around the American River and passing Goose Prairie, William O.'s summer home. All the way down I rehearsed what I'd say or sing to him in case he still felt no interest in me. I had no assurance that he would be there, because Watergate was going on in Washington, with the Supreme Court involved with the Nixon tapes.

Goose Prairie is a post office in a diner off the road. I sat down, ordered pie, and it turned out the waitress used to work for Douglas. "He was okay, nothing special," she said. Everyone at the counter acted very casual about this giant, as I perceived him. "He's a good ol' boy. He'll be comin' down pretty soon for his mail."

One of the guys spoke up suddenly. "There he is."

In he walked, dressed in a workshirt, no jacket or sweater, and went to pick up his mail. He nodded to us at the counter, not recognizing me, and left. I found out everything I could. He lived seven houses down, not deep in the woods as I had pictured. "You'll recognize his house by the open fence."

I found the entrance, went through a screen door up onto the porch, knocked and stepped back. Slow steps approached the door and Douglas opened it. Opting to play it light, I told him, "I came up to sing you a song." Based on a story of the

first fish Bill Douglas ever caught, here is what I had prepared
to sing:

> *A little boy stood, and then he sat,*
> *Side of a stream, the little Klickitat,*
> *Finally he hooked him an eight-inch trout,*
> *His very first fish, a rainbow trout.*

> *Fish looked at him, said, "I love my life,"*
> *Boy put away his little sharp knife,*
> *Said, "Just for that,*
> *Back you go in the little Klickitat."*

William O. had a puzzled expression when I announced
my intention to sing; so instead, I introduced myself. "I'm Earl
Robinson."

"Oh. Oh, yes," he said. Not a smile, but no animosity either.

Emboldened, I said, "I'd love to sing you the cantata I
wrote for you. Have you got a piano? No? All right, I can
bring my guitar, if you like." Leaving it up to him, I said I
could come back after I went to Spokane. A 200-mile drive
seemed like nothing with his acceptance imminent. I realized
how sharp his mind was as he reviewed his schedule. Something doing every minute: One day Seattle, next day Yakima,
and he was sending in to Washington, D.C., his opinions on
the Nixon tapes. He didn't attend the court unless absolutely
necessary, so he could spend time up in the mountains of
Washington state.

We made a date the following week, this time, finally, an
invited guest in his house. I sang him the whole 18-minute *Ride
the Wind*, kind of rough with just a guitar. That granite face
just stared out the window. I spotted two and a half smiles
cross his face. When I finished, he asked one question: "Where
do you live?"

I had trouble answering, for at the time I had three addresses: Spokane, Los Angeles, and Mommer's house in Seattle,

because I was thinking seriously of moving back to the Northwest. Interestingly, he chose the Seattle address, and explained, "I have a person whom I trust, who wants to do a TV show about me, and I want to suggest you to do the music." Wow! That sign that he liked what I had done fell like music upon my ears. (The show, however, never got made.)

Thus began a much improved phase of our relationship, though nothing could ever top that solo performance I gave with guitar to William O. Douglas in a cabin in Goose Prairie off American River.

Mostly dissents these days

A couple of months after my visit, William O. had his stroke, his left side paralyzed. It happened that way, I believe, so that his right hand could keep on writing. After several weeks in a New York hospital he returned to the bench again, temporarily. He felt a strong responsibility to prevent the Republicans from stacking the court with conservatives. During the time of his stroke therapy, our relationship truly ripened. In March 1975 I visited New York for some concerts, and called his wife Cathy. She said, "When could you come?"

I brought a guitar and *Ride the Wind* to sing if appropriate. Well, it was very appropriate. I sat at the foot of his bed where he lay thin and wizened, Cathy by his side, and sang and sang. I did *Ride the Wind* twice, and in between, besides "Black and White" and "Joe Hill," some songs of Joe Hill and the IWW which he especially liked. "Casey Jones" and "Pie in the Sky" were close to his experience. It might be expected that William O. would be sympathetic to the Wobblies, who had been persecuted for organizing the One Big Union. As he put it, "I thought the powers that be were persevering unnecessarily against them." I guess he thought of me as an IWW, though I never joined it. But very sympathetic, of course. His blazing blue eyes—and Cathy's too—clouded over with tears during much of the singing. My performance turned into a concert. Doctors and other patients crowded into the room to listen.

A few weeks later, I returned to find William O. dressed in a tie and jacket and seated in a chair. If you didn't look at the brace on his left ankle, you couldn't tell a thing was wrong. I asked why he wasn't sitting in the court in Washington. He explained airily, "Oh, I send it in. Takes me a short time. Because all I have to do is tell the truth. All those other guys, it takes them a long time to think up a variation on the truth." He added, "It's mostly dissents these days."

"You mean you send your decisions in to the court from this rehabilitation hospital?"

"Oh, yes," he replied. "It's easy when you vote right."

I saw him a couple more times, even sang for him and Cathy and their Goose Prairie neighbors. He retired from the Court in November 1975. Then he worked steadily on his book about the Supreme Court, which got published before he passed on in 1980.

Ride the Wind is a good piece, orchestrated as a cantata for chorus and soloists, though never definitively produced. Though William Orville Douglas has not the inherent universality of an Abe Lincoln, I know of no other music celebrating his life.

Note

1. Andrew G. Bjelland, *Spokane Daily Chronicle*; Les Blumenthal, *Spokane Spokesman-Review*, both September 5, 1974.

1976: MY YEAR

Patriot of a different stripe

The year 1976 turned into a sweet celebration for me. On January 9, at a party in my house on Calle Cita in Santa Barbara, I tripped on LSD for the first time. I felt exhilarated and exalted enough, in the midst of a group hug, to see and proclaim myself as God. The day after, I sang my William O. Douglas cantata for the local Sierra Club.

On January 27 I attended the Paul Robeson memorial service in New York City. I took part in no less than thirteen celebrations of Big Paul's life in the four-month period following. These included appearances at the Mark Taper Forum in L.A.; at the Unitarian Church in Santa Barbara, where I produced, played, and sang, with a speaking-singing chorus, a two-hour show based on Pablo Neruda's magnificent "Ode to Paul Robeson"; at Rutgers University, Robeson's alma mater, in a singing-talking show with Brock Peters; Detroit, New York, Toronto, Purdue University, and elsewhere. The last of these appearances took place in Athens, Greece, May 19-21.

At a time when all of Paul's breadth and power got fully discussed—his position as a leader of his people, a revolutionary fighter against injustice, as well as an incredible singer/actor—I found myself extolling and defending his humanness, his gentle and vulnerable deeper self. I had a section in "Ode to Paul Robeson" where I reported him crying in London over his separation from the America he loved. His son Paul, Jr., did not like any softening of his father's image, any suggestion of him as less than the great man of steel. Which of course he was, but also much more than that.

The American Bicentennial year served as a nice reminder of my work. The first week of May I went to Fresno, honored as a VIP composer by the music department of California State University. The Fresno high school band played my *Soul Rhythms*, and two concerts by a combined university and high school chorus presented *Ballad for Americans*. Some of my published works went on exhibit, and I offered myself for talk and consultation.

Something important happened in Fresno during my week there. I got a good look at the magnificent statue of David of Sassoun in Courthouse Park downtown. Twenty-eight feet high, two and a half tons of bronze and pounded copper. I talked with the sculptor Varas Samuelian about the significance of this 8th-century folk giant of the Armenian people, David of the passionate glance, him on his rearing horse, brandishing his sword with the holy light in his eye. "That's an opera!" I exclaimed. Less than two months later I took positive steps toward making that a reality.

On May 8 I flew East to Rutland, Vermont, for a patriotic concert at the high school. Rank Smith, former principal of Elisabeth Irwin High School, was the sponsor and guiding force. Something very satisfying struck me about singing "The House I Live In," "Free and Equal Blues," and *Ballad for Americans* in this old New England setting. I had always felt uncomfortable with the narrow "bombs bursting in air" type of patriotism, and I took pains to introduce myself as a patriot of a somewhat different stripe.

On May 10 I flew back across the country to Wenatchee, Washington, to help prepare an all-Robinson program on the 16th. Malcolm Seagrave conducted the Wenatchee Valley College-Community Symphony Orchestra and Chorus splendidly. The program consisted of the orchestral *To the Northwest Indians*, which I narrated, the William O. *Ride the Wind* (concert premiere), *Lonesome Train*, and *Ballad for Americans*.

Not my time to leave

Immediately after this concert I hurried back to New York to catch a Soviet plane going to the Athens Peace Conference. Pete Seeger, originally invited, couldn't make it. Harold Leventhal worked it out for me to go instead. I missed the plane, so I paid $800 for a commercial flight to Greece. The conference was sponsored mainly by Third World and socialist countries, and therefore boycotted by the U.S. It began with a demonstration—permissible now under a government newly freed from the colonels' fascist grip. Special posthumous honorees of the conference were Robeson and Gregorios Lambrakis, the Greek politician murdered in 1963 and played by Yves Montand in the Costa Gavras movie Z.

After I sang at the conference, I took a bus from our Aegean seaside hotel into the center of Athens, and from there walked through 4,000-year-old streets to the Acropolis. Like the Empire State Building, the locals pay it no attention, but visitors must go to the top.

I arrived at the Acropolis on the wrong side. Fences surrounded the base of the mountain, but it looked like I could negotiate them quite readily. Beyond, a stream bed filled with bushes and other things to grab onto made the ascent an easy climb. So before you could say Earl Robinson, I was over the fence and on my way to the top for a short 15-minute climb.

I soon encountered a vertical section fifteen feet high. I took a long look. It's climbable, rough in spots; if I had a rope it would be a cinch. But rather than go back down to the proper entry place, I carefully cased the mountain. About twenty feet to my right was the edge of an oblong wall. I looked around the corner of it, and sure enough, about a hundred yards over, I could see a pipe construction job leading to the top over a path. Now some people wouldn't call it a path: You couldn't walk straight forward on it. But it had hand holds and foot holds, and by hugging the wall you could sidestep your way. The fact that the drop fell some 200 feet didn't bother me at all. Before you know it, I was right out on the wall making my way along.

I took good care to check my hand and foot holds. But about halfway to the pipe construction job, a rock came loose in my right hand. I was relying on these holds, and this fraction of a second terrified me. I could have fallen. If I was ready to go, that would have been the place and the time.

Well, I was pushed right back up against the wall. Truly. I checked this later with Dr. Peebles, and he said, "Oh, yes. We did that. It was not time for you to leave yet."

Safe, I still felt some scared. Come with me away from the wall for a few moments while I explain what I did about that. Back at the hotel, I would wake up each morning early and meditate. The next morning I looked closely at why I had been scared. I didn't like it, and I decided to get a handle on my fear. I imagined myself—positioned myself, so to speak—out in the air away from the wall, the loose rock in my hand. In my hotel room I'm perfectly safe, see? but I watched my astral body fall to the rocks below. Without even having to feel it crash. That was it. I had solved my own fear. Some time later in New York I told this story to Larry LeShan, who wrote the beautiful book *How to Meditate*, and he called me very wise to handle fear that way. I liked that.

Now back to the wall. The stone still in my hand, I was scared to drop it: I didn't want to hear it falling. So I deposited it at my feet. And I made those last few steps to the pipe construction. When I reached it I grabbed on with both arms and both legs, making my way slowly up to the top.

There I saw the Parthenon, and I started toward it. From my right a Greek in uniform came running at me. I thought for a minute, I'm caught. How did the police—or FBI—ever get up here? This fellow waved for me to accompany him. Too shaken to resist, I followed, protesting quietly. He led me away from the Parthenon and then he started down some steps. That did it. After all I'd gone through to get *up* here, I refused to go *down* any steps. I screamed, "Tell me what you want!"

He turned around. "You must buy ticket. Thirty drachmas."

That noble adventurous climb, reduced to a mere attempt to get in free! I paid him for the ticket and went back to bathe in the democratic spirit of the Parthenon.

Thrown out of the USSR

While in Athens I pursued a plan that had been germinating in my mind since before my visits to East Germany. I made contact with all the socialist countries represented at the conference, with the idea of setting up a conducting tour. It seemed best to work through the Soviet Union, the center of world socialism; and in addition they owned the planes supplying transportation to and from the conference. I buttonholed the delegates from Poland, Bulgaria, Hungary, Romania, Czechoslovakia, the GDR, and particularly the Soviet Union, about being invited to come and conduct. To this end I spent a lot of time and energy with the woman in charge of the Soviet delegation. She was friendly, but difficult to pin down. She kept telling me that everything looked fine for my return trip: I would fly in to Moscow on Saturday and leave for America on Monday.

"But I would like to stay longer in Moscow," I pleaded. "I want to meet with cultural and symphonic producers. I want to be able to call the numbers in Prague, Warsaw, Bucharest, and elsewhere that I've just obtained at the conference."

After several talks, she said, "It looks like I've got you through till Wednesday, and once you get there you will be able to work your way around and extend your stay if necessary." So I arrived in Moscow Saturday morning, staying in the biggest hotel rent-free. I set about making contacts and extending my time there, outlining my hopeful plan of remaining at least a week, as a paying guest at the regular Intourist rate. Neither objective proved simple. The folks from the Peace Committee politely insisted on my leaving *Monday*.

I had been given a nice young woman as interpreter, who started getting on the phone for me. I soon learned a shocking fact. Moscow, a city of eight million, had no phone book! She had to call for numbers each time. I had her try to reach a friend in Czechoslovakia, but she couldn't. We dialed numbers in Poland, Hungary, and Romania with no luck. In Moscow we located a number for the composer Kabalevsky, whom I had met in New York. He was out in the country, sick and unreachable. Another contact, head of English-language radio in Moscow and a relative of newscaster Vladimir Pozner, was busy.

I did manage to reach Pozner and his wife in Paris. I might be able to stay with them in case I had to get out of the S. U.

and didn't want to leave Europe. Aeroflot could drop me in Paris, where Soviet planes stopped every day, and they could pick me up any time for the final leg home. Which is exactly what happened after my short weekend in Moscow. I gave up the struggle to stay, and on Monday, May 24th, they "threw me out"—an exaggeration, but that's how I felt. I emerged still a friend of the Soviets, but with some sobering, ambivalent thoughts. Whatever they say good about the Soviet Union is true. Whatever they say bad, is true also. I'm reminded of a joke, which I wouldn't have told too many years ago. What's the difference between capitalism and communism? Well, capitalism is a system of man exploiting man. Under communism, it's just the reverse!

In Paris, Vladimir Pozner was just leaving town, and their house had been rented. I remembered another friend, the art connoisseur Felix Landau, who for a time just before the blacklist was my concert agent in California. He recommended the Bon Hotel, which proved ideal: within walking distance of his apartment, and just two blocks down from the Hotel Le Sevre, where Helen and I had spent a charming week seventeen years before, studying French and wandering the streets and shops and restaurants of the Left Bank. Near the Bon Hotel, I entered a cafe where Helen and I had spent some time in '59, learning about *vin ordinaire*. The clerk at the Bon had no trouble reaching through on the phone to Prague, where they could do nothing about a conducting tour, and to Warsaw, where they invited me to come and discuss the matter. It was incredibly simpler to reach the socialist countries from capitalist Paris than from socialist Moscow!

I flew to Warsaw. An impresario who spoke excellent English welcomed me, and we discussed when and how I would come back to Poland to conduct. After two days I returned to Paris, but I never followed through. A profound change took place in me at this point. I had been convinced of the importance of becoming a do-it-all Leonard Bernstein type, conducting as well as composing and singing. But it dawned on me that conducting, and the struggle to realize myself that way, was just not as much fun as I had imagined. So in Paris in '76 I decided: Should I ever be in demand as a conductor, I could do it with some grace and adequate merit. But at composing and singing I felt most expert and happy.

A most lovely personal thing happened in Paris. After a few days, I began to realize that Helen was *there with me!* She appeared in a remarkable dream, fat, round, hale, and healthy. I remarked how well she looked, in contrast to how sick she had been last time I saw her. Two things I wanted from her. First a kiss, which we consummated well. And I wanted to say something to her about all the other women while we were married. I had just begun when she spoke out strongly, "I don't want anything to do with this." She refused to discuss that aspect of our marriage and the dream ended.

Turned out, Aeroflot came to Paris much less often than I had been told, and that stuck me there for a week. Which was a good thing. I went with Felix Landau to a restaurant where they played guitar and a Greek bouzouki. In this nonharmonic playing, they sing and play the same melody with instrumental embellishments. Completely entranced, it struck me as perfect for my Armenian opera.

Still in a free Soviet plane, I stopped in London to spend some time with my former stepson Michael Martin. Mike had stayed there ever since our *Banjo Concerto* trip to the GDR three years before, struggling to make it musically in Europe. He added to my year-long 1976 celebration by inviting me to take part in two softball games, where I hit well and enjoyed a momentary reincarnation of my past athletic self.

More wonderful strokes came my way in June at a pre-birthday party that my son Perry held for me in New York. He literally played the hell out of "Happy Birthday" on that golden-toned clarinet of his: Twists and turns and squirrelings on the old "licorice stick" did things to that tune that have never been heard before or since.

Seth and me

As an important part of '76, I began acknowledging myself as a growingly psychic person. About the time of Big Paul's passing, I discovered the Seth books. I avidly read and reread *Seth Speaks* and *The Nature of Personal Reality*—I had taken both of them to Europe. In fact, I had tried to reach their author, channel Jane Roberts, in the spring before the trip, but without success. But I felt ready for her, and for Seth, because I got right through to her after arriving in New York.

I had been intrigued to meet Jane Roberts not just because of her channeling Seth—acting as a medium through whom Seth communicates—but also channeling the Sumari, a "family" of consciousnesses who communicate through music and poetry. I imagined that this music, brought through Jane, would help me in my Armenian opera. I traveled to the home of Jane Roberts and Robert Butts up in Elmira on a Saturday night—the wrong time to meet Seth, which I had no hope of doing, because he only came through on Mondays and Wednesdays. Which is when they got the material for the books.

Before going into the Sumari, Jane sang the Irish folk song "Molly Malone" in a dry, crinkly, off-key croak, demonstrating most eloquently the sad fact that she had no voice. So I urged her to get on to the Sumari, which could not be any worse than "Molly Malone." In fact, it was incredibly better. She sang like an angel, high birdlike warblings one minute, the next the deep powerful voice of a Russian alto, altogether enchanting. Robert had the tape machine on, and a good thing he did, because Seth came through to me three times that evening, directly and incontrovertibly.

In the books, Seth never talked about love, a pretty important subject with me. I asked Robert, in between Sumaris, a simple question: "Do you love Seth?" This seemed to bother him, as if he had never considered it. He hemmed and hawed, and all of a sudden Jane's voice changed to a lower range and there was Seth, explaining about not using the word "love."

We do not use that—uh—expression-uh. It does not serve their own purposes, or mine-uh. From the beginning-ah they would have been in aw-w-we-uh of-ah my eve-r-y wo-r-d-uh and they would not have-ah questioned-ah me-yuh in the way-uh that they had-ah to question-ah. For when they questioned-ah for themselves they questioned-ah for others, and the particular tur-urn-uh of their minds-ah was-ah and is-ah important. They treat me-ah very kindly, and I treat them-ah very kindly. They are, however, distant enough so that-uh they preser-rve-ah their own sense of independence. It is highly important to them, and to me. I am simply letting you know-uh that I am here, and I give you-ah my greeting-ah. I am glad that you like-ah me. I like-ah you.

I undertook to imitate his speech for Jane when she came out of her trance and had her in stitches. A little later I was discussing, lamenting probably, my falling asleep so often, and Seth came through in such a clarifying way that I reproduce him completely. For although Seth addressed himself to me in a very personal manner, his message may be helpful to others:

You have all the energy that you need, at your command. Creatively, as a creator, you understand. However there is somewhere within you a division between the person and the creator, and that portion is afraid, and it drives you so that you force your energy, and you need rest. Your body is very wise, very kind-ah. And so although you dr-rive yourself with nervous energy, it replenishes itself, it says to you, "Shut up and calm down-nuh and-ah *be*."

Now musically-ah you know this. One of your songs said it-uh creatively. But you do not follow your own-ah advice always. But your body follows that advice. And it *stills* you as a child-ah is stilled-uh and so you sleep. There is no great problem. You need only realize-ah that you can indeed-ah let yourself go, and you will go! You will not fall, or dissolve into nothing. Creatively again, you realize this, but you do not-ah follow your own advice, and when you do not, your body kindly takes over and hushes you and sings you a lullaby.

Now if I were truly-ah truly in form-ah I would graciously do an interpretation of you-ah as-ah you did for me. However, I do not have a beard on Rubert's face.*

Seth continued, most handsomely:

My best wishes go with you, and listen-ah. You like-ah me because I represent the hidden aspects of yourself that you know-ah but have not met. The hidden aspects and power of your own reality that exists, which you express through your music, and yet through your music you have never fully expressed. You can, however, and that music can open up still further and fall like-uh raindrops upon the earth.

(I was breathing real deep at this point.)

Do not hold it too tightly. Let it flow out, whether through political messages or elsewhere. Do not constrain it. Do not say you must speak on this subject or that subject. But let your music flow out of the back of your head, or your elbow, or your penis or your belly, as it will-ah. Do not consign it automatically to "causes." Let it also find its own cause, for it *is* its own cause, regardless of the cause for which you think it speaks.

At this point I exclaimed, "Ah, Christ," and screamed out, "Thank you, Seth. Thank you. Thank *YOU!*"

I believe this was one of the last times Jane channeled. She had created for herself a physical disability of bending forward, stooping low to walk, that was obvious that evening (except when she channeled Seth). After she "died" Robert Butts

*Seth calls Jane Roberts "Rubert" and Butts "Joseph." He obviously noticed my beard, which I was wearing at the time.

claimed that Seth doesn't come through any more, but I have felt in touch with Seth often—several times through another channel, Tom Massari. I was told he comes to visit me in my studio from time to time. I guess he likes-ah my music.

Dr. Peebles

I got home the end of June in time to help rehearse *Ballad for Americans* at the Hollywood Bowl on July 4th with Zubin Mehta and the L.A. Philharmonic, undoubtedly the climax of 1976. I was introduced from the stage for the first time since *The Lonesome Train* there thirty years before. Brock Peters sang the solo well and movingly. He sang that year on a United Artists record with *Ballad* and *Lonesome Train* (with Odetta) on opposite sides, the first time my two major cantatas appeared on a single album. Leonard de Paur admirably conducted a *Ballad* rearranged by Luther Henderson with a new overture.

My psychic potential had been primed by meeting Seth. Back in L.A. I met William Rainen and the extraordinary person-spirit he channels, the Scotsman Dr. Peebles. The good doctor came by his title legitimately, having practiced in San Francisco during his last incarnation at the turn of the century. William Rainen is a talented and volatile, mercurial being. Downs follow ups and vice versa with amazing swiftness. A book could be written about him. On the whole I am happy to accept that he does his best, which much of the time is excellent.

Dr. Peebles is a sturdy promoter of right action, continually urging people to maintain present-time awareness and to love themselves. He always comes through in a high piercing voice totally different from William's baritone. The doctor proclaims, "God bless you, Dr. Peebles. It is a blessing when man and spirit join together in search of the greater truth and awareness." And he does it all with a sense of humor.

Always knowing—apparently intimately—the people in the room with him, he addressed me this first time, September of 1976, "Earl, you are what we call an 'old soul.'" And he proceeded to recount a number of my incarnations, all very validating. I paraphrase a couple.

I was an artist, who painted many beautiful pictures, but my father did not approve. He wanted me to join his shipping business. I persisted on my path, the conflict developing until, in desperation, he had my hands broken so I could no longer paint. But I found a way of realizing my work with the help of friends. And I never did join the shipping business. (Incarnationally, Robinson was always the rebel. These days I am more into seeking agreement.)

Another time I led a band of underground dissidents trying to live under a fascist-style dictatorship. As the one responsible for these rebels I was apprehended and taken into custody. I was tortured for information that could lead to the capture of some of my followers and the undermining of the movement. I resisted the torture for a time. Then my mind slipped and I gave in and named names and places. Once they had this information they executed me. But I found a way of communicating from beyond with my followers, so that the information I gave proved useless to my captors.

This kind of material elevated my ego highly. As I soared somewhere in the stratosphere, the Doc casually remarked, "Of course, old souls are actually nothing more nor less than slow learners."

I laughed for a long, long time on that one. I realized I had spent forty years of this present life locked into a struggle against something my mother had put out when I was a teenager, "Men are beasts, and women don't enjoy sex." I spent a lot of "old soul" time subjecting myself to other people's authority in the Communist movement. I had for so long neglected to take account of the spiritual side of life. Who can predict what further development of my consciousness still awaits? Yes, wisdom does come so painfully slowly.

Dr. Peebles became a brother and friend, my doctor physically and mentally, my adviser on everything from Abraham Lincoln to sex. He has been extraordinarily helpful. Often I have passed on his advice to friends. William Rainen moved up to Seattle not long after me, so I can conveniently consult him whenever I wish.

There is no such thing as being "faithful" or "loyal" to Dr. Peebles, or to any spirit. I am on good terms with a number of spirits channeled by different people, and some I am able to call upon myself. To those who think I have lost it, I can only say that channeling has often given me solid, practical help and guidance that others seek from psychiatrists, priests or social workers. From time to time all of us can use the perception of someone outside ourselves who can listen to our problems, then frame them in a new light. It's a way of reaching down a little deeper, to a level that isn't immediately accessible, into what we already know and feel.

MY AMERICA

After the vast distances I had covered in 1976, both geographically and psychically, I spent 1977 quietly writing my Armenian opera. I should mention one piece of television work, a 1977 script, "Appalachian Spring," for the show *What Really Happened to the Class of '65*. With Irwin Coster I adapted some regional folk songs for that, and revived my acting career, appearing as a Southern Mountain farmer and folksinger. I even joined the Screen Actors Guild, and am still a member.

My potentially most important contact at the beginning of 1978 was Leonard de Paur, whom I knew from the all-black de Paur Infantry Chorus back in World War II. We had reached each other again in 1976 with the Brock Peters recording of *Ballad for Americans* and *Lonesome Train*. In his new capacity as head of programming for Lincoln Center outdoor summer shows, we began discussing a beautiful idea: To take *Ballad* and expand it into a complete evening of American history, for performance in August at Lincoln Center. I put *David of Sassoun* aside for a few months to concentrate on this new project. We had *The Lonesome Train* as a natural Civil War finale for the first act, and "Joe Hill" to finish the labor section in the second half. I filled out the *Ballad* from the Civil War to the present with essentially all new material, including a "Moving West," a "Robber Barons" section, "She Always Lights a Candle" about Eleanor Roosevelt, a "Watergate Madrigal," and a finale, "To My Northwest," saluting my homeland. Topping it all would be "The House I Live In," sung perhaps by me.

I sent Leonard scenes as I wrote them. Ed EmanuEl from Fresno State College was producing and directing *David of Sassoun* and seemed an ideal choice to direct *Earl Robinson's America*, as we were calling it. In the end, the project fizzled. De Paur canceled it, for reasons I never learned.

Skip ahead two years after the Lincoln Center mishap to May 1980 and a performance of *Earl Robinson's America* in Virginia—Virginia, Minnesota. A man I'd known in Los Angeles, Chuck Rowland, now a professor of drama at Mesabi Community College, asked me if I had anything new I wanted produced. I had earlier served as artist in residence at the college, when Theatre Mesabi presented *The Lonesome Train* in 1974. With high purpose and noble resolve, Chuck mounted this work there in "da iron range" country of northeastern Minnesota, some sixty miles up from Duluth. With musical direction by Jay Carlsgaard, and a talented cast of college kids, Chuck put on an enormous show: 57 characters, chorus of thirty, five dance sequences, a huge set with a thrust stage, and hundreds of projections on two screens showing scenes of American history from before the white man's arrival up through Watergate.

I had structured the musical around two main performers: Character, whose identity shifts between an American working-class Everyman and such historical figures as Jefferson, John Brown, and Lincoln; and Land, the female lead, who portrays the American soil itself, plus people such as a Civil War widow, Sojourner Truth, and Eleanor Roosevelt. Luckily, Chuck blessed me with two magnificent actor-singers for these roles, Gary Carlson and Denisse Hoole.

This whole production died in the hinterland after only five performances, the problem being the lack of money to properly produce the work, let alone publicize it. With a budget of $1,500, they could only pay my expenses for a week before opening night. I arrived April 30th, my bags packed with orchestrations (stepson Mike Martin assisted me) for sixteen musicians. After one sad, incomplete rehearsal, the plan dwindled down to one piano—and harpsichord played by the composer.

Still, Rowland, Carlsgaard, the cast, the pianist, and Robinson shared a warm, loving communication. In the inevitable editing of the script, we had full discussion, understanding, and agreement. Carlsgaard's religious convictions did not allow him to go for Joe Hill and the Wobblies' anticlericalism. I put up quite a struggle to include "Pie in the Sky"—and lost. But we remained good friends, with respect for each other, and the

main idea of *E.R.'s America* came off resoundingly. At the end
I left my harpsichord and went up on stage to sing "The House
I Live In" with the chorus.

"The show, which had to close because of College schedules after its five performances, could perhaps have run another week in view of the audience's praise, full houses, and
standing ovations," wrote one reviewer. Another rave spoke of

> an evening of joy for us, a musical that is unabashedly
> patriotic, served up with just the right amount of wit,
> tenderness and sophistication. *Earl Robinson's America*
> is "Everybody's America." The heroes are all there.
> Whether you are a member of NOW or of Project De-
> mocracy, you will find your favorite feminist or states-
> man honored in this giant musical history of America.[1]

The money problem, however, made it impossible to advertise outside of Mesabi and "da range." No outside producers
saw the show, and we made no recording of it. So I cling to the
idea that *Earl Robinson's America* will yet be done properly—
fully, professionally, sensationally.

Note

1. Unsigned, "Virginia Premieres Big, Beautiful Hit," *Arrowhead
Arts*, July 1980; Mickie Scholtus, "*Robinson's America* Is Big, Beautiful!," *Mesabi Daily News*, May 7, 1980.

INCARNATIONAL ARMENIAN

He overfulfilled his job

I mentioned visiting Fresno in May 1976 and seeing Varas Samuelian's sculpture of David of Sassoun. I studied the books written on David, such as *Daredevils of Sassoun* by Leon Surmelian. He and his book became both the inspiration and a stumbling block for my folk opera. In Surmelian, as in other published versions by Shalian, Aram Tolegian and Hovhaness Toumanian, David is presented as an incredibly naïve, some would say witless boy, a lover of animals, and a do-gooder, anxious to please, yet possessed of a bodily strength far beyond that of mere mortals. Fearless, quick to anger, quicker to forgive, he did not know or understand the miraculous power he owned but could not at first control. For instance, when he came home to Sassoun he played with the Armenian children; they teased him and, not meaning to, he broke the necks of three boys. They sent him to be a shepherd. David would nap, the sheep would stray, then in rounding them up, not knowing the difference between sheep and other animals, David would bring in hares, marten and fox, opossum and weasel, along with the sheep. "He is stupid. He is crazy," exclaimed the townfolk. "Clearly not a shepherd." Every job David was given, he overfulfilled, so to speak.

In time his mighty strength was put to use overcoming the enemies of Sassoun. As an unashamed killer, he first ascertained the facts of the situation, then dispatched these enemies with ridiculous ease.

I saw how David must be fleshed out into a real, more believable human being with weaknesses to go with his epic stature. This need showed itself crucially with the women in the story. With his father Meher, his grandfather Sanasar, and his son Pokr (Little) Meher, in all four parts of the legend David would perform amazing feats, turning back Sassoun's enemies with much slaughter. This accomplished, they were ready for women, who were to be found as princesses in adjoining or

377

faraway kingdoms. There the men would go, overcome enormous obstacles, win the ladies, and bring them back home.

I altered, indeed revolutionized this process by creating
Vardanoush Khanoum, bright in face, form, and mind, educated beyond her young years, a peasant but unsuspected aris-
tocrat. She and the Widow Barav became supporters, advisers,
and friends of David; and Vardanoush goes on to be a leader of
her people in the struggle to defeat Misra Melik, wicked leader
of the Assyrians. Our hero, who starts out the utter and complete individualist, gradually learns, first the alphabet with
Vardanoush, then to trust the animals, and finally to work
with his Sassounian people to resist and overcome Melik.

The story of getting all of this on stage—the psychic background, the limitations of the college drama department in
Fresno, the personality conflicts with the director, not to speak
of attempting to satisfy the private and public preferences of
the 20,000 Armenians living in Fresno—this story requires
more space than I can give here.

The most profound conflict involved the music. I operated
from the start on a basic method of getting words and story
down on paper before going at the music. Working away from
the piano, I sat myself at Howard Johnson's in Santa Barbara,
and later at the Pepper Tree. The waitress would bring me a
coffee pot and leave it on the table, where I wrote out large
parts of *David* longhand, lyrics as well as scenes.

I spent some time with Tom Bozikian, an excellent oud
player. Something like a mandolin, the oud was not originally
an Armenian instrument, but they adopted it, and I intended it
as an integral part of the sound of my opera. I also worked
with Gia Aivasian, researcher at UCLA, who translated for
me, and introduced me to modal Armenian church music; and
with Leon Surmelian the writer, who argued, angrily even,
that his book *Daredevils of Sassoun* was a more than sufficient
libretto for the opera. Why did I need to spend all this time
writing? Seemingly jealous of anything outside of his book, he
wouldn't hear any of my elaborations, though I took the name
of his sister Vardanoush for my heroine.

Producing the play, sabotaging the opera

As the production of *Earl Robinson's America* that Ed
EmanuEl hoped to direct never happened at Lincoln Center,
he could schedule *David of Sassoun* sooner than expected.
Auditions and casting took place the first week of September
1978. The first rehearsal rolled around on September 25th, and
Robinson, whom Ed had arranged to hire as music director for
$2,000, wasn't quite ready. I arrived late for that all-important
occasion. I had scheduled a psychic channeling that morning in
L.A. to prepare me for the production spiritually, but hadn't
left enough time to drive to Fresno.

My high expectations were destined not to be realized. I
had prepared a "hit" for the chorus, "Song of Sassoun." But
when I got there I met not a chorus but fragments. The entire
chorus, a central idea to the whole production, did not get together completely until two weeks later, when Ed needed them
for the staging. He had arranged staggered rehearsals for 5, 6,
and 7 o'clock to meet the individual needs of the chorus people, but without regard to my need to work with them all together. I'd meet with eight or nine voices for an hour, perhaps
five the next hour, and so on. I knew I had to work with singing actors, rather than acting singers, and this suited me all
right. Except I had no chance of achieving a balance of soprano, alto, tenor, and bass because of the fragmentation. As a
result, we accomplished little those first weeks. I felt patheti-
cally grateful when I got an hour with the whole cast intact,
once Ed started stage rehearsals. As might have been expected,
when he stood them up on stage, the inadequately rehearsed
songs fell apart. One quite beautiful three-part phrase for
women's voices never did get learned clear through opening
night. I simply never had six women—the minimum for doing
this properly—together long enough.

Ed EmanuEl, a genius of stagecraft, I freely admit, was in-
capable of understanding and making proper use of the music
in this folk opera. He produced an exciting *play*, bringing out
most of the values of my script. Yet he sabotaged the *opera*,

though not consciously, I believe. It only began with the mis-
management of the chorus.

Well into the rehearsal schedule he informed me that I'd
have no pit orchestra. The plus or minus fifteen pieces I had
counted on had to be cut to no more than five, and they had to
be backstage, unseen. And he had no money to pay the players, who had to be professional level. EmanuEl began creating
his own score, consisting of a rehearsal pianist and drum beats
played by unoccupied actors to punctuate the beginning and
ending of scenes. My contribution to the orchestration kept
getting reduced. He cut the number of musicians down to
three, and I went on a search for players of the oud and clarinet (hopefully doubling duduc, the Armenian double reed
oboe-like instrument). I finally found an amateur oud player,
and brought my clarinetist son Perry out from New York for
the run of the production; he could learn the duduc. I got two
timpani from the music department, plus a couple of gongs.
Meantime, Ed had become so used to piano and drums that he
had a hard time, not with the oud, played very softly in only
two numbers, but with Perry, who was used to playing out,
loudly at times. Ed would repeatedly turn down the micro-
phone on Perry, thereby insuring that the audience heard only
the softest piano background and some mumbling woodwind.
Probably a lucky thing, the borrowed duduc broke down
shortly after Perry tried it out; its penetrating tone would have
pained Ed's tender ears.

My differences with Ed EmanuEl went beyond music. For
instance, I planned and wrote *David of Sassoun* in three acts. I
never learned till more than halfway through rehearsals that he
had no intention of staging more than two acts. Ruthlessly he
compressed three into two. I realize that the feelings of the
playwright sometimes need to be overridden in the interest of
a successful production, but the manner of doing it left much
to be desired. I never knew from one day to the next what
would be cut and what left. Once the pressure of production
began, we had little communication or consultation between
us.

The limitations of a college production applied particularly
to casting. Robert Beltran, the beautiful young man who
played David, gave a solid performance. But he was physically
not big enough; his voice was that of a singing actor, without
the range, depth, and power that I had sought.

Vickie Shagoian as Vardanoush, on the contrary, had a
lovely strong soprano, and gave promise of being the true
soulmate and equal partner of David. Here I need to reveal
something of myself. When I went against the David folk tradition of male supremacy and created a mate for him, I did this
with love in my heart. I fell in love with the character Vardanoush before I ever met the performer. I prepared myself to
totally love the woman chosen to play her.

I made a huge mistake confiding this fantasy to Ed
EmanuEl. For although he had his girlfriend in the cast, he
could not countenance my creating a similar relationship with
one of *his* actors. I don't know what hidden puritan streak surfaced in him with my revelation, but it was very real. At his
instigation the head of the drama department called me in for a
talk. He strongly advised me not to make passes at anyone. It
might be all right in the circles I presumably moved in, but it
was improper here at this school. This possibility must have
obsessed Ed. Up to the final production week his communication with me had little to do with problems musical or otherwise, but with warnings against making a date with Vardanoush.

He made his attitude even clearer, once the show began
running successfully, when we discussed what got cut and what
should be kept in any future version of the opera. He concluded that Vardanoush had no real presence in the script and
advised cutting her out entirely!

With all the carping, it must be said that *David of Sassoun*
was an exciting production that captured much scholarly attention. An international symposium on the David legend took
place at the university November 30th and December 1st, with
panelists from several countries. In face of one of the most difficult jobs ever, so he said, Ed EmanuEl performed theatrical

magic on stage. A huge sixteen-section mirror, suspended above the entire stage at a 45-degree angle, provided additional sightlines and allowed David and his horse Jalali to "fly" through the sky in the second act. It helped make the epic confrontation between Melik and David more real. Casting dancing-singing actors, he filled the stage with motion at all times. Neither of us managed to please all the Armenians, but enough liked it and came back to see it several times. Critic Carolyn van Schaik did not care for David's prayer for peace at the end, but "the music," she wrote, "when it was allowed full development, was enveloping and beautiful. . . . The words were fun and wonderful as they transposed the 10th century into modern day vocabulary."[1]

An interesting conflict came out as a result of my rewriting the legend. After the climactic moment when David kills Melik, I bring David back as a man of peace, through the lovely theme "Song of Sassoun." I felt this was inherent in David's higher self and that it was appropriate. Some Armenians, and one reviewer, felt that David must remain unrepentant to the very end. Let the arguments roll.

In the end, I blame no one for the outcome of this production. Going with a college production in Fresno, mostly because of the large Armenian population there, I set myself up for an inadequate treatment of the material. Once again I had chosen for myself a "losing script." Thinking ahead to a future production, I would like a cast of acting singers organized as a chorus to give stability and presence to the music. I'd like David and Melik to be more like giants physically, with voices and epic acting ability to match. I'd like a Regina Resnik type to play the Widow Barav, and a singing Anthony Quinn as Uncle Ohan. I'd like an orchestra, minimum twenty pieces, plus oud and duduc. And finally, I'd like a director with full musical understanding to create theatrical magic on the stage.

I am struck by how Wagnerian it all sounds, beginning with the single mind that creates both music and text out of old legends about national ethos. I suspect several factors here: First, my early exposure to Wagner in Mrs. Van Ogle's class at the University of Washington. Second, this is a deeply patriotic opera. Having spent much of my life committed to the idea of America, I found in the late 1970s, with Vietnam, Watergate, and the havoc we wrought in Chile behind us, that patriotism rang too hollow for me. So for artistic purposes I "switched countries," trying to find in the Armenian epic a cause worthy of celebration. Last, I was affected by Soviet aesthetic theory. With all their different republics and ethnic groups they had to come up with a formula for keeping narrow nationalism in check. "National in form, socialist in content," they said. Now *David of Sassoun* is not socialist, but it does affirm positive human values, which it would need if it were ever produced in Armenia (and which I fondly hoped). It's mind-boggling to realize what changes have taken place there since 1978!

Maybe you will find this obvious by now, but *David of Sassoun* confirms something about Earl Robinson that has not changed. I am a seeker trying to get at the truth, about myself and about the world. I often cast this truth in the persona of a liberating hero—Joe Hill, the Uncle Sam of *Ballad for Americans*, Abe Lincoln. I don't throw a lot of personal introspection and emotionalism into my work in the manner of the typical hair-tearing romantic, but I do remain open to new philosophies and ways of perceiving. I have tried to express these perceptions in music, whether Communism in my songs of the Thirties, or industrial democracy in *Ballad for Americans* and *The Lonesome Train*, racial justice in "Black and White," the human potential movement in "Four Hugs a Day," ecology in *Ride the Wind*, or psychic reality in *David*. At times in our history my seekings have exactly corresponded to the mood of the nation. I like to feel that these times are not over.

Note

1. "David of Sassoun: Struggling to Fly," *The Daily Collegian*, December 1, 1978.

DYLAN AND ME,
AND MORE LEE HAYS

A sense of timelessness

When John Higgins and Randy Polak of the Santa Barbara
Repertory Theater came to me in July 1979 about a Bob Dylan
production, I was cool at first. They hadn't, after all, proposed
my songs. Given a choice, I'd rather push my own than anyone else's—a narrow, selfish trait that may be understandable,
but not exactly fine and noble. Also, the truth is that I admired
Dylan more as a poet and conveyor of concepts than as a
songwriter. His manner of singing didn't turn me on, as it obviously did millions of his followers. Maybe I felt a little jealous. Add to that the fact that earlier that year I had taken a
spill, landing on my wrist, and from then on my guitar playing
was never the same. So I couldn't and needn't compete any
longer with all the young folk guitarists. The fall didn't affect
my piano playing, however.

The pay offered to me as music director was also nothing
special. But I'm glad I took the job. I received a very special
education. By the time the show rolled onto the boards, I discovered a kind of musical sophistication in Dylan that had es-
caped me, for he is right there with whatever he needs to put
his words and ideas across. I had personally known Dylan for
fifteen years, from appearing with him for one cause or another, but working directly with his songs, I felt closer to him
than ever.

John Higgins really created the show, out of the mountain
of published Dylaniana—interviews, poetry and anecdotes contained in the liner notes to Dylan's twenty or more record albums, and his book *Tarantula*. The show featured eight singing
performers plus Peter Landecker, who perfected Dylan's dis-
tinctive speech as the narrator. I was more than twice the age
of anyone in the production. All recruited from local talent,
they seemed at first like a motley, unprofessional crew, but
they shaped up wondrously into a sharp-witted ensemble.

385

I didn't always agree with Higgins as to what songs should be included. I listened repeatedly to "Like a Rolling Stone" and "Chimes of Freedom" and couldn't see their importance. The cast voted to keep "Rolling Stone." I coached them to emphasize all its bitterness, and I came to appreciate it as an outrageously different, true original. Then, during "Chimes of Freedom," Higgins showed slides of antinuclear demonstrations and had the cast shout "Diablo!" (in reference to the plant at Diablo Canyon), and that convinced me of that song's necessity. Shows what a theatrical presentation can often achieve. At my insistence we got "Lay Lady Lay" into the show: I liked its unexpected chord changes, and the imagery of a laboring man whose clothes are dirty but whose hands are clean appealed to me.

We scheduled *Words and Music of Bob Dylan* to run at Santa Barbara's Alhecama Theater for only one week, but it attracted growing audiences, and it kept getting extended, until five weeks had passed. Part of the attraction involved the sense of timelessness in Dylan's work: Antinuclear rallies in Southern California had only recently included "Blowin' in the Wind" and "The Times They Are A'Changin'" as prominent musical commentary. But finally the theatre had to make way for another production. We made a videotape and I set out to get Dylan's permission to have the show considered for Broadway.

There seemed to be a lot going for this at first. A friend wanting to take a crack at agenting me two years before had got a lovely quote from Dylan for a publicity flier:

> Earl has never been much of a taker; he is a giver. He gives a lot of help to his friends, and a lot of great music to everybody.
>
> —Bob Dylan, March 1, 1977

Bob also supported me when I began working on the show: Word came back that he approved of "anything Earl Robinson does."

After this auspicious start, however, I ran up against road-blocks. I made trips down to Malibu, where he had an estate, but all I could do was leave messages. I got the videotape to him through an assistant, and received an inconclusive answer. I also contacted one of Bob's agents, without response. I don't know to this day whether Bob liked or didn't like the video—or ever saw it.

I took some time off in between Dylan promotion to do songs for a charming TV production by my old collaborator dating back to the 1944 Roosevelt campaign, Chuck Jones—an animation special called *The Pumpkin Who Couldn't Smile*. It aired on CBS Halloween night, and gets repeated fairly frequently. Kids eat it up.

That November I made a special trip to Portland, Seattle, and Spokane, where Dylan was concertizing, in an attempt to see him and get permission to move with the show. I attended his concerts, went backstage in all three towns, and eventually struck out. Up into 1980 I was getting good feedback on the video from three New York producers, but they eventually lost interest because I never could obtain the go-ahead from Bob.

The only reason for this that I've been able to discern is that he got heavily into his born-again Christian phase, for a time not even singing the protest numbers so important to his audience. And naturally I could not stay forever excited about a project where I arranged and produced the songs of another composer. Still and all, it's kind of sad.

The Thing

When Lee Hays cleared out of our home in Brooklyn to make room for Helen's father, he moved to uptown Manhattan. After that, he took up his last permanent home in Croton-on-Hudson, where he revived his art of raising vegetables for the table. From there he wrote to me so tenderly when my father passed on, not too long after he and Mommer had celebrated their 60th anniversary: "Earl," Lee said, "of the myriads of stars that have streaked across the abyss between the eternities, if that is what I mean, your dad surely gave out a fine light."

Up in Croton is where, bowing to the onslaught of diabetes, Lee had first a little toe, and then one leg and then the other amputated at the knee. And where he also turned off on me, for reasons undetermined. Writing him a cheery poem about his losing a leg, I intended to encourage him to view it not just with equanimity but to regard it as a positive boost to his now being able to get at some of his "posthumous works." Which he had been joking about for years, looking ahead to a time of leisure removed from the pressure of day-to-day events. Actually, he had written a poem himself, which he called "In Dead Earnest":

> If I should die before I wake,
> All my bone and sinew take.
> Put them in the compost pile
> To decompose a little while.
> Worms, water, sun, will have their way,
> Reducing me to common clay.
> All that I am will feed the trees,
> And little fishes in the seas.
> When radishes and corn you munch,
> You may be having me for lunch.
> And then excrete me with a grin,
> Chortling, "There goes Lee again."
> 'Twill be my happiest destiny
> To die and live eternally.

He could joke about not feeling bad at losing a leg, because he had not been able to see his toes (over his big tummy) for years, but no one else was allowed to see humor in this.

Another possible reason for his turnoff might have come from a visit I made to him up in Croton. There he showed me a story he had recently written, and instead of giving him wholehearted praise, I came up with suggestions on how it

could be improved. I thought I was helping, but I may have
had the opposite effect.

Anyway, shortly after this he found a way to criticize me
about something. It may be that a newly developed habit of
mine—of taking positive responsibility for what happens to
me, and expecting others to do the same—went too far for Lee
to handle. "The things you say, particularly your remarks to
Toni and Fran, are so offensive as to defile the glory of life,
and thus border on the obscene," he wrote to me testily. "I
won't have any part of it."

I never understood what he was talking about, and I never
did learn who Toni and Fran were, but that was the last I
heard from him for a long time. I'd send letters abjectly beg-
ging forgiveness, and he'd return them unopened. I took to
sending him notes through friends, but this had no effect either.

This sad, locked-in position got jarred open by a Scottish
spirit named Tom McPherson, who is one of Shirley Mac-
Laine's advisers. Hearing of my miscommune with Lee, Tom
seemed to understand immediately and suggested a gift to Lee.
Nonthreatening, nonjudgmental. Well, I had been considering
buying for myself a fascinating piece of art which the excellent
Santa Barbara sculptor Elijah David Herschler had lent me for
a while, a sort of small airplane-propeller-shaped mobile
mounted on a thin pointed spire, which would rotate at the
touch of a finger. Hypnotic to watch, it seemed like it might
soothe Lee. I wonder if you can appreciate how unusual, bi-
zarre even, this situation was for me, never being an art collector—I seldom if ever had money to spend that way. And Elijah
had this mobile listed at $1,200. But when the action is right,
the tune plays itself.

First I got Elijah to cut his price in half, and made arrangements to pay it off in installments. Then the question
arose, how to get the gift to Lee so he would accept it. I talked
with Pete Seeger. He asked why Lee was angry and I told him I
didn't know. Understanding Lee better than I, Pete said, "Lee

believes in the Eleventh Commandment. Never forgive a grudge."

At Pete's suggestion, I wrapped the sculpture carefully, put it in a box and sent it to Pete, who got this innocent, unobjectionable gift to Lee. This miraculously drew an answer. A card came from Lee:

> Dear Earl:
>
> Pete carried The Thing around for weeks before remembering to drop it off. We have put it in the back room so nobody will have to see it. I presume it is a work of art but no one is quite sure. All we are really sure of is that it scares cats, and that is to its credit. Thanks for sending it, I think. Lee

This communication was pure gold to me. It had broken the ice surrounding us. Only a couple more notes passed between us, in which "The Thing" was never mentioned. I couldn't make the Weavers' final Carnegie Hall concert just after Ronald Reagan's 1980 election. Shortly thereafter, Lee left the physical before I had a chance to find out if he had forgiven me or not. After his memorial celebration in October 1981 I got the sculpture back.

SECTION SEVEN
1982 to Now

A GRAND SWIM-IN PICKET LINE

The Law of Allow

Flowing out of a growing interest in animals, particularly in communicating with animals, I met, through a spirit channel, Yuka the dolphin. From my channel's larynx came a series of high, singing "ah"s. "Ah-aah-ah-ahhh-AAah-ahh-aaahha," developing through different tones, dips and swoops, shades of feeling—sadness, pain, pleasure, joy, rejoicing. Thus Yuka sang on and on, and I found myself joining her. I sang higher notes—not as high as Yuka—but higher than I'd ever sung in my life, and we had a most exciting dolphinian conversation which went on for eight or ten minutes.

We both came to a stop. After a moment of quiet, in her high voice Yuka said, "Ahh-ah-aaah-ah-eye LOVE—You!!!"

Well! I went up in smoke. Her first English words, the most sensitive and beautiful in our language. I incoherently returned the love message. And so began a relationship which can be expressed, ridiculously inadequately, as beyond orgasm. From February 1980 on, I met with the channel and talked with Yuka every two weeks when possible. She started speaking more and more English.

Our commune grew apace. I studied with her, all manner of things dolphin and whale, of the sea, and of love. She became my guide and adviser. Along about June of 1980, Yuka came up with an amazingly practical suggestion. Psychically knowing that I was still locked into two moderate unsuccesses, *Earl Robinson's America* and *David of Sassoun*, she proposed that I take two weeks off and look at writing a dolphin musical. Clever of her! I took the two weeks, and with her ongoing help, four months later I had *Listen for the Dolphin*, the story of a baby dolphin trying to communicate with people. Besides Yuka, it drew on books by John Cunningham Lilly (*Man and Dolphin* and *The Mind of the Dolphin: A Nonhuman Intelligence*), and *The Lure of the Dolphin* by Robin Brown. I had also

393

been profoundly moved by a squib in *The New York Times*
(March 9, 1980) that became the finale.

> ### 4,000 Dolphins Force
> ### Japanese Boats Back
>
> Iki Island, Japan—About 4,000 dolphins
> massed around this island today, forcing fishing
> boats back to port, a day after fishermen from
> the island slashed and stabbed about 200 dol-
> phins to death after trapping them in nets.
>
> Meanwhile, an American environmentalist
> was formally charged in Nagasaki with freeing
> some 250 dolphins that had been trapped in the
> bay at Iki Island where the others were killed,
> the Prosecutor's Office announced.
>
> A spokesman said the conservationist,
> Dexter Cate, 36 years old, of Hawaii, was
> charged with obstructing fishermen's business
> by force and damaging equipment by cutting
> nets.
>
> There was no explanation for the massing
> of the dolphins around the island.

That last line fascinates me. What indeed can explain the
dolphins' action? My theory leads me into the psychic arena.
Their brains are more than a quarter size larger than the human brain, which establishes in John Lilly's mind and research
that dolphins are at least our equal in intelligence. One is
tempted to ask, If the dolphins are as smart as they seem, what
are they doing around Iki Island at all, where they can surely
see they will be met with sharp knives?

Every observer, scientific or not, is turned on by how so-
ciable, playful, cooperative, loving, and helpful are the dolphins. They have willingly "carried" the tuna to the tuna fishermen—hovering over the schools of tuna so the fishermen
know where they are—in the process allowing themselves to be
killed in large numbers. Dolphins persist in saving us from

drowning: Documented evidence goes back 2,000 years. And they have led countless ships and sailors, lost in fog and storm, home to a safe port. They allow themselves to be exploited for human purposes of many kinds—entertainment, scientific, military.

How did 4,000 of them gather on March 8th around Iki Island? They knew exactly when to arrive. They showed up early enough in the morning to greet the fishermen, and they made a demonstration with precision and power. They succeeded in their peaceful picketing, and the fisherman had trouble crossing their picket line.

Where did they find this very human tactic? Did they learn from César Chávez, or take a leaf from Martin Luther King, Jr.? What made this most gentle of animals act so organized and forthright, risking the guns and knives of the fishermen and the killing propensity of the human race? What made them so sure they could get away with this demonstration?

While these questions are beyond answering, we can see some results of the dolphin action. Our compassion is energized and worldwide attention begins to perk up. The body count on whales and dolphins goes down, the tuna fishermen figure out ways to lower the nets so the dolphins can swim over. And the Japanese are pressured to take a nonviolent look at their practices. The reeducation process goes on. Dexter Cate is indicted, but later freed, the Japanese authorities deciding that he was mainly, uh, impolite.

Our brothers and sisters in the ocean are speaking strongly to us. Responding not with violence, they instead offer us friendship, peace. They understand the Law of Allow. They allow man every conceivable abuse, even slashing and grinding them up for fertilizer. As psychologists supreme (though I think they cannot do it any other way) they grasp that this is the only way we will learn. If we don't, it is we humans who will vanish, not the dolphin.

In the process of completing *Listen for the Dolphin*, I came into contact with Dexter Cate, the dolphin saver. Now, working on this book, I am saddened by his sudden passing, at age

47, while leading a protest by boaters and surfboarders in
Keauhou Bay against a project backed by the State of Hawaii
to build geothermal power plants in the Wao Kele O Puna rain
forest. Flipping out of his kayak, he drowned August 23, 1990.

Writing in the sky

In *Listen for the Dolphin* I set a series of scenes aboard a
tuna boat, in a dolphinarium, at a naval exercise, a beach, and
finally at Iki Island. Producing the show took up the first half
of 1981. It opened at the Garden Street Theater in Santa Barbara on June 12th and ran three weekends. Julie McLeod, cho-
reographer of the dolphin dancers on stage and a member of
the original *West Side Story* company, continually gave her all.
Mayri Sagady LeVeille, director and lighting person extraordinaire, had reservations about *Dolphin* from the start, and never
did put her entire self into the production. But I got her to a
session with Dr. Peebles and with that spiritual encouragement, she saw it through.

Besides writing words and music, I was nominal producer,
singer, actor, and conductor. Faced with a budget of $6,000, I
raised a third of that amount in Santa Barbara, the rest from
friends in L.A. and elsewhere, then had to make up a $2,000
overdraw out of my own pocket. Our plan for the dolphins to
be danced live on stage while the humans remained more card-
boardy in the background called for me to sing-talk at a piano
behind a scrim that would occasionally light up, and conduct a
band of eight mainly amateur musicians who are also called
upon as a singing chorus and for some spoken lines. Some of
these acted more temperamentally by far than would have
been the case with union musicians, whom we could not afford
to pay at scale. On top of this we had an incredibly "down"
series of dress rehearsals, leading to a Friday night opening at
once horrendous and inspiring.

Having the commendable idea of taking the audience
"under water" in the beginning with whale and dolphin sounds
plus pictures on the scrim, we had to keep the windows closed,
as it was still light outside. The hot June night produced a

temperature of close to one hundred in the theatre. We staggered out into the cooler back yard at the half, more dead than alive, to be greeted by *writing in the sky*! Someone remembered they were testing missiles at Vandenberg Air Force Base, which struck everyone as a bad thing, except me. For some reason I felt OK about it, and pushed through the trees to get a better look at the "cloud formation." And we all saw an astounding phenomenon. The sky writing had taken the shape of a dolphin, and the tail of a whale diving! I took a picture of it.

A full explanation came at the next Dr. Peebles session. "Oh, yes," the good Doc said, "we wanted to salute your production." A team of spirits had gathered, including Doc Peebles, Yuka, and two dolphins, to rearrange the missile vapors into those beautiful, prophetic shapes.

"It was easy," Dr. Peebles said. "Up in the air there is no resistance, and we decided you could use some support on your fine project." Which comforted us no end, and made the whole production hassle most worthwhile.

The reviews were mixed. One, by Ted Berkman, totally understood what we tried to do.

> *Listen for the Dolphin* is not afraid to take chances. Provocative in theme and bold in execution, the new . . . offering at the Garden Street goes out on a tenuous limb and makes its way home safely, overcoming limited physical resources to create a buoyant evening of entertainment. . . .
>
> It mixes music, masks and mime with ballet, puppets, projection and stroboscopic lighting devices to fashion an end product that defies categorization. Reflecting Robinson's long background as an artist-activist, it has elements of Brechtian political theater. But it is also part 17th-century morality play, part Americanized Kabuki and with its sonorous chants could even be regarded as a throwback to the stone amphitheater of ancient Athens. The one thing it is not [is] a conventional dramatic work. . . .
>
> *Dolphin* is a delight to the informed ear . . . , a score that is in turn rollicking, fervent, tenderly lyrical, and

crisply dramatic, mingling traditional sea chanteys with talkin' blues and stretches of avant garde opera. . . . Because the Process production speaks to us in a theatrical language that is different and for many persons unfamiliar, some may be put off by its free-swinging approach. Last Saturday night's audience was not. Applause began early in the first act, continued throughout and was topped off by several lengthy curtain calls.[1]

Not long after *Dolphin* closed (fortunately we made a video of the whole production), I sang some concerts up in Seattle, and Patricia Foote of the Seattle *Times* interviewed me. I explained to her about being a dolphin myself in a previous incarnation and how then, too, I had been an entertainer, performing for sailors.

"What would you say to those who would believe you're bonkers?" she asked me.

I laughed, then answered, "You may be right. All creative people are a little bonkers. If we all allowed ourselves to be a little bonkers . . . , the world would not only be a more peaceful place, but more fun."[2]

Spirits, friends, and publishers

During the time I wrote *Listen for the Dolphin*, my friend and collaborator Yip Harburg had a memorial at the Mark Taper Forum in Los Angeles. He met a sudden end on March 6, 1981 in a car crash on Hollywood Boulevard. I sang our "Free and Equal Blues," and spoke about Yippur as a perfectionist and true original. I added, "Yippur is here. All his friends and musical personalities around, everyone celebrating him and his work? He wouldn't miss it! Yippur is here!"

Afterward, a young psychic lady came up to me and said, "You're right. I saw him. He was here till the last number." It so happened that they got hold of the last song Yip wrote and put it on at the end of the program. Now that song had not quite come out of Yip's top drawer; it hadn't yet reached his idea of perfection. So he quietly left, didn't stay for that one performance.

September of '81, 125 people showed up for a fundraising party in L.A. to support the Earl Robinson Foundation. I got to sing my heart out, concentrating on Old Left material more than New Age, for that same day, labor united in a massive solidarity demonstration in Washington against Reagan's anti-union schemes.

The Foundation did good work for five years or so. As one of its projects, it hired Gwen Gunderson, herself a talented singer and songwriter, to organize my papers at the Southern California Library for Social Studies and Research, a fine institution on S. Vermont Avenue in Los Angeles, devoted to archiving the history of people's movements. Gwen also undertook a series of interviews, with me and others, toward this eventual autobiography. She bowed out, however, and not too much later, the Foundation sort of tuckered out. Alas, it never lived up to its intentions of preserving and promoting Robinson music, and of giving grants to encourage other composers to use my work as an inspiration.

At present the Foundation is history, but in keeping with my philosophy that there is no "death," a new Friends of Earl Robinson has emerged to address many of the same goals. Maurice Peress is the President—he is Professor of Music at the Aaron Copland School of Music at Queens College, CUNY, in Flushing, New York, and can be reached there if you need to find him. My new book collaborator Eric Gordon is the Secretary, and Leonard Bernstein agreed to serve as Honorary Chair. "I'll be happy to help to the extent that I can," he said.

The Friends' first project was to research and publish a composer brochure, a short catalogue of all my works available for performance. This brochure, the first ever in my career, came together with the noble old music publishing house of G. Schirmer in New York, which in my 80th year took me on as "their" composer. Schirmer now represents works of mine that had been previously unassigned to other publishers; and when copyrights mature on my other works, Schirmer will take them over. It's a satisfying feeling to have all my work consolidated this way.

Notes

1. Ted Berkman, "A Song for Sea Angels," *Santa Barbara News and Review*, June 18, 1981.

2. Patricia Foote, "Songwriter Robinson Says Humans Should Listen to Dolphin," *Seattle Times*, July 25, 1981.

I SING OF ATLANTIS, J.C.,
AND FRANCIS (OF THE SAINT VARIETY)

I invent strange magick

The year 1982 began with a trip to Mexico, where I went without any engagements, but with names to look up. I spent some time with a blacklist refugee, Cedric Belfrage, and his wife Mary, who had established a home in Cuernavaca where liberal and left-wing writers felt comfortable. With Pablo and Jesucita O'Higgins I enjoyed the most satisfactory and indeed uplifting part of my trip. Pablo (formerly Paul O'Higgins of Wisconsin) had gone to Mexico to live artistically, socially, and politically far more gratifyingly than he could in the States. He became a high-level painter and worked with the Mexican artists' collective, Taller Gráfico. I had met Pablo when he came back to the U.S. in the 1940s to paint a mural for the Ship Scalers Union in Seattle. What a constant, gentle, serving spirit.

The Mexican experience with Pablo and friends gave me an immense spiritual opening which made possible my new music drama *Song of Atlantis*. As I climbed the pyramids of Teotihuacán outside Mexico City, I found myself communing with souls upon souls involved in the construction. This helped set in motion the finale, which is the building of a pyramid.

The people Jesucita and Pablo attracted to their home offered a tremendous boost for *Atlantis*. One guest, Miguel León-Portilla, had edited a book, *Native Mesoamerican Spirituality*, which gave me an invaluable springboard.[1] My central character, The Rascal, took both his form and sense of wonder from this book. Here, after the opening Garden of Eden Singing Flower dance sequence, is how he introduces himself:

> *I speak to you as the Rascal,*
> *The Queen Quetzl, the Coatl Bird Rascal,*
> *A precious feathered Serpent,*
> *I'm the rattlesnake Bird of the agile neck. . .*
> *I invent, I invent strange magick. . . .*

Working on *Song of Atlantis*, I discovered some of the literally thousands of books written on that subject. The majority try to prove that Atlantis did or did not exist. A peripheral
book such as León-Portilla's stimulated me more. The book by
the king of channels, Edgar Cayce's *Atlantis*, was the most useful of all. More than books, however, I needed to experience
Atlantis in my own body and spirit. As it was, as it is. I needed
to probe, go there in person.

I found this by a process of channeling called "regression."
With the help of Verna Yater, talented Santa Barbara channel,
I would lie down and allow myself to be mildly hypnotized,
being conscious the whole time. Together we went back
10,000 years to Atlantis, where I re-experienced my own and
other scenes, talking them onto a tape she had running. By this
felicitous method I would live, as the leading character of Rascal but in a number of successive incarnations, through the
timespan of that fabled continent. Scene after scene of Atlantis
came alive; I transferred some of them almost verbatim to the
Song of Atlantis script. I made contact with my Atlantis friend
Regis, who is an integral part of the drama. Not one to short-
change my experience, I actually joined up with and became
one of the Sons of Belial, the "evil" denizens of Atlantis. Thus I
told the story, a parable if you will, of a land in many ways
ahead of us today—with their lighter-than-air trains, their healing temples, their use of ESP as a natural form of communication—which nevertheless blew itself into the water by the mis-
use of atomic power. In the world today, I believe, many wiser
reincarnations from Atlantis are with us in the anti-nuclear
movement, trying to prevent the same kind of end to our civilization—and so far succeeding.

With an extended Garden of Eden sequence in the opening, elements of Star Wars in the body of it, and the grand-
opera building of a pyramid at its close, I envision *Song of Atlantis* as a film some day, with music telling the story. I have
made two mighty attempts at presenting this music drama.
With some excellent pro singer-actors, Lombodaro Das and
Takako Wakita, a small orchestra and me at the piano singing-

talking the Rascal, we presented and recorded the work as a
Robinson birthday celebration in July '83. Five weeks later I
conducted a performance from the piano at the Cornish
School in Seattle. There we had a powerful acting-singing chorus of four voices, including basso profondo Leon Lishner and
Valerie Yockey, soprano. I added my son Perry on clarinet—
him being in Seattle from New York for gigs and family get-
togethers—and Lishner's son Paul on electric bass.

A glowing love

December 1982 was the month of my mother's passing,
and I think on it with some sense of wonder. It seems peculiar
to write about her again only when she is finally ready to go,
at the age of 93. After two marriages and so many mistakes in
life, for which I accept full personal responsibility, I was able
to stop blaming my mother for whatever unhappinesses I have
suffered in my personal life. Once I finally began to "grow up,"
we got along much better. I could level with her, and she with
me. In time we became real friends in the truest sense. Many
families aren't. When Mommer finally chose to go, we both
felt more prepared as a result of this nice communing kinship.

I had agreed to fly to New York to sing at Will Lee's memorial. I had enjoyed his ongoing friendship going back nearly
fifty years to the Workers Laboratory Theatre. I took joy in
Willy's later success—twelve years on "Sesame Street," and as a
teacher of acting, a man who inspired laughter and love.

I got word from Seattle that Mommer was in the hospital
with cancer. So I flew there before going to New York. Our
love glowed when I sat by her bed, comforting and singing—
"Spring Song," which she always loved, "Joe Hill" and the entire *Ballad for Americans*, all unaccompanied. (She felt especially proud of knowing Paul Robeson.) They tried to push
food on her which she didn't want. "Can I really not eat this?"
I took some pleasure giving her permission to refuse.

In New York the next afternoon I sang songs that I had
taught Will Lee forty-eight years before, helping him discover
a high tenor he never knew he had. The next day, back in

Santa Barbara, I learned that Mommer had passed on quietly, gently, without pain. It seemed as if, having seen me one last time, she had stayed long enough.

Your brother and friend

In November 1984 a contest in Wausau, Wisconsin, attracted me: A high school advertised for a work for chorus and strings, encouraging a religious theme. Now I write well for chorus, and I understand high school strings, harking back to my playing in the West Seattle H.S. orchestra; and most important, I was in direct touch with Jesus through a channel in Santa Fe, and wanted to speak of him musically.

I did not win the contest. But from singing the piece around, and from some beautiful, deep new commune with Himself, I felt ready to expand it into a musical.

I am not a "born-again Christian," but I strongly desire to offer my understanding of Jesus as an ever-present, here-and-now loving friend. My position on Jesus is not to contradict the Bible unnecessarily, nor to claim *the* truth of the matter, nor to "expose" any wrongdoing in the creation and interpretation of the Holy Writ, but simply to put out the truth that *I* perceive from him. Hence the title, *I Been Thinkin' About J.C.*

Unfailingly modest, J.C. did not want to be regarded as God or the son of God. He came here to remind you *who you are*. It was his disciples who made a god of him. He told me: "The original concept of disciple was not a truly worthy idea. Do not deify me," he kept saying, "I am your brother and your friend."

I asked him about the Ten Commandments. He answered, "I am not all that comfortable about the word 'commandment.' Some people, you try to command them, they do just the opposite. How would you go for *suggestion*?" He was astoundingly simple in his reaction to the commandment on adultery. "Is there any possible fault to be found with love, as long as it is given lovingly and received lovingly?"

Here is a breakdown of some high spots in *I Been Thinkin' About J.C.* You'll notice certain affinities with Liberation The-

ology, or New Age Christianity. It begins with a dialogue between Jesus and Mark. (Jesus claims that the Book of Mark,
though it has been adulterated, is the most accurate.)

> *MARK: I been thinkin' about J.C.*
> *How he manifests, and about how he*
> *With such warm and gentle power*
> *helps me to be free. . . .*
> *Is it all right to call you J.C.?*
> *Speak up plain and familiar with you?*
>
> *JESUS: It's okay, it allows me to be*
> *Plain and familiar with you, too.*
> *So just be—who you are.*
> *Call me anything, oh J.C.'s fine,*
> *Just don't call me too late for dinner,*
> *I want to share our food together . . .*
> *I like to sit here at your table,*
> *Eat and talk, break bread together.*
> *Let's begin now—with a simple thought.*
> *Are you ready? There are no sinners.*

Healing, Jesus says, begins with the person to be healed.
And he introduces "To Be Perfect," sung by the Chorus, in
which J.C. attempts to eliminate the struggle for perfection
that Mark is into. As he says, "You are attempting to get out of
your head, and into the real you. This real you is, excuse the
expression, perfect. The struggle ends when you realize this."

"Jesus the Jew" (Part Three) is a dramatic cantata in itself,
begun by Mark's singing

> *I'm confused—about the Jews,*
> *A race refuted, persecuted,*
> *The Holocaust instituted,*
> *The Rosenbergs electrocuted . . .*

and answered by J.C.'s forthright

That's the big reason I became one.

In the song "He Said This," the Lord of Love comes down from above to live, work, and play. This song shows that J.C. favors the poor and the working people. He emphasizes that we are all working people, rich or poor, and can use all the celebration we can get.

"Just Imagine" is J.C.'s answer to Mark's accusation that he was manipulative when he allowed the violence to develop against the moneychangers in the Temple. "I don't manipulate," says J.C.,

> *But my followers needed learning,*
> *Always questing, violence testing,*
> *I allowed this show of might.*
> *Stop it too soon—would not be right.*
> *They must all be allowed to travel,*
> *March along to their own drumming,*
> *Find their way all unobstructed,*
> *On their own now, overcoming.*

Fantastic psychologist, J.C. Love means, among other things, allowing people the freedom to make mistakes. That's the way they learn.

One of J.C.'s finest "commandments," which made its way into the Bible in the form of the saying, "Love thy neighbor as thyself," is the subject of the next song, "Love Thyself." He gives a message that many of his followers are unable to hear:

> *Wait not, dear friend, for that second coming,*
> *Lift your eyes, open up, just allow,*
> *Your second coming IS HERE RIGHT NOW.*

Questioned by Mark on the "mystery period" where the Bible goes silent—"Just as you enter your teens you apparently disappear for almost twenty years"—J.C. says, "I left pieces of myself with people of fame, among them the noble entities you know as Buddha, Muhammed and others. But I also shared the Light with so-called ordinary people, becoming often a stable boy, a chambermaid, a slow-witted child, a professor of mathematics. . . ." He goes into the finale with

> *Do not envision me upon the cross,*
> *Hanging in pain, nails in my wrists,*
> *Stabbing my ankles.*
> *Rather envision Jesus here with you,*
> *Holding you lightly, warmly, strongly,*
> *My arms around you,*
> *Round your shoulders,*
> *Laughing and crying,*
> *Playing and singing and running and dancing*
> *And walking and talking together.*

Lombodaro Das sang a powerful J.C., and I played his friend Mark at the piano, when we recorded *J.C.* in July 1985. We had a vocal quartet for the chorus, and added a string quartet and bass fiddle.

No sound of birds

On Saint Francis's birthday, October 4th, 1982, my friend and concerned citizen Bert Schwarzchild made a pilgrimage to the shrine of St. Francis of Assisi, to feel and experience this remarkable man. Climbing Mt. Subasio, where Francis spent much of his time, he noticed the beautiful trees and plants, only gradually becoming aware of a missing element—no sound of birds. No birds at all. Then he saw shotgun shells on the ground. More and more of them, as he traveled up the mountain, confirmed a sad and horrifying thought. The birds of Francis were being hunted down, apparently by Italian sportsmen.

Bert's sense of outrage grew. After spending the night on the mountain, he came down to talk with the elders of Assisi. The result is now a worldwide campaign to restore the birds to Assisi. As part of this, I was commissioned in the fall of 1985 to compose a dramatic cantata. *A Concert for Francis (of the Saint Variety)*, I call it.

Like *J.C.*, my source material came . . . from the source. Unlike *J.C.*, this dialogue was largely unchanneled. After an immense amount of research on Francis, I found myself communicating directly with him. I got answers to questions about both the music and the content of the piece. I actually checked with him on chords and phrasing, and took his advice most of the time.

I increasingly gained a picture of Francis as a vulnerable, loving man, totally natural in his identification with God and his desire to make God available to all; a miracle worker who didn't realize he was making miracles; and a person who struggled with immense contradictions, never knowing their nature. This poet praised the Lord Sun, yet hid in dark caves. This saint could be so gentle with the wolf, as with all the inhabitants of the animal kingdom, yet castigated his own flesh. This troubadour hailed the power of love, but separated himself from women. As much as he sang praise to God for giving us our bountiful Sister, Mother Earth, with all the passion of the pagan he equally praised our Sister, Death. A fascinating person to sing about in all his contrasting inconsistencies.

Of the seven sections that form the *Concert for Francis*, the most rousing "audience precipitation" number is "Love, Love, Give Love," subtitled "Joy of Francis Blues," wherein Francis is completely understood as a Lover. Thus defined through all the contradictory miracles he has performed, he seeks to free us *from* this world so that we can be truly *in* this world. At the end we come back to the theme of "Where Are the Birds?" the question that inspired the cantata to begin with.

After I started *Francis*, Bert Schwarzchild didn't have the money for the commission. But a date to perform the piece in Berkeley in April 1986 solidified the project. I tried getting Joan Baez to sing the piece with me, but she was on tour at the time. As a matter of fact I've had no luck getting Joanie to perform anything of mine since she made "Joe Hill" her own at Woodstock. It has been difficult for me to push others to sing my songs, when I could do them okay by myself—a shortcoming I hope sincerely to remedy one of these days. I am reminded of my friend Bob Russell who spent 10 percent of his time writing and 90 percent plugging—and thereby became a very successful songwriter.

Anyway, I gave a 40-minute composer's run-through of *Francis* in Berkeley to good audience approval and a moderate review. The reviewer loved me and my singing, but was only medium impressed by the cantata. Friends in the Bay area, New York, Los Angeles, and Santa Barbara have heard it and encourage me with the work. It is arranged for soloists and chorus with piano, but could be orchestrated.

I have programmed it together with a 12-minute cantata for men's voices, *A Natural Human*, based on texts by gay poets, that I wrote in response to a call by the New York City Gay Men's Chorus for new works, thus adding my voice of support to the gay movement. There is a wonderfully affirming and growing movement of gay and lesbian choruses, though so far none of them has sung *A Natural Human*. That piece, *Francis*, and *I Been Thinkin' About J.C.* are all more or less patiently awaiting definitive productions.

Note

1. Miguel León-Portilla, *Native Mesoamerican Spirituality*, New York: Paulist Press, 1980.

WHAT I'VE BEEN UP TO LATELY

Alive and well

All through these years, sometimes in heavy spurts, I've kept up an active cross-country performing schedule. At one very special concert I gave at NYU, they feted me as Guest of Honor. Many old friends surfaced at the dinner beforehand, and I encountered at least one new friend, progressive New York State Senator Frank Barbaro. For the first time that I remember, I was introduced as a "living legend."

In the summer of 1984 I started in earnest to make a new recording in Santa Barbara. I planned to make it on a $10,000 gift from Jessie Lloyd O'Connor. More than a year later, in the fall of 1985, the record was almost finished, and had cost twice as much. I begged, borrowed, and had donated the other ten thousand, and put some of my own money into it as well (of which I hadn't much). But we got a good album, containing some of the best singing I have ever done, with excellent help from a number of other fine musicians and vocalists. It came out in 1986 on Aspen Records, it's called *Earl Robinson Alive and Well*, and I am proud of it. It contains some of my "hits"— "Joe Hill," "Black and White," "Same Boat, Brother," "Free and Equal Blues," "The House I Live In," and *Ballad for Americans*—plus two less familiar numbers, "He Built the Road" (from *The People, Yes*), and "A Man's a Man for A' That," my setting of a Robert Burns poem that Jessie particularly loved.

A number of celebrations honored my 75th birthday in 1985. The biggest took place at Lonnie Chapman's Theatre in L.A.'s Studio City. Greetings came in from Harry Belafonte, Pete Seeger, and many others. Norman Corwin emceed, retelling strong memories of Carl Sandburg. The most unexpected greeting came from Frank Sinatra. I had invited him to come and sing "The House I Live In," which he had been doing for more than forty years, though we had not been in touch most of that time. I never presumed on our friendship; particularly during the blacklist years, knowing that he had been burned, I

411

stayed out of his way. Anyway, he called to say that he was unfortunately busy for the birthday, but he would like me to write new words for "House," which they had scheduled him to sing in New York on July 4th, 1986, at the 100th-anniversary rededication of the Statue of Liberty. He emphasized that his own father and mother had come through Ellis Island, and he wanted to talk about that a bit. To the concert itself he sent a bottle of champagne and a note instructing me, "Think about Statue of Liberty, Think about Statue of Liberty," written about ten times.

Bowing before the fact of Lewis Allan's Alzheimer's debilitation, I undertook to write new lyrics for Frankie. I endeavored to maintain contact with him so that the new text would reflect him and where he was at, but he proved elusive to the end. I wrote him a letter with portions of the new lyric, attempting to enlist his cooperation in the creation process. This went unanswered. I made a date with him to go over my complete new version with suggested lines for him to speak. First the appointment got changed from his house to his office, later it was canceled, and he never contacted me again.

Next thing I heard, his singing at the Statue of Liberty was off entirely because he had taken sick, though the celebration committee told me they hadn't given up hope on him yet. In fact, the idea emerged that I might accompany him at the piano. In the upshot, he did sing, but none of my new verses. They never even invited me to attend until the last possible moment, and then just to sit in the cold bleachers on Governor's Island. So I stayed with friends on Shelter Island, and on TV we watched an under-par Frank struggle through the original words.

I drowned my disappointment in wine and assumed a philosophical position. Frankie was not always consistent, nor easy to get along with. But I continue to like him, and respect that he persists in doing his best no matter what.

Once my Earl Robinson album was released, I started thinking about another album, or really a series of albums, based on the labor songbook *Carry It On*, put together by

Robert Reiser, Pete Seeger, and a team of consultants. The first of these is called *Songs of the Working People: From the American Revolution to the Civil War*, and includes thirteen numbers. We rounded up an all-star cast: me, Pete Seeger, Ronnie Gilbert, Odetta, Alan Lomax, Tommy Makem, Steve Stanne, Chet Washington, and a dozen other vocalists and instrumentalists recruited from both coasts. You should hear how Ronnie and Odetta knock the hell out of "John Henry," and there are quite a few other gems on this album, too. Again, I acknowledge my old comrade Jessie Lloyd O'Connor as the angel for this project. Flying Fish Records released it in 1988 in all three formats. My first CD!

Impressed with his Rainbow message, I wrote a Jesse Jackson campaign song. A bit of a rouser, I sang it for increasingly enthusiastic groups of people committed to his candidacy during the 1988 primary season. Christmas Eve of '88, I got the news that Jessie Lloyd O'Connor, my benefactor, had passed on. A memorial took place in Little Compton, R.I. At the suggestion of Edith Tiger of the National Emergency Civil Liberties Committee—she has been supporting and advising me ever since my appearance before the Un-Americans in 1957—I arranged to be there with a new song. Which grew naturally out of my song for Jesse Jackson: The tune fit amazingly well, and some of the same words were appropriate. Jessie Lloyd O'Connor, like Jesse Jackson, was a "teacher, a listener and a preacher." At the service I sang "Joe Hill" and the new Jessie song.

Republicans again

One night in August 1988, while I was sitting at home in Santa Barbara watching a Dodger game, friends called me from New York, Seattle, and L.A., all saying that Gov. Thomas Kean of New Jersey, keynote speaker at the Republican National Convention, was reciting "The House I Live In," announcing to the nation that he had grown up with the song. I never got to hear the speech live, but I later saw a written transcript. That's how I realized the curious fact that of all the re-

corded versions, Kean recited a verse including the name of
Frederick Douglass that only Paul Robeson used.

Somehow the *Newark Star-Ledger* found out that I was
alive and well and living in Santa Barbara, and they conducted
a phone interview with me that appeared a couple of days
later. They brought out the "New Jersey connection" of
course—that Frank Sinatra was born in Hoboken, and that
both my sons Perry and Jimmy live in the state. I also wrote a
letter to *The New York Times*, where it appeared August 25th:

> As the alive and well composer of the song "The House
> I Live In," which was quoted very well by Gov. Tho-
> mas H. Kean in his keynote address to the Republican
> National Convention Aug. 16, I would like to make my
> position gently clear.
>
> Speaking for the writer of the words, Lewis Allan
> (who died two years ago), I need to say that we did not
> write the song for Republicans exclusively. Nor for
> Democrats or any other "ism," but rather for people of
> all stripes and colors, all or no political beliefs, "All
> races and religions, that's America to me."
>
> And while I probably will not vote for Mr. Bush
> this November, I wish to thank Mr. Kean and the Re-
> publicans for quoting from my song. It is living proof
> that a song may transcend politics and give a message to
> all Americans and people everywhere, as to what our
> country is all about.

Well, that's where this story might have ended. But comes
the fall, and Maurice Peress, the conductor, and Eric Gordon,
my co-writer, began sending out letters to several dozen blue-
ribbon types, asking for their sponsorship of the Earl Robinson 80th Birthday Celebration in 1990. They decided, what the
hell, if Gov. Kean is such a fan of my song, why not send a
letter to him as well? A few weeks later, Gov. Kean's appoint-
ments secretary called Eric and asked if I could go to Trenton
for a "courtesy meeting." I interpreted this to mean realistically
not more than five minutes.

In January 1989 I had a performance in Philadelphia, and I could stop in Trenton on the way back to New York without too much trouble. So we set a date for one o'clock. I got to Trenton and took a cab over to the State House. A man toting a gun greeted me at the door. He looked down his appointment sheet and said, "Yep, you're on the list." I went into a waiting room and sat down.

After a while, out came Marcia Golden, a beautiful black woman, the Governor's public events coordinator, who said, "The Governor will be with you shortly." At one o'clock precisely I got into his office. "The Governor's coming in that door there," she said, so I sat facing that way. The Governor's official photographer came in and we talked about the weather and why I had come.

Then the door opened, and in strode a tall, good-looking man who hailed me with great warmth. "Thank you very much for coming, Mr. Robinson. I've been looking forward to this. I'm a fan of Paul Robeson—he's a Jersey man, you know. I have every one of his records." So that's where he got "The House I Live In."

"I suppose you must have known him," the Governor said.

"Yes, I knew him well and worked and sang with him for a long time." After all these years, Big Paul formed a strong bond between me and Gov. Kean. Shortly we got onto the *Ballad for Americans*. I told him about its origins in the Federal Theatre Project, where the government paid writers to write and artists to paint, and he seemed to understand that.

"You wrote 'Joe Hill' too, didn't you? This is one of the most important songs ever written. It's about the laboring people. It tells it like it is."

Meanwhile, the photographer took pictures. The Governor pulled a chair close to me for this purpose. Then the press came in. The guy from the *Newark Star-Ledger* suggested we both get on the couch. Then he said, "Why don't you put an arm around the Governor?" And he told the Governor, "It would be better if you unbuttoned your jacket," so I unbuttoned mine too.

Kean kept saying, "Your pieces are worth listening to. My children want me to listen to rock. I can't understand half of the words, and the half I can, I'm not sure I like too much. But your music is good. It has a message." I told him about my recent record *Earl Robinson Alive and Well*, and he laughed appreciatively at that. A true lover of music, of the best in music. After all, he has every record of Robeson.

We spent twenty or twenty-five minutes together. Then he had to move on with his day.

"What can I do for you?" he asked in conclusion. I reminded him about my 80th Birthday Celebration and the sponsoring committee being put together. "Absolutely," he said, "I'd be delighted." We hugged one another at the finish— my instigation, but he accepted it wholeheartedly, and it felt totally right. And in between hugs we shook hands about four times. The mood was continuously loving. I left feeling I had made a good friend.

When I emerged from the meeting, Ms. Golden asked how I was getting back to the train. "Cab, I guess."

"Wait," she said, "I'll drive you." Which she did, and I made the two o'clock to New York. She let me in on a little story. When he heard he had been scheduled for just a short courtesy visit with me, Gov. Kean asked, "Can't it be longer?"

"House" is still ripe fodder for parodies. The Associated Press report on the Gridiron Club roast of 1992, where the Washington press corps gets to poke fun at officialdom, featured this spoof titled, "Song for a Democratic Congressman Who Declined to Speak on the Record":

> *What is America to me?*
> *Safe seat, good pay, and perks for free,*
> *Political plutocracy—that's America to me.*
> *The House we live in is more than just a bank.*
> *It's a monumental tribute to the privilege of rank.*
> *A parking space for members, no tickets and no fees,*
> *The right to be elitist, that's America to me.*[1]

Seattle celebrates Robinson

In the spring of 1989, after more than fifty years away, I moved from Santa Barbara back to old Seattle. I'd always thought of the Northwest as God's Country, but how was I supposed to make a living there? I had to be in New York or L.A. To celebrate this event, the King County Council passed a Motion declaring June 5, 1989, Earl Robinson Day. Nothing less than the combined houses of the Washington state legislature welcomed me by sponsoring me in a free concert open to the public in the Capitol Rotunda. The press covered it fully, and both the Washington Senate and the Governor issued appropriate proclamations bulging with whereas-es.

That year I won a contest for my song "Now," another of my New Age contributions emphasizing the importance of *knowing what you want now*. A composer named Lee McClure in New York runs a concert series called Eclectix! and sponsors a yearly Erik Satie Mostly Tonal Award. A superb black singer, Marion Cowings, dressed to the nines in a tuxedo, sang the prize song, as well as "Rose of Sharon" from *One Foot in America* and "One Sweet Morning." Composer David Hollister, who also had a piece on the program, accompanied. I couldn't be there, but Eric says he'd never heard my music performed so elegantly.

For quite a few years Seattle had a courageous little company called the Pioneer Square Theater. A musical booked there for the summer of 1989 canceled out. Phil Randall, a cast member of *Angry Housewives*, playing on one of the company's three stages, is an old Robinson fan, and he suggested that since I had come back to town, some kind of musical Robinsoniana could fill the bill. For three hours at the piano I ran through song after song for Phil and the director Lyn Tyrrell. Out of that resulted *The Earl Robinson Celebration*, a two-act retrospective at the theatre's Firststage, featuring me singing and telling stories at the piano, and a buoyant cast of seven actor-singer-dancers performing arrangements I prepared especially for the show. My occasional momentary memory lapses proved amusing—people never could be sure if it wasn't part of the act.

Part of one house sold to the local chapter of the Abraham Lincoln Brigade, who presented me with a plaque saluting me "for a lifetime dedicated to building a better world." At the end of each show we received a standing ovation, and people said they were ready to hear more. "Elegantly turned-out songs of hope, courage, loyalty, humor, justice, gratitude and generosity are worth celebrating," wrote Joe Adcock, theatre critic for the *Seattle Post-Intelligencer* on August 12th. "A rebirth and renewal of these qualities is passionately to be desired. And two hours of effective adult entertainment that doesn't exploit hatred and fear is a rare and joyous experience."

The show opened August 10th and ran for only three weeks. I showed up one night ready to go on, and found the door locked and a cancellation notice posted. It seems that with three theatres running simultaneously, Pioneer Square had overextended itself. The simple truth is, they went broke. A year later, June '91 in Portland, Oregon, Lyn Tyrrell directed the show again at Artists Repertory Theatre, with a new cast minus me under the title *Same Boat, Brother*. In light of the Persian Gulf War, my songs took on a painfully refreshed relevance.

In mid-September of '89 I spent ten days in New York to participate in a series of concerts at Merkin Hall called "Voices of Change." Five evenings of music revealed how rich and deep is our "American music of protest, politics and persuasion," as the series subtitle had it. My music appeared on two programs. On a "Workers of the World" concert, Neely Bruce and his American Music/Theatre Group revived my "Flying Squadron." Marni Nixon sang solo numbers, too—items from Blitzstein's *The Cradle Will Rock*, Harold Rome's *Pins and Needles*, and Copland's *The Second Hurricane*. What a harvest they uncovered. I felt transported back fifty years, right into the Composers' Collective scene.

A few nights later, as the series finale, the Workmen's Circle Chorus, a dynamic quintet called Sons and Daughters, the

North Jersey Philharmonic Glee Club (a black men's chorus), and the Gregg Smith Singers each did separate sets, then joined up at the end for a 50th-anniversary performance of *Ballad for Americans* conducted by Zalmen Mlotek, in which I sang the solo part I know so well. Though now when I do it, I include the American Indians left out of the original script, and for the first time I also mentioned "people of all sexual persuasions, gay, straight and lots more." The audience exploded with applause at that unexpected line. I guess I happily surprised them. In the *Village Voice*, critic Leighton Kerner referred to the *Ballad*—"that last 10-minute epic drawing together all the evening's singers (at their considerable best), and its composer somehow besting even Paul Robeson's historic recording. What a finish!" The picture accompanying his review was the one my son Jimmy took of me that I use for publicity. I don't know about comparing me to Big Paul, but there's nothing like a live performance to stir the soul. The melding of those interracial, interreligious forces was proof positive that "our country's strong, our country's young, and her greatest songs are still unsung."

My 80th

Soon it came time to think about my 80th birthday. Concerts of my music, receptions, and parties took place in a number of places. First, internationally: In Vancouver I helped celebrate with the Vancouver Jewish Folk Choir. In Freiburg, Germany, Gary Schneider conducted my *Banjo Concerto* with Mike Martin and an interesting ensemble: The woodwinds and brass were local musicians, and the string players came from a youth orchestra in Leningrad! My son Perry went and for the several days we were there, he and I joined all kinds of giddy late-night jam sessions and made quite a father-son splash.

In America: In Woodstock, New York, the Ars Choralis concert co-celebrated the 80th of my dear composer friend Herbert Haufrecht, who had over the years become an eminent scholar and collector of Catskills folk songs. New York City, under the superb management of Charlotte and Perry

Bruskin and Edith Tiger, organized a swell bash at the Douglas
Fairbanks Theater. Two hundred of "my closest friends" attended that night, July 23rd. Honorary Chair of the Friends of
Earl Robinson couldn't make it because of his conducting as-
signments, but sent a telegram:

> DEAR EARL, WHATEVER IT SAYS ON YOUR
> PLAQUE, COUNT ME IN AND DOUBLE IT.
> LENNY BERNSTEIN.

That message to me turned out to be one of his last from
this address. He passed over less than three months later.

You might have thought (I certainly had) that *Ballad for
Americans* had been performed by just about every conceivable
kind of group, but I found out the list has not been exhausted
yet: In Pittsburgh, with the help of my ever-young University
of Washington classmate Mary Lou Wright, the Centennial
Choir, an alumni group from the Western Pennsylvania
School for Blind Children, performed it as part of a big benefit
for the Self Help Group Network. (On that concert I gave the
first performance of part of my new *Ballad for Mother Earth*.)
And in Seattle, a proclamation from Mayor Norman B. Rice
declared my birthday as Earl Robinson Day. On a concert
with Pete Seeger and several veterans of the Pioneer Square
Theatre revue, a proudly mixed gay and lesbian chorus, in
their first public appearance, sang *Ballad* under conductor
Dennis Coleman.

When he was preparing the publicity on this concert,
Dennis asked me did I openly acknowledge being gay? I had to
tell him I didn't, because it wasn't so. Totally surprised, he had
assumed all along that I was. All I could say was a feeble, "But
some of my best friends. . . ." I told him I felt honored that he
had been deceived—he answered, "Yes, by your warm manner"—and I take it as a sincere compliment. As I do when people, knowing my work and name, but not my face, assume I'm
black. Maybe in my next incarnation.

Seventy-five years after the State of Utah executed Joe Hill, an organizing committee came together for a grand commemoration in Salt Lake City. Convenient that it coincided with my 80th birthday year. I attended, naturally. In conjunction, Smithsonian Folkways Records (which took over Moe Asch's Folkways label) put out a truly magnificent album called *Don't Mourn—Organize!* (SF 40026) that pulls together contemporary versions of Joe's songs, songs about him, and historic recordings. Al Hayes and my song is on the album twice, once sung by Paul Robeson, and once by yours truly, my old 1940 Timely recording with guitar from *Songs for Americans*. My rendition sounds rather four-square, and not too caressingly phrased. I know a lot more now about how to mold and move a tune, but the quality of the voice is remarkably similar to the way I sound today. It's amazing when I think about it—there aren't that many people who can hear their voices recorded more than fifty years ago.

In the lull following the 80th birthday celebrations, which continued through December 1990 with additional concerts in Santa Monica and Boston, I reviewed my life's work and put in order the compositions G. Schirmer will be publishing. When I came to *David of Sassoun*, I saw that I could not give Schirmer this material in the form in which I found it. Due to the vagaries of the Fresno production, some numbers had been left only half-composed; and by the time the director had finished slashing and cutting, other numbers had, so to speak, decomposed. Was it worth it now to try and make a viable work out of this epic? A quick consult with Dr. Peebles gave me a resounding YES. He said, "Besides, it will be fun." Eric told me, "Earl, you must do it. Who else will? Approach it as though *David of Sassoun* is the work you will be remembered by." Next to "Joe Hill" and *Ballad for Americans* that was some challenge. So in the spring of 1991 I completely reworked my Armenian opera and sent it off to Schirmer's.

My soul is unassailable

For a long time I have put out the notion of living to the age of 140. At that time I will look around and see how things are. If they're okay, I'll stick around. If not, I'll go someplace else. But I have lately decided there is nothing magic about the number 140. I might choose to go some sooner. Who knows?

With these thoughts in mind, the song "Message from a New Address" poured out a couple of years ago, a meditation based on Chief Sealth. I sing it at all my concerts now.

> *Think of me and I'll be present*
> *Together with you, never apart.*
> *Send me love, I'll be available,*
> *Saving myself just for you.*
> *For my soul is unassailable,*
> *I'll be in your mind and heart.*
> *Death is just a change of address,*
> *That is all, that's all.*
> *There's no death, just change my address,*
> *I live on, I live on.*
> *We live on, we live on.*
> *We live on, we live on.*

Is this the naïve defense of one afraid to face death?— the comfort of believing I am eternal? I feel it is a sincere expression of my belief in the undying soul. And having composed it, I feel . . . composed. Funny, isn't it? My dictionary defines that word as "calm, tranquil, undisturbed, self-possessed." That's just how I feel: My life's work has given me satisfaction. Oh yes, I have suffered disappointments, but personally I feel complete. For most of my life I have not been a tremendous fan of Richard Strauss, but in his "Four Last Songs," written at the very end of a very long career, he hit the note of well-earned peace beyond death that I have tried to express in this song. Beyond that, my only comment is that greater minds and talents than mine have addressed this theme with some success.

"O death, where is thy sting? O grave, where is thy victory?" saith I Corinthians.

My yoga is a very present-time part of me. I rely on it to keep me in the now. I conclude with a perplexing manifestation. I have been striving for more than a year to understand its meaning. In doing my yoga meditation at night in front of the mirror, I notice a strange effect. The outline of my body and my arms and legs appears, but my head vanishes. Reaching hands up to my head, I feel the solidity—the head is surely there—but it is invisible in the mirror.

Opening my eyes wide does not help, and squinting merely makes the body indistinct, as well as the head. When I continue to stare, lights begin to take the place of my face. A white light mainly, but a lavender light has begun to show, and occasionally orange and red. These I believe are part of my aura, which is freer to shine through in the absence of a recognizable head and face.

I may be in the process of moving from the denser physical self into a lighter, more spiritual and evanescent state of being. Red Hawk, a fine spirit who comes to me and helps with certain physical ailments, tells me that this state is comparable to that of dogs who can hear sounds higher than the human ear can hear.

All of this is very interesting, but it still doesn't tell me where my head goes in the mirror. So the mystery persists. Perhaps in time I will come to understand. Meantime, I can quietly celebrate the magick.

Clarity

Occasionally, some old-timer who hasn't kept up with me will attend a concert and express surprise or shock when they hear my newer pieces. Having come to the end of this book, you can appreciate the continuity of themes in my life. There is in fact no separation between the Old Left and the New Age Robinson. I point once again to the song "Joe Hill": That line "I never died" forms the natural bridge between old and new Earls. I don't need to give up one for the other.

For make no mistake about it, friend, there is no death. The time comes, for all of us, to make a change in our style of living. At that time our higher-level self, not always consciously, decides to create a . . . change of address. We discard a body, sometimes worn-out, but in any case not necessary to our new scene. And we remain right here if we choose. The essential "I" lives on and does what it needs to continue its education—the real reason we are here being to study and learn. If you ask me, Learn what? I would say, To properly love ourselves and others.

I thank whatever powers are responsible for leading me to the words of "Joe Hill." For that song brought me to this clarity.

Note

1. *Los Angeles Times,* March 29, 1992.

GOODBYE FROM TAMALPAIS

by Eric A. Gordon

In the two and a half years that Earl lived in Seattle before he died, I paid three visits to him, and enjoyed watching him re-acculturate himself to the city and to a new group of friends. He began, slowly, breaking down some of the walls between him and his sister Claire, from whom he had been alienated for some years, mostly over Earl's treatment of women. He became especially close to Bette Jean (B.J.) Bullert, who conveniently lived just two blocks away. With several PBS film credits under her belt, B.J. spent the last year or so of Earl's life working on a documentary, *Earl Robinson: Ballad of an American*. The completed film has been aired on public television and at a number of film festivals, garnering excellent and well deserved reviews.

The last time I saw Earl, the final weekend of March 1991, he was writing and composing a song called "I Choose Wilderness," his contribution to a campaign in Utah to declare large tracts of land as a federally mandated natural wilderness area. He played the song through for me, and asked for my opinion. It was too wordy, full of lists of trees and flying and running fauna; together we culled a few representative samples, and gave the song more of a story line. With its old-fashioned devotion to the topical folksong idiom, I kidded him about a certain resemblance to Woody Guthrie's "This Land is Your Land," and in the repeat of the last line on the refrain, to his own "Joe Hill." "Steal all you want . . . ," he grinned, knowing that I could recite the wrap, " . . . but only from the best places." At the end of April Earl sent me a printout of the song "by Earl Robinson, additional lyrics: Eric Gordon and Gibbs Smith" (the Utah organizer who had commissioned Earl).

(Refrain) I choose wilderness
My Utah wilderness,

Wand'ring this grand land
Takes hold of my soul, takes hold of my soul.
I walk the wilderness
My Utah wilderness
Praising this proud land
Body, heart and soul, Body, heart and soul.

I say, Glen Canyon, who altered your face?
Can we return to your ancient homeland?
Will the Eagle soar now, Can the river run free?
Time to restore now, this wild and pure holy place.

(Refrain, followed by three more stanzas.)

"They like it very much and I am recording on tape the latest version," he wrote. "The project is to get the Sierra Club to get the song to John Denver, in hopes." Earl continued with other news:

> I just sang two concerts, one to a private house party of opera listeners, the other to celebrate the centennial of the West Seattle Public Library. It is extraordinarily good for me to keep my hand in, so to speak, singing wherever and whenever with or without fee, although of course it is nice to be paid.

A few weeks later Earl's FBI file finally arrived, and he spent weeks reviewing its 1,050 pages. He kept it on hand until June, so that B.J. could film him looking at it, the black swaths of censored passages floating across each page like funeral ribbons. He sent me the carton of papers, almost a foot thick, with his pages of notes, in mid-June.

Earl traveled down to Portland, Oregon, that month for the opening of a new version of the Pioneer Theatre's revue of his music, *Same Boat, Brother.* There he met up again with his old friend Michael Loring, who first recorded "Joe Hill" back in the 1930s. He sent me the program and the published notice. "The review is not a rave," Earl wrote me, "but lukewarm is better than a pan I guess." In fact, the review read better than that.

Earl managed to keep himself busy, but more than once in the last couple of years, he asked my advice as to what he should be doing now. For me, of course, his priority lay in putting down on paper what we needed for our manuscript. I also helped him determine the absolute necessity of pulling together his scores for G. Schirmer, so that they could begin properly promoting his work. He completed revisions on *David of Sassoun* in the spring of 1991, inviting a small group to his home to hear the work in his own voice and piano rendition, which he tape recorded. And he supervised the reorganization of his archival collections at the University of Washington library. On my last visit to Seattle, Earl introduced me to the head of the archives, Karyl Winn, and I felt content that Earl's papers had found a good home.

Earl had begun expressing concerns about getting old and redundant, and becoming a burden on others. Active, self-reliant, and productive still, he faced the need for a cataract operation shortly. That, combined with his tendency to drift to sleep at unexpected moments—especially when not the focus of attention—caused him worry about how long he had left as a driver, as an independent person capable of getting around on his own (he had passed his Washington driver's test only after several tries). Some months before, his companion Joanne had returned to Santa Barbara, leaving Earl in search of another intimate relationship. Really for the first time in his life, Earl felt nonplussed by the lack of a sex drive. Like most of us, Earl feared becoming helpless.

He stepped out very briefly

Perhaps symbolically, Earl died without a cent in his pocket. When his friend Kathryn Butzerin happened to drive up Admiral Way just moments after the crash, she thought to herself, "That sure looked like Earl's car." She headed to Earl's house on 41st Avenue, found the door open, the lights on, and the TV going. Earl had obviously stepped out very briefly.

The body was cremated on July 24th. The divided ashes
went to Puget Sound, to Jim's back yard in New Jersey, and
with a grandson to Puerto Rico. Major newspapers across the
country and abroad published obituary notices. David Hinck-
ley of the *New York Daily News* concluded his "Remembering
Earl Robinson, Songwriter for Troubled Times," saying,
"Robinson's blacklisting was triggered by his membership in
the Communist Party, which he quit in the '50s and later suggested had lost touch with its constituency. But what really
made him dangerous were his songs . . . whose messages, it's
safe to say, will outlive us all." A few progressive radio stations
played his music.

Many people approaching the end of their lives turn toward religion and visions of the afterlife as a way of cheating
Death. Earl had the foresight to begin thinking about reincarnation and the indestructibility of the soul some twenty years
before. But he really needn't have worried about his long-term
survival: He lives on in the most meaningful way anyone could
hope for.

I once asked him, "Earl, with this no-death philosophy of
yours, when the time comes, should we have a memorial for
you or not?"

Without a second's pause, he said, "Oh yes, don't forget,
I'll be there!"

The family did not hold a funeral, but loving friends organized tributes to Earl's life and career in Seattle, Los Angeles,
and New York, attracting hundreds in each city who appreciated him and his songs. At long last, the Friends of Earl Robinson published its brochure on Earl and his works, sending it to
conductors of orchestras and choruses, in hopes of stimulating
renewed interest.

Though Earl and I shared an unconditional trust in the
power of our collaboration, and a sense of humor about his
life, the single question that came up most between us concerned choice and responsibility. Under the influence of the
personal growth movements, Earl tried to own responsibility
for all his actions. Don't blame others, he said, don't evade

your own role in creating the position you are in. We choose everything that happens to us. I answered, Is the three year-old African child dying from dehydration responsible? Does the bystander choose to be killed in a drive-by gang shooting? How about the homeless in America, are they to blame when we can clearly point to the Reagan-Bush zero housing policy?

Earl's answers did not satisfy me, but for him, his belief in the spirit world, in magic and revelation, offered a kind of cosmic balance. Earl affirmed his own responsibility up to a point; after that, he allowed the forces of the spirit world—the souls of those who have gone before—to determine his fate. More than once in the course of his book, he refers to these intervening spirits. In Athens they saved his life. They can also take us from this world into the next if our souls are needed for another incarnation. In a more conventional sense, some people see such intervention as the kind of thing God does or (for the more secular-minded) as the inexorable workings of the laws of science and history. In any case, there is no death, except by the most prosaic, literal definition.

Despite certain concerns appropriate to his age, Earl was a very lively 81-year-old, who in no outward way appeared ready to change addresses. When I saw him last, in March 1991, I wanted to witness the morning yoga exercises he conducted each day. Twice I joined him, and I can tell you we worked up quite a sweat together. He was writing and composing; he had this book to look forward to publishing; he had a new contract with the music publishing firm of G. Schirmer which might lead to some major performances of his works and a re-evaluation of his career; he was being filmed for a professional-level, hour-long documentary; and he had before him a steady calendar of concerts and appearances. He had already sent out announcements of an 81st birthday performance at the Unitarian church in Seattle on August 4th. The last letter I received from him—indeed a message from his new address, as I received it three days after he "moved"—talked about a whole weekend devoted to his music that we were planning in Madison, Wisconsin, in January 1992. (On the back of the envelope he had written, "I picked the pie cherries," a reference to the fruit tree in his yard and to the pies we had baked together two years before: At 81 Earl was still climbing trees!) This all-Robinson concert took place "without" him, ending with a tape of Earl singing his song "Message from a New Address," the chorus taking over from him on the final stanza.

Despite all this evidence suggesting that Earl intended to stay a while longer, I need to close his autobiography affirming his right to make his own choices in life, even as to the timing and manner of his passing over. Kathy Butzerin reports a strange conversation with Earl the day they met at a senior center in West Seattle about six months before he left. Kathy asked Earl where he lived, and he had trouble stating his address. Finally, and inexplicably, he said, "At the corner of Admiral Way and Manning," a spot probably twenty blocks from his house—but the spot where he had his crash months later.

A few days before he went, B.J. Bullert, the Seattle filmmaker, had a pre-birthday party which Earl attended. She shot a roll of film, and when she took it in for developing, nothing came out. The film was blank. Had B.J., a photographer with twenty years' experience, somehow misloaded the camera? Or had Earl's soul already departed? He died several days later, on B.J.'s birthday.

Mount Tam

For me, one of Earl's most moving chapters is his account of San Francisco, where the world's leaders had gathered (with the spirit of FDR) to form the United Nations. Part of the reason this passage affects me so is that I was born in early 1945. Just days before, my Dad had sat shivering in a foxhole in Belgium in the Battle of the Bulge; I have always felt that my own life was somehow destined to be one of struggle for liberation. Well, I had never been to San Francisco before. My friend Rick and I drove up scenic Route 1 from Los Angeles, and arrived on Friday, July 19th. In only two days I wanted to see all the sights of San Francisco, but most of all I wanted to go up Mt. Tamalpais, to see what Earl had seen when I was only four months old. On this splendid, magical day, Saturday the 20th, we saw the Presidio, Golden Gate Park, drove across the Bridge, visited Muir Woods to see my first redwoods, then drove up to Mt. Tam.

All of Earl's friends wanted him with us for many more years. But for his own reasons Earl—or some higher-level part of him not available to his conscious self—must have felt ready. For he chose to go at 7 o'clock that evening, just as I stood up on Mount Tamalpais, surveying San Francisco and the whole Bay area, and contemplating the fate of the world since 1945. To say that I could feel Earl's strong presence with me then would be a colossal understatement.

I believe it is not a coincidence that he chose that time and place to say goodbye. For now, as in 1945, we have before us a comparable euphoric opportunity to build that world of peace everlasting, that Age of Aquarius that Earl so clearly envisioned. Do we dare discard the comforts of our customary cynicism and embrace one another with respect and love? With the help of Joe Hill, and Abe Lincoln and Paul Robeson, Carl Sandburg, Franklin and Eleanor Roosevelt, and William O. Douglas, with the help of Jesus, St. Francis, Chief Sealth and the dolphins, and with "especially the people," we might just get it right this time.

LIST OF WORKS AND DISCOGRAPHY
BY EARL ROBINSON

Incompleteness is unfortunately the byword to this list. Too many recordings and publications—and their re-releases and reprintings—are scattered about, even to locate, much less include. As a general rule, individual songs from larger works are mentioned here only if separately published (**Pub:**) or recorded (*Rec:*). Works are listed in chronological order within each category, with many a guess as to date. In a few cases, works are listed here by title even though they appear to be lost. Additional items, corrections, and suggestions for this list may be submitted to Eric A. Gordon c/o the publisher for updating in a possible second edition. A composer brochure giving publisher, timing, orchestration, and other details, is available from Friends of Earl Robinson, c/o Prof. Maurice Peress, Aaron Copland School of Music, Flushing, NY 11367.

The following abbreviations apply:

Earl Robinson, *Songs for Americans*, Timely 500-504, 1940 = *Songs*.

Songs by Earl Robinson, Alco, 1944 = *Songs by ER*.

Earl Robinson Sings, Folkways FG3545, 1963 = *ER Sings*.

Earl Robinson, *A Walk in the Sun*, Folkways FA2324, 1957 = *Walk*.

Earl Robinson: Ein Porträt, Eterna, 1973 = *Porträt*.

Strange, Unusual Evening: A Santa Barbara Story, UAW-ER-101, 1970 = *SUE*.

Earl Robinson: Alive and Well, Aspen APN 30101, 1986 = *Alive*.

Text = t.

Earl Robinson = ER.

Orchestra and Band

Rhapsody in Brass, 1934.

Symphonic Fragment, 1934.

"Fantasie (After Images of a Movie)," piano and saxophone, 1940?

Bouquet for Molly, ballet suite for Lester Horton, 1949.

Black and White (marching band), 1955.

A Country They Call Puget Sound (t: "Acres of Clams," traditional song), 1956. Revised 1957 for orchestra.

Salt Water Song (concert band), 1960.

Banjo Concerto [Concerto for Five-String Banjo] (t: Lee Hays), 1967.

Flight to the Moon, 1969. *Rec:* Bell Records soundtrack.
Soul Rhythms (band), 1972. **Pub:** Belwin-Mills, 1972.
Piano Concerto ("The New Human"), 1973.
To the Northwest Indians (t: ER), 1974.

Piano Solo

"Jazz Lyric," 1940? **Pub:** "Lírica de jazz," *Boletín Latino-Americano de Música* 5:28-33, 1941.
"Dreamy Misty," n.d.
"Ballad of Molly Pitcher," n.d.

Chorus

"The Flying Squadron" (t: Peter Martin, Oscar Saul), 1934. **Pub:** *Workers Song Book 2*, 1935. Used in film *United Action*, 1939.
"Joe Hill" (t: Alfred Hayes), 1936.
Ballad for Americans (t: John Latouche), 1939. **Pub:** Robbins, 1940; as a narrative solo for baritone, arranged by D. Savino, Robbins, 1968. Used in *Born to Sing*, MGM film, 1942. *Rec: Alive*; Paul Robeson, RCA Victor 26516-7, 1940, re-released on RCA Victrola AVM1-1736, 1976, and on Vanguard CVSD 117/18 cassette and CD, 1989; Bing Crosby, Decca 134, 1940; Lawrence Tibbett; Odetta, Vanguard VSD-2057/VRS-9066; Brock Peters, United Artists, UA-LA 604G-0698, 1976; John Anthony, New York City Labor Chorus, *Live '93*, FLE 1, 1994.
The People, Yes (t: Carl Sandburg, Norman Corwin), 1938-41. Excerpts: *In the Folded and Quiet Yesterdays* (t: Carl Sandburg), 1941. **Pub:** Shawnee, 1964. *Rec:* Michael Loring, American People's Chorus, Keynote, 1942. "He Built the Road" (t: Earl Robinson), 1938, and "Tower of Babel," 1940: See Songs.
Battle Hymn (t: John Latouche, ER, based on Franklin D. Roosevelt), 1942. **Pub:** Chappell, 1943.
The Lonesome Train (t: Millard Lampell), 1942. **Pub:** Pickwick, 1943; text only: Erik Barnouw, ed., *Radio Drama in Action: Twenty-five Plays of a Changing World*, New York: Rinehart, 1945. *Rec:* Decca DA-375, 1944, re-released on Decca DL 5054; Odetta, Brock Peters, *Ballad for Americans*, United Artists, UA-LA 604G-0698, 1976.
That Freedom Plow (t: Lou Lerman), 1943.
Song of a Free People (t: Bernard Schoenfeld), 1943. *Rec:* See Songs.

"Same Boat, Brother" (t: Yip Harburg), 1945.

"Quilting Bee" (t: Jack Shapiro), 1949.

"If I Am Free" (t: Matthew Hall, aka Lewis Allan, aka Abel Meeropol), *Sing Out!*, October 1952; see also the correction in the December 1952 issue.

When We Grow Up (t: Roslyn Harvey [Rosen]), children's chorus, 1952. **Pub:** Chappell, 1952. Used as the score for a film by the same name, 1952.

"Black and White" (t: David Arkin), 1954. **Pub:** Shawnee, 1972, arranged by John Coates, Jr.

Giants in the Land (t: Joseph Moncure March), 1956. **Pub:** Piano-vocal score, Piedmont/Marks, 1962. Originally written as the score to a General Motors film by the same name, 1956.

Preamble to Peace (t: Lewis Allan, ER, based on the United Nations Preamble), 1960.

"My Fisherman, My Laddy-O" (t: Waldo Salt), 1962. **Pub:** Sanga. *Rec:* See Songs.

"Hurry Sundown" (t: Yip Harburg), 1966. **Pub:** MCA. *Rec:* See Songs.

Illinois People (t: Carl Haverlin, ER), 1968.

Ride the Wind (t: ER, after William O. Douglas), 1974.

A Concert for Francis (of the Saint Variety) (t: ER), 1985.

A Natural Human (t: Mark Hyatt, Isaac Jackson, Pat O'Brien), men's chorus, 1985.

Stage Works

Who's Got the Baloney?, 1934. Music director, actor.

The Young Go First (George Scudder [Arthur Vogel]), 1935. Actor.

The Crime (Michael Blankfort), 1936. Actor.

Who Fights This Battle? (Kenneth White), 1936, score by Paul Bowles. Music director.

Pink Slips on Parade, 1937. ("Doin' the Demonstration")

Stop That Tiger! (Jules Dassin, Nathaniel Buchwald), 1937. Composer.

Processional (John Howard Lawson), 1937. Composer.

Life and Death of an American (George Sklar), 1939. Co-composer with Alex North.

Hellzapoppin, 1938. Includes "Abe Lincoln."

Sing for Your Supper, 1939. ("Ballad of Uncle Sam," later renamed *Ballad for Americans*)

It's All Yours (Millard Lampell), 1942. Actor, singer.

It's Up to You (Arthur Arent), 1943. (Various songs written with
Lewis Allan, Woody Guthrie, and Hy Zaret.) Excerpts used in a
ten-minute film by Department of Agriculture, 1943.

Dark of the Moon (Howard Richardson and William Berney), 1947.
Composer.

Sandhog (t: Waldo Salt, after Theodore Dreiser), 1954. **Pub:** piano-
vocal score, Chappell, 1956. Separately **Pub:** "Twins," "Katie
O'Sullivan," "Johnny-O," Chappell, 1954; "Katie-O" (a version
of "Johnny-O"), Chappell, 1957; "Sweat Song," *Sing Out!*, Win-
ter 1955; "Katie O'Sullivan" and "Katie-O, Johnny-O" in *Erl
Robinson Pyesni*, Moscow: Muzgiz, 1963. *Rec:* ER, Waldo Salt,
Sandhog, Vanguard VRS-9001, 1955, includes "Come Down,"
"Johnny's Cursing Song," "Johnny-O," "Good Old Days,"
"Song of the Bends," "By the Glenside," "Sandhog Song," "Sweat
Song," "Fugue on a Hot Afternoon in a Small Flat," "Twins,"
"Katie O'Sullivan," "Work Song," "Death of Tim," "Sing Sor-
row," "Ma, Ma, Where's My Dad?," "The Greathead Shield," "In
the Tunnel," "Sam on the Stick," "Cursing Song (reprise),"
"Johnny-O (reprise)," and "Sandhog Song (finale)"; "Katie-O,"
Vince Martin, Glory 45-252, 1957.

One Foot in America (t: Lewis Allan, after Yuri Suhl), 1962.

The Gingerbread Boy (t: Elsa Rael), 1965.

Earl Robinson's America (t: ER and others; incorporates *Ballad for
Americans, The Lonesome Train*, etc.), 1976.

David of Sassoun (t: ER), 1978.

Words and Music of Bob Dylan, 1979. Music director.

Listen for the Dolphin (t: ER), 1981.

Song of Atlantis (t: ER), 1983.

I Been Thinkin' About J.C. (t: ER), 1985.

The Earl Robinson Celebration (t: various), 1989. Renamed *Same Boat,
Brother*, 1991.

Songs

"Down with Fascist Terror," 1934.

"Amter Election Song," 1934?

"Vote Red," 1934?

"I'm No Communist," with Ruth Burke, 1934.

"Song of the Pickets" (t: Stephen Karnot), 1934. **Pub:** *Workers Song
Book 2*, 1935.

"Death House Blues" (t: Peter Martin, from *Negro Songs of Protest*, collected by Lawrence Gellert), 1935.

"May Day Song" (t: Philip Cornwall), 1935. **Pub:** ER, Miriam Bogorad, Gertrude Burke, D. Hunt McCurdy, eds., *Songs for America*, New York: Workers Library, 1939; *Sing Out!*, April 1952.

"The Flying Squadron" (t: Lou Lantz, Peter Martin, Oscar Saul), 1934. Used in film *United Action*, 1939. See Chorus.

"Joe Hill" (t: Alfred Hayes), 1936. **Pub:** Bob Miller, 1938; Margaret Bradford Boni, *Fireside Book of Folk Songs*, New York: Simon and Schuster, 1947; Irwin Silber, *Lift Every Voice*, New York: Sing Out!, 1957; Olive Woolley Burt, *American Murder Ballads and Their Stories*, New York: Oxford University Press, 1958; Helga Sandburg, *Sweet Music: A Book of Family Reminiscence and Song*, New York: Dial, 1963; Erl Robinson Pyseni, Moscow: Muzgiz, 1963; Tom Glazer, *Songs of Peace, Freedom and Protest*, Greenwich, CT: Fawcett, 1970; Maggi Peirce, *Songs from Tryworks*, v. 2, New Bedford, MA: Tryworks, 1973; and many other reprintings. *Rec: Walk, SUE, Porträt, Alive, Songs* (re-released on *Don't Mourn—Organize! Songs of Labor Songwriter Joe Hill*), Smithsonian/Folkways SF 40026, 1990. Among the many other recorded versions: Michael Loring, Musicraft, 1938; Howie Mitchell, *Howie Mitchell*, Folk-Legacy FSI-2; U. Utah (Bruce) Phillips, *Nobody Knows Me*, Prestige/Int. 13040; Jean Ritchie, *The Appalachian Dulcimer: An Introduction Record*, Folkways FI 8352; Jean Ritchie, *The Best of Jean Ritchie*, Prestige/Int. 13003; Arlene Mantle, *In Solidarity*, Canadian Auto Workers, 1989?; Paul Robeson, *Songs of Free Men*, Victor, 1943; Paul Robeson, *Let Freedom Sing*, Othello L-301, 1954; Paul Robeson, *Favorite Songs*, Monitor MPS 580; Paul Robeson, *Freedom Songs*, Topic Records, Top 62, 1961, re-released on *Don't Mourn—Organize! Songs of Labor Songwriter Joe Hill*, Smithsonian/Folkways SF 40026, 1990; Joe Glazer, *Jellybean Blues*, Collector Records, cassette, 1980s; Joan Baez, Woody Guthrie, Arlo Guthrie, and Pete Seeger; Phil Ochs, *Tape from California*.

"Abe Lincoln" (also known as "Old Abe Lincoln") (t: Abraham Lincoln, Alfred Hayes, ER), 1936. **Pub:** Bob Miller, 1938; Waldemar Hille, *The People's Song Book*, New York: People's Artists, 1948. *Rec: ER Sings, Porträt, Songs*; Michael Loring, 1938.

"Old Man Noah" (t: Lesan, Gabrielson), 1936.

"Herbert C. Hoover Snaithe" (t: Alfred Hayes), 1936.

"I Kissed a Communist (Was My Face Red!)" (t: Lewis Allan), 1936.

"May I Dance Without My Pants?" (t: Lewis Allan), 1936.

"Tin Boxes" (t: Jules Dassin, Nathaniel Buchwald), from *Stop That Tiger!*, 1937.

"John Brown" (t: Philip Cornwall), 1938? *Rec: Songs*.

"Horace Greeley" (t: Jack Shapiro), 1938? *Rec: Songs*.

"Quiet Man from Kansas" (t: Mark Hess), 1938?

"He Built the Road" (t: Earl Robinson), 1938. *Rec: SUE, Alive*.

"Doin' the Demonstration" (t: Lewis Allan), 1939. **Pub:** ER, Miriam Bogorad, Gertrude Burke, D. Hunt McCurdy, eds., *Songs for America*, New York: Workers Library, 1939.

"Ballad of the Chicago Steel Massacre" (t: J. F. [Alfred Hayes]), 1939. **Pub:** ER, Miriam Bogorad, Gertrude Burke, D. Hunt McCurdy, eds., *Songs for America*, New York: Workers Library, 1939; *Sing Out!*, May 1954.

"A Man's a Man for A' That" (t: Robert Burns), 1939. **Pub:** *Sing Out!*, January 1953. *Rec:* ER, *Americana*, Keynote 132, 1945?, *ER Sings, Alive*.

"A Letter to a Policeman in Kansas City" (t: Kenneth Patchen), 1930s?

"Ludlow Massacre" (t: Alfred Hayes), 1930s? **Pub:** Alan Lomax, comp., *Hard Hitting Songs for Hard-Hit People*, New York: Oak Publications, 1967.

"Spring Song" (t: Harry Schachter), 1939. Used in film *Says Youth*, American Peace Mobilization, 1940? **Pub:** New York Council of the Arts, Sciences and Professions, 1952; Irwin Silber, *Lift Every Voice*, New York: Sing Out!, 1957; *Erl Robinson Pyesni*, Moscow: Muzgiz, 1963. *Rec: Walk*; Paul Robeson, Keynote K513, 1941; Ernie Lieberman and Hope Foye, Hootenanny Records, 1951; Ernie Lieberman, *Goodbye, Mr. War*, Amerecord ALP-101, 1955.

"In Memoriam" (t: Harry Schachter), 1930s?

"Tower of Babel" (t: Carl Sandburg, Norman Corwin), 1940. *Rec: Songs by ER*.

"When Plain People Meet" (t: Benjamin Franklin, Lewis Allan), 1940s?

"The Fascist Aviator" (t: Alfred Hayes), 1940s?

"Six-Hour Day and Five-Day Week" (from *The People, Yes*), 1941

"The House I Live In" (t: Lewis Allan), 1942. Used in *Follow the Boys*, Universal, 1944; and in a film *The House I Live In*, 1947. **Pub:** Chappell, 1942; *Erl Robinson Pyesni*, Moscow: Muzgiz, 1963; Judy Bell, *This Land Is Your Land*, New York: TRO, Ludlow

Music, 1972. *Rec:* ER, *Americana,* Keynote 132, 1945?, *Walk,
Porträt, Alive*; Frank Sinatra, *The Frank Sinatra Story in Music,*
Columbia CL 1130 and C2L6, 1945; Frank Sinatra, *Sinatra: A
Man and His Music,* Reprise 2FS 1016, 1960; Frank Sinatra, The
Voice, Volume 4, Reprise FS 5283, 1962; Frank Sinatra, *America,
I Hear You Singing,* Reprise FS 2020, 1964; Frank Sinatra, *"The
House I Live In": Early Encores: 1943-46,* vol. 2, Vintage Jazz Clas-
sics VJC 1007-2, 1990; *Duets II,* Capitol CDP 7243 8 28103 22,
with Neil Diamond; Paul Robeson, *Spirituals/A Robeson Recital
of Popular Favorites,* Columbia ML 4105; Paul Robeson, *Ballad
for Americans and Great Songs of Faith, Love and Patriotism,* Van-
guard CVSD 117/18 cassette and CD, 1989; Lauritz Melchior,
RCA Victor DM 1056-10-1225-B; Conrad Thibault, Decca
23346; Sammy Davis, Jr., B'nai B'rith Anti-Defamation League,
1957; other versions by Josh White, Sonny Rollins and Archie
Shepp, Eddie Fisher, Connie Francis, Sarah Vaughan, Ted
Nealy.
"Fight, America!" (t: Lewis Allan), 1942. **Pub:** Chappell, 1942.
"Kickin' the Panzer" (t: Lewis Allan), 1943?
"Porterhouse Lucy, the Black Market Steak" (t: Alfred Hayes), 1943.
   Rec: Songs by ER.
"Get the Point, Mrs. Brown" (t: Lewis Allan), 1943.
"We Can Take It" (t: Lewis Allan), 1943.
"Brother, There's a Job to Do" (t: Lewis Allan), 1943.
"Look Out of the Window, Mama" (t: Lewis Allan), 1943.
"Plain Men in Dirty Overalls" with Woody Guthrie (t: Woody
   Guthrie), 1943.
"It's Up to You" (t: Lewis Allan and Woody Guthrie), 1943.
"Song of the Free Men" (t: Millard Lampell), 1943.
"The Ostrich, the Turtle and the Eagle" (t: Jack Shapiro), 1943?
"Victory Begins at Home" (t: Hy Zaret), 1943.
"When You Gotta Grow" (t: Hy Zaret), 1943.
"Life Could Be Beautiful Without a Can Opener" (t: Hy Zaret),
   1943.
"We'll Hammer It Out Together" (t: Hy Zaret), 1943.
"We'll Hammer It Out Together" (t: Langston Hughes), 1943.
"Freedom Blues" (t: Bernard Schoenfeld), from *Song of a Free People,*
   1943. *Rec: Songs by ER.*
"That Man in the White House" (t: Lewis Allan), 1944?
"Danger! Men Working (Against Us)" (t: Bob Russell), 1944. **Pub:**
   American Theatre Wing Music War Committee, 1944.

"Free and Equal Blues" (t: E. Y. Harburg), 1944. **Pub:** Chappell, 1944; *Sing Out!*, Spring 1958. *Rec: Walk, SUE, Alive*; ER, Alco S-106; Dooley Wilson and ER, International Artists 2182; Josh White.

"Have You Heard About the Meeting?" (t: E. Y. Harburg), 1944.

"Same Boat, Brother" (t: E. Y. Harburg), 1944. **Pub:** *Sing Out!*, October-November 1962; *The Collected Reprints from Sing Out!*, vol. 8, 1965. *Rec: Songs by ER, ER Sings, Porträt, Alive*; Leadbelly, *Leadbelly's Last Sessions*, vol. 2, Folkways FA2942.

"Got To Get Out and Vote" (t: E. Y. Harburg), from film *Hell Bent for Election*, 1944. *Rec:* UAW-CIO, 1944.

"We're Keeping Score for '44," (t: Vern Bartlow [Partlow]), 1944. *Rec:* UAW-CIO, 1944.

"Texas Girl" (also known as "Marriage Song" or "You Can Give Marriage a Whirl"), (t: ER, Carl Sandburg), 1945. *Rec: Walk.*

"From Here On Up" (also known as "Hills Don't Get Any Higher"), (t: ER), 1945. *Rec: Walk.*

"Train Song" (t: ER), 1945. *Rec: Walk.*

"Hold Fast to Your Dream" (t: Sol Barzman), 1945? *Rec: ER Sings.*

A Walk in the Sun, film (t: Millard Lampell), 1945. Songs: "Ballad of the Lead Platoon," "Texas Division," "Waiting," "One Little Job," "The Platoon Started Out," "Six Mile Walk," "Trouble A-Coming," "Texas Division Blues," "They Met Hitler's Best," "Moving In," "Walk in the Sun." *Rec: Walk.*

California, film (t: E. Y. Harburg), 1946. Songs **Pub:** Paramount, 1946, include "California," "California or Bust," and "Said I to My Heart, Said I." Not published: "Lilly Aye Lady O" and "I Should'a Stood in Massachusetts."

"Pioneer City" (t: Millard Lampell), 1946.

The Romance of Rosy Ridge, MGM film (t: Lewis Allan), 1947. Songs **Pub:** "I Come from Missouri" and "Far from My Darling," Robbins, 1947; both in *Erl Robinson Pyesni*, Moscow: Muzgiz, 1963. Not published: "Fiddlin' for a Frolic," "Pig in the Parlor," "Lonely Lovers."

"Toward the Sun" (t: Lewis Allan), from film *The Roosevelt Story*, 1947.

Man from Texas, film (t: Joseph Fields), 1947. Unpub. songs: "My Darling," "El Paso Kid," "Sunday Song."

"If I Am Free" (t: Lewis Allan), 1947? See Chorus, 1952.

"Varsovienne" (also known as "Come Along") (t: Harry Schachter), 1947. *Rec:* Earl Robinson, *Hootenanny Tonight*, Hootenanny Records, 1954, rereleased on Folkways FN2511, 1963.

"The Quilting Bee" (t: Jack Shapiro), 1949. **Pub:** Cromwell, 1951, later The Richmond Organization; *Sing Out!*, April 1954. *Rec:* *ER Sings*; The Weavers, *Weavers' Gold*, Decca DL4277; The Travellers, Columbia FL261; Ernie Lieberman, *Goodbye, Mr. War*, Amerecord ALP-101, 1955.

"Good Morning" (t: Harry Schachter), 1949. *Rec: Walk*.

"My True Love" (also known as "Martian Love Song") (t: Lee Hays), 1952. *Rec:* Pete Seeger, Folkways FN2501; *ER Sings*.

"Power of U.E., The" (t: Waldo Salt), 1951. **Pub:** *Sing Out!*, January, 1952.

"It's a Clear Day" (t: Edwin Rolfe), from film *Muscle Beach*, 1952.

"My Fisherman, My Laddy-O" (t: Waldo Salt), 1952. Used in film *End of Summer*, 1952. **Pub:** *Travelling On with The Weavers*, Harper & Row, 1966. See also Chorus. *Rec: ER Sings*; The Weavers, *Reunion at Carnegie Hall*, Part 2, VRS 9161, 1963.

"Twins," "Katie O'Sullivan," "Johnny-O," "Katie-O," 1954. See *Sandhog* under Stage Works.

"The Animal Kingdom" (t: Mel Leven), 1950s?. *Rec: Porträt, SUE*.

"Side by Side" (t: Lee Hays), 1954. **Pub:** *Sing Out!*, Winter 1956.

"Black and White" (t: David Arkin), 1954. Used in "Crossroads Africa," CBS TV, 1960. **Pub:** *Sing Out!*, Winter 1956 (t: "Alan Roberts"); *The Collected Reprints from Sing Out!*, vol. 1, 1959 (the errata page corrects the text attribution to David Arkin); Alec Templeton, 1956; *Erl Robinson Pyesni*, Moscow: Muzgiz, 1963; rock version, Shawnee, 1972; Helga Sandburg, *Sweet Music: A Book of Family Reminiscence and Song*, New York: Dial, 1963; with illustrations by David Arkin, Los Angeles: Ward Ritchie, 1966; Ralph Rolls, *Everybody Sing: A BBC Songbook for Assembly*, London: BBC Publications, 1973; *1001 Jumbo Song Book*, New York: Charles Hansen Educational Sheet Music & Books, n.d. See also under Chorus. *Rec: Walk, Alive, Porträt*; Sammy Davis, Jr., B'nai B'rith Anti-Defamation League, 1957; Pete Seeger, *Love Songs for Friends and Foes*, Folkways FA 2453; The Spinners, 1971; Greyhound, 1971; Three Dog Night, *Seven Separate Fools*, ABC Dunhill DSD 50118, 1972; Three Dog Night, *Around the World with Three Dog Night*, ABC Dunhill DSY 50138, 1973.

"Rose of Sharon" (t: Lewis Allan), from *One Foot in America*, 1962.

"Right as Rain" (with Harry Simeone, David Arkin), 1963.

"Johnny Got His Gun" (t: Ray Golden), 1964?

"Nobody's There" (t: Ray Golden), 1964?

"Logan's Lament" (also known as "Who is There to Mourn for Logan") (t: Chief Logan), 1965. *Rec: Porträt.*

"Hurry Sundown" (t: E. Y. Harburg), 1966. **Pub:** Northern Music, 1966; *Peter, Paul and Mary Album*, New York: Pepamar. See Chorus. *Rec: SUE*; Peter, Paul and Mary.

"Johnny's Gone" (t: Waldo Salt), 1966.

"All the Words Are New" (t: Josef Berger), 1966.

"The People Painter" (t: Josef Berger), 1966.

"Janie in the Rain" (t: Josef Berger), 1966.

"Big World Now" (t: Josef Berger), 1966.

"How Can I Keep from Singing" (t: Lee Hays), from the *Banjo Concerto*, 1967.

"One Sweet Morning" (t: E. Y. Harburg), to the tune of "How Can I Keep from Singing" from the *Banjo Concerto*, 1971.

"Peace and Plenty" (t: David Arkin), 1972.

"I Appreciate Me" (t: Earl Robinson), 1972.

"Four Hugs a Day" (t: ER), 1973. *Rec:* Charlotte Diamond, *10 Carrot Diamond*, Hug Bug Records CDL 317, 1985.

"Suppose" (t: Bob Russell, ER), 1973? *Rec: Porträt.*

"Ode to Paul Robeson" (t: Pablo Neruda, ER), 1976.

"The Parents of Our Race" (t: John Andrew Storey, adapted by ER), 1976. **Pub:** *How Can We Keep from Singing*, Los Angeles: Hodgin Press of First Unitarian Church, 1976.

"Where It Is" (t: ER), 1970s.

"Parlier Sings" (t: ER), 1978.

"A Ballad of Jesus" (t: Aaron Kramer), 1980s?

"Build Fun City" (t: ER), 1980s?

"El Salvador" (or "Nicaragua") (t: ER), 1982?

"Valentine's Day" (t: ER), 1983.

"A Song to Ferraro" (t: ER), 1984.

"Now" (t: ER), 1986.

"Jesse" (t: ER), 1988.

"Jessie" (t: ER), 1988.

"Step by Step" (t: traditional Irish), 1988. *Rec: Songs of the Working People: American Revolution to the Civil War*, Flying Fish, LP, CD and cassette, 1988.

"A Place to Live" (t: ER), 1990?

"Song for the Earth Angels" (t: ER), 1990?

"Planet Earth Real Estate Company" (t: ER), 1990.

"The World Is My Garden" (t: ER), 1990.

"Message from a New Address" (t: ER), 1990.

"I Choose Wilderness" (t: ER, Eric Gordon, Gibbs Smith), 1991.

Words by Earl Robinson

"Which Side Are You On?," 1941 (about Morris Schappes).

"Joshua Fit the Battle of Jericho," 1942.

ER and Woody Guthrie, "When the Yanks Go Marching In," 1943, to the tune of "When the Saints Go Marching In." **Pub:** Robbins, 1943.

"The Unfriendly 19," 1947, to the tune of "Tam Pierce," also known as "Widdecombe Fair."

ER and Helen Robinson, "The Ballad of Dr. Dearjohn," 1962.

"This Land is Your Land," additional words to the song by Woody Guthrie. *Rec: SUE.*

"Roll On, McGovern," 1972, to the tune of "Roll On, Columbia" by Woody Guthrie.

ER, Sandy Arkin, and David Arkin, "Swingin' the Fifth," to a melody from Beethoven's Fifth Symphony, 1982.

Films, Radio, and Television

A. Films

People of the Cumberland, Frontier Films, 1938. Co-composer with Alex North.

United Action, UAW/CIO, 1939. Uses "The Flying Squadron."

Says Youth, American Peace Mobilization, 1940. Uses "Spring Song."

Born to Sing, MGM, 1942. Uses *Ballad for Americans.*

The Negro Soldier, United States War Department, 1943. Co-composer with Dmitri Tiomkin.

Follow the Boys, Universal, 1944. Uses "The House I Live In."

Hell Bent for Election, UAW (t: E. Y. Harburg), 1944. See Songs.

A Walk in the Sun, United Artists (t: Millard Lampell), 1945. See Songs.

California, Paramount (t: E. Y. Harburg), 1945. See Songs.

The Romance of Rosie Ridge, MGM (t: Lewis Allan), 1947. See Songs.

The Roosevelt Story (t: Lewis Allan), 1947. See Songs.

Man from Texas (t: Joesph Fields), 1947.

The House I Live In (t: Lewis Allan), 1947.

Whose Century?, Henry Wallace filmstrip, 1948.

When We Grow Up, Neighborhood Films, Irving Fajans, Carl Lerner (t: Roslyn Harvey [Rosen]), 1952. See Chorus.

Muscle Beach, Irving Lerner, Joseph Strick, 1952. See Songs.

End of Summer (t: Waldo Salt), 1952. See Songs.

Giants in the Land, General Motors (t: Joseph Moncure March), 1956.

Brücke über den Ozean (Bridge over the Ocean), Deutscher Fernsehfunk, 1958.

Up Tight, 1968.

Earl Robinson: Ballad of an American, produced by Bette Jean Bullert for the Public Broadcasting Service, 1994.

B. Radio

The Town Crier, ABC, 1946.

The Big Ol' Tree, NBC, 1947.

C. Television

Maybe I'll Come Home in the Spring (t: Bruce Feldman), ABC, 1970.

Great Man's Whiskers (t: E. Y. Harburg), NBC, 1973.

Huckleberry Finn (t: Steve North), ABC, 1975.

What Really Happened to the Class of '65, 1978.

The Pumpkin Who Couldn't Smile, Chuck Jones, 1979.

Books Edited by Earl Robinson

Young Folk Song Book, New York: Simon and Schuster, 1963.

Folk Guitar in 10 Sessions (later published as *Play Guitar in 10 Sessions*), New York: Macmillan, 1966.

Songs of the Great American West, New York: Macmillan, 1967.

The Brecht-Eisler Song Book (also listed as *Songs of Bertolt Brecht and Hanns Eisler*), New York: Oak Publications, 1967.

German Folk Songs, New York: Oak Publications, 1968.

Also: *Erl Robinson Pyesni* (Earl Robinson Songs), Moscow: Muzgiz, 1963.

Other Songs Recorded by Earl Robinson
(traditional, unless otherwise credited)

Songs for Americans, Timely Records 500-504, 1940
    "Grey Goose"
    "John Henry"
    "Jesse James"

"Kevin Barry"
"Drill, Ye Tarriers, Drill"

Bart van der Schelling and the Exiles Chorus (directed by ER), League
of American Writers 123-125
"Au Devant de la Vie" (music: Shostakovich)
"Els Segadors" (Catalan National Hymn)
"La Guardia Rossa"
"La Joven Guardia" (music: Saint-Filles)
"Wir Henterm Draht" (Eberhard Schmitt)
"Die Thaelmann-Kolonne" (music: Karl Ernst; t: Peter Daniel)

The Almanac Singers (directed by ER), *Dear Mr. President*, Keynote
K-111
"Reuben James"
"Dear Mr. President"
"Deliver the Goods"
"Round, Round Hitler's Grave"
"Side by Side"
"Belt Line Girl"

UAW-CIO, 1944
"We're Keeping Score for '44" (Vern Bartlow [read Partlow])

Americana, Keynote 132, 1945?
"The Frozen Logger"
"Sweet Betsy from Pike"
"Drill Ye Tarriers Drill"
"Jefferson and Liberty"

(untitled), Alco S-106
"Come in the Evening"/"Riddle Song"

Earl Robinson Sings, Folkways FG3545, 1963
"Red Toupee" (Art Samuels)
"Wild Goose" (Wade Hemsworth)
"The Pied Piper" (Malvina Reynolds)
"Kevin Barry"
"Casey Jones" (Joe Hill)
"42 Kids" (music: Merle Travis; t: anon.)
"Wanderin'"

Strange, Unusual Evening: A Santa Barbara Story, UAW-ER-101, 1970
    "Sit Down" (Maurice Sugar)
    "Hallelujah I'm a Bum" (Harry McClintock)
    "Pie in the Sky" (Joe Hill)
    "Solidarity Forever" (Ralph Chaplin)
    "Wanderin'"
    "Too Old to Work" (Kuppy Scott, Joe Glazer)
    "Which Side Are You On?" (Florence Reece)
    "Casey Jones" (Joe Hill)
    "Union Maid" (Woody Guthrie)
    "This Land is Your Land" (Woody Guthrie)

A Tribute to Woody Guthrie, Warner Brothers 26036, 1972
    "Mail Myself to You" (Woody Guthrie)

Earl Robinson: Ein Porträt, Eterna, 1973
    "Big Rock Candy Mountain" (Mac McClintock)
    "Pie in the Sky" (Joe Hill)
    "The Turtle Dove"
    "Shenandoah"
    "Old Paint"

Songs of the Working People: American Revolution to the Civil War,
    Flying Fish 483, LP, CD, and cassette, 1988. With other singers.
    Earl is heard on
    "Free Amerikay"
    "Jefferson and Liberty"
    "Step by Step" (new tune by Earl Robinson)
    "Jimmy Crack Corn"
    "Seneca Canoe Song with Words of Chief Seattle"

INDEX

Numbers in italics (*1-8*) indicate photograph pages.

ABOUT THE AUTHOR

Eric A. Gordon is the author of *Mark the Music: The Life and Work of Marc Blitzstein* (St. Martin's Press, 1989), in addition to hundreds of newspaper and magazine articles. He is a graduate of Yale University, and holds both an M.A. (in Latin American Studies) and a Ph.D. (in history) from Tulane University. In the 1980s he worked as Publicity Manager for the music publishing house of G. Schirmer. Since 1995 he has been Director of The Workmen's Circle/Arbeter Ring, Southern California District. A member of the National Writers Union, he serves on the Board of the Southern California Library for Social Studies and Research, on the Western Region Administrative Committee of the Jewish Labor Committee, and on the Editorial Advisory Board of *Jewish Currents* magazine. He lives in Los Angeles.